The Other One Percent

The Other One Percent

Indians in America

SANJOY CHAKRAVORTY
DEVESH KAPUR
NIRVIKAR SINGH

OXFORD
UNIVERSITY PRESS

OXFORD
UNIVERSITY PRESS

Oxford University Press is a department of the University of Oxford. It furthers
the University's objective of excellence in research, scholarship, and education
by publishing worldwide. Oxford is a registered trade mark of Oxford University
Press in the UK and certain other countries.

Published in the United States of America by Oxford University Press
198 Madison Avenue, New York, NY 10016, United States of America.

CIP data on file at the Library of Congress
Library of Congress Control Number: 2016954561
ISBN 978–0–19–064874–9

3 5 7 9 8 6 4
Printed by Sheridan Books, Inc., United States of America

To our children

Shourjo Chakravorty, Maya Kapur, Kunal Kapur,
Bhairav Singh, and Keshav Singh

CONTENTS

PREFACE

In June 2012, Rajat Gupta, retired chief executive of McKinsey, was convicted on three counts of securities fraud and one count of conspiracy for passing along confidential boardroom information to a hedge fund. Leading the prosecution was Preetinder Singh "Preet" Bharara, the U.S. attorney for the Southern District of New York. Both Gupta and Bharara were naturalized citizens who had been born in India and came to the United States in the early 1970s, the former after graduating from IIT-Delhi and the latter as a child immigrating with his parents. Both had received status-boosting educations at Harvard University and were highly ambitious. Gupta had become, in 1994, the first worldwide managing director of McKinsey born outside the United States and was a pioneer in the first generation of Indian Americans to break through the glass ceiling in corporate America. Bharara was the first Indian American to occupy that U.S. attorney's office—considered the most prestigious crime-fighting position in the country—and his actions appeared to ensure an even more promising future for an already prominent public figure.

The trial vividly captured "The Rise of the Indian-American Elite" (the subtitle of Anita Raghavan's account of the story) and overlaid an even larger story—namely, a half-century of one of the most selective immigrations in modern history.[1] It illustrated David Ben-Gurion's wry observation that "for Israel to be counted among the nations of the world, it has to have its own burglars and prostitutes," and appeared as a milestone marking the emergence of the Indian-American community as part of mainstream America.

We wrote this book on the fiftieth anniversary of one of the most significant laws enacted in postwar America. The U.S. Immigration and Nationality Act of 1965 abolished the national-origins quota system established in the 1920s and replaced it with a preference system based on skills and family relationships. The quota system had excluded people from the Global South and favored Europeans. Now, for the first time since WWI, the doors of the United

States were partially opened to people of color; but unlike the earlier big immigrant waves, this official opening was less to the "huddled masses" and more the skilled immigrants and those fortunate to already have family members to vouch for them. Unofficially, of course, the huddled masses came anyway. The impact of this new skill bias of America's immigration policy was profoundly manifest in one immigrant group: Indians. The next half-century—especially its final two decades—saw the most selective immigration (of skilled and educated workers) into the United States from any one country. Half a millennium after Christopher Columbus thought he had discovered India and encountered "Indians," the Indian-American population was 50 percent larger than the native American (Indian) population, and earned, on average, three times as much.

People of Indian origin—whether they are born in India, the United States, or somewhere else—make up about 1 percent of the American population. Despite its small size, this community has been called (along with several other Asian-American communities) a "model minority" that has been unusually successful in pursuing the American Dream through careers in high-skill occupations and entrepreneurship. How did a population from one of the poorest countries halfway around the world, with distinctive linguistic and religious characteristics and low levels of human capital, emerge as arguably the richest and most economically successful group in one of the richest and unarguably the most powerful country in the world—and that, too, in little more than a single generation?

There are several anecdotal and journalistic accounts of the professional and entrepreneurial achievements of Indians in America (along with the occasional high-profile crime), a number of scholarly studies on specific subgroups of the population (such as taxi drivers in New York or motel owners of Gujarati origin), but no single study has looked at the whole community, including its marginal or less visible members. The community has also not attracted much attention in the burgeoning literature on immigration. When Maritsa Poros (herself the daughter of Greek immigrants) decided to study Indian immigrants, she "was told by a prominent migration researcher and sociologist. . . that 'Indians are not a problem'. . . in that as a group they were not poor, segregated, unemployed, exploited, illegal, criminal, or even culturally different enough to be perceived as one of the more 'problematic' immigrant groups in American society. Their presence in the United States neither appealed to any need for social justice nor seemed to spark much anti-immigrant sentiment."[2] So why study a nonproblem?

If for no other reason, Indians in America deserve scholarly attention for demographic reasons. In 2014, India was the largest source of new immigrants to the United States and the second largest source of total immigrants. Providing over 147,000 new immigrants in a single year, India was a bigger source than China (about 132,000) and Mexico (about 130,000). These latest additions raised the total India-born population to 2.2 million, making it the second largest foreign-born group in the United States (after Mexicans). The scale and speed of this inflow becomes even clearer when we note that in 1990, people born in India were not even in the top ten of foreign-born populations in America. Something large was afoot and it was necessary to understand what it was.

This book is a serious attempt at creating that knowledge. It aims to provide a reasonably comprehensive account of this community, the life and work of its members, its increasing visibility and its not insignificant "invisible" component, and, importantly, what explains its specific characteristics. We use the characterization "reasonably comprehensive" with due caution, since for reasons of space, expertise, and approach, there are important issues we do not cover, especially the following two.

First, unlike much writing on Indian Americans in the humanities traditions, we do not focus on the discourse centered on race and identity, nor on questions of how Indians do (or do not) fit into American racial categories and the politics of racialization.[3] Race is an important category, and we give it significant attention, but it is not the only or necessarily most important dimension of identity for everyone. Diversity among Indian Americans is a leitmotif for us. Rather than see "Indian" as a homogeneous category to be somehow placed in the American racial system and its dynamics and differences, our approach includes a disaggregation of the category "Indian" into its linguistic and class components, to discuss their dynamics and differences. We show, at many points in the book, that these categories from "home" are more meaningful in terms of outcomes in the host. We submit that this approach reverses the analytical orientation—we look at Indians in America from an Indian perspective rather than an American one.

Second, we elide the cultural expressions of being Indian in America, ranging from the more recognized ones of artistic creation and performance to the less recognized ones of consumption practices from clothing to cuisine, from housing to hospitality. We believe that scholars trained in the humanities traditions are epistemologically better equipped to address these subjects.

Our approach is rooted in the social science disciplines and methods. It includes serious and substantive interrogations of the two most important processes in immigration: *selection* and *assimilation* (extending to its contemporary avatar, *acculturation*), where each has economic, social, and spatial dimensions. Our method is to rely on data to find patterns and explanations, including the American Community Survey (ACS) and the Public Use Microdata Samples (PUMS) of the U.S. Census; a survey of Asian Americans (including Indian Americans) by the Pew Foundation; an original survey of Indian-American professionals and entrepreneurs undertaken for this project; and individual interviews with a range of Indian Americans. Finally, it is important to note that this work is interdisciplinary by definition. The theoretical foundations come from our disciplinary trainings and include insights from economics, political science, and geography. The analytical and presentation methods we use are similarly diverse.

Selection and Assimilation

A comprehensive account of any immigrant group must begin by investigating who immigrates. Immigrants are rarely representative of the sending country's population. And, while many may desire to enter another country, only a few are allowed. Immigrants have specific characteristics that both allow them to leave their country of origin and be suitable for admission to the receiving country. These characteristics can be both observable (such as age, gender, education, religion, language) and unobservable (such as ambition, grit, luck). In short, immigrants are always selected: for leaving the country of origin *and* for being allowed to enter the destination country.

In large part, the story of Indians in America is one of selection. While this is true for all immigrants, those from India stand out in the degree of selection on human capital relative to both the destination country and the country of origin. In the first, pre-1965 phase of immigration, when few Indians came to the United States (for a number of reasons, including nativist and racist policies and barriers), they were largely laborers in the early part of the twentieth century, though a handful of students and more educated people did trickle in. Those who managed to enter post-WWII were well educated but few in number. In the post-1965 period, when U.S. policy favored both family unification and higher skills, the India-born population immigrated in three waves. *The Early Movers* (from the mid-1960s to the late 1970s) were highly educated (45 percent had or later acquired professional degrees, especially in medicine, or graduate degrees, especially in what has come to be called the STEM fields). There was greater variance in the human capital of *The Families* cohort (from the beginning of the 1980s to the mid-1990s), in which family unification became the dominant mode of entry. The most recent period, from 1995 to 2014–2015 (when this book was written), saw the arrival of what we call *The IT Generation*, a group selected specifically for its specialized skills in the information technology sector or other science and technology (STEM) fields. They also arrived in much larger numbers—at five times the rate of the Early Movers and twice the rate of The Families initially, and more than three times that rate when this book was being written.

Critically, what did not happen is also important. Distance kept Indians with low human capital from entering the United States illegally in very large numbers (in contrast to illegal immigrants from more proximate locations like Mexico and Central America). Also, India's democracy meant that the vast majority of those who left India did so voluntarily, unlike many immigrants from other developing countries who came as refugees or asylum seekers to escape political chaos or persecution. And since they were not escaping, Indians tended to be more connected to "home." These characteristics, in combination with the very high volume of skilled-worker immigration after 1995, made Indian immigrants "outliers" in the degree to which higher education, especially in technical fields, and the U.S. labor market played larger roles relative to other selection mechanisms of U.S. immigration policy.

Indians in America did not resemble any other population anywhere: not the Indian population in India, nor the native population in the United States, nor any other immigrant group from any other nation.[4] They were triply selected: in India, first through a social hierarchy that generally restricted access to higher education to groups with high socioeconomic status, then through an examination and education-financing system that further limited the number of individuals who received the inputs that made it possible to become eligible for immigration to the United States, and finally in the United States, selected though an immigration system that was geared to admit students and workers who matched the country's high-end labor market needs.

A major focus of this book is on demonstrating and understanding the multiple selections that shaped the Indian-American population. These selections applied not only to education (that, in terms of attaining college degrees, made the India-born population three times more educated than that in the host country and nine times more educated than the home country's population) but also to class and caste (favoring, by large margins, the "upper" and dominant classes and castes of India), profession (engineering, IT, and health care), and both the region of origin (Gujarati and Punjabi were overrepresented in the first two phases, and Telugu and Tamil in the third phase) and region of settlement (in specific metropolitan clusters in and around New York City, the San Francisco Bay Area, Chicago, Washington, D.C., and Houston and Dallas).

In addition to direct selection is what we call the "selection+" advantage: we suggest that group characteristics or norms, such as the fact that Indians had the highest propensity to live in married-couple households of any major immigrant group, added to the advantages of being an already selected group. We show, in particular, how family norms were useful in keeping the Indian-American poverty level low (under 5 percent) and family income high (the highest in the United States). It is also likely that the selection process enabled, without explicitly intending to, the generation of high levels of social capital (through linguistic/ professional networks such as Gujarati entrepreneurs in the hotel industry, Telugu and Tamil workers in the IT industry, IIT engineers, Malayali nurses, Bengali academics, etc.). Several linguistic subgroups, many with caste or clan affinities, with moderate to high levels of human capital, were also successful in creating "bonding" social networks and capital that enhanced their status.[5] Even low-income groups, such as Punjabi taxi drivers in New York, were able to create some social (bonding) capital. Several professional subgroups without kinship or linguistic affiliation—doctors and engineers, for example—were able to organize and prosper by creating bridging social networks and capital. Selection—broadly understood—is present as a primary or secondary theme in much of this book.

If the subject of *selection* covers the question of who immigrates, the subject of *assimilation* covers what happens after immigration. We are cognizant that, like selection, assimilation has multiple meanings whose salience varies across generations and issues(economic, social, or political). First-generation, or India-born, immigrants faced assimilation issues that were distinct from those faced by their children, the second generation, or America-born; and both in turn have differed from those faced by the so-called 1.5 generation—those who moved to the United States as children. History matters, as does geography. Early immigrant cohorts and those that moved to smaller towns faced very different contexts of reception from those who came later or settled in large cities. And while economic assimilation has proceeded rapidly, social assimilation has lagged.

Assimilation is a wide umbrella that covers a swathe of social and cultural issues, from marriage, gender, and child-bearing norms, to political participation, faith, and language preferences. The intergenerational differences on some of these dimensions can be stark and often the basis for anxiety and intergenerational conflict. For the first generation in particular, assimilation had significant economic and spatial dimensions, from occupational to settlement choice (or, absence of choice); and these choices (or compulsions) had consequences. Like selection, the theme of assimilation runs through the book, but is especially important in the second half.

The Organization of the Book

Our account of the immigration of Indians to America has three major elements: deep history, recent history, and the second generation. In chapter 1, "A Short History of Small Numbers," we begin at the turn of the twentieth century, when a small number of people from what was then the British Empire in the Indian subcontinent began to arrive (mainly from Punjab and going to the West Coast, but also some from Bengal and going to the East Coast) before it was shut tight after the passage of race-based immigration restriction acts. We include concise studies of the hybrid Punjabi-Mexican communities in the Central Valley of California and their Bengali counterparts on the East Coast, as well as the rare Indian intellectual trying to engage Americans in the struggle against British colonial rule in India. But, of course, at the time there was no "India," at least as an independent political entity; and being Indian was a civilizational ethos whose political boundaries were an external construct of the British Empire, in which identities were as yet more local than national.

As the title of chapter 1 indicates, the numbers of Indian immigrants in the United States were very small before 1965. So, the larger part of our story is the recent history—the half-century after the mid-1960s, the broad trends in the growth of the Indian-American population in that half-century, and the policies in both the United States and India that have shaped these changes. These shifts have transformed a miniscule community that grew by less than 300 per decade in the early twentieth century to one that grew by more than 300 a day by the end of the first decade of the twenty-first century. This dramatic increase in numbers transformed an "invisible" minority into a "visible" one, especially in some key locations and professions.

It is important to note that the visibility of the community is a recent phenomenon—about three-fourths of the India-born population in the United States arrived after the mid-1990s. We discuss several reasons that explain this surge, including technological changes (generalized phenomena such as the revolution in communication and information technology and specific events like the Y2K problem that initiated the demand for Indian IT professionals); higher education policies in the United States and India that facilitated the movement of the "best and brightest" from India to the United States in high-skill fields; and policy changes (such as the 1991 structural reforms and rapid privatization of higher education in India and the adaptations of the H-1B visa program in the United States).

Chapter 2, "Selected for Success," is an account of this large transformation with a focus on the "selection" processes both in the United States and in India that have made this an economically successful outlier community. We carefully detail the selection process and establish the "outlier" status of the Indian-American population, especially its economically active and demographically dominant India-born segment. We show that the India-born had the highest levels of educational attainment, worked most intensively in skill-based industries and occupations, and had the highest family incomes in comparison to all subgroups and national origins in the U.S. population. At the same time, because the higher levels of education and income were combined with norms imported from the subcontinent that emphasized marriage and family cohesion, Indians were largely insulated from the structural inequalities of American society.

Three facts are highlighted. First, *Indians were entering the United States in unprecedented numbers.* At the time of this writing, about 110,000 Indians were entering each year through the skill-based paths (60,000 through H-1B visas focused on computer-related occupations, 20,000 through L-1 visas, also focused on computer-related occupations, and 30,000 through F-1 student visas focused on STEM disciplines). Another 10,000 to 20,000 India-born were entering every year through the more traditional paths: family sponsorship and family reunification. Together, the annual rate of entry was well in excess of 120,000 individuals.

Second, *the increasing significance of skill-based entry paths ensured that this population was highly educated.* Almost every one of the skill-based annual entrants had at least a bachelor's degree when he or she entered, or acquired the degree soon thereafter, and well over half either already possessed or soon acquired a graduate degree. As a result, the proportion of college or higher degree holders among Indian Americans jumped from 48 percent in 1990 to 69 percent in 2010. This was the root cause of the rise of Indian Americans into the highest-educated and highest-earning group.

Third, *the new entrants spoke different languages and lived in different places than earlier immigrants.* The linguistic composition of the Indian-American population began to change fundamentally from the mid-1990s. Telugus and Tamils increased rapidly in numbers, joined later by Hindi speakers. They entered in large numbers using skill-based paths, whereas the traditional leaders (Gujaratis and Punjabis) remained reliant on the traditional mode of entry (family-based paths), and were rapidly losing their once-dominant shares.

These shifts came about as a result of major technological changes—the communication revolution that continues to restructure the process and location of production and value addition on a global scale—and policy changes that both reacted to and further enabled this particular form of economic globalization. We present a detailed account of the immigration policy shifts in the United States, especially as they applied to Indians, and emphasize that this was a necessary but not sufficient condition to generate the flow of IT workers from India. On the supply side, in India, there were policy shifts in higher education associated with liberalization beginning in 1984 and strengthened in 1991. These policy shifts had a distinct regional orientation—states in South India were early adapters, where private engineering colleges first mushroomed—which is why there was a regional turn in the composition of Indian immigrants to the United States. Changes in the stock and flow of these immigrants was one of the many elements of global economic restructuring that included, in India, the rise of the IT industry to one-twelfth of that country's economy, and the industry's growth in cities ranging from Bangalore to Gurgaon, and Pune to Hyderabad.

Our examination of the stock and recent flow of Indians continues into chapter 3, "A Coat of Many Colors," in which we discuss the diversity of Indians in America by disaggregating the national-level data along two intersecting dimensions of geography: the geography of origin in India (expressed through language spoken) and the geography of settlement in the United States. That is, where in India did the Indians come from, where in the United States did they settle, and what do these specific movements imply for the Indian-American population? We study these questions at disaggregated scales (states, counties, municipalities, metropolises, and places) in order to detail the variances within the Indian population in the United States—its clusters, concentrations, and inequalities.

We identify the large Indian clusters in the New York–New Jersey metropolitan region (especially in Queens County, New York, and Middlesex County, New Jersey), in Santa Clara County in California, in and around Chicago-Schaumberg in Illinois, and in the suburbs of Washington, D.C., and Houston and Dallas. We argue that the concentration of Indians in a handful of occupations—the IT sector alone employed more than one-fourth of all Indians working in the United States in the early 2010s—along with the clustering of these occupations in a few places in the United States had created a new, specialized settlement form that we call "ethno-techno-burb." This new settlement form is different from the "ethnic enclave" of old—the Chinatowns and Little Havanas and Little Sicilies—and different yet from the "ethnoburbs" of recent decades, because along with a clustering of co-ethnics in selected suburbs was the fact of their specialization in technical fields.

It is a paradox. Despite the decline in housing discrimination and institutionalized racism in the United States, and an almost unlimited freedom of location choice (conditional, of course, on income), a large proportion of Indians were spatially constrained by the work they did to residential choices in a small number of specialized suburbs. They were like workers in the coal industry, concentrated where the coal seams were.

Our method allows us to see where the IT professionals lived, as well as the doctors and money managers, the retail workers and farmers, the highly educated and the less educated, and the very rich and the poor—and the size of the gap between these groups. It is necessary to emphasize that there was substantial variance within the Indian community, with extremes at the two ends. At the time of this writing, it was estimated that there were as many as a quarter of a million undocumented individuals from India, roughly one in twelve of the adult population had less than a high school education, one in ten households did not have a single person older than fourteen who spoke English well, and one in eight individuals did not have health insurance.

We identify these polarizations and juxtapositions in specific ways. For instance, we show the extreme polarization in the New York metropolitan region, which had two of the four and five of the twenty highest-income settlements of the India-born, even as it harbored two of the three and seven of the twenty lowest-income settlements. Similar, albeit less stark, juxtapositions existed in California between the high-tech, high-income cluster in Silicon Valley, where more than half the India-born population had advanced degrees, less than a hundred miles from locations in the Central Valley, where fewer than one in ten India-born had advanced degrees and most worked in low-income agriculture.

These different combinations of data allow us to identify an emerging story of India's different linguistic groups and their distinct histories, geographies, and occupations in the United States. For instance, Punjabis specialized in the transportation and retail trade sectors; Gujaratis dominated in the hotel/restaurant and retail trade sectors; Malayalis were strongly concentrated in the nursing sector; Bengalis were disproportionately employed in the education sector; and the IT sector had a high concentration of Telugus and Tamils. Physicians were more evenly divided among the languages, a rare case of linguistic evenness.

We show that the three phases of Indian immigration also had distinct linguistic patterns. The Early Movers and The Families in the first two phases were composed primarily of Gujaratis and Punjabis (and to a lesser extent, Malayalam and Urdu speakers); we call this group Settlers 1.0. On the other hand, the IT Generation (which we call Settlers 2.0) was dominated by Hindi, Telugu, and Tamil speakers (and, to a much lesser extent, Kannada, Marathi, and Bengali speakers). Settlers 2.0 were much more educated and earned about 50 percent more, on average, than Settlers 1.0. So different were these groups that a comparison of the top and bottom by income (Kannadigas or Telugus vs. Punjabis) could lead to the conclusion that, other than the country of origin, they had almost nothing in common. At the time of this writing, the demographic dominance of Settlers 2.0 within the community made it the driver of the key characteristics of settlement, education, income, and linguistic composition for the overall Indian population, and appeared poised to create new Indian-American identities.

The work in chapter 4, "Becoming American," examines the multiple pathways—economic, social, cultural, civic, political—that all immigrants travel to "become American," maintaining some aspects of their distinctive identities while shedding others. We interrogate this story from multiple angles: naturalization, civic engagement, and forms of political participation. How did discrimination—from blatant racism to more subtle glass ceilings—shape the forms and degree of assimilation? What does assimilation mean for the second-generation Indian American and how is it manifested through exogamy, fertility decisions, occupation choices, and different forms of civic and political engagement? Is there a "regression to the mean"—that is, is the second generation becoming more like the average American? The quintessential immigrant story in the United States is of first-generation immigrants coming with education and incomes below the home average, and taking several generations to rise up to the host average. But, in the case of Indian Americans, the first generation already had considerably higher averages than at home and host; hence, for the second generation, a regression to the mean could only mean downward mobility. Is that the case? With relatively limited evidence—because the second generation was so young (five out of six were younger than twenty-five)—we argue that the answer is negative: there was no downward regression to the mean. Therefore, because of the rising significance of high-skilled labor migration into more developed economies, our findings invite a fundamental reexamination of some accepted precepts of immigration theory on assimilation.

Assimilation is not, of course, simply a second-generation issue. We examine some specific questions about first-generation immigrants: whether, for instance, greater familiarity with English, relatively low levels of illegal immigration, and higher levels of education have facilitated economic assimilation, at the same time that different religious and linguistic identities have impeded cultural and social assimilation. How have cultural mores and social practices impeded or adapted assimilation? Our analysis of gender relations examines whether the patriarchal norms prevalent in India have "traveled," and on what dimensions they have changed and how? We find mixed evidence of change (for instance, in child gender ratios), but also surprisingly, how the U.S. visa regime itself, with its differential labor rules regarding "worker" and "spouse," reinforces patriarchy.

Professional and entrepreneurial success, however, go only so far as indicators of assimilatory success. A presence in politics, public life, and popular culture are the other signs of a community's assimilation. While the gubernatorial success of Bobby Jindal and Nikki Haley might signal the community's arrival in politics, they also point to an important barrier—religion—that has hobbled this ambition. And religion, we argue, might also explain why Indian Americans appear to vote against their class interests by shying away from the Republican Party and voting overwhelmingly for Democratic candidates—at rates higher than most groups other than African Americans.

Given the sheer diversity of India—languages, cultures, religions—it is unsurprising that the "Indian" in "Indian American" is contested terrain, as reflected in the multiple and distinct sites where the community congregates to worship (temples, gurdwaras, mosques), to be entertained (Bollywood and regional language films and live shows), and sites of cultural reproduction (language, performing arts, and religious-instruction schools for second-generation children). Indeed, one of the biggest divides is between activists (including academics based in the humanities) and those claiming to speak for (and represent) the majority community. The contestations of self-identity are manifest in many ways—through the reinvention of names, for instance—as immigrants seek to "fit in." We try to understand a critical subjectivity involved in assimilation, namely ethnicity and identity. What do we make of the range of hyphenated identities as, for example, Gujarati, Gujarati American, Indian American, Asian Indian, South Asian American, Asian American, or just American? In examining this issue we also shed some light on what we term "the diaspora in the diaspora"—the roughly 10 percent of the Indian 1 percent who were born neither in India nor in the United States.

Unlike earlier waves of immigrants, Indians arrived in an America that was more tolerant of hybrid identities. While this has meant that, for example, Indians have not Anglicized their last names, they have yielded ground on first names, picking two-syllable names that can be pronounced by their children's peers and teachers. Are these types of practices emblematic of a new hyphenated American, representing a more liminal cosmopolitanism, or simply a veneer masking more chauvinistic identities? The answers are not easy or clear; as we discover in multiple ways and places, to be Indian in America is not one thing, not a single identity that is "conservative" or "liberal," or any of the simplifying polarizations that dominate the discourse. We struggle to reach some understanding, trying always to not be reduced by the need to be conclusive.

Next, in chapter 5, "Entrepreneurship by the Numbers," we turn our attention to entrepreneurship. For a long time, the image of Indian-American success was found in the professions—successful doctors and engineers who epitomized the suburban good life, though some of these professionals were also small business owners, running their own practices, individually or in partnerships. A second pillar of the community—the entrepreneurs—was concentrated in ethnic businesses such as Indian grocery stores and restaurants. The educated middle class was risk averse and held on to a traditional (Indian) class aversion towards entrepreneurship. This began to change in the 1980s and 1990s, with the emergence of entrepreneurial initiatives in hospitality, trade, and even manufacturing, in places like Boston and Chicago, Houston and Washington, D.C. But the most visible manifestation was the rise of the Silicon Valley innovators/entrepreneurs who created successful software or hardware companies. While these tech companies and their founders were more visible in the media, the leading industry sectors for entrepreneurship, we find, were not necessarily those in which Indian Americans work (like computers and technology), but in industries requiring less skilled labor (restaurants, grocery stores, convenience stores, hotels, etc.) and in franchise ownership across a host of service industries. We are able to outline a story of the diversification of Indian-American entrepreneurs, from traditional ethnic enterprises into new industry sectors, and from community strongholds into uncharted terrain.

We are as interested in the entrepreneurs as we are in entrepreneurship. Our data (which include original surveys and interviews) allow us to describe patterns of education and migration, linkages with India, motivations, and cultural norms. The patterns we look at go beyond individual variables to examine how different characteristics of individuals are related to their entrepreneurship choices and the outcomes of those decisions. We analyze "generational differences" in terms of both chronological age and the degree of remove from the displacement of immigration, and "motivations," including reasons for moving and for becoming entrepreneurs. We compare the patterns we find with those of other studies of Indian Americans, of immigrants, and of other entrepreneurs to understand the differences, as well as the basic similarities. For example, does education trump culture in explaining choices and predicting success? Do distinctively "Indian values" matter, or are they just personal characteristics that happen to be prevalent among this select group of immigrants? These questions are particularly germane given current debates on the contributions of immigrants to creating new firms in the United States.

Our analysis of both U.S. Census data and survey data on Indian-American business owners suggest that there is no obvious "secret sauce" in their entrepreneurial success. Education and familiarity with English are important determinants of success. High levels of education persist for the second generation, even though there is a broadening of choices of field in education and of sector or industry in subsequent careers. The census data from 2007 suggest that women entrepreneurs still do not do as well as men, on average, but the survey data from 2013 indicate that the playing field may be leveling, at least at the high end. Again, education seems to play an important role in allowing Indian-American women access to successful careers, entrepreneurial or otherwise. The survey data do not provide any evidence for special roles played by networks or values in the success of Indian-American entrepreneurs. Of course, both sets of factors play a positive role in success, as emerges from survey responses. But the processes do not seem especially distinctive from those operating for any other well-educated ethnic immigrant group.

Chapter 6, "Entrepreneurial Narratives, Niches, and Networks," uses individual interviews conducted for this study, as well as interviews available in print and other media, to anchor the Indian-American entrepreneurial story with specific examples. The prototypal Gujarati motel and hotel owner business community has leveraged a classic ethnic network, one that is based on social identities (particularly caste affiliations) and norms of trust and reciprocity. A large number of these business owners came from a narrow segment of the Gujarati population, namely Patels and a couple of related caste groups. On the other hand, the success of Indian-American entrepreneurs in Silicon Valley appears to have been aided by a conscious attempt to create a pan-Indian (indeed, pan–South Asian) network of information sharing and mentoring. No doubt, there are regional ethnic networks that continue to operate, and alumni networks (particularly that of IIT graduates) that are very important in the technology sector, but institutions like The Indus Entrepreneurs represented a significant innovation for Indian Americans, though preceded by similar efforts by Taiwanese and Chinese Americans.[6]

Individual stories of Indian-American entrepreneurs also reveal some of the challenges of assimilation. The American Dream can include conspicuous consumption and self-promotion, and some of the perils of this path are illustrated in chapter 6. A strong message of this chapter, as in preceding chapters, is of diversity: the Indian-American entrepreneurial experience is widely varied. The stories of Silicon Valley and the Gujarati motel owners are well known, and revisited here, but there are also gas station owners, taxi drivers, comic book aficionados, and more. Diversity also shows up in social entrepreneurship, with the classic philanthropy of the older generation, aimed at their home country, complemented in various local efforts by younger Indian Americans, where the nature of their enterprises is unrelated to their national or ethnic backgrounds. Younger Indian-American entrepreneurs are also venturing into more varied fields and bring with them more global experiences. While many Indian immigrant entrepreneurs have come from privileged social backgrounds in India, the first generation arrived almost empty-pocketed (as a result of India's foreign exchange controls and not necessarily family penury); recent arrivals are less financially pressed. There are also rags-to-riches stories sampled in this chapter. The case of Sikhs, as a religious minority within a minority, further illustrates some of the diversity of experience among Indian-American entrepreneurs.

Finally, in chapter 7, "Host and Home," we turn the lens in the other direction: the relationship of Indian Americans with the country of origin—India. The economic success of Indian Americans within a single generation has implications that go well beyond the immigrants themselves, affecting both their countries of origin and of settlement; on the relationship between the two; and on the vexing subject of immigration policy. We first examine how Indian Americans have affected their country of origin, through trade and investment, financial flows in the form of remittances, cross-border philanthropy, and the flow of information and ideas. We argue that their success in the United States has had reputational externalities, which has given them access as interlocutors in both countries. While not the driver, they have helped put a proverbial foot on both the accelerator and the brake in the relationship between the world's largest and most powerful democracies. And as the geopolitical tectonic plates shift in Asia, this community has helped facilitate stronger U.S.–India relations.

Of all the drivers of contemporary globalization—trade in goods and services, flows of investment, information, and people—it is the last that is the most politically contentious. What are some implications of the economic success of Indian Americans in what is still the most powerful country: for immigration policy, both in the United States and more broadly? Are the key factors that have led to this outcome—selection and the context of reception—replicable or even normatively desirable? The evidence in this book strongly suggests that *how* one comes into the country is critical to the likelihood of economic success and upward mobility. We argue that the immigration literature has underplayed the importance of the manner of arriving in the United States. Even among legal immigrants, those coming in as students or on work visas have much better access to labor markets than those who enter as refugees or through family sponsorship, and this fundamentally affects their long-term economic prospects, as well as their economic contributions. It is also less conflictual, since the immigrants' assimilation path is less contentious.

But this amplifies the privileges of those already relatively privileged. New factors, such as the rise of dual citizenship, greater global economic opportunities, and easier links with the country of origin make "circulation" more feasible, giving mobile human capital greater bargaining power and the rents that come with it. For immigrants, how these trends are affecting assimilation characteristics and what they mean for citizenship in the twenty-first century is unclear. And for immigrant-destination countries, the importance of economic factors relative to the weight of other factors in deciding whom to allow in has more or less become a form of social engineering whose effects will reverberate well into the future on fundamental conceptions of citizenship and nationhood.

We end the final chapter and the book with some crystal-gazing about the future of Indians in America. Because of the vicissitudes of globalization and national policies, it is not possible to project with any degree of certainty how many more Indians will immigrate to the United States. We do know, however, that the recent Indian immigrants have been young people (two-thirds are between 20 and 35 years old), in the prime of fertility and reproduction. We are also sure of one number: the children already born in the United States to Indian parents. They are already here. This cohort of second-generation Indians will more than double in size by 2030. Considering the new entrants and the reproductive patterns of existing and new arrivals, it is possible that the Indian-origin population in the United States could double in a couple of decades, from a little over 3 million to about 6 million. Thus, the "other one percent" will then become the "other two percent," with its second generation forming a population of significant size and voice. Perhaps, by then, this book will need to be rewritten, with an updated title and by authors who are the progeny of the first generation. But that outcome is not only some time away, it is by no means certain, as Indians and other immigrants in the United States negotiate their way through these anxious times.

ACKNOWLEDGMENTS

This book has its antecedents in a grant provided by the Government of India's Ministry of Overseas Indian Affairs (MOIA, subsequently merged with the Ministry of External Affairs in January 2016) to the Center for the Advanced Study of India (CASI), School of Arts and Sciences, University of Pennsylvania, on research related to the Indian diaspora. That grant resulted in three reports: Sanjoy Chakravorty, "The Indian-Born Population in the United States: Distribution and Characteristics"; Randall Akee and Devesh Kapur, "Characteristics and Uses of International Remittances: A Comparison of Non-Resident Account Holders with Average Migrant Households"; and Nirvikar Singh, "Entrepreneurship and the Indian-American Community." The background work that resulted from this grant provided the seeds that sprouted into this book project.

A project of this scope results in many debts. Our foremost debt is to the staff of the Center for the Advanced Study of India (CASI) at the University of Pennsylvania, who helped manage the grants, workshops, student research assistants, and myriad other operational issues with especially good cheer and support. Their own families' immigration experiences from around the world were a constant reminder of this quintessential American experience.

At the University of California, Santa Cruz, particular thanks are due to Professor Robert Fairlie of the Economics Department; Susan Leach, department manager; and graduate students James Chubb and Arshad Mirza. At the University of Pennsylvania, Aashna Desai and Alex Polyak conducted painstaking historical research and data for chapter 1. Megan Reed and Apoorva Jadhav put together data and analysis that was especially helpful for chapter 4. And Mollie Laffin-Rose painstakingly went through the copyedits. At Temple University, Liv Raddatz provided invaluable assistance in collating data for chapters 2 and 3 for the MOIA report.

We are also deeply grateful to the South Asian American Digital Archive, and in particular Samip Mallick, the Co-Founder and Executive Director, who has put together an invaluable resource. John (Jack) Boulet, Vice President of Research and Data Resources, Foundation for Advancement of International Medical Education and Research, very generously shared data and insights on Indian-origin and Indian-trained physicians in the United States. Yash Jaggi, a high school student, patiently put together data on scholastic achievements of young Indian Americans. And Neelanjan Sircar was always there to both bounce ideas off and serve as a crucial data analysis guru.

Parts of the book were presented at various seminars, and we are grateful to the participants at seminars at Boston University (arranged by Professor Min Ye and co-sponsored by the Frederick S. Pardee Center for the Study of the Longer-Range Future, in cooperation with the Center for the Study of Asia and the East Asian Studies program), the Social Science and Policy Forum at the University of Pennsylvania, the South Asia Institute at Harvard University (arranged by Professor Akshay Mangla), the annual Board meeting of the International Advisory Board of CASI, and Vijay Advani at his home in California.

A first draft of the book was discussed at a day-long seminar held at CASI. We are grateful to Tanya Carey, Georgette Rochlin, Juliana Di Giustini, Apoorva Jadhav, Megan Reed, Neelanjan Sircar, Milan Vaishnav, and Sadhana Kapur for their thoughtful comments. Some results from the book were also presented at a workshop on India's Political Economy at CASI, where Lant Pritchett suggested an idea that resulted in a modification to figure 3.16, and several other participants provided valuable feedback.

A Short History of Small Numbers

In 1948, a year after India's independence, Jagjit (J. J.) Singh, a prosperous immigrant entrepreneur from India who had lived in the United States since 1926, complained in a letter to the *New York Times* that "Columbus Had Word for the Natives Here and It's a Nuisance to Visitors from India."[1] JJ, as he was popularly known, had led the India League of America since 1941 and had parlayed his status as a successful, urbane Manhattan businessman into an influential "envoy" on behalf of India's cause.[2] The linguistic confusion over the word *Indian* had seemingly linked the fates of two countries half a world apart. "Destiny," President Harry Truman stated while welcoming Prime Minister Jawaharlal Nehru on his maiden visit to the United States, had "willed it that our country should have been discovered in the search for a new route to yours."[3]

Columbus, as we shall see, was hardly alone in his linguistic confusion about a group called "Indian." Half a millennium after Columbus's epic voyage, the original "Indian" "in Columbus's discovery—now renamed "Native American" and sometimes "American Indian"—languishes at the bottom of the socioeconomic hierarchy in the United States, a poignant testament to the ravages suffered by the original inhabitants of the Americas. Meanwhile, the Indians from the part of the world whose riches Columbus was chasing have emerged as one of the most economically successful (and arguably *the* most successful) immigrant groups in the United States by the early part of the twenty-first century, even while the country they left has just a modicum of the riches that Columbus was looking for.

That a simple linguistic reversal—from American Indians to Indian Americans—also reverses education and income, the modern markers of life's chances, at one level simply reflects the ironies of human history. But at another level it presents a curious puzzle. How did an immigrant group from halfway around the world, from a country with the largest concentration of the world's poor, end up being so successful in a country that fought for much of the twentieth century to keep them out?

This book seeks to address this puzzle and to detail the rise of the Indian-American community, with the evolution of U.S. immigration policy as the backdrop. As Hannah Arendt observed, "sovereignty is nowhere more absolute than in matters of emigration, naturalization, nationality and expulsion."[4] Visions of the political community—"the people" who constitute "the nation"—have been fundamental in shaping immigration policy all over the globe. In the case of the United States, immigrants have been at the core of its self-conception as a nation. In his 1958 essay on the contribution of immigrants to American society, John F. Kennedy argued that "every American who ever lived, with the exception of one group, was either an immigrant himself or a descendant of immigrants."[5] At the same time, however, for "two-thirds of U.S. history, the majority of its population was explicitly excluded from citizenship based on ascriptive criteria such as race and sex."[6] Those exclusions, unsurprisingly, were intimately intertwined with immigration policy.

This core tension provides the backdrop to our story, which unfolds over the *longue durée* of the twentieth century during which the economic and educational status and the domestic economy and politics of emigrant countries shaped people's propensity to leave; who was welcomed (or not) in the immigrants' destination countries; international politics that influenced bilateral relationships and international norms that underpinned attitudes regarding immigrants, race and ethnicity; and economic and technological changes that molded the demand for labor and skills. But history also unfolds because of chance, contingencies, and unintended consequences, which is abundantly the case here as well.

Until 1882, the United States did not have an immigration policy: anyone who came could stay. However, there was ambivalence about new arrivals depending on where they came from. While this ambivalence was initially centered on "culture" or "assimilability," later on race emerged as the central concern. Benjamin Franklin had worried about the Germans, alarmed that "Pennsylvania, founded by the English," might "become a colony of aliens, who will shortly be so numerous as to germanize us instead of our anglifying them."[7] Later generations worried about Irish immigrants, then Italians, Jews and Eastern Europeans, subsequently the "Orientals," and most recently, Hispanics and Muslims.

Beginning with the Page Act in 1875, which prohibited the entry of immigrants considered "undesirable" (defined as any individual coming as a forced laborer from Asia, any Asian woman who would engage in prostitution, and anyone who would be regarded as a convict in his or her own country), and particularly after the first Chinese Exclusion Act of 1882, the doors for immigrants from Asia began to close. Initially, Chinese laborers were the only group specifically targeted by immigration statutes before 1917. However, the substantial influx of less educated immigrants from southern and eastern Europe in the years prior to World War I drove a growing nativist and xenophobic sentiment, especially on the East Coast. On the West Coast, growing intolerance targeted immigrants from Asia, especially from China and Japan, and later Korea and what was then British-ruled India.

The result was steady increases in restrictions on immigration. The 1917 Immigration Act created the "Asiatic Barred Zone" (see figure 1.1), virtually terminating immigration from Asia. It culminated in the 1924 law, which created a highly restrictive system of national-origin quotas favoring northern European immigrants and set limits on others that were steadily tightened as the Great Depression set in. These severe restrictions would be gradually loosened after World War II, but it was not until the 1965 immigration reform act that the doors really opened to immigrants without specific regard to their race.

The doors had closed in response to a confluence of factors, including anti-Asian nativist and xenophobic sentiment, a post–World War I recession that amplified opposition from labor, and theories of racial superiority propagated by "intellectuals" involved in the eugenics movement. But underlying some of this, ironically, was an expansion of democracy as elected officials responded to popular labor movements. The Zeitgeist of "the morbid age" (in historian Richard Overy's characterization of the interbellum, or interwar, period) had much to do with the growing alarm of "the foreign," whether it involved trade, money, or people.

It would take the horrors of World War II to completely thoroughly delegitimize the eugenics movement. Subsequently, the civil rights movement further undermined the intellectual arguments that had underpinned the racial bias in immigration laws. Lobbying by ethnic groups whose numbers had been limited by country-of-origin quotas also played a role. But perhaps the decisive factor that curbed congressional opposition to the removal of racial immigration quotas was the cold war—this was an opportunity to deny the Soviet Union the facile propaganda victories it had been reaping from the racist underpinnings of American immigration policy.[8]

The resulting policy shift—the Immigration and Naturalization Act of 1965 (also known as the Hart-Celler Act)—would transform immigration into the United States, and along with it the Indian-American community. Although analyzing this transformation is the main subject of this book, one needs to understand the earlier history of migration from the Indian subcontinent. Figure 1.2 provides a timeline of the key events in this history until 1965.

Pre-1965

There are three notable features of the Indian-American presence prior to 1965: first, it was minuscule; second, despite their tiny numbers, the immigrants encountered virulent animosity; and third, there was a high degree of

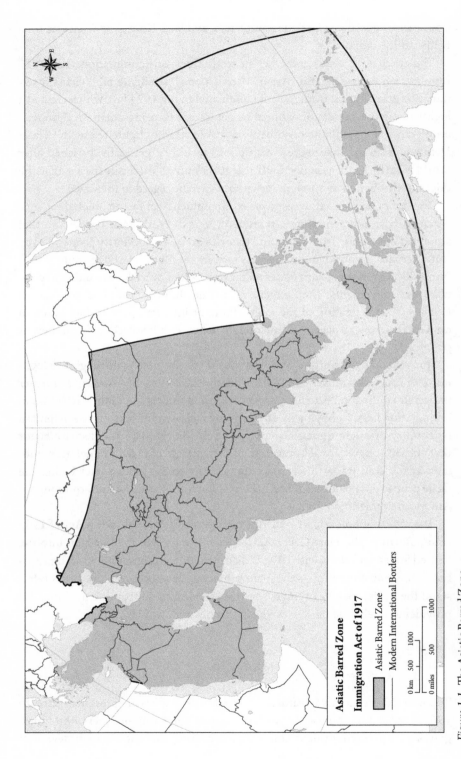

Figure 1.1 The Asiatic Barred Zone.
Source: Wikipedia.

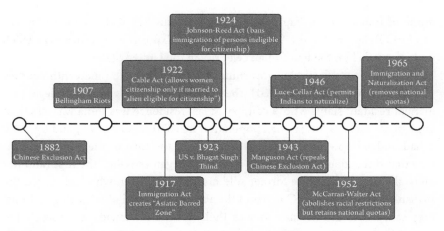

Figure 1.2 Timeline of Major Events in the Immigration History of Indian Americans.

ignorance and confusion among Americans about people from the Indian subcontinent.

Trickling In

Although people from the Indian subcontinent had been migrating to other lands during much of the last millennium (with those currently known as the Roma being perhaps the first major emigrant group), large-scale migration began only after the abolition of slavery in the British Empire in 1833, which created a demand for cheap labor. Most migrants from India went to South or Southeast Asia—about 42 percent settled in Burma, another quarter in Ceylon, a fifth in British Malaya, and the rest went to Africa, the Caribbean, and Fiji. Indian migration to the Caribbean— about half a million strong—was mainly in the form of indentured labor for the sugar plantations of Guyana, Suriname, Jamaica, and other Caribbean islands. Some of these people's descendants would later make their way to the United States, but that would not occur until the latter decades of the twentieth century.

The few Indians who arrived in the United States in the nineteenth century often came as sailors on ships plying waters between Indian and American ports. According to one source, the first recorded mention of Indians visiting America was "six or seven Indian sailors" brought to New England seminaries in the 1820s.[9] Surprisingly for a society that was extremely conservative with regard to women's education, two women (who were also cousins) traveled to and studied in the United States in the 1880s: Anandibai Joshee, who graduated from the Woman's Medical College of Pennsylvania in 1886 (and apparently "startled her American student counterparts by appearing in a sari in her first anatomy class"),[10] and Pandita Ramabai, a social reformer. Both returned to India. Another early visitor from India was Swami Vivekananda, "the Hindoo monk of India," whose "rapturously received addresses at the fair's Parliament of World Religions," at the World's Columbian Exposition in Chicago in 1893, perhaps made him the first Indian celebrity in the United States.[11]

According to official U.S. government data, during the nineteenth century (the data is available from 1820), the number of persons obtaining legal permanent resident status whose country of last residence was India was less than ten a year. The U.S. India-born population in 1870 was just 586, and by 1900 it had nudged upward to 2,031. It was only at the turn of the twentieth century that three identifiable groups of Indians began arriving. The first (and numerically dominant) were former soldiers and policemen who had served the British colonial forces in China and the Far East. Instead of returning to India, they sailed east and decided to seek their fortune in Canada and the United States. They were largely from Punjab, were male, and were predominantly Sikhs (with some Muslims), although American officials (and the U.S. Census) classified them as "Hindus." They were later joined by young men from farming communities in Punjab who settled on the West Coast, in the region stretching between Vancouver and Seattle to Portland and south to San Francisco. Initially recruited by the Western Pacific Railroad to construct railway lines in the Pacific Northwest, they gradually branched out to working in lumber and construction, and as they moved farther south, they worked as agricultural laborers. Another set of immigrants were students—in this case, mainly Hindu with some Sikh and Muslims, almost all males—studying at Stanford University, the University of Washington, some midwestern and East Coast universities, and the University of California, Berkeley. The last, with its $15 annual fee, was a favorite.

Recent historical work has identified another group from rural Bengal, mainly Muslim men, who often worked as stokers on British merchant vessels and who jumped ship when their vessels were berthed in U.S. ports. Many were sojourners and most returned to the subcontinent after working for a while in the United States. Those who stayed married African-American, Creole, and Puerto Rican women, and settled in places as varied as New Orleans, Detroit, western Baltimore, and Harlem, in New York City. But unlike their Punjabi counterparts, they did not form visible enclaves nor leave much of a trace in the way the Punjabis on the West Coast had.[12]

During the first two decades of the twentieth century, these new arrivals amounted to only 300 immigrants annually, with many returning to India. From 1910 to 1920, the Indian-American population barely increased, from 4,664 to 4,901, less than 300 over a decade. Despite these minuscule numbers, however, their presence generated a backlash. Ironically, a century later, when the Indian-American population increased by more than 300 every day, there was limited backlash. This stark difference in response to the Indian-American presence encapsulates the transformation not just of the community but also of the United States itself.

Race: The First Frontier

In the beginning of the twentieth century, there were many differences between the United States and India. But they shared one deeply pernicious historical legacy. In both cases, ascriptive identities—caste in India and race in the United States—had created extremely stratified societies whose troubling legacies have meant that even today, to echo William Faulkner, "The past isn't dead and buried. In fact, it isn't even past."

The arrival of "Hindus," as all people from the Indian subcontinent were officially termed regardless of religion, was in part a by-product of Indian immigration to Canada in the first decade of the twentieth century. Most were farmers and laborers from the Punjab, where Canadian companies seeking contract labor in British Columbia had publicized the economic opportunities in the country. Some 2,623 Indians entered Canada in 1907, and opposition quickly mounted. Fear of labor competition drove nativist and xenophobic opposition, leading to anti-Indian riots. Deploying skillful subterfuge in its immigration laws—specifically a requirement of "continuous voyage" from the country of origin to Canada—the Canadian government effectively ended this Indian immigration in 1909, in which year only six Indians were admitted.

The passage of highly restrictive immigration laws in Canada increased fears in the United States that there would be a greater influx of immigrants from the subcontinent who would otherwise have proceeded to Canada. It also provided grist for the mill among opponents of Indian immigration in the United States, given that Canada had chosen such restrictive policies despite being part of the British Empire along with India.

The competition for jobs amid fears that the new immigrants were willing to work for less money further fueled nativist antipathy. The arrival of Chinese labor, followed by the Japanese in the late nineteenth century, had already created a racist backlash. The president of the American Sociological Association warned in 1901 that Asian migration would lead to "race suicide" for whites. The Chinese Exclusion Act of 1882 and the 1908 Root-Takahira "Gentleman's Agreement" had severely restricted immigration from those two countries. The "Hindus" were soon caught in the anti-Asiatic maelstrom, fueled by the arrival of 127,000 Japanese between 1901 and 1908. Beginning in 1907, California's rural areas began pressing for legislation that would exclude Orientals from land ownership. A widely publicized report by the chief investigator of the Immigration Commission on the Pacific Coast in 1910 concluded that Indians were "the most undesirable of all Asiatics and the peoples of the Pacific states were unanimous in their desire for exclusion."[13] The Asiatic Exclusion League (AEL)—formed by the merger of Japanese and Korean Exclusion Leagues in 1905—whose constitutional objective was "the preservation of the Caucasian race upon American soil," announced with alarm that there were over 10,000 "Hindus" in California (in fact, the total in all the Pacific states was less than 6,000) and demanded that the federal government exclude them.[14] The league warned that Japanese and Italian immigration had mushroomed from similar modest beginnings.

Unsurprisingly, the immigrants from the Indian subcontinent began facing increasing discrimination and nativist hostility. In 1907, the Oregon State Legislature enacted a law prohibiting Indians from acquiring permanent residency in the state.[15] A major riot in the town of Bellingham, Washington, in 1907 was a landmark. On a September night that year, a mob of six hundred lumber-mill workers, incited by the AEL, attacked the compounds of immigrant workers from India. A news report on the riots at the time commented that the rioters struck with excessive violence to "impress upon employers the resentment of the laboring men against the importation of Hindu workmen."[16] A hysterical article in *Overland* warned that America faced an inundation of "Hindus," since the Vedas obliged them to "cover the earth."[17] The AEL held the Indians responsible for the riots, claiming their willingness to work for low wages and that their "filthy and immodest habits" invited reprisals.[18]

Bellingham had witnessed ethnic cleansing in almost identical fashion a few years earlier, when white workers drove out Chinese immigrants. Despite the pleas from the mayor of Bellingham, who "urged the Hindus to remain, and assured them of the city's protection," and the promise of mill owners to pay the Indians on a par with whites, most Indians from Bellingham and neighboring towns fled to Canada, traumatized after seeing their shacks destroyed and their belongings vandalized.[19]

The Bellingham riot was followed by other acts of violence in the Northwest, a sign of growing racial intolerance toward Asians. The "problem presented by the natives of India [was] not, as in the case of the Japanese and Chinese, a race problem." . . . They were at least "Aryan, not as black as frequently characterized in the press."[20] Instead the problem was "industrial." Thus, while Indians were perceived as undesirable, as those who "live in dirt and filth," competition in labor markets that was seen to be driving down wages appeared (at least initially) as the prime factor driving the antipathy toward the group.

These immigrants were entering a United States that was undergoing a momentous demographic upheaval. Starting in the 1880s, an enormous wave of immigration had begun, and it continued unabated until the outbreak of World War I. Between 1900 and 1915, 15 million immigrants entered the United States, equal to the number who had arrived in the prior four decades.[21] In 1900, the U.S. population was 76 million; by 1915, the population had increased by one-third to over 100 million.[22] Moreover, these immigrants represented a significantly different demographic from prior immigrant groups. Whereas the nineteenth century saw large-scale migration from western and northern Europe, the late nineteenth- and early twentieth-century migration stemmed largely from eastern and southern Europe.

The arrival of ethnic, linguistic, and religious groups who were different from earlier immigrants generated much unease about the character of immigration, particularly since it was concomitant with the massive upheavals generated by the second industrial revolution. Upheavals breed anxieties that often transmute into fear and hostility against "the Other."[23] The nation of immigrants was now having serious qualms about the effects of immigration on its national character.

These anxieties were magnified by the concerns of the progressive movement of the early twentieth century. At a time when social Darwinism and eugenics were in intellectual vogue, the progressive movement supported efforts to restrict immigration from those parts of the world that challenged the perception of America as a homogenous entity composed of western European, Christian (preferably Protestant) stock. The rapid arrival on the West Coast of Asians, first from east Asia and subsequently from south Asia introduced major new racial demographics into a nation with congealed black-white binaries. The East Coast saw a large inflow of Jews, Italian Catholics, Greek Orthodox, and other religious groups, creating apprehensions among Protestant elites, who feared the influence of these other religions on American public life. In particular, the arrival of millions of eastern and southern European Catholics, on the heels of a substantial influx of Irish Catholics, frightened many observers concerned with possible "divided loyalties" between the immigrants' adopted country and the Papacy.[24]

With the AEL fanning fears of a "Hindu invasion" of the West Coast,[25] the U.S. Congress House Committee on Immigration and Naturalization Congress held "Hindu Immigration Hearings" on February 13, 1914. In Congress, Representative Denver S. Church, from California's seventh congressional district and elected with the backing of the AEL, led a determined and vitriolic campaign for exclusion. Church groups joined hands with Senator Ellison D. "Cotton Ed" Smith of South Carolina and introduced measures in 1914 to exclude "Hindu" laborers.[26] An Indian immigrant, Sudhindra Bose, spoke on behalf of a delegation that had been sent by two Indian organizations (the Pacific Coast Khalsa Diwan Society and the Hindustan Association of America), stating that "Hindus [*sic*] come to this country precisely for the same reason as the millions that come to this country from other countries. To us America is another name for opportunity."[27] He then narrated his own story as someone who had come as a laborer, obtained a doctorate within a decade, and was at the time, at the age of thirty, a lecturer at the State University of Iowa.

In his testimony, Anthony Caminetti, the Commissioner General of Immigration, repeatedly insisted that "Asiatic" and "Hindu" immigration" were "a menace to the country, and particularly to California."[28] When asked how many of them were in the country, recognizing that his reply—6,656—might not appear menacing enough, he insisted that there must be more of them, especially in California's San Joaquin Valley. A range of reasons why they were a "menace" were laid out. The immigrants were accused of both being at risk of becoming public charges and working too hard for too little and driving out employment for (white) labor; not assimilating (especially through marriage), even as anti-miscegenation laws forbade it; and of not being literate.

A key reason to stop entry was to protect the American people from disease that the Indians were perceived to carry (especially hookworm). The hearings placed on record a "scientific" document that argued, "The question of the protection of the white race makes a study of the diseases of these people more important than even their economic or social characteristics. If the eastern immigrants are likely to deplete the vitality of our people, as the Negro has done, it is a far more serious question than if they merely force an unwelcome economic competition upon us."[29] And if their apparent inability to assimilate was seen as a major problem, successful assimilation was seen as posing an even more frightful prospect, since it would encourage another three hundred million to move to the United States!

Some of the most hostile reactions came from Representative Denver S. Church, who claimed that "those of us who come into contact with the Hindus, and I think it is universal, regard them as a menace. Now, regardless of how people feel on the immigration of other nationalities into this country, I stand here to say that everybody who has come in touch with this class of immigrants, who sees them and knows them, is in favor of their exclusion."[30] "They are a thick-headed and obtuse sort of people and can hardly appreciate those things . . . they cannot read our language any more than a horse can."[31] A century later, that same 7th Congressional District in California would be represented by Representative Amiresh Babulal "Ami" Bera, a second-generation Indian American whose parents had emigrated from Gujarat in 1958.

The overt racism was compounded by a lack of the most elemental knowledge of the immigrants' social and cultural backgrounds, as this exchange illustrates:

MR. CHURCH: They have their religion; in fact, it seems to be about all there is to a Hindu, his religion.
THE CHAIRMAN: Is that the Mohammedan religion?
MR. CHURCH: As I understand.[32]

Indeed, such sentiments had become relatively mainstream by the mid-1910s. The *Los Angeles Times* carried an article in 1915 with the headline: "Hindu Invasion Is Headed Off." It spoke in approving terms of the local campaign by the state immigration service to deport illegal Hindu migrants and prevent their entry into the state from the Mexican border.[33]

Although Church's demands were not initially met, the exclusion of "Hindus" was accomplished through the immigration law passed in February 1917, overriding a veto by President Woodrow Wilson. Intended primarily to restrict immigration from southern and eastern Europe, this act stipulated a literacy test requirement. It also established what came to be termed as the "Asiatic Barred Zone" (see figure 1.1). The Immigration Act of 1917 banned from admission into the United States for purposes of settlement all inhabitants of the continent of Asia "west of the 110th meridian of longitude east from Greenwich and east of the 50th meridian of longitude east from Greenwich and south of the 50th parallel of longitude north."[34] Essentially, this prohibited immigrants from most of Asia, including all of British India. In the congressional debate, despite the strong fears expressed by church officials and other California representatives of the threat posed to American labor by immigrants from Asia, the proponents of the measure failed to support their theory with any specific numbers. But that did not matter. By now, nativist and xenophobic sentiments had become pervasive.

Public sympathy for the community was further undermined by the well-publicized "Hindu German conspiracy" trials that commenced shortly after passage of the Immigration Act. Eight Indian nationalists, some of whom were members of the Gadar ("Revolt" or "Revolutionary") Party, were charged with conspiring with agents of the German government and Irish nationalists to overthrow British rule in India, and thereby violating American neutrality laws. For several years Indian immigrants had been organizing against British rule in India, hoping to capitalize on the strong anticolonial sentiments in American society.[35] The British government had been anxious, for the same reason, to ensure that Indian nationals did not immigrate to the United States in large numbers. The arrests came on the eve of U.S. entry into World War I, and the German link cast them as enemy agents. Nonetheless, although the Gadarites were jailed, American authorities staved off British pressure to extradite them to India, bowing to domestic public pressures that were still instinctively anticolonial.[36]

Between 1900 and 1924, after which Indian immigrants were legally proscribed from naturalizing, officially 8,115 immigrants from what was then British-ruled India entered the United States.[37] This immigration was part of a wider trend of Asian immigration to the West Coast during this time. In 1920, for example, there were 1,948 resident East Indians in California, compared to 28,812 Chinese and 71,952 Japanese.[38] What is particularly notable about the Indian populace as compared to other Asian populations is its extremely skewed gender ratio. By 1930, for every 100 Chinese women, there were 298.6 Chinese men; for every 100 Japanese women, there were 137.6 Japanese men; but for every 100 Indian women, there were 1,572.3 Indian men.[39]

The Wall Goes Up

By the early 1920s, anti-immigrant sentiment reached a new high in the United States. Biological theories of eugenics now provided scientific authority to exclude certain races because of their "proven" biological inferiority. If the 1917 Act closed the door to immigration, a Supreme Court ruling in 1923 stopped naturalization as well. In a decision that exemplified the tenacious hold of race in U.S. society, the Supreme Court ruled in *United States v. Bhagat Singh Thind* that immigrants from India settled in the United States were not eligible for naturalization as U.S. citizens.[40] Bhagat Singh Thind had immigrated to the United States in 1913, and then after a stint at U.C. Berkeley, enlisted in the U.S. Army when the United States entered World War I. In 1917, he petitioned for the right to hold U.S. citizenship.

Thind was granted citizenship twice, in 1918 and 1920, only to have the Immigration and Naturalization Service (INS) cancel his naturalization each time on the grounds of Section 2169 of the Revised Statutes of the Naturalization Act of 1790. This act, dating from the First Congress of the United States, had been revised after African emancipation and read as follows in 1923: "That any alien, being a free white person, who shall have resided within the limits and under the jurisdiction of the United States for the term of two years, may be admitted to become a citizen thereof . . . and be it further enacted, that the naturalization laws are hereby extended to aliens of African nativity and to persons of African descent."[41]

Though Thind had arrived in the United States prior to the 1917 Act that created the Asiatic Barred Zone, it was in the context of that act that Thind's case was heard before the Supreme Court. In a decision written by Justice George Sutherland, the Supreme Court examined Thind's claim that as an "ethnic north Indian Aryan" he was Caucasian and therefore eligible for naturalization as a "free white person." A year earlier, the court, in *Ozawa v. United States*, written by the same Justice Sutherland, had held that a Japanese man, though white of skin, was ineligible for citizenship under the Revised Statutes of 1790 because he was not Caucasian. In a remarkable *volte face*, Sutherland now wrote that Thind, though of Caucasian ethnicity, could not be naturalized because he was not "white" in the "popular" meaning of the term.

> What we now hold is that the words 'free white persons' are words of common speech, to be interpreted in accordance with the understanding

of the common man, synonymous with the word 'Caucasian' only as that word is popularly understood. . . . The children of English, French, German, Italian, Scandinavian, and other European parentage, quickly merge into the mass of our population and lose the distinctive hallmarks of their European origin. On the other hand, it cannot be doubted that the children born in this country of Hindu parents would retain indefinitely the clear evidence of their ancestry.[42]

Thus, a white man was not white because of the color of his skin or Caucasian ethnicity but, rather, in the court's view, in the "understanding of the common man"—a phrase Justice Sutherland judiciously chose not to define with any precision. Thind now did not have the legal right to be a U.S. citizen. Shortly thereafter, the INS and the Justice Department moved to rescind the citizenship of naturalized Indian immigrants.[43] In addition, the Immigration Act of 1924 implemented a national-origins quota system that specifically banned the admission of all groups that could not legally be naturalized in the United States.

Given the centrality of race in the construction of American nationhood, it was hardly surprising that the U.S. government struggled for nearly a century to find the appropriate racial box to classify Asian Indians. Early Asian Indians pointed to their Aryan roots in U.S. courts as a basis for attaining "white" status—based on the 1790 statute that naturalization could only be granted to "white persons and persons of African descent"—hoping to secure citizenship by virtue of being classified as "white." From 1880 to 1910, the U.S. Census Bureau vacillated between labeling Indians as "white" and leaving them in the "Other" category. A footnote in the 1910 Census, in which Asian Indians were reclassified as "Other," elucidates the official attitude the government adopted toward Asian Indians. The footnote reads that although

> pure-blood Hindus belong ethnically to the Caucasian or white race and in several instances have been officially declared to be white by the United States courts in naturalization proceedings . . . in view of the fact that the Hindus, whether pure-blood or not, represent a civilization distinctly different from that of Europe, it was thought proper to classify them with non-white Asiatics.

The debates within the Census Bureau on classifying people from the Indian subcontinent reflected the legal battles in the U.S. judicial system. Asian Indians were ruled "white" by courts in 1910, 1913, 1919, and 1920, but were declared nonwhite in 1909 and 1917.[44] With the Supreme Court ruling in the *Thind* case, Indians continued to be classified as Hindus in the 1920, 1930, and 1940

Censuses, despite the fact that many of the Indian pioneer immigrants—espe-cially on the West Coast—were Sikhs and Muslims from Punjab.

The combination of the 1917 and 1924 Immigration Acts effectively throt-tled immigration from India—the few who trickled in were largely students who managed to stay behind—which of course had been the intent of this legisla-tion. Some immigrants returned to India, unable to bear the racism and limited opportunities. As a result, the Indian population in the United States dwindled to 2,405 by 1940. The 1940 Census contained a footnote indicating that the Asian-Indian community had become significantly older by this time, and many in the population were illiterate and working as farm laborers. It found that the educational level for Asian Indians was the *lowest* of all reported racial and eth-nic groups. Ironically, as we document in chapter 2, Asian Indians now have the *highest* educational attainment of all racial and ethnic groups in the United States. But at that point, the community had shrunk to such an extent that Indians were no longer separately counted in the 1950 and 1960 Censuses; rather, they were shuffled back into the "Other" catch-all category with other Asian groups that included Thais and Malays.

In contrast, the metamorphosis in the immigration landscape of the United States after the 1965 Immigration Act led the U.S. government to establish "gov-ernment wide standards for ethnic and racial data collection" by standardizing categories for the 1970 Census.[45] This restructuring particularly affected South Asians. The Federal Interagency Committee on Education (FICE—a division of the U.S. Commission on Civil Rights) established a Committee on Racial and Ethnic Divisions, which debated whether to classify South Asians as Asian or white—Asian because South Asians are from Asia, or white because they are Caucasian, albeit with darker skin. In a reversal of terminology from the *Thind* decision in 1923, FICE concluded that because South Asians were Caucasian, they were to be classified as white.

But if, a half century ago, immigrants from the subcontinent fought to have themselves classified as white, ironically during the 1970s, in the post-civil rights era, they fought to avoid this classification. What had been a door to naturaliza-tion now became a cage that denied them minority status, and hence disqualified them from civil rights protections. Although the new cohort of immigrants was highly educated in contrast to their predecessors, racial discrimination, while less overt, was still rife. Indian-American community organizations launched a campaign to secure minority status for the community, arguing not only that the denial of minority status would have negative implications for access to ben-efits in employment, housing, and education, but also that classification of the Indian-American community as white would camouflage more subtle forms of racial discrimination—observed, for instance, in "glass ceilings" in corporate management. These efforts eventually prevailed, and the 1980 Census classified the community as "Asian Indian."[46]

The U.S. Supreme Court's ruling in the *Bhagat Singh Thind* case led to a series of court cases filed by naturalized Indians in an attempt to regain their citizenship. Sakharam Ganesh Pandit, the lawyer who had defended Thind, represented a fellow Indian migrant in the first case contesting the *Thind* ruling, but he lost, with the presiding judge ruling that "an alien when he lands on the shores of this country, comes with no right at all of any natural kind to have extended to him the privilege of citizenship."[47] Shortly following this court case, the government filed a petition to denaturalize Ganesh Pandit, the attorney himself.

Pandit's defense makes for a revealing anecdote. He noted that he had conducted himself as a responsible member of society: he had practiced law in California courts for over ten years and owned a $15,000 home (worth $2.6 million in 2014 dollars), and therefore derived both land and property from activities that could only be engendered by citizenship. If he were denaturalized, not only would he lose his occupation (foreigners could not practice law) and his property (from California Alien Land Law stipulations), but his marriage to his American-born wife could also be nullified.[48]

This last provision was a particularly odious feature of the anti-immigrant frenzy of the times. The Cable Act of 1922 (named after its chief sponsor) had partially attempted to liberalize existing marriage laws concerning the union of an American female and a foreign spouse. Hitherto, American wives would lose their U.S. citizenship and be forced to take up the citizenship of their husband; this former law was amended by the act to enable American wives to retain U.S. citizenship, but only if the alien spouse was himself eligible for U.S. citizenship, effectively rendering American wives with denaturalized husbands stateless in their own country.[49]

The denaturalization proceedings ultimately went to the Supreme Court, which in 1927 refused to grant a writ of certiorari to the government case. As a result, the Justice Department dropped all pending denaturalization cases against Indian migrants. However, it was not until the Luce-Celler Act of 1946 that Indian immigrants became fully eligible for naturalization. (The Cable Act was repealed earlier, in 1936.)

The 1924 Immigration Act banned Indians from immigrating, including those from outside the Asiatic Barred Zone, who were barred because they could not be naturalized. Interestingly, the United States had a quota for immigrants from India—but it was utilized by British and other Europeans residing in India! In the next two decades, over 1,000 Europeans entered the United States under India's quota.

The 1924 Immigration Act was a high point in the progressive movement. The *San Francisco Examiner's* pronouncement on the Act—"This is not race prejudice. This is race preservation"—exemplifies the zeitgeist of that era in the United States.[50] Perhaps indicative of the tidal shift in both race relations and U.S. views of India, in 2011 the same *San Francisco Examiner* published a guest column titled "Send us your best and brightest students yearning to study here." The columnist, Dale McFeatters, advocated granting green cards to foreign students in the United States, arguing that "people forget that for a couple hundred years we didn't so much grow Americans as make them out of immigrants ... [and] if the top Indian schools don't have room ... we'll take [them] and if [they're] like so many other immigrant students, someday we'll be glad we did."[51]

However, unlike earlier racially biased immigration laws, the 1924 Immigration Act was keenly felt in India. The rise of national consciousness within India meant that the actions of the United States would now invite a response. In retaliation, the central legislature in New Delhi passed the Indian Naturalization Act of 1926, which prohibited Indian citizenship for nationals of a country that did not permit naturalization of Indians. The law was clearly directed at the United States.[52] The legislative debates in India included many references to the *Thind* decision.

The plight of Indians in the United States was further dramatized in 1929, when India's (and Asia's) first Nobel Laureate, Rabindranath Tagore, abruptly cut short a lecture tour owing to discourteous treatment by U.S. immigration officials, which he believed reflected the anti-Oriental bias encouraged by the 1924 law. Like other educated Indians in that era, Tagore had earlier looked to the United States as a beacon of democracy and anticolonialism, but had become disenchanted.

From Exclusion to Symbolic Quotas

The *Thind* ruling had a nearly immediate effect on the land holdings of Indian immigrant farmers. Ulysses S. Webb, the long-serving attorney general of California and a leader in the anti-Asiatic movement, boasted that the "menacing spread of Hindus holding our lands will cease."[53] He further instructed California district attorneys to view any contract that sold land to East Indians as void under the Alien Land Law. Finally, Webb told all Indians owning land in Yuba and Sutter Counties to dispose of their properties and terminate all the land leases they then held.[54] (Nine decades later, Kamala Harris, Webb's successor [after twelve others] as California's attorney general, had an Indian heritage, her mother having emigrated from Chennai and her father from Jamaica.)

Between 1919 and 1931, as the Alien Land Laws took effect, there were more prosecutions and litigations brought against Indian defendants by the state and by white landlords; 46 percent of civil cases featured an Indian defendant and a non-Indian plaintiff, compared to 21 percent before the law took effect. At the same time inter-Indian legal actions fell from 53 percent of all cases involving Indian immigrants to 17 percent of cases.[55]

Not surprisingly, some enterprising immigrants creatively skirted the California Alien Land Laws by having Anglo friends take over the title to their land while returning the profits to their Indian cultivators. However, this arrangement was flawed for its reliance on the good intentions of the Anglo owners to abide by the agreement.[56] Other immigrants registered their American-born children at an early age as the legal owners of the family's farm-land; through a creative legal manoeuver, the parents would then petition the probate courts to register the parents as guardians of the children until they came of age, thus extracting the legal right to manage their children's property.[57]

The immigrants who managed to remain—about four thousand farmers and farm laborers in California, with a handful of professionals, businessmen, and laborers in urban areas—assimilated in a circuitous way. Because the numbers of eligible Indian women were few, owing to the skewed gender ratio, the Indian men, especially Punjabi farmers, married women of Hispanic descent. Anti-miscegenation laws played a role in this selection process as well, for while it was illegal to grant a marriage license to an Indian man and a white woman, it was viewed as permissible for "brown" races to mix. Hence, Punjabi-Mexican marriages became a norm in the West.[58]

The children of these marriages, however, often faced bigotry, derided as "half breeds," especially among the white elites in the region. In California, discrimination was rampant and segregation was a part of everyday life. Swimming pools, barber shops, schools and other public facilities were segregated.[59] Punjabi-Mexican children were typically sent to inferior schools for nonwhite children, where they faced much hostility from their peers, reflecting tensions between Indian and Mexican immigrants despite the intermarriages. By the 1920s, this divide was seen through an economic lens, as Indian immigrants moved from being laborers to landowners, while Mexican immigrants disproportionately continued to work as field hands on Punjabi-owned farms.[60]

After the enactment of the 1917 and 1924 Immigration Acts, immigration of Indians virtually ceased, although some continued to trickle in through the porous border with Mexico. The Gadar Party, in a remarkable recalibration of its mission, became heavily involved in assisting with the illegal entry of Punjabi immigrants into the country. The 1917 and 1924 Acts had essentially precluded legal entry; therefore, the only means of entering the country was by surreptitiously crossing the border. The Mexican border was the entryway of choice, as California's Imperial Valley, with its substantial Punjabi population, offered illegal immigrants both the support they needed and the ability to diffuse easily in a relatively homogenous population. For the Gadar Party leadership, illegal migration served as a means to bolster the party's finances.

Accounts of this illegal immigration indicate that the price for facilitating entry into the United States and providing a local safe house to live in was $200 if the immigrant was willing to shave his beard and cut his hair; it was double that for those who wished to maintain their traditional garb and keep their facial hair.[61] Narrative accounts suggest that the discount deal's pricing attractions won out. One successful illegal immigrant appeared to sum up the views of many when he declared that "he was willing to die for his religious faith, but he was not willing to be deported from the United States for it."[62] Altogether, it is estimated that between 1,800 and 2,000 illegal immigrants of Indian extraction entered the United States between 1920 and 1935.[63]

The transformation of religious and cultural life was also noticeable. The Sikh Temple in Stockton, California, which opened in 1912, was one of the first major cultural and religious centers for the Indian-American community in the United States, catering not just to Sikhs but also to other ethnic Indians.[64] Dalip Singh Saund noted that his first home in America, upon his arrival in 1920, was at the Stockton Temple, where a clubhouse provided free lodging for all Indian students studying at the University of California.[65] During the 1930s and 1940s, fierce debates over appearance and assimilation raged in this prominent community center. By the late 1940s, the temple had received special dispensation from religious authorities in Amritsar (the Sikh holy city in Punjab) to seat congregants in chairs and for the sacrament ("prasad") offerings to be served on paper plates. The fiercest debates were over the appropriateness of shaving beards and forgoing the turban, two central distinguishing tenets of the Sikh faith. In the late 1940s, the Stockton Temple elected its first clean-shaven secretary and its first clean-shaven treasurer.[66]

The effects of the intracommunity discord during India's partition in 1947 initially had a negligible effect on relations between Sikhs, Hindus, and Muslims in California. However, even though all groups had strongly supported independence, the virus of the partition of colonial India into an independent India and Pakistan slowly infected the community. The Muslim members of the community found their identity newly demarcated and no longer felt it proper to participate in events at the Stockton Temple. In May 1947, the Muslim community in Sacramento opened its first mosque, and in 1950, the Pakistan National Association was inaugurated in California. These two events marked the beginning of a distinct Pakistani identity among the then resident Muslim immigrants from the subcontinent.[67]

While some of the Indians established themselves in agriculture, others began to make a mark by climbing the time-tested immigrant ladder of social mobility: higher education. Presaging the predominance of engineering among Indian students coming to study in the United States a century later, the first Indian student came to the Massachusetts Institute of Technology (MIT) in 1882, and at least 100 Indians received degrees from that institution prior to 1947. Between 1930 and 1940, thirty-two Indians received degrees from MIT (of which nearly half were from the princely state of Bhavnagar).[68] However, most of these students returned to India. But some students from other institutions remained.

Dhan Gopal Mukerji came to U.C. Berkeley at the age of twenty, in 1910. Over the next few decades, he established himself as a writer of children's books and won the Newbery Medal in 1928 for *Gay-Neck: The Story of a Pigeon*. Battling loneliness and depression, he committed suicide at the relatively early age of 46. Yellapragada Subbarow came to the United States in 1922 and was a biochemist researcher at Harvard Medical School. He discovered the function of adenosine triphosphate (ATP) as an energy source in cells, and developed methotrexate for the treatment of cancer. Nonetheless, he was refused tenure at Harvard. "Any one of these achievements should have been enough to guarantee him a professorship at Harvard. But Subbarow was a foreigner, a reclusive, nocturnal, heavily accented vegetarian who lived in a one-room apartment downtown, befriended only by other nocturnal recluses."[69] Gobind Behari Lal, who came to study at U.C. Berkeley in 1912, went on to become the science editor of the *San Francisco Examiner* and, in 1937, was the first Indian American to win the Pulitzer Prize for journalism. Noni Gopal Bose, a physics student at Calcutta University, was arrested and imprisoned for his opposition to British rule in India. He escaped and fled to the United States in 1920, where he married an American schoolteacher. Their son, Amar Bose, was born in Philadelphia and rose to become one of the world's foremost researchers in acoustics at MIT, and a billionaire entrepreneur whose company, Bose Corporation, is synonymous with quality acoustic systems.

And Dalip Singh Saund, a Sikh, came to study agriculture at U.C. Berkeley, but eventually received his Ph.D. in mathematics. After graduation, he took up farming and became financially prosperous, and was eventually elected as the first Asian-born member of Congress in 1956. His election reflected a changing attitude among the electorate, something Saund had taken note of when he ran for judge in Westmoreland County in 1952. At the time, his close friend and the school board president admitted to Saund that despite their longstanding friendship and joint community work, he did not think himself capable of supporting him for judgeship. "I'll be frank with you Saund," the friend reportedly said, "I want an American to be the judge." However, Saund was unperturbed, for he had noticed a change in the attitude of younger voters. "This man (the school board president) had a large family and I found out that while he voted against me, ten younger members of his family voted for me. And that generally was the pattern—most of the young people voted for me while the older ones, my generation or older, on whom I thought I could depend for support, went against me."[70]

Indeed, Saund's success in politics stemmed from his successful assimilation into an American society that was still very conscious of race. Having worked as a farmer in the Imperial Valley, he understood the daily lives of his neighbors. He married the daughter of Czech immigrants, served in civic organizations, was a member of the county debate club, and held relatively mainstream political views. His election in 1956 as the first congressman of South Asian origin within California's then heavily Republican 29th Congressional District was striking not only because of his ethnic background but also because he ran as a Democrat. The U.S. government heralded Saund's election internationally, with the U.S. Information Agency (a government agency tasked with "public diplomacy" during the cold war) producing a film on Saund's election that was distributed worldwide, particularly in India, where his reputation as a "native son" soared.[71]

By around 1940, the locus of activity of the Indian-American community began moving eastward. In 1910, 95 percent of all Indian immigrants lived on the West Coast, but that figure dropped to 75 percent in 1920, and by 1940, to 65 percent. In 1940, Indians were registered as residents in forty-three U.S. states.[72] While the West Coast was still dominant, Indians began to settle in urban centers across the country, particularly in the mid-Atlantic states. A notable population emerged temporarily in the 1920s in Detroit, through the offices of the Ford Motor Company. As the company expanded its international operations, it opened a school to train "service executives" who would be sent to supervise Ford Motor operations in foreign nations. By 1925, over a hundred Indians were enrolled in the training course, representing one of the largest nationality pools in the program. However, pay discrimination, whereby white trainees received higher salaries than the Indian contingent, ultimately led to a lack of interest in the program.[73]

Detroit also served as the launching site of the first mosque in the United States in 1921 by a visiting preacher from as-yet undivided India. Muhammad Sadiq, sent by the Ahmadiyya movement on a proselytizing mission, summarized his achievements in America as having "opened two mosques and converted around a thousand Christians."[74] Ironically, despite his achievements in the United States, after partition the Ahmadiyyas would be declared non-Muslims in his native region, which had now become part of Pakistan.

During this period the community sought solidarity with other oppressed groups in the United States, most notably Irish Americans and African Americans. While there had been contacts with Irish nationalists before World War I, the collaboration deepened following the founding of the Gadar movement in San Francisco in 1913. *Free Hindustan* (the newspaper of the Gadar Party) was first printed on presses belonging to the *Gaelic American*, a major newspaper of the Irish-American community, which also supported the Gadar Party with funding. Indeed, an anti-British pamphlet printed in 1916 had an article by Gadar leader Ram Chandra, referring to himself and his compatriots as "Hindu Sinn Feiners!"[75] In 1920, the St. Patrick's Day parade in New York City included an Indian contingent with banners that read: "Up! The Republic of India" and "315,000,000 of India with Ireland to the Last." That same year, addressing the India freedom dinner of the Friends of Freedom for India, in New York, Éamon de Valera, the Irish leader then visiting the United States to build financial and political support for the Irish cause, compared India and Ireland's colonization by the British. Invoking George Washington's message linking American independence with the Irish cause, "Patriots of Ireland, your cause is identical with mine," he declared. "Is it not directly in accord with Washington's thought then that speaking for the patriots of Ireland I should say here: 'Patriots of India, your cause is identical with mine?' "[76]

The relationship of the community with African Americans was more complex, in large part because of deep differences among members of both communities "over whether being black is like being colonized or like being untouchable."[77] A prominent Indian nationalist leader, Lala Lajpat Rai, who lived in the United States in exile between 1914 and 1919, immersed himself in black politics and befriended leaders such as W. E. B. Du Bois, Marcus Garvey, Fredrick Douglass, and Booker T. Washington. In his travelogue, *The United States of America* (1916), he drew parallels between race in the United States and caste in India, linking the predicament of blacks in the United States with untouchables in India. However, as the nationalist movement gained momentum, he emphasized how "Indians and blacks stood united in the fight against 'white imperialism,' " which could take either the form of domestic racism or the subjugation of foreign nations. In either case, it was "the greatest world menace known to history," compared to which "the caste cruelties of India" were relatively unimportant.[78]

In contrast, B.R. Ambedkar, the former "untouchable" who studied with John Dewey at Columbia University and would later emerge as a key architect of the Indian Constitution, and the preeminent leader of the Dalit (the self-identification of the former "untouchables") community in India, stressed the parallels between race and caste. In India, contentious (but also cordial) debates between Gandhi and Ambedkar—two giants of twentieth-century India— reflected deep tensions between prioritizing the goals of sovereignty and of social justice.[79] However, the former view became dominant in the next few decades. Black intellectuals like Du Bois, Garvey, and Paul Robeson saw the issue of race in the United States as part of the wider struggles of nonwhite races in the colonized world, and of course India at the time was the world's largest colony.

Indian-American intellectuals such as Kumar Goshal and Haridas Muzumdar continued Lajpat Rai's mission of educating blacks about Indian nationalism, subordinating the evils of casteism to the perceived greater evil—imperialism.

An important factor was the perception of Mahatma Gandhi's moral leadership and nonviolent struggle against British colonial rule, a view strongly influenced by two books that came out at the time. Richard Gregg, an American who went to India in the later 1920s, published *The Power of Non-Violence* in 1934; and Krishnalal Shridharani, who came to pursue graduate studies in the United States in the 1930s, published *War without Violence* in 1939. Both had spent time by Gandhi's side and hoped blacks in the United States could adopt the framework for nonviolent political action they had proposed in their works.[80]

After Pearl Harbor, India took on a new significance for Americans who were looking for Indian cooperation in the war against Japan. Some quarters in official Washington looked upon India as a crucial test of the vaguely phrased pledge of self-determination in the Atlantic Charter. This provided a rationale for recognizing China's contribution to the war effort in 1943 by repealing the Chinese exclusion laws. China was granted an immigration quota and its nationals were given naturalization privileges.

A similar argument began to be made for immigration from India. Since the 1930s, a number of voices of Indian opinion had emerged in the United States: the India League of America, the National Committee for India's Freedom, the Indian Association for American Citizenship, and publications such as *India News* and *The Orient and the U.S.A.* The most influential group, the India League, led by the aforementioned J. J. Singh, and through its monthly *India Today*, represented the cause of the Indian National Congress.[81]

World War II and the Beginning of the End

Despite multiple efforts through court petitions and congressional advocacy, the Indian-American lobby made little headway until World War II. Indeed, it was events in British India that catalyzed the changes that Indian Americans had striven for ever since the *Thind* decision. By 1945, it was clear that the twilight of British rule in India was at hand. The war had demonstrated India's notable contributions to the Allied cause, in both men and resources. Politicians in the United States, if unconcerned about the plight of people of Indian origin residing within U.S. borders, were becoming aware of the economic and political implications of the impending independence of a nation of 350 million people. The winds of change were blowing in from abroad, and a new course for immigration policy had to be charted.[82]

The shift began with the Luce-Celler bill, which was first discussed in a congressional committee in June 1945. The bill sought to provide an annual quota of 100 for Indian immigration to the United States while also extending the immigrants the right of naturalization. The bill received broad backing (even the British government privately supported it) and was approved unanimously by the Senate and signed by President Truman on July 2, 1946—some twenty-three years after the *Thind* decision denaturalized Indians, and some twenty-two years after the 1924 Immigration Act banned the entry of Indian immigrants.

Virtually excluded since 1917, Indians were now eligible for naturalization and immigration into the United States, albeit in miniscule numbers. By the time direct diplomatic relations at the ambassadorial rank were established between the United States and the Congress Party–led government of India in October 1946 (a year before independence), some of the most contentious immigration and naturalization issues had been addressed to a degree.[83]

Despite considerable public sympathy for millions of displaced Holocaust survivors, refugees from war zones, and escapees from behind the newly risen Iron Curtain, postwar public opinion in the United States was strongly opposed to increased immigration quotas at a time when millions of returning service-men were looking for jobs, prices were increasing as wartime price controls were removed, and labor unrest was mushrooming. However, this time, unlike after World War I, the doors to immigration would remain ajar. For instance, the 1945 War Brides Act, which facilitated the entry of aliens engaged, married, or born to U.S. servicemen, had widespread public support.

But perhaps more than anything else, the transformation in the standing of the United States in the postwar global world order meant that the world's new super power had numerous international responsibilities that necessitated more internationalist sensibilities.[84] The Naturalization Act of 1952 (known as the McCarran-Walter Act) repealed the 1917 Asiatic Barred Zone and enabled peoples of Asian origin and ancestry to immigrate on equal terms, although it still maintained a tiny quota of 100 per Asian country. Nonetheless, it established a principle that marked a shift away from nativist isolationism and set in place a new approach on immigration that would later form the basis of the 1965 reforms.[85]

By the postwar years, the geographic distribution of Indian Americans had altered dramatically. The 1950 Census revealed not only that half of all Indians in the United States were living elsewhere than on the West Coast but also that the demographic momentum was shifting toward the East Coast. In 1950, while the average age of an Indian American in California was fifty-seven, it was just thirty-four on the East Coast. And while the majority of those on the West Coast were still settled in rural areas, on the East Coast they were largely urban residents.[86]

Concomitantly, occupations began to diversify as well. Increases in land prices in the 1940s, together with the introduction of the Bracero program (which brought in thousands of Mexicans as guest workers, especially on farms), led many second-generation farmers to shift out of farming-related occupations and into commercial, nonagricultural occupations, from running small shops and grocery stores, to operating taxi services and becoming engineers.[87] Some Indians of Gujarati ancestry, a newer immigrant group in Sacramento and Stockton, opened a number of small hotels. In 1955, twenty-one hotel enterprises were operating in San Francisco alone, fourteen owned by Gujarati Hindus and the rest by Muslims from the subcontinent.[88]

Nonetheless, the numbers of Indian Americans were still tiny. Prior to the passage of the 1965 Act, the official count of the Indian-origin population as per the 1960 U.S. Census was 12,296.[89] India scarcely registered in the American imagination, and what did was feverishly imaginative. Writing in 1953, W. Norman Brown, a distinguished Indologist and Sanskrit scholar who established the first academic department of South Asian Studies in the country (at the University of Pennsylvania), observed,

> A large number of Americans . . . have a picture of India as a land of meditating omphalopsychites, hypnotic swamis, naked ascetics, bejeweled princes of fabulous wealth and incomparable harems, gross superstition, bare-skinned, poverty-stricken, famine-ridden masses, where everyone is a beggar and caste is more important than life, the countryside terrifying with Bengal tigers, the houses and fields infested with hooded serpents, a land where disease and depravity are rampant.[90]

That view would soon change—albeit slowly.

The Great Pivot

The Immigration and Naturalization Act of 1965 was an extraordinary shift in American immigration policy. The immediate impact would be to transform the level of immigration inflow and the country of origin. The foreign-born population as a share of the U.S. population had dropped from 14.7 percent in 1910 to 5.4 percent in 1960, and to 4.7 percent—its lowest level—in 1970. Since then, it has been climbing upward, reaching over 13 percent in 2013. The second impact would be to dramatically change the ethnic and racial mix of immigration into the United States. In 1960, Europeans accounted for 75 percent of the foreign-born population, while a half century later, that share had dropped to 15.8 percent (table 1.1).

The long-term consequences—most of which were unanticipated—would reverberate over decades, not only on virtually all aspects of American life but also on many countries of origin. But to understand its consequences for Indian Americans, one must first understand the parallel changes occurring on the supply side—that is, the country of origin, India. International emigration from

Table 1.1 **Naturalization by Region**

Decade	Europe	North America	South America	Oceania	Africa	Asia (total)	India
2001–2010	873	2,173	515	35	429	2,522	446
1991–2000	677	2,246	407	19	168	2,087	227
1981–1990	341	580	143	10	55	1,081	94
1971–1980	439	343	74	6	26	475	35
1961–1970	700	234	25	5	12	145	3

Note: All figures are in thousands.

Source: U.S. Department of Homeland Security, Office of Immigration Statistics, *Yearbook of Immigration Statistics* (various years).

independent India was initially driven by the large demand for unskilled and semiskilled workers in the United Kingdom following World War II. These labor shortages drew large numbers of Indians, mainly from Punjab and Gujarat, and a modest number of professionals and traders. Their numbers were supplemented by "twice migrant" East African Asians into the United Kingdom in the late 1960s and early 1970s, and some subsequently to the United States.

Three unrelated events sparked the next major flow of Indian emigration from the late 1960s onward. First, a sharp increase in oil prices and the resulting economic boom created a large demand for overseas labor in the Middle East. The majority of migrants were unskilled or semiskilled, along with some skilled workers. Because the policies of the Middle Eastern countries restricted permanent settlement, Indian migration to this region was temporary. Though most eventually returned home, some skilled migrants moved on to other countries such as Australia, Canada, and the United States.

Second, the liberalization of U.S. immigration law in 1965 led to the emigration of skilled professionals and students seeking to study and eventually settle in the United States. These people would constitute one of the most selective emigrant flows out of a sending country (India) into a destination country (United States), which we examine in detail in the next chapter.

Third, while the opening of the U.S. immigration door encouraging inflows was a key "pull" factor, there was an equally important "push" factor—namely, the transformation of the social basis of political power in India as a result of universal franchise. Over time, this resulted in the political ascendency of hitherto socially marginalized groups and a diminished political status for the upper castes. This erosion of social and political power of erstwhile social elites led them to seek greener pastures abroad.[91]

The passage of the 1965 Immigration Reform Act led to a surge of immigrants into the United States. Among them, those from India emerged economically successful to a remarkable degree, considering they were coming from one of the poorest countries, and entering a society that was still very conscious of racial differences. Yet, they achieved this success within a single generation. The next chapters provide compelling evidence that the economic success of Indian immigrants was the result of the selection bias in the 1965 Act by determining who could enter, the selection processes of higher education in India, and even the prior selection on who could access education, all of which combined to determine who came to the United States from India. This "triple" selection of Indian immigrants—and its consequences—forms the subject of the next chapter.

2

Selected for Success

The Immigration Reform Act of 1965 was the starting point of an immigration story that was by turns ordinary and exceptional, simple and complex. The simplest part of the story we tell in this chapter is about the uniqueness of the Indian-American population. At the time of this writing, there is little doubt that the Indian-American population is, by several important measures, the most successful racial or national subgroup in the United States. It is the most educated of all subgroups, exceptionally so in the fields of science and technology, and therefore is extraordinarily concentrated in a handful of high-skill, high-wage professions. Consequently, Indian Americans constitute the highest income group in the country. It is a population of outliers.

The explanation for this exceptional material success is also simple: We argue that it is not inner, personal characteristics like drive or hard work that explain the "exceptionalism"—because without drive and hard work, it is difficult to succeed at anything, anywhere—but a combination of selection processes that have made a critical difference.[1] The first two selections took place in India, where the social system created a small pool of persons to receive higher education, who were urban, educated, and from high/dominant castes; and also where there was an examination system that selected individuals from this socially selected pool to receive higher education in technical fields. This doubly-selected pool of individuals then became eligible for selection by an U.S. immigration system that favored individuals with specific skills, especially, in recent years, in information technology as that industry zoomed to prominence. It is this combination of selections—a triple selection—that has rapidly created this unique population. In essence, Indian Americans have been selected to be outliers—they have been selected for success.

At the same time, the story is not so simple. The selection in India was extreme in the earliest phase of immigration to the United States, but as we show in this chapter, with higher education in India becoming increasingly accessible by a broader cross-section of society, and growth in the volume of immigrants to the United States, the selection process has been moderated to some degree. If the selectivity of engineers (the most important degree in this population) was less than 1 percent of the eligible population in 1965, by 2015 it was closer to 3 percent. At the same time, as argued in this volume's preface, there have been likely some positive externalities of selection—what we call "selection +" effects—that arose from specific group characteristics. For example, as we show in this chapter, a combination of gender and marriage norms traveled to the United States from the Indian subcontinent, and that led to greater financial stability for Indians. In later chapters, we show how linguistic and professional networks were able to generate social capital that added to the advantages of selection.

As much, if not more, complexity arises from the diversity of the Indian-American population, reflected in discussions and disagreements within the community and among scholars about what to call it. Many names are in use, including Indian American, Asian Indian, South Asian, South Asian American, and Desi.[2] This abundance of names (unlike, say, the obvious names for Filipino Americans or German Americans) comes from a combination of Columbus's confusion about the location of India and the changing and vivisected geography of India itself (from the "crown jewel" of the British Empire to SAARC, the South Asian Association for Regional Cooperation, that includes Bangladesh, Bhutan, India, Maldives, Nepal, Pakistan, Sri Lanka, and the newest member, Afghanistan). Though we use the term "Indian American" to identify all people in the United States with Indian heritage, we argue that there are deeper geographical reasons to be careful about nomenclature.

First, there are three distinct populations that can be called Indian American, based on country of birth: those born in India, those born in the United States, and those born in a third country that nonetheless can or do claim an Indian "racial" or "ethnic" identity. We show that, at the present moment, as far as economic analysis is concerned, it is necessary to focus on the "born in India" group because it is the one that is economically active and clearly identifiable. The "born in the United States" group is very young and needs separate attention (which we provide in chapter 4); the "born in a third country" group is too amorphous, fragmented, and small for sustained analysis (though we do return to it, briefly, also in chapter 4).

Second, the India-born population, which comprises about three-fifths of all the people who can be called Indian American, is itself distinguishable by native language, or "mother tongue" (which is a proxy for the state or region of origin within India). Some languages, such as Gujarati, Punjabi, Telugu, and Tamil, are overrepresented in the United States, while some others, such as Bengali, Marathi, Kannada, and Hindi, are underrepresented. Not only that, but these language groups have distinct characteristics regarding educational attainment, income, age, occupation, geographical location, and length of tenure in the United States. So much so that some groups, such as Punjabis and Telugus, have little in common except their country of birth.

These distinctions between subgroups of Indian Americans are especially significant because the linguistic subgroups have grown at very different rates over time. In fact, one of the most distinguishing features of the India-born population is its remarkable rate of growth from the mid-1990s; as of this writing, almost three-fourths of the population living in the United States came during this period. It is necessary to clearly understand the significance of this rapid growth in Indian immigrants, and that is probably best done in a historic framework. We argue that there were three distinct periods or phases of Indian immigration to the United States in the nearly five decades after 1965. Figure 2.1 shows the broad outlines of this periodization, which we name as follows:

Phase 1—The Early Movers (1965–1979)
Phase 2—The Families (1980–1994)
Phase 3—The IT Generation (1995 to date)

The *Early Movers* of Phase 1 arrived from 1965 to 1979.[3] After a slow start in the initial couple of years, the flow became a steady stream that brought around 12,000 India-born immigrants to the United States every year. This was a group of very accomplished individuals who gained legal entry based on their education and skills. Forty-five percent of them already possessed or later acquired graduate or professional degrees, especially in medicine. Gujaratis were by some

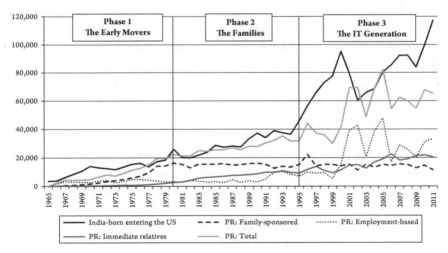

Figure 2.1 India-born Settler Streams in Three Phases, 1965–2011.
Notes: PR: Permanent Resident (or Green card). The PR Total does not include the data for refugees/ asylees (see Figure 2.8 for details). The Indian-born entry numbers reflect individuals who were alive and present in the U.S. for the ACS 2007–11 or PUMS 2012 (see below). The original numbers would have been higher, especially in the early years, because the recent estimates do not take account of mortality in this population nor the returnees. For the PR data: before 1977, the year end was June 30 and it became September 30 in 1977, which means that the 1977 data is reflective of 15 months. Sources: The Indian-born entry numbers in 1965–2006 are from ACS 2007–11; the data for the last five years (2007–11) are from PUMS 2012.

distance the most overrepresented subgroup in this population; they were the first among the Early Movers.[4]

The *Families* of Phase 2 arrived between 1980 and 1994. The immigrant flow began to shift in the mid-1970s (perhaps in 1976–1977) and the new stream of the India-born was established by the early 1980s, as many of the Early Movers began to pull in their families at the same time that skill-based immigration (especially for doctors) became more difficult as a result of U.S. policies enacted in 1976. Annually, about 30,000 India-born immigrants entered the United States in this phase—that is, at about two and half times the rate of the Early Movers.

The dominant mode of entry was, of course, using family-related categories. As a result, the by-now established subgroups, Gujaratis and Punjabis (the latter having been in the United States the longest), were the clearly overrepresented populations. These Phase 2 settlers were educationally accomplished, too, by both Indian and American standards, but markedly less so than the Early Movers. About one-third already possessed or later acquired postbaccalaureate degrees (compared to 45 percent earlier), while the share with professional degrees or doctorates was half that of the Early Movers.

The *IT (or Information Technology) Generation* (1995 to date) began arriving in the early 1990s, with a noticeable spike in immigration that began in 1995; and despite large dips during the recessions of 2001–2002 and 2008–2010, it averaged around 65,000 new entrants per year—more than twice the annual rate of the Families cohort and more than five times that of the Early Movers cohort. By the end of our study period, the annual rate of entry was well over 120,000—more than three times the rate of the Families phase.

Employment- and skill-related visas again became the most important entry category at this stage. A significant linguistic shift also took place, whereby languages from South India rose to prominence. Telugus were the most dominant in this cohort, which also included increasingly large numbers of Tamils. This, too, was a highly educated group; about one-third of its members already had or later acquired master's degrees, but the numbers with professional and doctorate degrees that marked the Early Movers did not increase from the previous generation.

We note that the first two phases of immigration—the Early Movers and the Families—followed the classic migration pattern seen in a wide variety of settings, most notably in rural-to-urban migration. Generally, the relatively young and relatively skilled tend to move first, and their families join them later. However, the third phase—the IT Generation—was a major departure from theory and history. This was the result of an exogenous shock, a significant technological change that jolted the U.S. labor market and initiated several international responses, including a change in immigration policy in the United States, and education and labor-skilling processes in India. The net result was a massive and unprecedented flow of India-born IT and science and technology workers and students to the United States. Indeed, this was the fundamental dynamic of the early twenty-first century. This new labor force was helping to redefine the identity of the Indian-American population, with new skills and new languages.

It is important to take note of the changes in immigration numbers. The details are discussed in the following pages, but the point can be easily made: Had this book been written in the year 2000 (a mere fifteen years ago), it could have been titled "The Other Half Percent." If it is rewritten fifteen or twenty years from now, it would likely be titled "The Other Two Percent."

Large demographic transformations have been taking place among Indian Americans at a rapid rate—in both size and internal linguistic composition—and much of the received wisdom on this population is simply out of date. One of the objectives of this chapter is to provide a much-needed corrective. In the three sections that follow, we detail this story of immigration, selection, and success. And whether or not one considers higher education and high income to be signs of "success," at least from an ecological perspective one should be persuaded that a population that doubles every fifteen years must at least be quite adaptable.

In the first section of this chapter, we discuss the diversity of the Indian-American population—by national origin and by regional origin in India. We show why it is necessary to focus on the India-born population to understand the fundamental dynamics of social and economic outcomes. In the next section, we establish the outlier status of the India-born population as a highly educated, well-paid, family-centered group that does not resemble any other population, anywhere—not the Indian population in India, nor the American population in America, nor any other immigrant group from any other nation. We establish the uniqueness of the Indian-American population using comparisons with other groups of immigrants and with native-born populations. In the final section, we focus on the explanation for this outlier condition, especially the considerable material success of Indians in America—that is, the demand and supply factors that have driven this specific immigration process, viewed in the context of the three-phase model we have identified.

Given that the modern-day United States is the highest-income major nation in the history of the world, and that Indian Americans are the highest-income group of any significant size, it may not be too extreme to argue that this select minority is an outlier of previously unknown magnitude. This requires some explanation and understanding.

The Composition of Indian Americans

Who is an Indian American?

We begin with a direct question: Who or what is an Indian American? The answer is not simple. Let us say that everyone living in the United States with ancestral roots in India is an Indian American. However, the "ancestral roots" part of the definition creates difficulties not dissimilar to the question of "blackness" in American history.[5] Let us assume, for now, that the presence of any identifiable person from India in an individual's family history allows us to label that individual as Indian American.

Based on this assumption, the category Indian American includes three subcategories:

- Individuals born in India (we use the terms "India-born" or "born in India" or "first-generation" to recognize this group in the rest of this book).
- Individuals born in the United States with Indian ancestry (we use the terms "America-born" or "born in the United States" or "U.S.-born" to refer to this group).
- Individuals born in a country other than India or the United States, with Indian ancestry, living in the United States (we do not investigate this group in any detail, for reasons explained later in this section; where we do, it is called the "born-elsewhere" or "diaspora in the diaspora" group).

There are subpopulations of these subgroups that do not, for temporal reasons, meet stringent tests of inclusion in this categorical system. This includes subpopulations that are in the United States temporarily (for instance, on short-term visas, such as tourists), many of whom can be expected to lose the "American" side of their hyphenated identity soon, or have had little connection with India for several decades, so that the self-identified Indian connection may be tenuous to nonexistent (for instance, immigrants of Indian origin who came to the United States from Latin America, having left India generations ago, often as bonded or indentured labor). And finally there are complications regarding individuals who were born in "undivided India," before August 15, 1947, in regions that are now in Pakistan or Bangladesh. They and their descendants cannot be categorized neatly.

The U.S. Census is our only source of comprehensive national data on the Indian-American population.[6] The census has historically focused on the primary cleavage in American society—race—as discussed in chapter 1 and by several observers.[7] The racial categories used in the U.S. Census have changed steadily for well over the last century, usually reflecting (and critics argue, refracting) prevailing ideas about race and identity in American society.[8]

In the early years of the U.S. Census there was no category to capture the population of Indian origin. As discussed earlier, the first category that could be used, imperfectly, was "Hindu." It appeared first in the 1910 Census (2,545 "Hindus" in the United States that year) and continued through the 1940 Census (2,405 "Hindus" then, fewer than in 1910).

Largely as a result of the smallness of this population, the next three censuses (1950, 1960, 1970) did not have any racial category to identify Indian Americans. In the 1980 Census, the category "Asian Indian" was introduced, and given this awkward label to distinguish this population from "American Indian." This is the category that continues to be used in the census. It includes all three subpopulations identified above—India-born, America-born, and born-elsewhere—as well as individuals of mixed race for which at least one parent is identified as "Asian Indian." This category is, in our view, the largest container of people who can be called Indian American.

The census added one other term in 1980, called "ancestry." This variable was meant to capture information on self-identified ethnic/linguistic "roots" or "heritage." It was an experiment that appears to have had mixed results. About one-fifth of the population does not report ancestry; another large fraction identifies the ancestry as "American" (quite likely because there is so much intermarriage that it is difficult to identify any one or two ancestries). The ancestry question was not asked in the 2010 Census, but this information continues to be collected in the annual American Community Surveys; see appendix 1. We do not think that this variable provides good or usable information for our purposes. The available data are shown in table 2.1, but not used henceforth.

There are long-term data of unknown quality on the remaining category, the India-born. Gibson and Jung compiled a long series on the India-born population beginning in 1870, with only two census years missing (1940 and 1950).[9] Thus, 1950 is the only census year for which we do not have any estimate of the Indian population in the United States. For 1940, we have an estimate of the number of Hindus (2,405), and for 1960, we have an estimate of the number of India-born (12,296). It is reasonable to estimate that the number of immigrants who could be called Indian American in 1950 was in the range of 8,000 to 10,000.

Note how small the numbers of Indian Americans were until the 1970 Census, the first conducted after the U.S. immigration reform of 1965 removed racial quotas and opened the doors to skilled Indians. In the first full decade after the reforms, the 1970s, the number of India-born quadrupled from 51,000 to 206,000. The contemporary period began in 1980, at which point the Indian-American population was growing rapidly and, because of its increasing size and economic significance, was accounted for in detail in the census.

The Stock of Indian Americans in the Early 2010s

Before we begin a discussion of the current composition of Indian Americans, it is necessary to acknowledge the complexity and variation introduced by the data-collection methods used in the U.S. Census from 2005 onward. This is an

Table 2.1 **Long-term Population of Indian Americans (three definitions)**

	Indian by Race	Category	Born in India	Indian by Ancestry
2010	2,843,391	Asian Indian	1,678,765	n.d.
2000	1,678,765	Asian Indian	1,022,552	1,546,703
1990	815,447	Asian Indian	450,406	569,338
1980	361,531	Asian Indian	206,087	312,000
1970	n.d.		51,000	n.d.
1960	n.d.		12,296	n.d.
1950	n.d.		n.d.	n.d.
1940	2,405	Hindu	n.d.	n.d.
1930	3,130	Hindu	5,850	n.d.
1920	2,507	Hindu	4,901	n.d.
1910	2,545	Hindu	4,664	n.d.
1900	n.d.		2,031	n.d.
1890	n.d.		2,143	n.d.
1880	n.d.		1,707	n.d.
1870	n.d.		586	n.d.

n.d. No data available.

Sources: The historic data are from Campbell Gibson and Kay Jung, "Historical Census Statistics on Population Totals by Race, 1790 to 1990, and by Hispanic Origin, 1970 to 1990, for Large Cities and Other Urban Places in the United States," February 2005, U.S. Census Bureau Working Paper No. 76. The 2010 data are from the U.S. Census website.

important subject—how Indian Americans are and were counted and measured, and what these counts and measurements mean—and is discussed at length in appendix 1.

In 2005, the U.S. Census Bureau shifted from a system in which it undertook the census once every ten years to additionally doing it every year using a 1 percent sample. This new method is called the American Community Survey (ACS), the single-year estimates from which are also released as Public Use Microdata Samples (PUMS). This small sample is less robust in estimating small populations, such as Indian Americans, and even less so in estimating subgroups within this small population, such as the number of Tamils, or Guyanese of Indian descent. The estimates are available, but they have high standard errors.

The alternative is to use pooled data gathered over several years; three-year and five-year pooled data are available from the census. These provide more robust and detailed estimates. But there are two problems with multi-year pooled data. First, it is not possible to attach a specific year to the data. For instance, in this chapter (and chapters 3 and 4), we have made much use of the pooled ACS 2007–2011 data, the latest and most detailed data available when we began our analysis. We cannot, however, state that this data was an average or that it applied to the midpoint (2009). It is what it says it is, a coverage of the period 2007 to 2011.

This creates the second problem: that we are unable to get a robust, very recent estimate of rapidly growing populations, such as Indian Americans. On balance (as shown in appendix 1), the arguments in favor of using multi-year pooled data frequently (but not always) outweigh those against using it. A gain of two or three years in the timing of an estimate is often less important than its robustness, reliability, and disaggregation.

Figure 2.2 shows the most recent estimate available—from PUMS 2012. The Asian-Indian population (which is the largest definition of Indian American) was about 3.3 million in 2012—the "one percent" of all Americans in the title— of whom about 3.06 million were "Asian Indian alone" and about 250,000 were of mixed race (Indian with white, black, other Asian, and so on).[10] Note that as this book goes to press, the Census Bureau made available the data from the 2014 PUMS. The number of "Asian Indian alone" went up to 3.448 million, plus 223,000 mixed race, making a total of 3.682 million Indian Americans. Of these, 2.209 million were born in India. The proportions of India-born, America-born, and born-elsewhere remained roughly the same. We do not use these data in the remainder of the book because there was no time to update all the figures and tables.

We find the mixed-race population estimate to be unreliable, so we ignore it in the remainder of this discussion.[11] Of the 3.06 million single-race Indians, roughly 1.8 million (about 59 percent) were born in India, 850,000 (28 percent) were born in the United States, and 400,000 (13 percent) were born somewhere other than India or the United States. It is possible that this total included perhaps as many as 240,000 undocumented or illegal aliens.[12]

The Need to Focus on the India-born

How, if at all, are the three subpopulations of Indian Americans different? We examined two key characteristics (age and education) of the India-born, America-born, and born-elsewhere using data shown in figure 2.3. We argue that

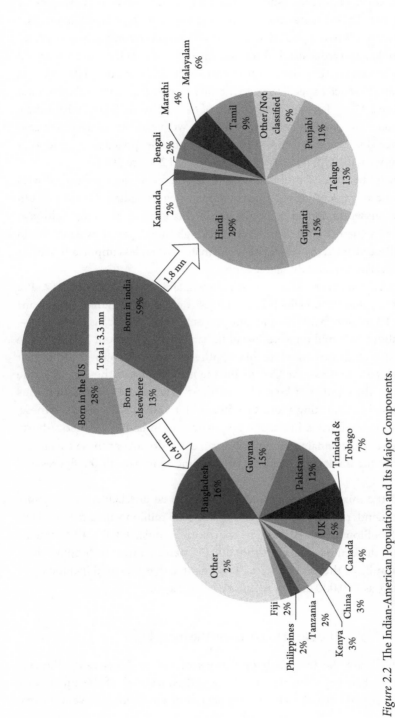

Figure 2.2 The Indian–American Population and Its Major Components.

Notes: The total single-race Indian population is 3.06 mn; the total including multiracial Indians is 3.3 mn. For details see Appendix Table 2.1.

Source: Calculated from PUMS 2012.

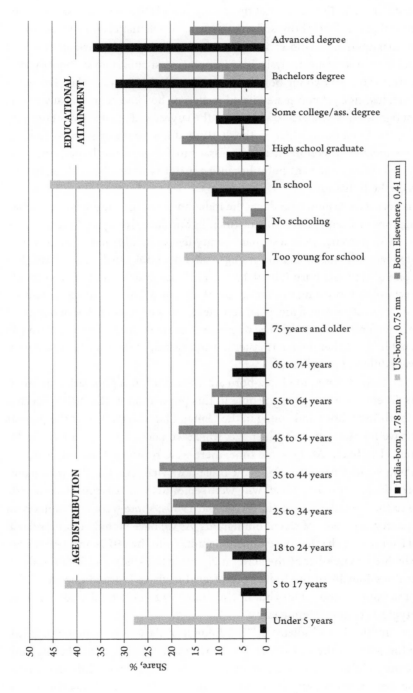

Figure 2.3 Age Distribution and Educational Attainment of Indian Americans by Country of Birth.

Source: Calculated from ACS 2007–11.

these are distinct subpopulations and have to be studied and treated in separate and distinct ways. The smallest of these subgroups is the born-elsewhere. Later, we show that the data for this subgroup may be problematic; and because of the substantial internal variation arising from its disparate national origins, it is least amenable to systematic analysis. The second largest subgroup is the America-born. This was a very young population in the early 2010s, a very large majority of which had not yet completed its education or become economically active. This subgroup was in sharp contrast with the largest and most active of the sub-groups, the India-born, which in the 2010s had few youth or seniors, and was highly educated. Therefore, it was necessary to focus on the India-born sepa-rately. This is an important point because a majority of this book does, in fact, focus on the India-born.

It is necessary to understand that the India-born and the America-born Indian populations are demographically distinct. In our data, five of six America-born Indians (83 percent) were less than twenty-five years old, and close to three-fourths were still in school or too young to attend school. On the other hand, less than one of six India-born (about 13 percent) was under twenty-five years old or in school or too young to attend. Therefore, more than five of six India-born were over twenty-five and most had completed their education. About one-third (31 percent) had at least a college degree, and more than another one-third (36 percent) had a higher degree (master's, professional, or doctorate). These were two very different populations.

In the United States, the India-born are, by definition, a population of immi-grants. There were few young people in this population in the 2010s because to be both India-born and young in the United States suggests that the parents must have immigrated at an older age, which we know from the migration lit-erature is less likely. At the same time, there were relatively few seniors in this population—less than 8 percent of the India-born were over 65. This was an out-come of the fact that individuals who were senior in the 2010s must have largely come to the United States in the 1970s and 1980s; some were undoubtedly in the country as parents of recent immigrants. As we have hinted before, and will detail later in this chapter, the early immigrants from the 1970s and 1980s were overwhelmed in number by the newer migrants in the 1990s and 2000s. Indeed, about three-fourths of the India-born arrived in these last two decades. They were too young to be seniors but not so young as to be school students. They were typical economic immigrants.

The America-born Indians are the children of these economic immigrants. Since the total for the India-born was heavily weighted by recent immigrants, it was their children who were abundant in the distribution. This was a pop-ulation several years away from coming of age. How young was this popu-lation of America-born Indians? Only about half of 1 percent was older than sixty-five. There were fewer than 12,000 total that were over fifty years old. Indian Americans who have become public figures—politicians like Bobby Jindal and Nikki Haley, or creative or media personalities like Mindy Kaling, Kal Penn, and Sanjay Gupta—come from a very small population base. As this base grows larger at a rapid pace, it is likely that the Indian-American face will become a more visible one in America, as more and more individuals choose careers that make them visible.

It made little analytical sense to group all three subgroups of Indian Americans and study the whole. Instead, we had to focus on the India-born because they are the drivers of the migration-assimilation-achievement process. America-born Indians are important too, and will become more so over time. (If this book is revised after two decades, it will need to give equal attention to both subgroups.) We discuss America-born Indians in chapter 4. Though chapters 5 and 6 deal with America-born Indians as well, the overall focus of this book is on the India-born.

The Facts and Puzzles of the Born-elsewhere

It is useful to take a closer look at the smallest subgroup, the born-elsewhere population. Contrary to a common perception—that the born-elsewhere Indians in America tend to come from England or East Africa—the data show that half originated from four other countries. Two of those countries are neighbors of India: Bangladesh (16 percent) and Pakistan (12 percent) provided over one-fourth of the total; two Latin American countries—Guyana (15 percent) and Trinidad and Tobago (7 percent)—provided over another one-fifth of the total.[13]

We expect there to be distinct differences between Indian Americans from these two subgroups—from South Asia versus Latin America—the most important of which may be the unquantifiable sense of "attachment" to the homeland. The immigrants who came via Latin America, we expect, were several generations removed from India, whereas the immigrants via South Asia were probably not. Also, some unquantified proportion of the born-elsewhere population may indeed have come from India, as examples of a globally-circulating elite. As a result of these two factors—the diversity of country of birth and variation in the date of leaving India—the born-elsewhere population is the hardest to characterize and comprehend.

This problem is compounded by a puzzle regarding the born-elsewhere populations from Bangladesh and Pakistan. A close inspection of these figures reveals that roughly 40 percent of the Bangladesh-born and 22 percent of the Pakistan-born identified themselves as Indian by race.[14] That is, they were born in Bangladesh or Pakistan, but identified themselves as Indians by race (even when the census allowed them to identify themselves as Bangladeshi or Pakistani by race). Age does not provide an adequate explanation. That is, the vast majority of these individuals were not old enough to have been born in undivided India; as shown in figure 2.3, only about 7 percent of Indian Americans were seniors (over 65 years in age). Part of the explanation may lie in how the census asked the question; "Asian Indian" was a boxed category that could be ticked (like Chinese, Japanese, Filipino, Korean), whereas Pakistani and Bangladeshi had to be written in. However, we are not convinced that this methodology (that biased responses toward "Asian Indian") fully explains this anomaly.[15]

It is a puzzle that merits deeper analysis, and perhaps some speculation. We do argue, however, that the born-elsewhere population of Asian Indians may be slightly overestimated in the census. As a result, the counts of Asian Indians, and therefore Indian Americans, are overestimated too, whereas the counts of Pakistani Americans and Bangladeshi Americans are underestimated. As a result of these difficulties—the variable counts, the diversity of national origin, the issues with racial self-identification—we do not explore this population in any depth. There is a small discussion in chapter 4 ("Becoming American"), but not much beyond that.

The India-born as Outliers

Let us now try to understand how the India-born compare to other significant groups—other foreign-born populations and a couple of basic racial categories in the United States. Our objective here is to underline the distinctiveness of the India-born from other groups, a distinction that arose primarily from the selection of the India-born for paths that led to the United States. We initially looked at nine groups for comparison: six were defined by their countries of birth (China, Taiwan, the Philippines, South Korea, Japan, and Germany), one was a group of all foreign-born, and the final two groups were racially defined (white and black, or African American, which together make up 75 percent of the U.S. population). We chose these comparators based on the size of the population from a given country[16] and with an emphasis on Asia.[17] We chose Germany as the sender of the largest number of foreign-born from Europe. The seven countries we compared together sent one-fourth of all the foreign-born in the United States, excluding Mexican Americans. Table 2.2 provides some basic demographic information on these comparator groups, alongside summary data on the key categories of interest: education, occupation, income, and disadvantage. The table is self-explanatory; we do not discuss each variable individually. Instead, we highlight three key themes and findings.

Table 2.2 **The India-born in Comparison with Other National Origins and the U.S. Population**

	Born in							All Foreign-born	White[b]	Black[b]
	India	China[a]	Taiwan	Philippines	S. Korea	Japan	Germany			
Basic Demography										
Total population, millions	1.881	1.653	0.361	1.826	0.625	0.322	0.602	40.451	230.706	39.200
Median age, years	37.7	43.7	47.2	47.6	41.9	45.3	61.7	42.0	40.0	32.7
Male, %	52.5	44.5	42.8	40.3	43.3	33.9	36.3	49.0	49.4	47.7
Average Family size	3.46	3.44	3.18	3.87	3.30	3.02	2.74	3.86	3.13	3.46
Families as share of households, %	82.1	73.1	71.8	80.2	70.8	53.4	53.6	76.7	65.7	63.0
Married couples as share of families, %	76.7	60.5	58.9	60.4	57.5	43.3	42.7	55.0	51.3	27.6
Entered U.S. after 2000, %	51.6	46.3	24.6	33.5	35.1	39.4	17.6	35.9	33.2[c]	40.9[c]
Education & Occupation										
College degree and above, %[d]	75.1	44	69.9	49.4	53.4	48.4	33.9	27.4	30	18.3
Graduate or professional degree, %[d]	41.7	26.1	39.3	8.5	19	16.6	17.6	11.3	11.2	6.5
Management, business, science, and arts occupations, %[e]	70.6	48.9	65.5	42.7	47.9	56.1	49.9	29.0	37.7	28.2
Professional/scientific services, %[e]	26.0	12.3	15.8	8.2	12.0	14.7	13.8	12.4	10.8	9.0

(continued)

Table 2.2 **Continued**

	Born in							All Foreign-born	White[b]	Black[b]
	India	China[a]	Taiwan	Philippines	S. Korea	Japan	Germany			
Income										
Median household income	99,133	52,340	80,856	81,334	53,040	58,256	49,831	47,420	54,929	34,406
Per capita income	52,521	30,968	48,488	35,653	32,528	37,874	41,640	28,848	30,137	18,316
Disadvantage										
Less than high school diploma, %[d]	8.2	25.8	5.3	8.0	7.8	6.6	10.8	31.3	11.9	17.5
Poverty rate, %	4.2	13.5	7.9	4.8	11.7	6.6	4.8	18.1	8.9	23.8
Without health insurance, %	12.9	18.9	13.2	13.0	28.3	9.1	7.2	33.5	13.4	17.7
Female-headed households, %[f]	8.9	23.7	25.3	27.9	27.0	37.9	42.2	26.5	28.7	49.8

Notes: a. Excludes Hong Kong and Taiwan; b. "White" and "Black" are single race and include all national origins; that is, foreign-born whites and blacks are included; c. Applies only to the foreign-born among the white and black populations; d. Shares of the population older than 25; e. Shares of the labor force (of population older than 16); f. Female-headed households include those with and without children.

Source: ACS 2010–12.

Outliers on Achievement Scales

For almost every variable we studied, the India-born had either the highest or the lowest value, often by large distances. To begin, consider the standard measure of material achievement—*income*; the standard source of that achievement—*education*; and the standard channel through which education is converted into income—*occupation*. There is little doubt that the India-born had the highest levels of educational attainment, worked most intensively in skill-based industries and occupations, and had the highest incomes. The India-born were distant outliers to the majority community: white Americans. Comparing adults, the India-born held graduate and professional degrees at an almost four times higher rate, held bachelor's degrees at almost twice the rate, and had a median household income almost twice as high as the white population. The channel through which higher educational attainment is converted to higher income—the professions—was well recognized and apparent in the data. Over two-thirds of the India-born workers were in high-status, high-income occupations (in management, business, science, and arts), and over one-fourth were in the highest-paid sector: professional, scientific, management, and administrative services. These are very broad categories, but useful for a general understanding at this stage. We discuss details of this occupational concentration and its implications later in this and the next chapter.

The India-born were also almost as distant outliers to every immigrant group we used as comparators. The only group that came close in terms of educational attainment and material achievement were the Taiwan-born, but they were always behind, despite having been in the United States for a longer period and being significantly older than the India-born. The Philippine-born, despite educational attainment levels significantly below the India-born, also had strong material achievements, but were older and had larger families. It may be reasonable to argue that when the India-born population is ten years older, its material achievements may be even further ahead of the other groups shown here.

But it is necessary to ask whether the outlier status of the India-born, especially the group's educational attainment and income, is an artifact of the comparators we chose. That is, did these achievement gaps hold up if we compared the India-born to *all* possible subgroups in America? To answer this question we identified the leading foreign-born populations, regardless of population size, on two critical dimensions: attainment of postgraduate degrees (master's, professional, and doctorate) and family income.[18] These leading groups and a selection of other major sending countries, shown in figure 2.4, were identified from a list that included all places of birth identified in the census—50 U.S. states and 167 countries. The India-born led both rankings of educational attainment and income. They were the clear, consistent outliers.

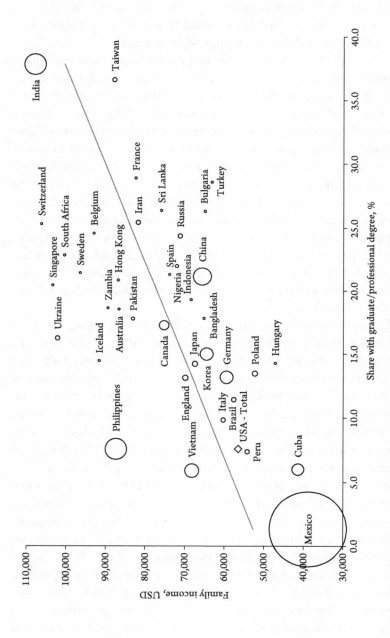

Figure 2.4 Educational Attainment and Income for the Leading and Significant Groups of Foreign-born.

Note: The countries shown include the ten with the highest attainments of advanced degrees (India, Taiwan, France, Turkey, Sri Lanka, Bulgaria, Iran, Switzerland, Belgium, Russia), the ten with the highest family incomes (India, Switzerland, Singapore, Ukraine, South Africa, Sweden, Belgium, Iceland, Zambia, Taiwan), and a cross-section of other significant countries for reference and comparison.

Source: Calculated from PUMS 2012.

The postgraduate education ranking shows a leading club of two foreign-born groups we have already identified; more than one-third of the India-born and the Taiwan-born had postgraduate degrees. This pair of populations stood apart from the next group (born in France, Turkey, Sri Lanka, Bulgaria, Iran, or Switzerland), about one-fourth of whose U.S. residents had postgraduate degrees.[19] Similiarly, there was small group of income-earners that was comparable to the India-born. At the highest level, with family incomes above $100,000 in 2012, were individuals born in five countries: India, Switzerland, Singapore, Ukraine, and South Africa. At the next level down, in the $90,000 to $100,000 range, were individuals born in three countries: Sweden, Belgium, and Iceland. We defined this "club of eight" as the leading income-earning group in the United States, and added Zambia to it (ninth on the list) because its high ranking was unexpected and merited additional scrutiny.[20]

Looking at this group, one could argue that the India-born were simply leaders but not outliers, that they appeared to be outliers only in comparison to the Asia-born and native populations. On the other hand, if we used the gap between "home-country income" and "U.S. income" as the measure of dispersal or exception, there is little doubt the India-born were far outliers. We calculated (but do not show the details here) that the per capita income of the India-born in the United States was ten times higher than in the home country. For the other nations (with the exceptions of South Africa and Zambia), there was no such gap; in fact, Singaporeans earned more on average at home than in the United States.

It is possible to modify our argument to state that, as far as income is concerned, the India-born were part of a small group of outliers in the United States. But within that group, the India-born were more than three times as numerous as the combined populations of the eight other leaders. Therefore, what made the India-born *exceptional among these outliers* was the size of its population in the United States.

Family Norms Derived from Home, not Host

India-born family norms—regarding marriage and gender, in particular—differed significantly from those of American society in general, as well as from those of most other immigrant groups except their regional neighbors in South and West Asia. That is, the family norms of the India-born were derived from their home region rather than from their host country. For instance, the India-born were the only group among the comparators (in table 2.2) in which men outnumbered women. This may appear to be "normal" given the known propensity of males to migrate, but this normalcy did not apply to the other immigrant groups shown in the table. The India-born also had by far the highest rates of marriage among the comparators. More than three-fourths of all the India-born lived in married-couple family arrangements; the closest any other group came to this proportion were the China-born, at about 60 percent. This appeared to be a curious combination—a marked preponderance of married males—and we investigated it further using the entire Asia-born population in the United States. The results—the gender balance and marriage rates among the Asia-born in the United States—are shown in figure 2.5.

The results are rather striking, and suggestive of a geography of patriarchy. The western half of Asia (especially Saudi Arabia, Jordan, and Yemen), stretching through Iraq and Iran into Pakistan, India, and Bangladesh, is a region that sends more males than females to the United States. The eastern half of Asia, beginning with Myanmar through Southeast Asia (Malaysia, Indonesia) and stretching most intensely into East Asia (China, Korea, and Japan), sends more females than males to the United States. The "married couple" data were just as stark. Of the thirty Asian countries for which data were available, the six with the highest proportions of married couples in the United States were, in order: Bhutan, Nepal, Bangladesh, India, Pakistan, and Sri Lanka—which, to be exact, is the subcontinent of South Asia.

Therefore, the marriage and gender norms of the India-born may have appeared to be exceptional in the United States, but were not outliers in the context of their region of origin. Rather, the India-born were members of two clubs: one is a West Asian club in which gender inequality is high; the other is a South Asian club in which marriage is a strong cultural imperative. There is little doubt that gender inequality in West and South Asia is significantly higher than in East and Southeast Asia. The rankings of nations on the gender-inequality dimension of the Human Development Index (HDI), however debatable the method of ranking, leaves no space for argument on this.[21] At the same time, there is no question that marriage is a bedrock institution in Asia, where almost all adults are married.[22]

Some norms and behaviors were changing back home; for instance, the critical "age of first marriage"—which has a big effect on women's health, education, work, and fertility—was increasing in South Asia.[23] But stark differences remained between South and East Asia, with a gap of four to eight years in the age of first marriage and a gender gap in schooling that was quite substantial at the age of secondary education.[24] When we consider the other cleavages in Indian society—by caste, religion, region, and urbanization—the large differences in opportunity structures by gender become apparent. And the selection process that brought Indians to the United States, a subject we discuss next, created a population that was at the same time both the *crème de la crème* and "just folks"—a thin, relatively privileged layer of Indian society with access to higher education (and therefore access to the United States) that nonetheless

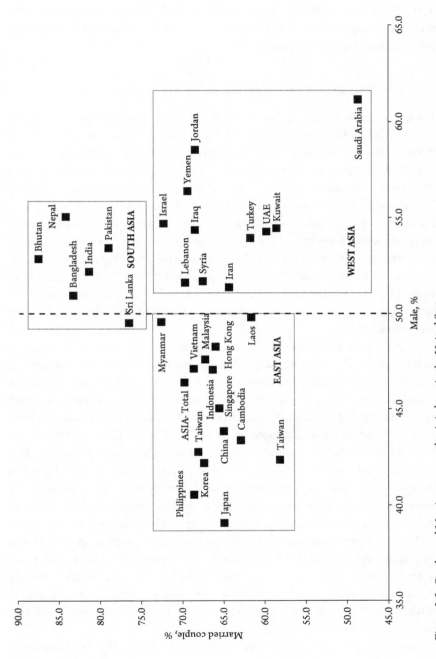

Figure 2.5 Gender and Marriage among the Asia-born in the United States.
Source: Calculated from PUMS 2012.

tended to follow the norms of the society they were born in, at least during their early years in the U.S. diaspora—that is, until perhaps some "assimilation" or "acculturation" took place (subjects we take up in chapter 4). But by the time the assimilation happened, if it did, critical life events like education and marriage and childbirth had already taken place.

Insulated from the Structural Inequalities of America

It is necessary to note here that we do not make the strong claim in regard to inequalities that we made earlier about the India-born being outliers in the distribution of achievement and advantage. In fact, as far as disadvantages are concerned, the India-born were not outliers. As shown in the data, their poverty level was low, but not very different from that of several other immigrant groups. The lack of health insurance in the India-born population was not widespread, but was not low, either; it was higher than for the Japan-born and Germany-born, and about the same as for the Taiwan- and Philippines-born, as well as the majority white population. Where the India-born did stand apart was in the share of female-headed households; less than one-tenth of the India-born households (with or without children) were headed by females; the closest comparator group was the China-born, almost one-fourth of whose households were female-headed.

There are two key ideas on why this matters. First, the combination of very high income with indices of marginalization and poverty that were low but not exceptionally so suggests that there was a fairly high degree of inequality in the India-born population. We did not have the data to calculate the level of inequality, but expect that it was expressed less through the size distribution of income in the population (typically captured by indices like the Gini coefficient) and more through differences between the top and bottom income earners. That is, the extremes mattered; the population was polarized. These data also led us to expect that there was a significant spatial dimension to this inequality. We show that this was true in the next chapter by identifying the clusters of high and low income and education among the India-born. Second, we argue that while the primary reason for the India-born to largely stay out of poverty was their high level of educational attainment and income, there was an important secondary reason. This is the fact that the India-born lived overwhelmingly in married-couple family arrangements, as a result of which they were able to diminish the well-recognized economic difficulties of single-parent, especially female-headed, households.

This is an important point. There is a large literature on the "feminization of poverty": the argument that poverty is disproportionately concentrated among women, especially in female-headed households.[25] At the core of this reality in the United States are two phenomena: gender inequality in the labor market that includes differential opportunity structures in education and occupation, and wage discrimination; and family composition and organization, especially the weakening of marriage as a social institution. To summarize, women earn less than men; therefore, when a family is dependent on a single woman's income, it is more likely to be poor. This is arguably the most significant contributor to poverty in the American black population (see table 2.2). The India-born, with their exceptionally high rate of marriage, were largely able to avoid the female-headed household poverty trap. It is ironic that the patriarchal norms of South Asia that led to high rates of marriage also led, at the same time, to low rates of family poverty.[26]

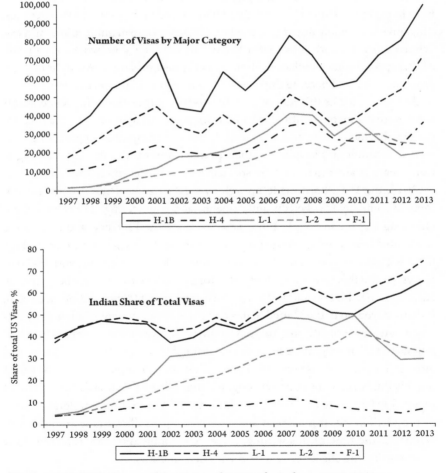

Figure 2.6 The Significance of the H, L, and F Visas for Indians, 1997–2013.
Source: Calculated from data tables in http://travel.state.gov/content/visas/english/law-and-policy/statistics/non-immigrant-visas.html. Website of the U.S. Department of State.

The Selection Process

The India-born stock was over 1.8 million individuals in 2012 (and had grown to 2.2 million in 2014, in data released by the Census Bureau in PUMS 2014 in the weeks before this book went to press). It was the result of close to five decades of immigration that began as a trickle, then became a steady flow, and finally turned into a torrent in the last two decades.[27] In the three to four years before this book was written, in the aftermath of the Great Recession of 2008–2010, the torrent became a flood, with Indians entering America in unprecedented numbers, at rates of over 120,000 individuals per year. In terms of absolute addition, at somewhere around 800,000, the decade of the 2000s saw easily the highest growth of the numbers of India-born immigrants. Around three-fourths of all the India-born living in the United States in 2012 had arrived in the previous two decades. This spike was widely noted in a number of Census Bureau publications and was echoed in media outlets like *USA Today* and several TV networks. As a result of this spike, Indians replaced Filipinos as the second-largest Asian immigrant group in 2012, and became the largest, displacing the Chinese, in 2014.

As remarkable as this rate of growth was its composition. The new entrants were more distinctly identifiable by education and occupation—with a preponderance having college and advanced degrees in computers, engineering, and related technology disciplines—than perhaps any other international migration stream at any other time. So specialized was this group of immigrants that by 2013, the India-born made up well over 10 percent of the American labor force in some fields (like computer science and engineering, and electrical engineering and technology). These new arrivals—the IT Generation—entered the United States along two major paths: as students in science and technology fields with F-1 visas or as workers in computer-related professions with H-1B or L-1 visas; and their corresponding status for immediate family members (spouse and children), the H-4 and L-2 visas. We estimate that 90 percent or more of all Indians stayed on in the United States and became permanent residents (by getting green cards) or citizens. This new immigration stream was enabled by adaptations to U.S. immigration policies (most notably the H-1B visa program, and more briefly, the L-1 visa program) and higher education policies in India (most notably the burgeoning of private engineering colleges). The latter had a distinct regional orientation, as a result of which the IT Generation immigrants came disproportionately from South India (especially Andhra Pradesh and Tamil Nadu). At the time of this writing, these new immigrants were fundamentally restructuring the character of Indian-American identity.

In this section we detail this unique story—of the growth from an immigrant trickle to a torrent, and the very specialized occupational structure of these new immigrants—by focusing on the selection processes that enabled this immigration. We argue that this is a new phenomenon, this large stream of techno-immigrants flowing from one country to another, and that it is a response to an exogenous technological shock—specifically, the information and communication revolution that has restructured production and distribution on a global scale. If this shock had not happened, this book probably would not have been written, certainly not with this title. Indian Americans would not have risen to constitute 1 percent of the American population. The dominance of Gujaratis and Punjabis in a much smaller population would have persisted through regular use of the family-based visa system (which is what most immigrant communities do), and stereotypes of Indian Americans would have continued as doctors, motel owners, and professors in belonging to both a "model" and an "invisible" minority.

The H-1B, L-1, and F-1 Visas

The surge in entry of Indians into the United States was fed by two large streams: (a) India-born workers, especially in computer-related fields, who largely entered with employment-based H-1B visas (and for a brief period, with a spurt in L-1 visas); and (b) India-born students who entered with F-1 student visas.[28] Both are nonimmigrant visas, but as is well known, they serve as entry points or pathways to permanent residency and citizenship.

Let us consider the H, L, and F visa systems to understand how they were primarily responsible for the surge in Indian-American immigration. In the period under study, the H-1B visa program was designed to temporarily allow U.S. companies to hire foreign workers in specialty occupations. It was a "dual intent" visa, which meant that the holder was expected to have the intent to change to immigrant status. The H-1B visa was initially valid for three years and could be extended for another three years. The minimum educational qualification was a bachelor's degree (exceptions were made for minor categories like fashion model, but those made up less than 1 percent of the H-1B pool).[29] There was an annual cap on the total number of H-1B visas allocated; this cap tended to change from year to year, largely as a result of special top-ups and additions authorized by the U.S. Congress—and in essence may have been a meaningless number.[30]

Despite a sharp drop in the quantity of H-1B visas issued during the 2008–2010 recession, the annual average granted to all nationalities from 1997 to 2013 was 125,000. Half these visas—over 62,000 per year—went to Indians; the rest of the world got the other half. Toward the end of the period (after 2010), over two-thirds of all H-1B visas went to Indians. Almost half of the H-1B visas were granted for computer-related jobs; and it is possible that almost all of those went to Indians. It may be fair to argue that the H-1B visa—which has been called the "outsourcing visa" by its critics—was used primarily to get Indian computer-sector workers into the United States.

The L-1 visa was similar to the H-1B, with the proviso that it applied to intra-company transfers.[31] This visa was rarely used, by Indians or other nationals, until 2000, after which and until 2007 (before the Great Recession), it went through a major expansion. For the period covered in figure 2.6, almost 21,000 L-1 visas went to Indians on an annual basis, which was about one-third of all such visas granted. As with the H-1B visa, the India-born were by far the primary users of the L-1 visa at its peak of issuance.

Although our focus is on employment-related visas in this discussion, it is useful to note the sizes of the visa categories for spouses and children associated with these two visas (H-4 and L-2 respectively). Close to 40,000 and 16,000 immediate family members were annually granted visas in these two categories over the whole period. By the end of the period, over 53,000 and 25,000 Indians were entering annually using the H-4 and L-2 categories. Since L-2s were allowed to work, it is possible that new workers, not just family members, were being added to the U.S. labor force through this system. Between these worker visas and the associated "immediate family" visas, it is possible that at the time this book was written, in 2014–2015, over 150,000 Indians were entering the United States on an annual basis.

The other big stream of Indian immigrants entered the United States using the F-1 student visa. For the period under study, about 28,000 Indian students annually came in with F-1 visas (plus another 2,000–3,000 in the J-1 visa category). We were given access to a detailed study of the period 2008 to 2012.[32] In those five years, 168,000 F-1 visas were granted to Indians, an average of over 33,000 per year. The vast majority of these visas, about 80 percent, were for master's degrees. Doctorate and bachelor's degree students more or less equally shared the remaining one-fifth. About 70 percent of these students were in STEM disciplines (science, technology, engineering, and mathematics), including one-third in engineering and one-fourth in computer-related fields. Therefore, over at least the last dozen years, a large number of Indians entered as students every year; this is larger, as we show below, than the total number of Indians who used to enter in previous decades, and they were extraordinarily concentrated in a small number of computer- and engineering-oriented disciplines.

Permanent Residents

In the long run, the inflow of India-born may change for any number of reasons: the H-1B and the L-1 visa programs may be withdrawn or diminished, the demand for computer-sector workers may weaken in the United States, wages in the Indian computer-sector may become more competitive, higher education in

India may become more competitive and retain more students, restrictions or caps could be placed on student visas, and so on. Therefore, to understand the lasting inflow of the India-born, it is necessary to know their paths to permanent resident status, which is typically required before citizenship can be acquired. It is all the more important to have a sense of the "permanent" addition of Indian Americans because when the ACS enumerates the India-born, it does so for all who fit the category at the moment they are enumerated, regardless of whether an individual is there for a week as a tourist, or has entered illegally, or is planning a lifetime as a U.S. citizen.

The U.S. immigration system offers four broad paths to permanent residency: (a) family sponsorship,[33] (b) employment-based sponsorship (typically for priority workers, professionals with advanced degrees, investors, etc.), (c) immediate relatives of U.S. citizens (spouses, children, and parents), and (d) a mix that includes diversity, refugee or asylee status, and other very specific methods (such as for some Nicaraguans, Haitians, Iraqis, etc.). Figure 2.7 summarizes information for the critical decade and half (1997–2012) on how the India-born attained permanent resident status.

The turning point in the history of India-born permanent residents took place in 2000–2001. There are three points to note. First, the volume of India-born who got permanent residency went through a major shift, more or less doubling from the low-30,000s per year before the transition to the mid-60,000s per year after it. Second, there was a large spike in the employment-based category during these two years. After the spike, there was significant annual variation in its use, but the average remained high. Third, the spike from the mid-1990s can be almost entirely attributed to the growth of the India-born in the professional services sector, and more specifically, in the computer subsector embedded in it.[34]

Why did this transition take place at this time? This is a well-known story but worth going into here. The "Y2K" problem, also known as the "millennium bug," was the catalyst. This was a glitch in older computers, in which the "year" in the date field was represented by two digits, and would turn to 00 in 2000. The fear was that this would throw the world's entire data system into turmoil. The Y2K problem was solved in large part by using Indian labor in both India and the United States.

That the Y2K problem catalyzed the growth in India-born computer-sector workers is a widely accepted view. By 1995, at the beginning of the abovementioned spike, U.S.–India trade in software services was on a solid foundation. Rafiq Dossani, among others, has shown that this trade had its beginnings as early as 1974, when Burroughs, the mainframe manufacturer, imported programmers from its Indian sales agent, Tata Consultancy Services, to install system software. But in statist India, the industry was not even considered an "industry" in those years and was subjected to large general tariffs. It failed to

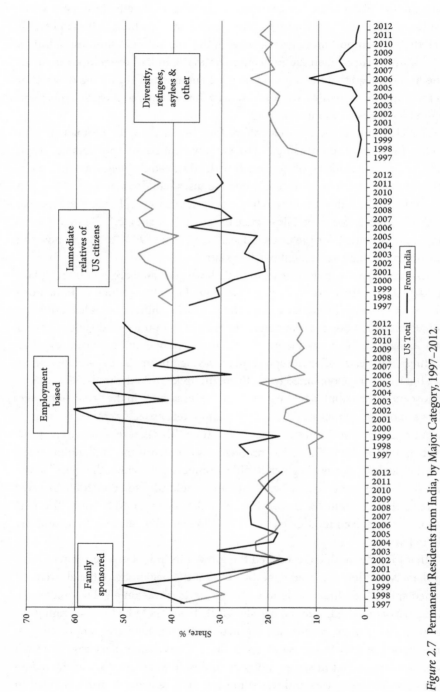

Figure 2.7 Permanent Residents from India, by Major Category, 1997–2012.

Source: Compiled and calculated from INS Yearbook of Immigration Statistics (different years). Available at http://www.dhs.gov/yearbook-immigration-statistics.

take off until the first regulatory reforms in 1984. By 1995, with the continuing growth in demand from U.S.-based firms, about 100,000 programmers were working in India.[35] In other words, a sizable and appropriate labor force already existed in India when the Y2K crisis arose, and it enabled a major shift in labor movement in the industry. AnnaLee Saxenian, who has studied the Indian information technology sector in Silicon Valley and Bangalore, wrote about "the post-Y2K recognition in the West that Indian firms offered high-quality services, not just cheap labor."[36] This Y2K cohort, which began entering the United States in large numbers around 1995, started using the employment-based category in applications for permanent residency five years later, around 2000.

After 2000, the employment-based track became by far the most important one for the India-born to get permanent resident status. This was quite different from elsewhere in the U.S. immigration system, where this path tends to be the least important, below even the refugees/asylees track (see figure 2.7).[37] In 2012, the last year for which we had detailed data, close to one-fourth of all permanent residencies granted in the employment-based category went to Indian citizens. Indeed, no other immigrant group came anywhere close to the more than 33,000 Indians who used employment to obtain permanent resident status in 2012; and this was true for all but one of the dozen years after the 2000–2001 transition.[38]

In the post-transition period, from 2001 to 2012, about 1.05 million individuals were annually granted permanent resident status in the United States. About 67,000 of those individuals (6.3 percent) were India-born. Over 31,000, or close to half of them, qualified in the employment-based category.[39] It is clear that the large pool of professional Indian Americans created by the H-1B and F-1 student visa programs was seen again, a few years after initial entry, seeking permanent residency by using their professional status, with large proportions of them in computer-related occupations. Figure 2.8 shows the rapidly increasing dominance of computer-related occupations in the India-born labor force after 1995.[40]

To summarize, up to the mid-1990s, about 40,000 India-born who became long-term stayers were entering the United States every year. From 1995, their numbers started increasing rapidly, reaching a peak of around 90,000 in 2000. Thereafter, there were two short periods of decline: in 2001–2003, as a result of the resolution of the Y2K problem and a mini-recession in the United States (the "dotcom bust"), and in 2008–2010, during the "Great Recession" (after the crash of the subprime housing market). Despite these troughs, the overall trend was of a significant upswing. The number of entering India-born, which followed the same trend as the number of new H-1B visas granted to Indians, peaked in 2012 (the last year for which we had data) at close to 120,000.

Note that some proportion of the India-born entering the United States do not become long-term stayers. For a number of reasons, including immigration

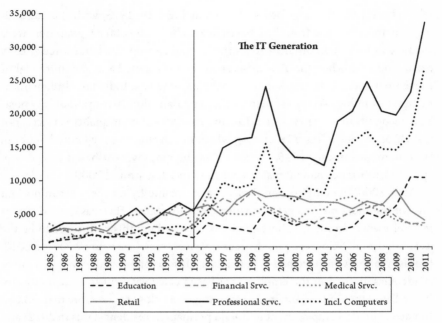

Figure 2.8 Industry of Occupation of the India-born Population, 1985–2012.
Note: The "Professional Services" industry sector includes the sub-sector "computer systems design and related services" which has been shortened to "Computers" in the chart.
Source: Compiled and calculated from PUMS 2012.

wait times, labor market issues in the United States and India, and personal choice, they do not become permanent residents. We do not know the exact percentage of India-born who remain permanently in the United States, but our reasonable calculations suggest that it is very high;[41] it was possibly as much as 90 percent in the early 2000s, but with anecdotal reports of increased circulation between India and the United States, it may have declined somewhat in recent years. Therefore, at this writing, it is likely that the India-born population that becomes long-term residents is growing at over 100,000 individuals per year. In the first years of the twentieth century, about 300 India-born entered the United States every decade. By the end of the first decade of the twenty-first century, more were entering the United States on a daily basis.

Language and Education of the New Immigrants

The very large group of new Indian immigrants that arrived after 1995 not only brought new skills in a new industry (information technology) but also represented new language groups (Telugu and Tamil), with a new and distinct educational pattern (emphasizing master's degrees in engineering). The linguistic shift, in particular, was quite remarkable.

India's linguistic diversity has always been obvious among Indians in the United States, but the languages were never represented in anything close to the same proportions as they are in the homeland. Some languages were overrepresented— Punjabi and Gujarati, in particular. In the 1980s, in fact, these were the fastest-growing groups; as a result of their initial stock in the population— Punjabis had the longest tenure in the United States, and Gujaratis were first among the Early Movers, followed by close to two decades of family-preference immigration.[42] But the dominance of Gujaratis and Punjabis declined in the 1990s and 2000s.

Figure 2.9 shows the changing linguistic composition of the India-born. In Phase 3 (The IT Generation), growth in Hindi speakers and in Telugus and Tamils in particular, almost mirrored the growth in the "computer" sector, shown in figure 2.8, whereas the numbers of those speaking the traditional dominant languages, Gujarati and Punjabi, grew at much lower rates. Among the fast-growers, Hindi is a notable case. Among the Early Movers and the Families, Hindi speakers were usually the largest group, but they were proportionally far less than in India. In the IT Generation, Hindi speakers became a more dominant group. They still did not equal their proportion in India, but they clearly showed a sharp growth path. Even more notable was the growth of Telugus in the IT Generation. In the Families phase, fewer than 1,500 new Telugus entered every year; by the time the IT Generation was in full swing, around 15,000 new Telugus were entering every year, a tenfold increase.

There was some increase in the number of Gujaratis in the IT Generation, but not much in the number of Punjabis. When we initially wrote this, it was simply a matter of time, perhaps less than three years, before Telugu would displace Gujarati as the second language among Indian Americans and Tamil would push

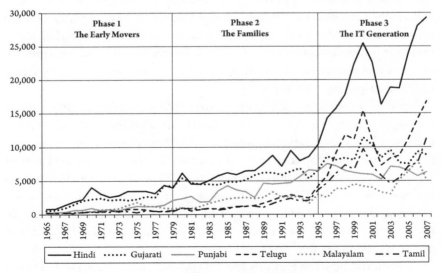

Figure 2.9 Settlement Streams by Phases and Language Groups, 1965–2007.
Source: Compiled and calculated from PUMS 2012.

Punjabi from third to fourth.[43] (Note: as this book was going to press, the PUMS 2014 data became available and showed that Telugu, with 270,000 speakers, had indeed surpassed Gujarati, with 259,000 speakers, to become the second language of Indians in America.)

Later in this chapter we return to the subject of languages and growth, and we show that this reshaping of the linguistic makeup is explained by the reshaping of immigrant flows into new occupations. These new skill-based occupations favored regions in India where private institutions of higher education, especially in engineering, blossomed first—the southern states, in general—and this fundamentally restructured the linguistic identity of Indian Americans.

Figure 2.10 shows the distinct patterns of educational attainment of the India-born during the three phases of immigration. The Early Movers were a highly educated cohort. Close to half the population possessed graduate or professional degrees (at arrival or acquired later). For a brief period in the mid-1970s, professional degree holders (almost all in medicine) were equal in number to master's degree holders. That came to an end with passage of the Health Professions Educational Assistance Act (HPEAA) of 1976.[44] Thereafter, the number of new professional and doctorate degree holders remained steady, at around 2,000 per year for each. The number of master's degree holders was steady too, at around 4,000 per year, in the 1970s and 1980s. Then the numbers began to climb—first to around 8,000 per year in the early 1990s and later to around 25,000 to 30,000 per year in the 2000s.

Not only was the IT Generation dominated by master's degree holders (among advanced-degree holders), but the India-born were present in numbers far out of proportion to the U.S. labor market as a whole in some key fields. In electrical engineering/technology and computer science/technology, India-born college graduates supplied 10 to 25 percent of the degree holders in these fields in the United States.[45] While it was not clear that these large numbers had yet translated proportionally to faculty positions in institutions of higher education (it may be too soon for the full effects to be manifested), there was growing evidence that Indian Americans were beginning to attain the top administrative positions in leading institutions.[46]

Figure 2.11 combines information on arrival phases and degrees attained with languages spoken. The patterns are unmistakable. Punjabis and Gujaratis had the lowest levels of educational attainment in all three phases of arrival, and, this is especially noteworthy, their levels of educational attainment declined in every succeeding phase. That is, among Punjabis and Gujaratis, the Early Movers were the most educated, the IT Generation the least. Among Punjabis, the attainment of advanced degrees dropped from over one-fifth to less than one-tenth from the Early Movers to the IT Generation. Among Gujaratis, this share dropped from over one-third to less than one-fifth.

The contrast between Punjabis and Telugus was quite noticeable. In the first two phases of immigration, about two-thirds of Telugus had advanced degrees.

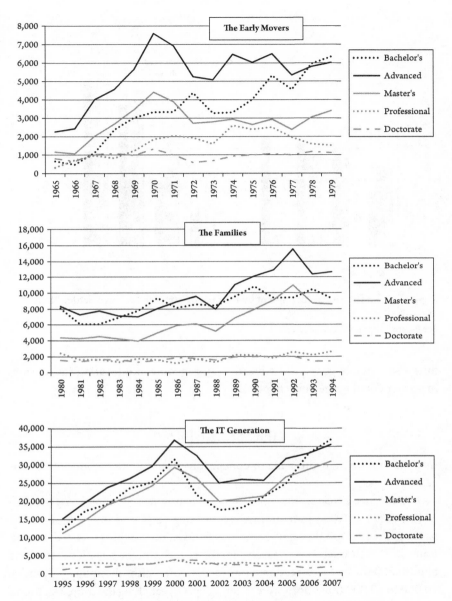

Figure 2.10 Educational Attainment of the Three Settler Phases, 1965–2007.
See Figure 2.1 for notes and sources.

The population base was small—only a few hundred Telugus were entering annually during those years—but it was a remarkably accomplished group. In the IT Generation, when close to 15,000 Telugus were entering every year, over half possessed or later acquired advanced degrees. During that same period, less than one-tenth of Punjabis had advanced degrees. These were two very different populations. They may have come from the same country, but they shared

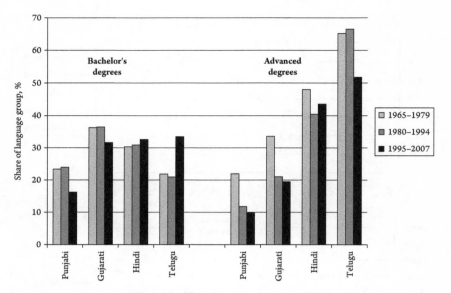

Figure 2.11 Educational Attainment by Language Group in the Three Settler Phases, 1965–2007.

See Figure 2.1 for notes and sources.

little else—not language, nor education, nor income, nor location (as we show in greater detail in the next chapter).

Three Stylized Facts

In summary, we draw three major conclusions from the discussions in the preceding pages.

1. *Indians were entering the United States in unprecedented numbers.* By the early 2010s, about 110,000 India-born were entering each year following the skill-based paths (60,000 through H-1B visas focused on computer-related occupations, 20,000 through L-1 visas, also focused on computer-related occupations, plus 30,000 through F-1 Student visas focused on STEM disciplines). Another 10,000 to 20,000 India-born were entering every year along the more traditional paths: family sponsorship and family reunification. Together, the annual rate of entry was in excess of 120,000 individuals. (Note that as of this writing, the first set of Indian immigration data that began to become available for 2012–2013 suggested an even more massive increase, perhaps to a level of 150,000 or more per year; the census data in PUMS 2014 too reflected this latest spike.)

A very significant proportion—perhaps as much as 90 percent—of the new "temporary or nonimmigrant" entrants could be expected to eventually change its visa status to something more long-term, typically permanent residency. The sustained entry of Indians in such large numbers was rapidly changing the balance of old and new, so that the dominant characteristics of the Indian-American population were increasingly being determined by the dominant characteristics of the new Indians.

2. *The increasing significance of skill-based entry paths ensured that this population was highly educated.* Almost every one of the 110,000 skill-based annual entrants had at least a bachelor's degree when they entered; or, in the case of the undergraduate F-1 student visa holders (4 percent of this pool), acquired the degree soon. Also, 90 percent of the F-1 visa holders later obtained graduate degrees, and we estimate that 40 to 50 percent of the H-1B visa holders already had graduate degrees when they entered. Therefore, well over half of the skill-based new entrants either possessed or soon acquired a graduate degree. As a result, educational attainment, as measured by the proportion of college or higher degree holders, among Indian Americans jumped by over 20 points in two decades—from 48 percent in 1990 to 69 percent in 2010—getting close to the educational attainment levels of the very accomplished Early Movers cohort.[47] This is a considerable fact. It is the root cause of the rise of Indian Americans into the highest-educated and highest-earning group, immigrant or native, in the United States.

3. *The new entrants spoke different languages and lived in different places from earlier immigrants from India.* The linguistic composition of the Indian-American population began to change fundamentally after 1995. Hindi speakers and Telugu and Tamil cohorts increased rapidly in size, as they entered in large numbers using the skill-based paths, whereas the traditional leaders (Gujaratis and Punjabis) continued to rely on the traditional mode of entry (family-based paths) and were rapidly losing their dominant shares. In chapter 3, we show that this demographic shift was also creating a new spatial arrangement: old Indian-American clusters in New York and Michigan were declining, being replaced by larger clusters in California and New Jersey especially, as well as other locations from Texas to Virginia, Georgia to Arizona. A new map of Indian Americans was being drawn.

The Supply Side Story

At one level, the explanation for the surge in Indians coming to America is simple. There was a technological change (the rise of Information Technology) which was a shock to the structure of the labor market in America (i.e., there was a shortage of appropriately-skilled labor) that was partially mitigated by importing labor, from India far more than anywhere else. But this explanation does not answer the question: why India? There are facile answers, such as: educated

Indians speak English or Indian labor is inexpensive. We argue that these explanations were possibly necessary but certainly not sufficient to explain the surge.

Proficiency in English was surely an advantage (which is why Ireland and Israel were early leaders in business process outsourcing from the United States), and the low wages in India could explain why work would go to India, but not why the share of that work done physically in the United States was done by labor from India (because there was little if any wage advantage inside the United States). Most important, it does not explain why India—not known until the IT revolution for its expertise in high technology or work of international quality—was able to supply the labor that was demanded in the United States. India was the land of the Ambassador car. How did it position itself on the cutting edge of information technology?

The deeper answer comes from changes in the supply side—that is, the system of higher education in India. By the mid-1960s, India had created a small network of good-quality institutions of higher education, even as primary education for the masses was neglected. However, as India's economy stagnated during the 1960s and 1970s, the demand for the highly-skilled graduates of these institutions was tepid. Beginning in 1965, though, they had access to another economy—one that had the capacity to absorb large numbers of talented individuals from all over the globe.

Graduates of the Indian Institutes of Technology (IIT) were among the first to take advantage of this. The IITs are elite institutions. Their acceptance rate is between 1 and 2 percent from a pool that is already highly selective. An analysis of the "brain-drain" of the graduates of IIT Bombay in the 1970s reveals that nearly one-third settled abroad (compared to a general migration rate of Indian engineers of around 7 percent). Data from the early 2000s confirms the overwhelming dominance of the United States as the preferred overseas destination of graduates of the IITs. Roughly, seven out of eight graduates of the IITs working overseas were in the United States.[48] The skill level of these individuals can be gauged from the fact that the five original IITs were among the top twenty-five global institutions providing computer science faculty in the leading institutions in the United States.[49] This extreme selection bias in emigration (favoring elite engineers) from India also existed in other disciplines like medicine.[50] We return soon to this point about selection.[51]

But elite institutions like the IITs could not possibly provide the tens of thousands of Indian engineers who emigrated in the IT Generation. For that to happen, a broader base of potential emigrants had to exist; a new system of higher education had to be created. The Indian system of higher education had, after independence, followed the Nehruvian vision of industrialization along the Soviet model, and invested significant resources in public-sector engineering colleges.[52] In 1960, 85 percent of the limited number of seats in engineering were in public institutions. But by the early 1980s, the Nehruvian vision was being challenged, first hesitantly when the Rajiv Gandhi government was in power (1984–1989), then openly with the liberalizing reforms of 1991 by the Narasimha Rao government.

At this point, higher education was among the sectors opened to private investment. By 2006, 85 percent of engineering seats in India were in private institutions of widely varying quality. By the mid-2000s, the total system was producing approximately 75,000 graduates annually in computing and electronics, and another 350,000 graduates in other science and engineering fields in universities and polytechnics.[53] By 2014, these numbers had grown even larger: about 325,000 students were enrolled per batch in computer science and related fields like electronics and electrical engineering, plus another 100,000 in other engineering and 250,000 in science fields.[54] In other words, by the early 2010s, India's system of higher education was producing around 650,000 new workers per year that could be suitable for meeting the needs of the information technology industry in India and the world, particularly the United States.

In the United States, the demand for IT labor had developed by the mid-1990s. Concurrently, the supply of IT labor was growing in the Indian education market. The final piece of the puzzle was the transaction agent that matched demand and supply. This role was played by dozens of India-based firms, some of whom became exceptionally successful at managing this transaction. Firms like Tata Consultancy Services and Infosys quickly became skilled at arbitraging the wage differential between the two countries to help grow both: (1) a stream of offshored work from the United States to India, and (2) a stream of IT workers from India to the United States.[55] From the U.S. offshoring of IT work was born India's IT industry, now the nation's largest export industry, with annual revenues of over $100 billion making up close to 8 percent of the Indian economy by the early 2010s. Millions of lives and dozens of settlements, from Bangalore to Hyderabad, from Pune to Gurgaon to Cuttack, were transformed by this industry. From the latter was born what has been called the "body shopping" industry—the pipeline of IT labor between India and the United States.[56]

This massive expansion of the private sector in higher education (especially in engineering and technology), and the massive growth of the IT industry had two distinct effects. On the one hand, the expansion in higher education enrollments was inevitably associated with a dilution of the extreme selection that existed among the Early Movers. By 2014, in India as a whole, almost one-fifth of its eighteen- to twenty-three-year-olds were enrolled in college. Yet all segments of the population did not benefit equally; enrollment rates of Scheduled Castes and Scheduled Tribes—Dalits and Adivasis—were two-thirds to half that of the majority groups, nor were these college students evenly distributed among the Indian states.[57] As in much else, states in East India were well below the mean;

the lowest among the major states was Jharkhand, with an enrollment rate of
8 percent. In North India, the enrollment rates were somewhat below the mean,
while in West India they were somewhat above it. In South India, especially
Tamil Nadu, Andhra Pradesh, and Karnataka, enrollment rates were well above
the national mean. In Tamil Nadu, one-third of eighteen- to twenty-three-year-
olds were enrolled in college.[58]

This marked orientation to South India, in turn, guided the linguistic shift
of Indians in the United States (from Gujaratis and Punjabis to Telugus and
Tamils). For a number of historic reasons, including a national policy that concentrated infrastructure for IT and institutions of technological excellence (such
as the Indian Institute of Science, the Indian Space Research Organization, and
Hindustan Aeronautics Limited) in Bangalore, as well as an independently chosen regional policy that created a mushroom–field of private engineering colleges, South Indian states had a head-start in and an accumulating advantage,
including ICT clusters, over most other Indian states in these computer-related
fields.[59] By the early 2010s, there were around 1,500 engineering colleges in
South India; industry-boosters claimed that 1.5 million of the 2.5 million IT
workers in India were "from the south;" as well as 5,000 IT firms in Bangalore,
2,500 in Chennai, and 2,000 in Hyderabad.[60]

Not only was South India home to a disproportionately large share of engineering colleges and the IT industry, it was just as disproportionately the source
of Indian students who came to the United States. During the period for which
detailed data are available (2008–2012), over 32 percent of all students from
India who went to the United States came from Andhra Pradesh (including the
restructured states of Telangana and Andhra Pradesh), and over 8 and 7 percent, respectively, came from Tamil Nadu and Karnataka.[61] In short, the roots of
the linguistic shift of Indians in the United States reach down to education and
industrial policy shifts in India.

The Triple Selection

We end this chapter with a summary of the key findings and a reiteration of
one key argument. Let us begin with a clear understanding of the demography
of Indian Americans in their two geographical contexts: India and the United
States. There are, we argue, two fundamental variables that underline the distinctiveness of these relevant populations: age and education.

Figure 2.12 shows the key elements of these two variables: youth (share of the
total population younger than twenty-five years) and education (share of total
population with at least a college degree) for the four populations of interest: the

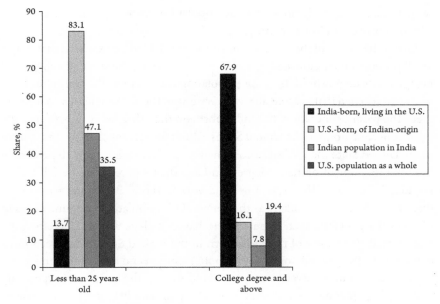

Figure 2.12 Four Distinct Populations, Two Outliers.
Sources: The U.S. figures (for the whole population, its Indian-born segment, and its Indian-origin U.S.-born segment) are calculated from ACS 2007–11. The "Indian population in India" figures are from the Indian census, 2011.

India-born living in the United States, the America-born of Indian origin, and the general populations at the origin (India) and the destination (the United States). It is clear that these populations of interest shared little, if anything. They were distinct.

Consider youth first and begin with this question: What is the "usual" distribution of youth in a population? India is considered a young country, with a "youth bulge" that is expected to provide a demographic dividend in the next two to three decades as the youth of today join the productive labor force. In these 2011–2012 statistics, close to half of India's population was less than twenty-five years old, compared to about one-third of the U.S. population. The America-born Indian population then had to be considered very, very young, because 83 percent (or five out of six) of them were less than twenty-five years old; a significant majority was still in school or college; very few had entered the labor force.

We can only begin to imagine the demographic dividend that this population may provide when it comes of age, a dividend that was being provided by its parent generation, the India-born in the United States, that had very few youth and even fewer seniors—about one in seven of the India-born were under twenty-five years and one in thirteen was over sixty-five.[62] If the America-born Indians were youth preparing to join the labor force, the India-born *were* the labor force. These two populations were completely distinct in demographic terms. At the same time, they were distinct from the populations from which they came or in which they lived, in India or America.

Given the youth of the America-born Indians, it is to be expected that only a small proportion had finished its education; as a result, the share of college and postgraduate degree holders in this population was very small—only about one in six had reached that age and almost every one of them had at least a college degree. The parent generation, the India-born, on the other hand, constituted the most educated group in the United States. About 68 percent of all the India-born in the United States had at least a college degree, whereas less than 20 percent of the full U.S. population had a degree, and less than 8 percent of the full Indian population had one. Therefore, the India-born in the United States were about three and a half times as likely as the general U.S. population and nine times as likely as the general Indian population to have a college degree. Therefore, the educational attainment of the India-born in the United States was exceptional compared to the general population at both its origin and its destination.

Since the primary correlate of income is education, the India-born expectedly had very high incomes. As we showed earlier, their family income was the highest of any group in the United States; it was about twice as high as the general population. Their per capita income was substantially more than twice as high as in the general U.S. population, and depending on how U.S. dollars are converted to rupees (using currency exchange or Purchasing Power Parity rates), ten to forty times higher than in the population in India.

These, we conclude, were the core facts about Indian Americans:

1. There were two major groups of Indian Americans: those born in India and those born in the United States. They need to be treated and analyzed separately. There were language subgroups that were also distinct on several dimensions (timing of immigration, for instance, and educational attainment and income), but these distinctions were not as stark as between the India-born and the America-born Indians. We tackle the America-born Indians separately in chapter 4 and language-based differences in chapter 3.

2. The India-born population is of primary interest because it is the one that was economically active and growing rapidly. Over half the India-born living in the United States in 2012 had arrived after 2000, in a mere dozen years; over three-quarters had arrived after 1990. The single most important event that catalyzed the spike in arrival of Indians into America was the Y2K problem, solved largely with Indian labor that began arriving in the mid-1990s and getting permanent residency in the early 2000s. This influx had grown to 60,000 to 90,000 new Indians coming to work in the United States annually, most of them in the single most important industry for Indian workers: information technology. This was the defining process starting about 1995, and these workers were supplemented every year by more than 30,000 students from

India, the vast majority of whom obtained master's degrees in engineering and computer science.

The "revolution" in communication and information technology that had supposedly made the world "flat," broken up and globalized the value chain in production, led to the "rise of the rest," as well as increased skill premiums and inequalities around the world, had also created a new immigration system for Indians to come to America and created a new and different Indian American.[63] This was not a trivial process. One could argue that this is a special form of globalization—this international movement of highly skilled labor—enabled by patterns of elite interdependence and interpenetration; that it led to new social formations and clusters of a hypermobile "creative class", if not quite an elite class, that was establishing new and unpredictable feedback loops into policies and politics that could affect future trends in economic globalization itself. Certainly, this is a subject deserving of separate, detailed analyses.

3. As a result of the rapid rise in the numbers of highly educated, technically skilled, and well-paid India-born workers in the United States, the Indian-American population changed from what used to be considered an invisible "model minority" to an outlier group of high-achievers that was becoming increasingly visible. The India-born were the most-educated and highest-income group of significant size in the highest-income major country in the world. They did not fit into any population, whether back home in India, or in the United States, or among the foreign-born or other Asians in America. The India-born in the United States truly were outliers.

This "exceptionalism" is worth noting, but not particularly puzzling. The U.S. immigration system was designed to admit skilled workers. One of the skills in greatest demand was in information technology. Indian firms have provided workers to meet this demand, while the Indian system of higher education expanded, especially in South India, to create graduates in those high-demand fields. It is easy to see this narrative now, in hindsight, but it is a model of path dependency. Other things could have happened but did not. And once this labor model was seen to be effective, it became the norm. Nothing succeeds like success.

What puzzles us instead is the tendency to ascribe individual characteristics like thrift or hard work or special psychological features to the success of Indian Americans and other ethnic minorities. Consider, for example, the contemporary trope of the "triple package"—a superiority complex, insecurity, and impulse control—that supposedly explains the economic success of some minority groups, including Indian Americans, that is proposed by Amy Chua and Jed Rubenfield.[64] We cannot offer an explanation for any other group's success, because we have not studied them, but as far as the Indian population is concerned, there is little doubt that their success arose not from some imprecise "psychological" characteristics, but from the fact that they were selected to succeed.

Not only did the U.S. immigration system make possible a selection of India's most educated population, but that base population out of which the Indians were selected had itself been selected through decades and centuries of caste and other forms of hierarchy and discrimination. Earlier in this chapter we showed how the selection process in India works in higher education, particularly for degrees in engineering or medicine. Add to that Devesh Kapur's findings on the caste composition of Indians in America. In 2003, the socioeconomic group with the highest status and income in India, which represented less than 3 percent of India's population, accounted for almost 45 percent of Indian immigrants to the United States. In contrast, while the lowest socioeconomic groups in India accounted for one-third of India's population, only 1.5 percent of U.S. immigration came from them. High castes (like Brahmins) and dominant castes (like Patels in Gujarat and Kapu and Kamma in Andhra Pradesh) constitute over 90 percent of Indians in America, distilled from a base of around one-fourth of the Hindu population in India.[65]

In fact, it is possible to suggest a form of "triple selection" that created this unique population. First, India's social hierarchies and historic discriminations selected certain groups like Brahmins and other "high" or "dominant" castes for education, ranging from the primary level all the way up to college. Second, the rationing of seats in higher education enabled a high-stakes, examination-based selection from within the already-selected group. Third, the U.S. immigration system selected within this doubly-selected group when it favored skills, especially skills in engineering and technology, to award employment and student visas. Thus, an increasing majority of Indians in the United States were triply selected.[66]

It is likely that if the number of Indian immigrants keeps growing, the selection effect will be moderated. On the supply side, in India, the growth of higher education has certainly benefited a larger population, drawn from a broader social base. The groups that were historically most marginalized remain so, despite affirmative action policies, but now about one in eight Dalits and Adivasis of college-going age are attending college. Nevertheless, the selection effect remains very strong—according to recent data, 19 percent of the eligible pool of eighteen- to twenty-three-year-olds are attending college, of whom 15 percent are studying engineering—that is, less than 3 percent of the eligible population. And as detailed earlier, this small minority is concentrated in South India. The overall selection effect changed from extreme to very strong, with the most-marginalized social groups and furthest-lagging states remaining most-marginalized and furthest-lagging.

The selectivity of immigrants by age, education, and skill is a well-known process that plays out over and over again in a wide range of systems, with many and different barriers to mobility.[67] The barrier to legal entry into the United States is a high one; it takes more than psychological fortitude to surmount it. The vast majority of Indians, perhaps over 90 percent of them, did not have a chance of surmounting it. The U.S. immigration system was relevant to the remaining 10 percent, the urban, educated, high/dominant caste, young men (more than women) who could speak English. When these traits became dominant in the immigrant population because of the selection process, which is exactly what happened as a result of the rise of information technology, the outcome was what we have described in this chapter: the formation of a younger, more educated, higher income population that was rapidly growing larger and rising to prominence in America.

3

A Coat of Many Colors

Not four miles from where two of the authors of this book live and work is the borough of Millbourne, Pennsylvania. It is a small community, one-third mile along Market Street stretching west from central Philadelphia. On these four or five blocks of Market Street are two stores that sell halal meat (specializing in goat), a Sabzi Mandi, Sonia's Beauty Place that does eyebrow threading for $3, and a Malayali-run insurance franchise. One block off Market Street, behind a Dollar Tree store, is a gurdwara and center of the Philadelphia Sikh Society. One could visit Millbourne on any warm evening and see families sitting on their porches and chatting with their neighbors in Punjabi or Malayalam or Bengali, or strolling along Market Street with their children, wearing salwars or saris and dupattas or turbans. It could be a neighborhood in Delhi.

Millbourne had a population of slightly over 1,100 in 2012. Over 400 of them were of Indian origin, of whom over 300 were born in India; another 110 were born in Bangladesh. It is a working-class community; many of the Indians, as we shall see later, were taxi drivers. The median household income in Millbourne in 2011 was under $34,000, significantly lower than the nationwide level of $53,000. Millbourne is bordered by Upper Darby, one of Pennsylvania's oldest industrial cities. With almost 83,000 residents, Upper Darby is much larger than Millbourne. Over 3,000 of Upper Darby's residents were of Indian origin in 2012, and there were another 600 to 700 residents each of Bangladeshi and Pakistani origin.

Signs of deindustrialization and distress are commonplace in Millbourne and Upper Darby. Emblematic of the financial stresses on the community is the Tower Theatre, which sits one block beyond the western corner of Millbourne, inside Upper Darby. David Bowie, Genesis with Peter Gabriel, and Bruce Springsteen's E Street Band all made their debuts at the Tower. Many iconic albums were recorded live here, including one by Paul Simon. But those heady days are long gone. The Tower is a run-down movie multiplex where at least one screen is dedicated to showing recent Bollywood movies.

Millbourne is one of dozens of "little Indias" in the United States. However, it is atypical in at least three ways. First is the very small size of the community, though, if Upper Darby were added, the community size would be more in line with "typical" Indian settlements in the United States. Millbourne's small size leads to the second oddity—the very large proportion of the community that is of Indian origin, close to 40 percent. This is unusual because there are only a limited number of communities—seven, to be exact—in which Indian Americans constitute more than one-fourth of the population.[1] The third feature that makes Millbourne unusual is its low income level. This is low relative to U.S. standards, and as we showed in the previous chapter and detail in this one, it is far lower than Indian-American standards. Millbourne, therefore, is a cluster of Indians of a specific type—uncommon, but as we show later, not rare.

There are different ways of identifying the varying concentrations or clusters of the Indian-origin and India-born populations in the United States. For instance, in 2008–2012, the New York–Northern New Jersey–Long Island metropolitan region, with an overall population approaching 19 million, had over 540,000 people of Indian origin, of whom over 300,000 were born in India. These Indians were not spread evenly through this large region. There were some big and dense clusters, such as in and around Edison and Jersey City in New Jersey, and in Queens in New York City and Hicksville on Long Island, the latter both in New York State. Similarly, in California, the region stretching from San Francisco into Silicon Valley had about 245,000 Indian-origin inhabitants, of whom 165,000 were born in India. There were especially large concentrations in Cupertino, Santa Clara, Fremont, and Sunnyvale, all in Silicon Valley. Elsewhere in California, there were concentrations of Indian-origin populations in communities ranging from Yuba City and Fresno and Bakersfield (all agriculture-based, low-income settlements), to high-tech, high-income communities like Cerritos/Artesia and San Ramon in southern and northern California.

These large and micro clusters differ greatly with respect to income, educational attainment, and occupation. For instance, in Glen Cove/Oyster Bay, communities on Long Island in the New York metropolitan region, the average family income of the 1,800-odd India-born population was about $273,000. At the same time, in a community in Fresno, California, the average family income of the 3,200-odd India-born was under $24,000, an eleven-fold difference. In a cluster of about 2,500 India-born people living in San Diego, about 70 percent had advanced, postgraduate degrees; another cluster in Yuba City, also in California, had a population of over 5,900 India-born, of whom less than 4 percent had advanced degrees, a nineteen-fold difference. In terms of occupation and industry, too, there were large differences at the state level (and, of course, clusters within states); California and New Jersey had a preponderance of India-born computer-sector workers, while in New York and Illinois, the India-born specialized in the health-care sector. New York City, specifically the borough of Queens, had concentrations of both India-born taxi drivers and medical-sector workers. India-born pharmaceutical workers were concentrated in the suburbs of Philadelphia. And so on.

To this range of income, education, and occupation variables can be added the linguistic diversity of the Indian-American population. According to the PUMS 2012 data, Punjabis were concentrated in California (Yuba City, Bakersfield, Merced) and New York (Queens), Gujaratis in New Jersey (Edison-Iselin, Jersey City) and Illinois (Schaumberg, Aurora), and Telugus in Virginia (Reston-Tyson's Corner) and Texas (Irving). Punjabis specialized in the transportation and retail trade sectors; Gujaratis specialized in retail trade and entertainment (hotels, restaurants); Malayalis were strong in the health-care sector (specifically nursing); Bengalis were disproportionately employed in the education sector; and the computer sector, the most significant one, had a high concentration of Telugus and Tamils. Since these different sectors require different education and skill levels, there were significant differences between Indian language groups by education and income.

This is a rich and varied tapestry. In this chapter we examine the details of this tapestry. We focus first on the geographical distribution of the Indian-American population at different spatial scales, from states to small communities. In the second section, we focus on the spatial distribution of the population by income, educational attainment, occupation, and language. We explore how these key variables interact with each other. We continue the argument laid out in chapter 2 that the India-born came to the United States in three phases: the Early Movers (1965–1979), the Families (1980–1994), and the IT Generation (1995 onward). We argue that the Early Movers and the Families cohorts can be combined into a single group, *Settlers 1.0* (1965–1994), composed primarily of Punjabis and Gujaratis (and to a lesser extent, Urdu and Malayalam speakers). The IT Generation (1995 onward) can be called *Settlers 2.0*, and they were primarily Telugus, Tamils, and Hindi speakers (and to a lesser extent, Kannadigas, Marathis, and Bengalis).

These two groups were distinguishable by age, tenure in the United States, educational attainment, industry and occupation, and income. At the extremes—such as Punjabis and Telugus—the group outcomes were so different that one could argue they shared a country of origin, but little else. Settlers 2.0, largely selected through the process discussed in chapter 2, were increasing in demographic dominance at this writing, and driving the key characteristics of settlement, education, and income for the overall Indian population. At the same time, the educational attainment and income differences between Settlers 1.0 and Settlers 2.0 raise serious questions about fragmentation in the Indian-American population and the long-term effects of such divergent paths.

We end this chapter with a discussion of the question of "spatial assimilation"—a recurring one in the literature on immigration in the disciplines of sociology and geography. For instance, what spatial strategies do immigrants use to assimilate in their host country? Where do they find work? Where do they live? Do they cluster and why? Are these strategies to enhance security, or to sustain ethnic businesses, or to create a sense of community, or generate social capital through proximity and thereby overcome a lack of access to formal capital that is typically available through "old boy" networks? Or is it all of the above?[2] Do these clusters persist over time? Are the spatial strategies used by Indians part of an overall or generalizable immigrant strategy, or is there something distinctive about their settlement patterns?

We show that the Indian American in the 2010s could be seen in multiple settings, from "ethnic enclaves" (in areas of inner cities, as in Queens County, in New York City), to "ethnoburbs" (like Santa Clara County, in California), to "invisiburbs" (in hundreds of interchangeable suburbs, the "geographies of nowhere," in which they were numerically so insignificant as to be invisible).[3] Therefore, unlike older immigrant groups from Europe (the Italians, Irish, and Russians, for example), but like other newer Asian immigrant groups (the Chinese, Filipinos, Koreans, and Vietnamese, for example), Indian Americans were less likely to be bound to inner-city enclaves and ghettos. On the face of it, they had more spatial choices.

We question, however, whether the new Indian immigrant working in the computer technology sector had any more ability to live in a "community of choice" than did the older Indian immigrant who gravitated to ethnic enclaves in the old urban centers. The techno-immigrants of the 2000s had little choice, we argue, about their place of settlement; they had to live where their industry was located, which happened to be, for reasons discussed extensively in the literature in economic geography, in the suburbs of a handful of American cities. They lived, we suggest, in a new kind of space: what we call—awkwardly, for lack of a better term—the "ethno-techno-burb." They responded, as they had to, to the new geography of work in America. As a result, the India-born were spreading to new states and new suburbs, and forming new "little Indias" at the same time that they were concentrating in larger numbers in some special and specialized locations and forming bigger "little Indias."

Concentration and Variation at Multiple Scales

U.S. Census Geography

Before beginning this discussion, it is necessary to have a clear idea of U.S. Census geography. The technical aspects of this geography are detailed in appendix

1, and the reader will find it useful to consult that before continuing with this chapter. The "census tract"—which holds about 4,000 people—is the scale at which much spatial analysis, especially urban analysis, is done in the United States.[4] However, this scale is too small for our analyses, for two reasons: first, the estimates of subpopulations (such as Indian Americans) are unreliable; second, the underlying places are unrecognizable.[5] We use an approach, instead, that seeks to minimize both problems by using larger, named geographical units to mitigate the data-reliability and place-recognition issues. But both problems cannot always be solved simultaneously, because valuable micro-level information is often lost in the process. Hence, we use a mix of geographical scales, as appropriate.

States and their primary subdivisions—*counties*—are two important scales. These are independent political units, and all data are available at these scales. In addition, we use subunits embedded inside counties, called *minor civil divisions* (MCDs) or *census county divisions* (CCDs); these can be thought of as *municipalities*.[6] Several municipalities—like New York City and Philadelphia— are themselves very large and can be decomposed into what the Census Bureau calls *census designated places* (CDPs), which are identifiable *places*—spatial units that are recognizable but that do not have independent legal existence. The Census Bureau also identifies *metropolises*, which are not legal entities in the sense that there is no governance or taxation that takes place at this scale.[7] These metropolitan regions are usually made up of more than one county, and they frequently cross state boundaries. For example, the Philadelphia metropolis is composed of five counties in Pennsylvania and three counties in New Jersey, which together have well over 200 municipalities and several thousand places in them. To summarize, census data are available at several scales, some of which are units of government (states, counties, and municipalities); and others that are more loosely identified spatial units that do not have local governance at those scales (metropolises and places).

We present some data at all these scales as needed and as available. In addition, we present data at the scale of the Public Use Microdata Area (or PUMA), which is a statistical geographic unit defined specifically for the tabulation and dissemination of the U.S. Census. The disadvantage of the PUMA scale is that these are not commonly recognizable units;[8] the advantage is that the most detailed micro-geographic information (say, on the number of Telugus who have professional degrees who live in and around Sunnyvale in Silicon Valley) is available only at this scale. Therefore, we find this scale very useful for analysis, and when we use it in the following discussions, we attempt to give the reader a good sense of the recognizable geography or named places underlying the PUMAs.

The basic data on the Indian-origin and India-born populations are shown in the five tables attached to table 3.1 and four figures that follow.[9] The Indian-origin population is what is identified as single-race "Asian Indian" in the Census; that is, the sum of India-born, America-born, and born-elsewhere populations identified in chapter 2. The tables show the distribution of the populations at multiple scales: leading states, counties, metropolises, municipalities, and places. The figures (four maps) show one nationwide picture (at the county scale) and three regionally focused pictures for the most significant regions: the New York–New Jersey metropolitan region, California and its population cluster in and around San Francisco and Silicon Valley, and Texas and its clusters in and around Houston and Dallas. As in chapter 2, we begin the data presentation and discussion with both the Indian-origin and India-born populations. As we move further into the discussion, for reasons detailed in chapter 2 (principally that the India-born are of greater interest on economic matters because they were the economically active population), the focus narrows to the India-born population.

The State Level

Consider the state-level data in table 3.1a. We show data for two points in time—2005–2009 and 2008–2012—for the leading twenty states, for both the Indian-origin and India-born populations. Regardless of the year of counting and the population counted, these twenty states are home to over 90 percent of the Indian-American population. The remaining thirty states include less than 10 percent of the population; that is, approximately as many Indian Americans live in these remaining states together as in the state of Illinois. Therefore, we generally ignore these remaining smaller states in the rest of this discussion.

The data in table 3.1a (and the other series in the same table) point to two major patterns:

1. There was significant spatial variation in the distribution of Indian Americans, with a concentration of the population in a small number of states.
2. There was significant variation in the growth of the Indian-American population at the state scale, marked especially by a decline in some traditional leaders (New York in particular) and a rapid rise of other states, some of which were traditional leaders, whereas others were new.

Considerably more than half the Indian-origin and India-born populations lived in the five leading states of California, New York, New Jersey, Texas, and Illinois. Close to one-fifth lived in a single state: California. This is not unusual in comparison with other recent immigrant groups. John Iceland notes that "two-thirds of all immigrants lived in just six states in 2005," and that one-fourth of California's population was foreign-born.[10] Five of these leading states for all immigrants

Table 3.1a **Leading States for Indian-origin and India-born Populations**

	Indian-origin						India-born				
	Pop. 2005–09	Pop. 2008–12	Share of Indian-origin, %	Indian-origin share of total, %	Change in period, %		Pop. 2005–09	Pop. 2008–12	Share of India-born, %	India-born share of total, %	Change in period, %
USA	2,502,563	2,854,732		0.9	14.1		1,535,972	1,837,838		0.6	19.7
California	464,761	536,738	18.8	1.4	15.5	California	296,120	351,568	19.1	0.9	18.7
New York	333,190	325,401	11.4	1.7	−2.3	New Jersey	169,486	208,069	11.3	2.4	22.8
New Jersey	247,145	298,195	10.4	3.4	20.7	Texas	124,610	164,349	8.9	0.7	31.9
Texas	204,495	252,996	8.9	1.0	23.7	New York	140,111	146,895	8.0	0.8	4.8
Illinois	170,158	190,698	6.7	1.5	12.1	Illinois	114,228	131,154	7.1	1.0	14.8
Top 5 states:	1,419,749	1,604,028	56.2	1.5	13.0		844,555	1,002,035	54.5	1.0	18.6
Florida	117,197	127,261	4.5	0.7	8.6	Pennsylvania	58,406	73,224	4.0	0.6	25.4
Pennsylvania	87,948	105,883	3.7	0.8	20.4	Virginia	52,136	67,881	3.7	0.8	30.2
Virginia	83,734	103,252	3.6	1.3	23.3	Florida	58,359	65,365	3.6	0.3	12.0
Georgia	79,255	92,835	3.3	1.0	17.1	Georgia	50,590	61,381	3.3	0.6	21.3
Michigan	78,310	82,036	2.9	0.8	4.8	Michigan	48,975	52,716	2.9	0.5	7.6

Maryland	69,352	78,975	2.8	1.4	13.9	Massachusetts	42,027	50,805	2.8	0.8	20.9
Massachusetts	63,781	74,520	2.6	1.1	16.8	Maryland	42,831	50,351	2.7	0.9	17.6
Ohio	53,627	63,147	2.2	0.5	17.8	Ohio	37,398	45,778	2.5	0.4	22.4
Washington	48,298	59,458	2.1	0.9	23.1	Washington	34,006	43,727	2.4	0.6	28.6
North Carolina	46,999	56,610	2.0	0.6	20.4	North Carolina	30,649	38,857	2.1	0.4	26.8
Connecticut	39,974	47,750	1.7	1.3	19.5	Connecticut	26,363	32,139	1.7	0.9	21.9
Arizona	30,162	36,075	1.3	0.6	19.6	Arizona	20,984	24,883	1.4	0.4	18.6
Minnesota	29,481	33,756	1.2	0.6	14.5	Minnesota	18,681	23,409	1.3	0.4	25.3
Indiana	20,883	26,979	0.9	0.4	29.2	Indiana	14,844	19,857	1.1	0.3	33.8
Tennessee	19,830	22,352	0.8	0.4	12.7	Tennessee	13,933	16,531	0.9	0.3	18.6
Top 25 states:	2,288,580	2,614,917	91.6	1.1	14.3		1,394,737	1,668,939	90.8	0.7	19.7

Source: Compiled and calculated from Summarized Data in http://dataferrett.census.gov/.

were the top five for Indian Americans, too. The sixth state, which was also the sixth state for the Indian-origin population, is Florida. In fact, if the population of Florida was added to the top five, we could repeat Iceland's statement for the Indian-origin population—that close to two-thirds lived in just six states.

A second way to consider the data is in terms of the proportion of a state's population that is of Indian heritage. This method shows the relative signifi-cance, or visibility, of the Indian population at the state level. We use the term "visible minority" not in the way the Canadian census does (to distinguish this axis of difference from "invisible" axes such as language and religion, which can-not be identified by sight) but in the sense of being noticeable. We suggest that there is some (so far unquantified) threshold below which an immigrant group may be unnoticeable or invisible. This invisibility can have both positive conse-quences (such as less overt discrimination) and negative consequences (such as a lesser ability for political mobilization). In the United States, Asian community leaders (of Chinese, Filipino, Korean, and other national origins) frequently be-moan the political and public policy challenges faced by "invisible minorities."[11]

The clear leader using the shares or visibility method was New Jersey, where about 3.4 percent of the state's population was of Indian-origin and 2.4 percent was India-born. For the Indian-origin population, the next four states in order were New York, Illinois, California, and Maryland. Note that three of these four states were among the top five by population size. In these states and in Virginia, Connecticut, Massachusetts, Texas, and Georgia, the share of the India-born was higher than their national share of 1 percent. In these ten states (or, more accurately, selected counties of these states, as discussed below) the India-born formed a visible minority with differing degrees of visibility.

More remarkable than the state-level concentration of the Indian-American population—which really was not any more remarkable than the concentration of other new or older immigrant groups—was the rapidity of its recent growth (a subject we discussed at length in chapter 2), and the new spatial patterns of settlement of the new population. Let us focus on the India-born population in table 3.1a because they were the drivers of this growth. In the short period cov-ered by these data (2005–2009 to 2008–2012), this population grew by about one-fifth, which is a remarkable rate in any context. The rate of growth was even higher than this high average in several states, including leading states like Texas (32 percent) and New Jersey (23 percent), mid-level states like Pennsylvania and Virginia (25 and 30 percent, respectively), and smaller states like Washington, North Carolina, Minnesota, and Indiana, which had historically never attracted large numbers of India-born immigrants; for these, the India-born population grew by at least one-fourth in these few years.

The most dramatic effect of the rapid influx of large numbers of India-born on the settlement pattern was seen in the state of New York. New York used to be the first- or second-most important destination for Indian immigrants in earlier decades. In 2008–2012, with 11.4 percent of the Indian-origin population, it was ranked second. But in this brief period, during which there was rapid growth almost everywhere else, New York State lost Indians. If these trends continue, and in the short-term there are strong indications that they will, New York's Indian-American population could be overtaken by those of New Jersey and Texas by the end of the 2010s. New York, and to a lesser extent Michigan, were the two states of considerable but diminishing significance for the Indian-American population.[12]

Counties and Smaller Scales

Summary statistics at the county level are shown in table 3.1b for the Indian-origin and India-born populations separately. It is useful to read these tables in conjunction with the county-level population map in figure 3.1.[13] Additional data on other scales are provided in table 3.1c (at the metropolitan scale), table 3.1d (at the municipality scale), and table 3.1e (at the place scale). These tables should be considered in concert, as the following discussion ranges freely among these scales, as appropriate. The associated three regional maps (of California in figure 3.2, New York–New Jersey in figure 3.3, and Texas in figure 3.4) go along with these tables and should also be considered part of the same information and discussion set.

The principal feature of these tables is a confirmation of the primary findings at the state level—of the *spatially uneven distribution* of the Indian-American population and its *spatially uneven growth*. Our understanding of these spatial processes is deepened by this examination at these smaller scales, whereby it is possible to identify the key counties, metropolises, municipalities, and places where Indian Americans resided during this period and to which they were (or were not) moving.

Rise and Fall: New Jersey, California, and Texas vs. New York

The four most important counties for the Indian-American population were Queens County (which is part of New York City), Santa Clara County (which is part of Silicon Valley in California), Middlesex County (in north-central New Jersey, popularly identified with the township of Edison), and Cook County (where Chicago is located). These four counties—out of a total of 3,200 odd in the United States—were home to about one-sixth of the Indian-American population. It is instructive to examine the characteristics and histories of these

Table 3.1b Leading Counties for Indian-origin and India-born Populations

		Indian-origin (ACS 2008–12)						India-born (ACS 2008–12)			
County	State	Population	Change from ACS 2005–09, %	Share of Indian-origin in US, %	Share of county pop. %	County	State	Population	Change from ACS 2005–09, %	Share of India-born in US, %	Share of county pop. %
USA		2,864,433	14.1			USA		1,837,838	19.6		
Queens	NY	134,656	-8.8	4.7	6.0	Santa Clara	CA	84,904	19.8	4.6	4.7
Santa Clara	CA	119,463	18.6	4.2	6.7	Middlesex	NJ	74,283	27.4	4.0	9.2
Middlesex	NJ	106,089	25.9	3.7	13.1	Cook	IL	65,475	16.0	3.6	1.3
Cook	IL	94,925	13.7	3.3	1.8	Alameda	CA	49,713	17.4	2.7	3.3
Los Angeles	CA	79,108	5.0	2.8	0.8	Los Angeles	CA	49,005	11	2.7	0.5
TOP 5		534,241	8.7	18.7		TOP 5		323,380	18.8	17.6	
Alameda	CA	73,628	16.3	2.6	4.9	Queens	NY	48,537	-4.8	2.6	2.2
Harris	TX	49,949	8.3	1.7	1.2	King	WA	32,265	28.1	1.8	1.7
Orange	CA	45,306	8.6	1.6	1.5	Harris	TX	32,175	16.6	1.8	0.8
King	WA	42,790	26.2	1.5	2.2	Orange	CA	29,167	8.4	1.6	1.0
Fairfax	VA	42,784	12.9	1.5	3.9	Hudson	NJ	28,457	46.1	1.5	4.5

DuPage	IL	42,332	3.3	1.5	4.6	DuPage	IL	28,279	6.2	1.5	3.1
Nassau	NY	39,259	10.9	1.4	2.9	Fairfax	VA	28,189	22.3	1.5	2.6
Dallas	TX	38,892	20.5	1.4	1.6	Dallas	TX	27,385	42.7	1.5	1.2
Hudson	NJ	38,697	38.1	1.4	6.1	Middlesex	MA	26,499	23.8	1.4	1.8
Middlesex	MA	36,776	17.4	1.3	2.4	Nassau	NY	22,170	8.6	1.2	1.7
Fort Bend	TX	35,933	43.1	1.3	6.1	Maricopa	AZ	21,833	20.9	1.2	0.6
Montgomery	MD	32,394	5.2	1.1	3.3	Oakland	MI	21,697	11.6	1.2	1.8
Collin	TX	32,320	34.8	1.1	4.1	Fort Bend	TX	21,188	47.8	1.2	3.6
Maricopa	AZ	31,395	21.9	1.1	0.8	Collin	TX	21,022	35.6	1.1	2.7
Oakland	MI	31,014	10.7	1.1	2.6	Montgomery	MD	20,640	11.0	1.1	2.1
TOP 20		1,147,710	13.0	40.0				732,883	18.4	40.0	

Source: Compiled and calculated from Summarized Data in http://dataferrett.census.gov/.

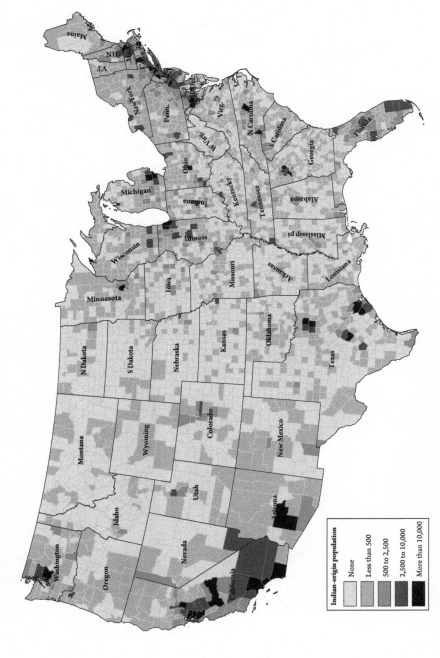

Figure 3.1 Distribution of the Indian-origin Population at County Scale.
Source: ACS 2007–11.

Table 3.1c **Leading Metropolitan Regions for Indian-origin and India-born Populations**

	Metropolitan population	Indian-origin population	India-born population	Share of Indian-origin in U.S., %	Share of Indian-origin that are India-born, %
New York-Northern New Jersey-Long Island, NY-NJ-PA	18,923,404	540,476	300,793	18.9	55.7
Chicago-Joliet-Naperville, IL-IN-WI	9,460,763	173,602	117,966	6.1	68.0
Washington-Arlington-Alexandria, DC-VA-MD-WV	5,603,696	127,235	80,873	4.4	63.6
San Francisco-Oakland-Fremont, CA	4,348,880	125,366	79,953	4.4	63.8
Los Angeles-Long Beach-Santa Ana, CA	12,861,864	124,414	78,172	4.3	62.8
San Jose-Sunnyvale-Santa Clara, CA	1,843,860	119,533	84,992	4.2	71.1
Dallas-Fort Worth-Arlington, TX	6,400,781	102,713	68,174	3.6	66.4
Houston-Sugar Land-Baytown, TX	5,962,416	96,297	59,544	3.4	61.8
Philadelphia-Camden-Wilmington, PA-NJ-DE-MD	5,967,349	93,705	64,219	3.3	68.5
Atlanta-Sandy Springs-Marietta, GA	5,291,701	76,981	49,194	2.7	63.9
Boston-Cambridge-Quincy, MA-NH	4,563,673	60,550	41,905	2.1	69.2

(*continued*)

Table 3.1c Continued

	Metropolitan population	Indian-origin population	India-born population	Share of Indian-origin in U.S., %	Share of Indian-origin that are India-born, %
Detroit-Warren-Livonia, MI	4,304,617	60,023	37,654	2.1	62.7
Seattle-Tacoma-Bellevue, WA	3,453,748	51,690	38,133	1.8	73.8
Miami-Fort Lauderdale-Pompano Beach, FL	5,598,297	41,145	19,335	1.4	47.0
Sacramento--Arden-Arcade--Roseville, CA	2,153,736	32,538	18,938	1.1	58.2
Baltimore-Towson, MD	2,715,650	32,454	20,226	1.1	62.3
Phoenix-Mesa-Glendale, AZ	4,210,193	32,269	22,256	1.1	69.0
Minneapolis-St. Paul-Bloomington, MN-WI	3,290,811	30,455	20,982	1.1	68.9
San Diego-Carlsbad-San Marcos, CA	3,100,500	26,044	17,237	0.9	66.2
Austin-Round Rock-San Marcos, TX	1,731,777	25,432	16,372	0.9	64.4
TOTAL:	111,787,716	1,972,922	1,236,918	68.9	62.7

Source: Compiled from the 2008-12 series in Summarized Data in http://dataferrett.census.gov/.

Table 3.1d **Leading Municipalities for Indian-origin and India-born Populations**

	Total pop.	Indian-origin pop.	India-born pop.	India-born as share of Indian-origin, %	Indian-origin as share of CCD, %
Queens borough, Queens County, NY	2,235,008	134,656	48,537	36.0	6.0
San Jose CCD, Santa Clara County, CA	1,666,871	117,690	83,795	71.2	7.1
Fremont CCD, Alameda County, CA	326,899	49,096	33,795	68.8	15.0
Houston CCD, Harris County, TX	3,081,338	38,115	25,068	65.8	1.2
Chicago city, Cook County, IL	2,702,471	30,656	18,424	60.1	1.1
Edison tnshp, Middlesex County, NJ	100,116	28,963	21,367	73.8	28.9
Jersey City city, Hudson County, NJ	248,435	28,352	20,258	71.5	11.4
Plano CCD, Collin County, TX	504,880	27,673	18,058	65.3	5.5
Sugar Land CCD, Fort Bend County, TX	250,040	27,487	15,635	56.9	11.0
Manhattan borough, NY County, NY	1,596,735	24,364	11,339	46.5	1.5
Seattle East CCD, King County, WA	556,572	24,329	19,137	78.7	4.4
Brooklyn borough, Kings County, NY	2,512,740	24,290	7,533	31.0	1.0
San Diego CCD, San Diego County, CA	2,266,727	22,962	15,339	66.8	1.0
Anaheim-Santa Ana-Garden Grove CCD, Orange County, CA	1,653,617	22,353	15,274	68.3	1.4
Southwest Dallas CCD, Dallas County, TX	913,038	22,145	15,802	71.4	2.4

(continued)

Table 3.1d **Continued**

	Total pop.	Indian-origin pop.	India-born pop.	India-born as share of Indian-origin, %	Indian-origin as share of CCD, %
Phoenix CCD, Maricopa County, AZ	3,003,292	21,945	16,001	72.9	0.7
San Fernando Vly CCD, Los Angeles County, CA	1,776,852	20,412	13,734	67.3	1.1
Philadelphia city, Philadelphia County, PA	1,525,811	19,571	12,374	63.2	1.3
Hempstead town, Nassau County, NY	759,197	17,659	8,953	50.7	2.3
Los Angeles CCD, Los Angeles County, CA	2,512,536	17,209	9,887	57.5	0.7
Northeast Dallas CCD, Dallas County, TX	1,466,176	16,747	11,583	69.2	1.1
Woodbridge tnshp, Middlesex County, NJ	99,695	15,299	11,463	74.9	15.3
Sacramento CCD, Sacramento County, CA	1,077,222	14,537	8,868	61.0	1.3
Roswell-Alpharetta CCD, Fulton County, GA	257,571	14,160	8,760	61.9	5.5
Bronx borough, Bronx County, NY	1,386,364	13,741	3,233	23.5	1.0
Schaumburg tnshp, Cook County, IL	131,290	13,333	9,793	73.4	10.2
Township 1, Charlotte; Mecklenburg County; NC	740,931	13,193	10,371	78.6	1.8
Dulles district, Loudoun County, VA	82,227	12,524	7,677	61.3	15.2
South Brunswick tnshp, Middlesex County, NJ	43,419	11,754	7,429	63.2	27.1
San Francisco CCD, San Francisco County, CA	807,755	11,631	5,668	48.7	1.4

Source: Compiled from the 2008-12 series in Summarized Data in http://dataferrett.census.gov/.

Table 3.1e Leading Places for Indian-origin and India-born Populations

	Total Pop.	Indian-origin pop.	India-born pop.	Indian-origin as share of local total, %	India-born as share of Indian-origin, %
Loudoun Valley Estates CDP, VA	3,025	1,195	796	39.5	66.6
Iselin CDP, NJ	18,763	6,730	5,292	35.9	78.6
Franklin Park CDP, NJ	12,815	4,093	2,745	31.9	67.1
Dayton CDP, NJ	7,603	2,424	1,566	31.9	64.6
Princeton Meadows CDP, NJ	13,840	4,226	3,088	30.5	73.1
Heathcote CDP, NJ	5,603	1,591	917	28.4	57.6
McNair CDP, VA	16,344	4,583	3,203	28.0	69.9
Cupertino city, CA	57,459	11,550	7,857	20.1	68.0
Kendall Park CDP, NJ	9,034	1,773	1,169	19.6	65.9
North New Hyde Park CDP, NY	14,626	2,620	1,403	17.9	53.5
Morrisville town, NC	17,313	3,053	2,158	17.6	70.7
Avenel CDP, NJ	17,639	3,015	2,137	17.1	70.9
Fremont city, CA	211,748	35,973	25,129	17.0	69.9
Garden City Park CDP, NY	7,874	1,328	909	16.9	68.4
Bradley Gardens CDP, NJ	14,203	2,190	1,441	15.4	65.8
Merrifield CDP, VA	15,215	2,315	1,602	15.2	69.2

(continued)

Table 3.1e **Continued**

	Total Pop.	Indian-origin pop.	India-born pop.	Indian-origin as share of local total, %	India-born as share of Indian-origin, %
New Hyde Park village, NY	9,661	1,468	927	15.2	63.1
Brambleton CDP, VA	9,333	1,379	703	14.8	51.0
Sunnyvale city, CA	138,436	20,148	15,789	14.6	78.4
Madison Park CDP, NJ	7,318	1,065	391	14.6	36.7
Livingston city, CA	12,899	1,824	1,125	14.1	61.7
Woodbridge CDP, NJ	19,937	2,814	2,324	14.1	82.6
Carteret borough, NJ	22,623	3,152	2,498	13.9	79.3
New Territory CDP, TX	16,351	2,268	1,478	13.9	65.2

Note: CDP stands for Census Designated Place. CDPs resemble incorporated places such as cities and towns but do not have independent political boundaries or governance.

Source: Compiled from the 2008-12 series in Summarized Data in http://dataferrett.census.gov/.

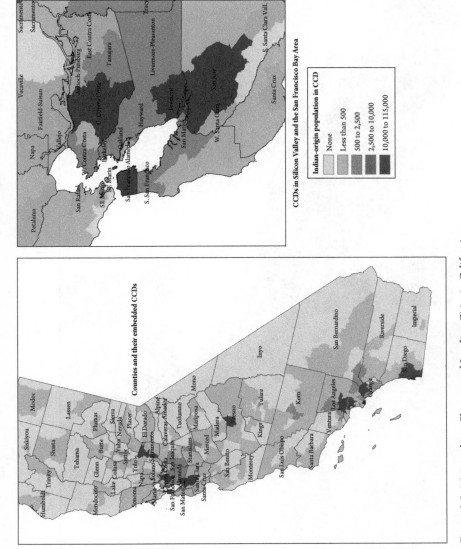

Counties and their embedded CCDs

CCDs in Silicon Valley and the San Francisco Bay Area

Indian-origin population in CCD

None
Less than 500
500 to 2,500
2,500 to 10,000
10,000 to 115,000

Figure 3.2 Metropolitan Clusters and Leading Cities in California.
Note: County boundaries are in dark lines, CCD boundaries are in grey lines.
Source: ACS, 2007–11.

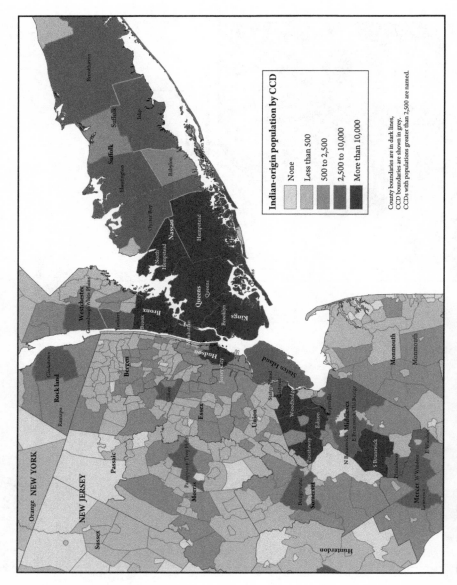

Figure 3.3 The New York–New Jersey Metropolitan Region and Its Leading Cities.

Source: ACS 2007–11.

CCDs in Dallas-Forth Worth Metropolis

Indian-origin population in CCD

- None
- Less than 500
- 500 to 2,500
- 2,500 to 10,000
- More than 10,000

CCDs in Southeast Texas metropolitan regions:
Houston–Sugar Land, San Antonio, and Austin

Figure 3.4 Metropolitan Clusters and Leading Cities in Texas.
Source: ACS 2007–11.

specific counties (and the other geographies associated with them), because they tell us much about the settlement patterns and trends of the Indian-American population in the United States.

Queens County had the largest Indian-origin population; about 135,000 people, close to 5 percent of the national total, resided in this single county. However, Queens had lost Indian-origin population in the period covered here, the only county in the top twenty-five to do so other than Kings County (Brooklyn), which is also part of New York City.[14] The decline of these two counties (especially Queens) was the primary reason for the decline of New York State as a residence for Indian Americans. This is a development of some significance and was driven largely by fundamental changes in the composition of the Indian-American population, created by the increasing and overwhelming dominance of the computer/ information technology sector. We discussed the extent of this fundamental occupation shift in chapter 2. Later in this chapter, after we present further details on the micro-geography of work, income, and language, we deepen the explanation for this phenomenon.

Middlesex County in New Jersey is also part of the New York–New Jersey metropolitan region, but its recent trends were in the opposite direction of Queens and Kings Counties. It was the fastest growing of the large counties (for both the Indian-origin and India-born populations). It was also the only county in which the Indian-origin population made up more than 10 percent of the local population; at 13.1 percent, the share of Indian Americans in Middlesex County was almost twice as large as the next densest concentration, in Santa Clara County, where Indian Americans made up 6.7 percent of the local population. In other words, *Indians in America were most visible in Middlesex County, New Jersey*.

There is little doubt that the state of New Jersey contained locations with the highest density of Indian Americans. In fact, a ranked order of all municipalities in the United States with respect to the share of resident Indian Americans showed that *all* of the top eight and fourteen of the top twenty were in New Jersey. Six of the top eight New Jersey municipalities were in Middlesex County: Edison, Plainsboro, South Brunswick, North Brunswick, Piscataway, and Woodbridge. Some of the densest places (CDPs) contained within these municipalities—like Iselin and Franklin Park and Dayton—where the proportion of Indian Americans exceeded 30 percent of the local population, were in this same stretch. Almost as dense with Indian Americans were some subregions of Silicon Valley—specifically, Cupertino, Fremont, and Sunnyvale, in each of which the Indian-origin population constituted between 15 and 20 percent of the local total. These two regions—Middlesex County, New Jersey, and Silicon Valley, California—were the largest "Little Indias" in the United States; they were large enough to have smaller "Little Indias" embedded inside them.

Consider now the share of India-born in Indian-origin in the two most important spatial units for Indian Americans: the New York–New Jersey metropolitan area and Silicon Valley.[15] On the New York side of the Hudson River, the boroughs that make up New York City had the lowest shares, not only as shown in Table 3.1d, but in the entire United States. In Queens, only 36 percent of the Indian-origin were India-born; the figures were 24 percent in the Bronx, 31 percent in Brooklyn, and 47 percent in Manhattan. Across the Hudson River, municipalities and places in New Jersey had some of the highest ratios of India-born to Indian-origin: 75 percent in Woodbridge, 74 percent in Edison, and 72 percent in Jersey City (these specific locations are identified in figure 3.3). This is a tale of two cities within the same metropolitan area: on the New York side was an India-born population that had arrived earlier—so much so that their children now outnumbered them. On the New Jersey side was a population that had arrived largely in the last two decades, and they outnumbered their children by factors of two to three.

The New York City story was increasingly the uncommon one. The New Jersey story, on the other hand, was visible in states and communities throughout the country. For instance, in Silicon Valley, the proportion of India-born in the total Indian-American population was 71 percent in San Jose (in Santa Clara County) and 69 percent in Fremont (in adjacent Alameda County). Similarly, it was 79 percent in Seattle East in King County (Washington State) and in Township 1 in Charlotte (North Carolina), 73 percent each in Schaumberg (in Cook County, Illinois) and Phoenix, Arizona, and 72 percent in Southwest Dallas, Texas.

The spatial narrative that emerges from these data is quite clear, and it builds upon the chronological narrative we established in chapter 2. We argued that it was possible to identify three distinct temporal phases of Indian immigration to the United States. The first two immigrant streams—the Early Movers and the Families—had disproportionately large numbers of Gujaratis and Punjabis, many of whom entered with family-oriented visas, and the workforce was dispersed among the professions, from entrepreneurial small business to retail trade and entertainment and education. The third and later stream (the IT Generation) had disproportionately large numbers of Telugus and Tamils, many of whom entered with employment or student visas, and created a workforce heavily concentrated in professional services, specifically computer services.

We can see that these two different immigrant streams had different spatial manifestations. One stark spatial implication was the decline of New York City (Queens County, in particular) and the rise of north-central New Jersey (Middlesex and Hudson Counties, in particular). On the West Coast, in California, there was a visible concentration of Indian immigrants in Silicon Valley, especially in Santa Clara and Alameda Counties. Some older destinations had cohered, such as those in Chicago-Schaumberg in Cook County, Illinois. And several new destinations—all suburban—were emerging or becoming larger in Texas, Washington, Virginia/Maryland, North Carolina, Arizona, Georgia, and Pennsylvania. Examples included Dallas, Fort Bend, Harris, and Collin Counties in Texas and the municipalities of Plano, Southwest Dallas, Sugar Land, and Irving; King County in Washington and the municipality of Seattle East; Fairfax and Loudon Counties in Virginia; Maricopa County in Arizona and the municipality of Phoenix; and the Roswell-Alpharetta region in Fulton County, Georgia, in greater Atlanta. These new settlements had not begun to approach the sizes of the old clusters, but several could stake a claim to being a significant new "Little India."

Income, Education, and Work

In this section we examine the spatial distribution of the India-born population in combination with key characteristics of income, education, and occupation/industry, followed by a subsection on the detailed distribution of language speakers. Note that henceforth we focus entirely on the India-born population. But this is not a restrictive condition. Because the vast majority of America-born Indians still lived at home with their parents, they get picked up whenever we discuss family or household-level characteristics (such as income). Since five in six America-born Indians were still students, it did not make much sense to discuss their educational "attainment" (as yet incomplete). As for work, since only one in six of the America-born Indian population was economically active—which meant that the economically active America-born population was approximately one-tenth the size of the economically active India-born population—adding that population to this discussion would contribute little analytical value. The core findings, then, of the preceding section are repeated here—namely, that there was great spatial variation in the India-born population, and consequently there were notable inequalities, at the same time that there were significant clusters of similar characteristics and outcomes.

Very High Incomes, But Not Everywhere

Detailed information on three forms of income-earning units are widely available from the Census Bureau: *personal* or *individual income* is obtained by summing eight types of income defined by the Census Bureau for each person fifteen years old and over.[16] *Household income* includes the income of the householder and all other individuals fifteen years old and over in the household, whether related to the householder or not. *Family income* includes the incomes of all household members fifteen years old and over who are related to the householder. To limit the exposition here, we provide information on family income and personal income;[17] and to use robust estimates, we follow the Census Bureau's cautions.[18]

There are two noticeable features in the family income data shown in figure 3.5. The first, which we noted in chapter 2, and that is often highlighted in even the most cursory coverage of Indians in America, was the income difference between them and the rest of the country. The average India-born family income of $103,000 was 1.8 times as large as that of the average American family. The personal incomes of Indians—not detailed here—was more than twice as high as in the general population ($48,000 vs. $23,000). Incomes of the India-born were higher in every state, for both definitions of income. There was no exception to this, nor was there any discernible pattern in the extent of difference between incomes of the India-born and overall U.S. incomes—that is, there was no regional pattern, nor was it possible to argue that the gaps were highest where incomes of the India-born were highest.[19] Neither was it possible to identify a pattern based on the size of the India-born population.

This leads to the second major feature in the data, which is less known and less discussed: the inequality within the Indian-American community. For example, the family incomes of the India-born in Texas and Illinois were lower by about $10,000 than the national average of India-born families, and lower by almost $25,000 compared to India-born family incomes in the leading states

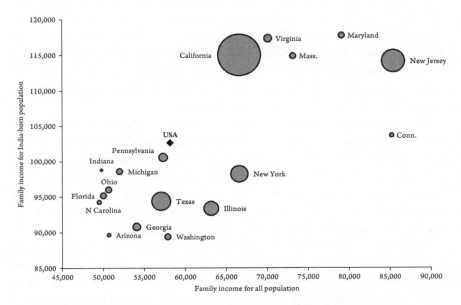

Figure 3.5   Family Income for India-born and Total Population in Leading States.
Note: States shown have at least 20,000 Indian-born. The size of the circle is proportional to the size of the Indian-born population.
Source: ACS 2007–11.

of Maryland and Virginia. In other words, the India-born families in Maryland and Virginia were significantly more well to do than their counterparts in Texas and Illinois, and even more so—with family incomes about twice as high—compared to the India-born families in southern states like Alabama and Mississippi.[20] In short, there was a significant level of income inequality between India-born families at the state level.

As expected, the spatial distribution of family income was even more unequal at a smaller geographical scale.[21] The only scale at which reliable income estimates could be generated for small populations like the India-born was the PUMA scale, which for the sake of convenience, we call *settlements*.[22] The following analysis is based on the 469 PUMAs (out of about 2,100 total PUMAs in the United States) that met the criteria of data reliability.[23] The results are shown in table 3.2 (in which the settlements with the highest and lowest family incomes for India-born families are identified) and figures 3.6 and 3.7 (in which we map family incomes at the settlement-level for the most important regions: the New York–New Jersey metropolitan area and the San Francisco–Silicon Valley metropolitan area).

It is clear that the India-born were distributed in a wide range of settlements with a wide range of incomes. A significant majority of the India-born settlements (a little under three-fourths of the total) had family incomes in the range of $75,000 to $150,000. This could be called the middle to upper-middle class range in the United States. The remaining one-fourth of the settlements were polarized. Fewer than half of this remainder (58 settlements) had family incomes over $175,000, while somewhat more than half (68 settlements) had family incomes under $75,000. In this polarized quarter of settlements, there was a wide range of family incomes, from under $24,000 in a part of Fresno (an agriculture-based city in California) to $273,000 on Long Island, around Oyster Bay and Glen Cove—an eleven-fold difference.

The characteristics of the lowest-income settlements are obvious. They are: (1) farming/semi-rural settlements like Fresno in Kern County and Stanislaus County (both in California); and (2) inner-city areas in New York City (Queens, in particular), Chicago, Houston, and Detroit. In this, the India-born were identical to the general American population, where poverty is concentrated in the inner city and rural areas.[24] American rural poverty is manifested more starkly in the southern states, but the India-born, as we have shown earlier, tended not to reside in those regions. Neither, other than in Fresno, were whole settlements of the India-born officially "poor," as the poverty line in the United States is around $24,000 for a household of four. The India-born low-income settlements were "low" relative to other India-born settlements, not by official U.S. standards. We remind the reader of a significant conclusion from the preceding chapter: *Very*

Table 3.2 **Settlements with Highest and Lowest Family Incomes for the India-born**

	Highest Family Incomes				Lowest Family Incomes		
Puma#, State	PUMA located in	Pop.	Income		Puma#, State	PUMA located in	Pop.	Income
Puma# 04202, New York	Long Island	1,764	272,801		Puma# 03301, California	Fresno	3,240	23,733
Puma# 06121, California	Los Angeles (Cerritos)	974	271,529		Puma# 04107, New York	Queens	2,571	35,650
Puma# 00201, Ohio	Springfield/Sylvania	781	247,236		Puma# 04112, New York	Queens	1,439	41,747
Puma# 03504, New York	Rye/Mamaroneck	625	228,231		Puma# 03503, Illinois	Chicago	4,688	43,474
Puma# 06126, California	Los Angeles (San Fernando)	492	211,266		Puma# 04113, New York	Queens	3,453	43,543
Puma# 02704, Florida	Tampa/Hillsborough	1,066	208,262		Puma# 03504, Illinois	Chicago	2,449	45,971
Puma# 01400, Mass.	Maynard	1,842	206,112		Puma# 00703, New Jersey	Bayonne/Kearney	2,755	45,978
Puma# 02707, California	Cupertino/Los Gatos	10,874	205,690		Puma# 04111, New York	Queens	7,407	48,728
Puma# 02505, Michigan	Birmingham	2,916	204,859		Puma# 04102, New York	Queens	5,540	49,227
Puma# 01705, Missouri	Clayton	1,562	199,757		Puma# 03806, Michigan	Wayne	1,372	49,228
Puma# 01801, Penn.	Allegheny County	1,092	198,383		Puma# 03406, Illinois	Chicago	850	49,512
Puma# 03501, New York	Westchester County	758	196,433		Puma# 04610, Texas	Houston	2,508	49,561

(continued)

Table 3.2 Continued

Highest Family Incomes				Lowest Family Incomes			
Puma#, State	PUMA located in	Pop.	Income	Puma#, State	PUMA located in	Pop.	Income
Puma# 01903, New Jersey	Plainfield	1,554	196,032	Puma# 03903, California	Kern County	649	49,660
Puma# 02600, Mass.	Wellesley/Needham	783	195,940	Puma# 02602, California	Stanislaus County	494	49,729
Puma# 02713, California	Santa Clara	5,856	195,628	Puma# 04101, New York	Queens	1,824	49,950
Puma# 04301, New York	Suffolk County	2,014	194,148	Puma# 05411, California	Los Angeles	3,204	50,871
Puma# 01001, New Jersey	Bridgewater/Plainfield	4,711	193,571	Puma# 04109, New York	Queens	3,074	51,015
Puma# 06101, California	Los Angeles (Desert View)	786	193,171	Puma# 01002, Florida	Alachua/Gainesville	1,353	52,084
Puma# 02105, California	Alamo/Danville	5,348	191,911	Puma# 01201, Georgia	Atlanta/N Decatur	1,920	52,381
Puma# 03503, New York	White Plains/Scarsdale	3,168	187,382	Puma# 00600, Mass.	Lowell	1,253	52,683

Note: These lists include only those PUMAS for which the standard error of family income was lower than 25 percent.

Source: Calculated and compiled from ACS 2007–11.

Figure 3.6 Income Distribution in the New York–New Jersey Region.

Notes: Income estimates with more than 25% standard error are "not reliable". The figure inside each PUMA is the average family income (in thousands).

Source: ACS 2007–11.

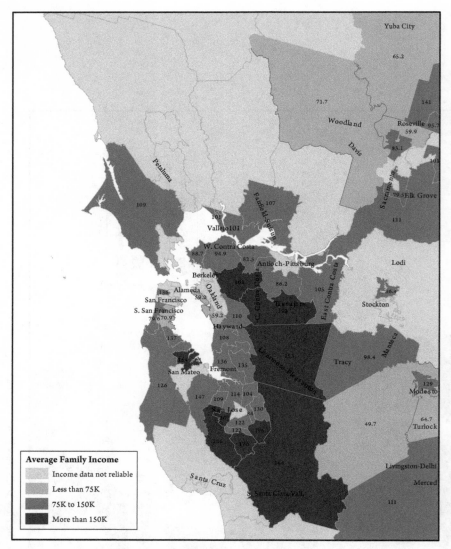

Figure 3.7   Income Distribution in the San Francisco Bay Area, California.
Notes: Income estimates with more than 25% standard error are "not reliable". The figure inside each
PUMA is the average family income (in thousands).
Source: ACS 2007–11

large majorities of the India-born did not have to struggle with the structural inequali-
ties and disadvantages in American society.

The spatial pattern of the highest-income India-born settlements is as obvious as that of the lowest-income ones. Generally, the high-income India-born
lived in suburban settlements like Long Island, Rye/Mamaroneck, and White
Plains in New York, parts of suburban Los Angeles County (Cerritos, San
Fernando) and Silicon Valley (Cupertino, Santa Clara, and Alamo/Danville)

in California, Plainfield and Bridgewater in New Jersey, and scattered settlements like Springfield/Sylvania in Ohio, suburban Tampa in Florida, suburban Pittsburgh in Pennsylvania, Maynard and Wellesley in suburban Boston, and Clayton in suburban St. Louis, Missouri.

The widest range of incomes was in New York State, specifically New York City and its suburbs (see figure 3.6). Two of the top four and five of the top twenty high-income settlements of the India-born were in New York, all in the suburbs of New York City, at the same time that two of the bottom three and seven of bottom twenty low-income settlements were in Queens County, in New York City. New York's income distribution stood in visible contrast to its neighbor New Jersey's distribution. Figure 3.6 shows the low-income cluster in Queens and its proximity to the high-income clusters on Long Island and in Westchester County, whereas the only low-income settlement in New Jersey on our list was Bayonne, right across the Hudson River from New York City. From figure 3.5 we know that the average family income of the India-born in New Jersey ($114,000) was considerably higher than in New York ($98,000). We have to conclude that New York had a spatially polarized income distribution for India-born families, while New Jersey had a relatively egalitarian one.

This geography of income distribution is the legacy of a history of settlement patterns. New York City was the original prime destination for the first and second phases of Indian immigrants, which included relatively large shares of less-skilled workers who earned low incomes. However, in recent decades, New York City has been supplanted by New Jersey, which is increasingly a magnet for the new (third) phase of Indian immigrants, increasingly larger proportions of whom have technical skills and earn higher incomes.[25] The simultaneous decline of New York City and rise of suburban New Jersey is a geographical narrative inscribed by the momentous changes in Indian immigration patterns that have taken place in the last two decades.

Remarkable Levels of Educational Attainment, Unevenly Distributed

In chapter 2 we showed that the India-born were the most educated group in the United States, in comparison to every native-born (racial) category and every foreign-born population tabulated by the census. Here, we briefly discuss the spatial distribution of educational attainment with a focus on the attainment of advanced degrees (master's, professional, and doctorate) in the twenty-four states that had at least 10,000 India-born, followed by an identification of the settlements that had the highest and lowest concentrations of India-born advanced-degree holders. The relevant data are in table 3.3 and figure 3.8.

Table 3.3 **Communities with the Highest and Lowest Concentrations of Advanced Degrees**

	Highest concentration of advanced-degree holders					Lowest concentration of advanced-degree holders			
Puma#	State	PUMA located in	Number	%	Puma#	State	PUMA located in	Number	%
08110	CA	San Diego	1,733	70.2	02601	CA	Ceres / Turlock	5	0.1
02304	CA	San Mateo	2,155	67.3	00800	CA	Yuba	220	3.7
02701	CA	Los Altos	3,952	63.5	03401	CA	Coalinga / Selma	134	4.9
03510	IL	Chicago	3,175	61.5	02006	WA	East Hill	138	5.3
01003	MD	Rockville	2,831	60.2	03100	CA	Los Banos / Merced	256	5.5
02505	MI	Birmingham	1,748	59.9	01505	CA	South Sacramento	120	5.9
02702	CA	Sunnyvale	9,269	55.0	03301	CA	Fresno	201	6.2
02708	CA	Bloomingdale	2,718	53.9	04102	NY	Clayton	373	6.8
00901	MD	Columbia	1,522	53.3	01902	CA	Stockton	166	7.8
02103	TX	Plano	3,851	51.9	03800	CA	Bakersfield	411	8.1
00305	VA	Oakton / Reston	6,838	51.9	02001	CA	Lathrop / Manteca	341	8.9
08111	CA	San Diego	2,163	51.5	04113	NY	Queens	366	10.7
07603	CA	Foothill Ranch	1,770	50.9	04109	NY	Queens	329	10.7
02703	CA	Santa Clara	5,977	50.7	00501	NJ	Clifton / Passaic	517	10.8

03305	IL	Buffalo Grove	1,537	50.5	03503	IL	Chicago	527	11.2
02700	MA	Waltham / Watertown	2,237	50.1	04101	PA	Philadelphia	667	11.6
02705	FL	Tampa	1,666	49.7	01506	CA	Galt / Rancho Cordova	324	11.6
02410	CA	Dublin / Livermore	3,240	49.6	07605	CA	Buena Park / Cypress	362	12.0
07300	CA	Irvine	3,040	49.5	03504	IL	Chicago	297	12.1
02302	NJ	Princeton	3,774	49.4	04107	NY	Queens	344	13.4
02102	TX	Richardson	3,094	49.3	03302	CA	Fresno	417	14.5
02707	CA	Cupertino / Los Gatos	5,321	49.3	04102	PA	Philadelphia	295	14.6

Notes:

Advanced degrees include master's, professional, and doctoral degrees.

To limit the number of communities listed here we used two cut-offs: the minimum number of India-born in a PUMA (2,000) to identify only the more reliable estimates; and the minimum share of advanced-degree holders in the local population (49% of the India-born population) for the "high concentration" group and the maximum share of advanced-degree holders (15%) to identify the "low concentration" group.

Source: Compiled and calculated from ACS 2007–11.

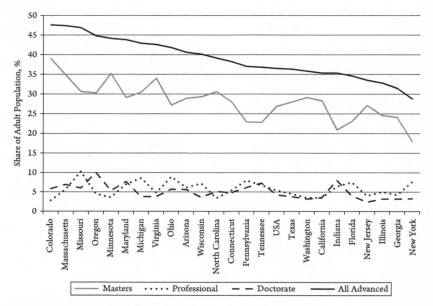

Figure 3.8 Distribution of Advanced Degrees (in Leading States).
Note: The shares are calculated for the adult population, 25 years and older.
Source: Calculated from ACS 2007–11.

We already know that over 36 percent of the India-born adults in the United States held advanced degrees, but this average was centered between a wide geographic range. In Colorado, Massachusetts, and Missouri, close to half the adult India-born population (about 47 percent) were advanced-degree holders. In Virginia, Michigan, Maryland, Ohio, Arizona, Minnesota, Wisconsin, and Oregon, more than 40 percent of the India-born population held advanced degrees. However, in all five of the most populous states for Indians (California, New Jersey, New York, Texas, and Illinois), the share of the India-born holding advanced degrees was lower than average. The lowest share (28.8 percent) was in New York. Note again that this is "low" relative to India-born in the United States, not by average American standards.

One of the more remarkable figures we found is the number of India-born doctorate-degree holders in the United States—over 73,000 in 2007–2011. (Note: As of this writing, the Census Bureau released the PUMS 2014 data, and this single-year sample estimates the number of India-born with doctorates at over 92,000. However, to maintain consistency, the discussion here refers to the older ACS 2007–2011 data.)[26]

There were almost 12,000 India-born doctorate-degree holders in California alone, another 5,800 in Texas, and about 5,000 each in New Jersey and New York. The highest concentration of doctoral degrees among the India-born was in Oregon, where, astonishingly, one in ten had a doctorate.[27] In Indiana, Maryland, Tennessee, and Massachusetts, 7 percent or more of the population of India-born held doctorates. Recall from chapter 2 that 70 percent of the India-born with student visas were in STEM disciplines (science, technology, engineering and mathematics), including one-third in engineering and one-fourth in computer-related fields. We estimate that, controlling for quality, it will take decades for India's system of higher education to simply match the U.S. stock of India-born doctorate-degree holders in the science and technology disciplines. In short, the stock of "Indian" intellectual capital in science and technology is overwhelmingly resident in America. This has serious policy implications for India.

The relationship between educational attainment and income is well known, but as a reminder we show its extent for the India-born and full U.S. population in figure 3.9. As expected, there was a pronounced skill-premium: the personal and family incomes for both populations tracked in harmony, showing rapidly increasing income with the attainment of advanced degrees.

At the bachelor's degree level, the personal incomes of the India-born were lower than for the overall U.S. population ($45,000 vs. $53,000),[28] but family incomes were considerably higher ($91,000 vs. $73,000). At the highest income levels, for professional and doctorate degree holders, India-born personal incomes were marginally higher than their overall U.S. counterparts, whereas family incomes were much higher. Incomes for professional degree-holding India-born families were over $196,000, while for their U.S. counterparts they were less than $141,000. The importance of the Indian family structure to income achievement cannot be overstated; Indian-American families were both larger and more stable. As discussed in chapter 2, India-born households were significantly more likely to be family households, and other arrangements, such as single-parent and female-headed households, were relatively uncommon. It is likely that, along with an education or skill premium, there was a family premium in the attainment of income. This is a dimension we identify as a "selection +" premium.

Like the distribution of income, the distribution of advanced degrees was spatially polarized. On the one hand, there were 141 settlements (or PUMAs) in which at least half the India-born population had advanced degrees. On the other hand, there were 83 settlements in which less than one-fifth of the India-born population had advanced degrees. At one extreme, there were four settlements with over 5,000 advanced-degree holders each; three were in Silicon Valley (Sunnyvale, 9,300; Santa Clara, 6,000; Cupertino, 5,300), and one was in suburban Washington, D.C. (Oakton/Reston in Virginia, 6,800). In addition, there were some extraordinary settlements. For example, one was part of the city of San Diego, where over 70 percent of the India-born had advanced degrees; and two settlements in Silicon Valley (in San Mateo and Los Altos), where over 60 percent of the India-born had advanced degrees.

At the other extreme, there were areas in Turlock, Yuba, and Coalinga (all in rural California), where less than 5 percent of sizable India-born populations

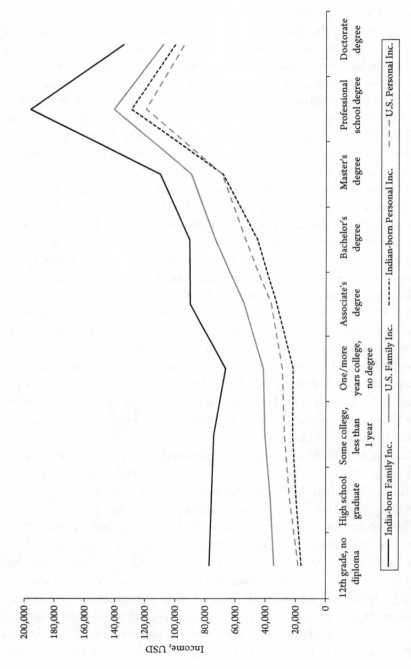

Figure 3.9 Educational Attainment and Income for India-born and U.S. Families.
Source: ACS 2007–11.

had advanced degrees. This polarization in the distribution of educational attainment existed within individual states (especially California and New York, and to a lesser extent, Texas) and individual metropolitan regions (especially New York, and to a lesser extent, Chicago and the San Francisco Bay area). Especially notable was a stretch in California—along Highway 99 between the San Francisco Bay area and Southern California—an agricultural belt that includes Stockton, Turlock, Merced, Fresno, Selma, Bakersfield, and other cities. This stretch—called the Central Valley—had sizable India-born communities (where, we shall see later, Punjabis were overrepresented) with low levels of educational attainment (relative to the overall India-born population certainly, but also relative to the native-born population).[29] At the same time, in Silicon Valley, the settlements of Sunnyvale, Santa Clara, Cupertino, Los Altos, San Mateo, Walnut Creek, and parts of San Jose had thousands of India-born advanced-degree holders. San Jose itself is a large municipality (the tenth largest in the United States, larger than the municipality of San Francisco) and includes neighborhoods that had both very large and very small proportions of India-born advanced-degree holders.

As we have come to expect, New York City had a high degree of polarization on educational attainment. Manhattan had a concentration of advanced-degree holders; in at least seven settlements inside Manhattan, more than half the India-born had advanced degrees. At the same time, Queens had large areas with relatively low educational attainment among the India-born; there were four settlements with less than 10 percent, and nine more with 10 to 20 percent who held advanced degrees. The Bronx and Brooklyn had similar but somewhat better numbers. Chicago was another example of the same phenomenon, with three settlements in the top category and two settlements in the bottom category of advanced-degree holders.

In closing this subsection, we take note of one important issue: a recognition that the polarizations noted here are not peculiar to the India-born but, rather, reflective of larger processes of polarization in American society and space. For example, Glaeser and Gottlieb write: "Bethesda, Maryland, is one of the richest urban areas in the country, and more than half of its adults have college degrees. By contrast, fewer than one in ten adults in the least educated metropolitan areas have college degrees." Similarly, in the mid-2000s, the per capita metropolitan product ranged from around $16,000 in Brownsville, Texas, to around $74,000 in Bridgeport, Connecticut (San Jose, of special interest to Indian Americans, was ranked third with about $68,000). The authors show that "differences in human capital account for about half of the variance in metropolitan-area wage levels."[30]

For Indian Americans and for the general U.S. population, Midtown Manhattan and Queens are physically separated by the narrow East River, but in socioeconomic terms the two are worlds apart, as are the two valleys in California, Silicon and Central. It was not surprising, therefore, to find that the India-born population in these spaces exhibited similar polarizations in educational attainment (or human capital) and income. In other words, the India-born population was geographically sorted along the same lines and for similar reasons as the general U.S. population. The U.S. housing market is finely graded, and the quality of public goods (especially schools) is embedded in the price of housing. Therefore, "good" places have good schools and high home prices, which prices out low-education, low-income families to inferior places with inferior schools. It is a model of cumulative causation that the India-born cannot affect but have to adapt to in making residential choices.

From Techies to Taxiwallahs: The Range of Occupations

Education and occupation are related variables that in combination produce income and welfare. Earlier we have provided a sense of the occupational structure of the India-born. We know that they had high levels of educational attainment strongly favoring science and technology fields. Here, we identify the specific occupational categories in which the India-born were over- and underrepresented, the distribution of workers in the leading categories and states, and some specific clusters of India-born workers in key occupational categories.[31]

The Pew Foundation's 2012 report titled "The Rise of Asian Americans" provided a data frame for us to compare the occupational structure of the India-born to the native-born and other foreign-born populations in the United States.[32] The data in figure 3.10 show two points of stark difference. First, the India-born were significantly underrepresented in low-skill occupations; only 13 percent of India-born labor was in this category, compared to over 35 and 50 percent, respectively, of the native-born and foreign-born populations. At the same time, the India-born were significantly overrepresented in the computer, engineering, and science (CES) category; it provided work for over 30 percent of the India-born but only 6 percent of the foreign-born and just 4.4 percent of native-born workers. This was the category that set the India-born labor force apart from everyone else.[33]

Figure 3.11 shows the occupational structure of India-born workers by major categories used by the Census Bureau, and changes in this structure in the period 2004–2012. The "computers" category was by far the most important for the India-born (full compositional details of the major categories are in

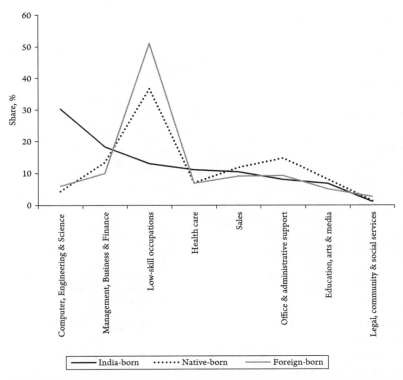

Figure 3.10 Distribution of U.S.-born, Foreign-born, and India-born Workers by Major Occupation Groups.

Note: "Low-skill occupations" include: Food preparation & serving, Cleaning & maintenance, Other general services, Farming, fishing & forestry, Construction & extraction, Installation, repair & production, Transportation & material moving, and Military.

Source: The native-born and foreign-born data are from the Pew report "The Rise of Asian Americans." The Indian-born data are compiled by the authors to match the Pew categories from ACS 2006–10.

the notes to figure 3.12). In the eight years covered by the data, the number of workers in the "computers" category increased from around 200,000 to around 350,000; the share of all India-born workers in this category increased from under one-fifth to around one-fourth of total workers. This is a number to be noted: *one-fourth of all the India-born in the United States worked in computer-related occupations.*

The second-ranked occupational category was "managers";[34] this grew at a similar pace and increased its share of all India-born workers from under 10 percent to over 12 percent—to about half the size of the "computers" category. The third- and fourth-ranked categories were "sales" and "medical services," both of which grew in size during 2004–2012 period but lost share, so that each employed a little under one-tenth of the India-born workforce in 2012. More than 55 percent of all India-born workers were employed in these

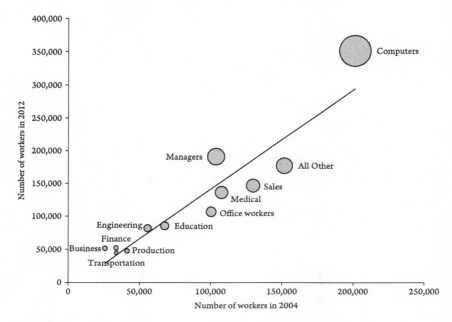

Figure 3.11 Changes in Occupational Distribution for Indian-born Workers, 2004–2012.

Note: The size of the circle is proportional to the number of workers in 2012. The full definition of the major categories in in Figure 3.12.

Source: Compiled & calculated from PUMS 2004 & 2013.

four leading categories. Three of these four (all but "sales") were high-skill, high-wage occupational categories (see table 3.4).[35]

The distribution of the India-born labor force at the state level has two notable patterns (see figure 3.12). One pattern could be called the national average for Indian labor, represented by California and New Jersey. These two states were strikingly similar in the occupational structure of the India-born, with a marked dominance of the computer sector. The second pattern was represented by Texas and Illinois (and at a smaller scale, Pennsylvania), states in which employment in the "computers" category was the largest, but the share of the "medical" category was relatively high (close to one-seventh in Illinois, for example). New York was in its own group, the only state in which the share of employees in "computers" was not the highest; but, rather, it was "medical," with one-fifth of all workers. Once again, New York stood apart.

Finally, in table 3.5, we took the analysis to a smaller spatial scale by identifying the settlements with the highest concentration of India-born workers, then further analyzing the leading settlements for four categories:

1. All workers.
2. "Computer systems design and related services," the leading occupational subcategory for the India-born, which was the major component of the

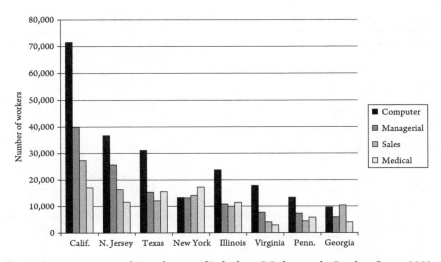

Figure 3.12 Occupational Distribution of India-born Workers in the Leading States, 2012.
Notes: The major categories in this and Figure 3.11 have the following composition: <u>CMM</u>:
Computer & Information Research Scientists, Computer Systems Analysts, Information Security
Analysts, Computer Programmers, Software Developers, Applications & Systems Software, Web
Developers, Computer Support Specialists, Database Administrators, Network & Computer Systems
Administrators, Computer Network Architects, Computer Occupations, Actuaries, Operations
Research Analysts, Miscellaneous Mathematical Science Occupations, Including Mathematicians &
Statisticians <u>MGR</u>: Chief Executives & Legislators, General & Operations Managers, Managers
of: Advertising & Promotions, Marketing & Sales, Public Relations & Fundraising, Administrative
Services, Computer & Information Systems, Finances, Compensation & Benefits, Human Resources,
Training & Development, Industrial Production, Purchasing, Transportation, Storage, & Distribution,
Farmers, Ranchers, & Other Agricultural work, Construction, Education Administrators,
Architectural & Engineering, Food Service, Gaming, Lodging, Medical & Health Services,
Natural Sciences, Property, Real Estate, & Community Association, Social & Community Service,
Emergency Management Directors, Miscellaneous Managers, including Funeral Service Managers &
Postmasters & Mail Superintendents <u>SAL</u>-First-Line Supervisors Of Retail Sales Workers, First-Line
Supervisors Of Non-Retail Sales Workers, Cashiers, Counter & Rental Clerks, Parts Salespersons,
Retail Salespersons, Advertising Sales Agents, Insurance Sales Agents, Securities, Commodities, &
Financial Services Sales Agents, Travel Agents, Sales Representatives, Models, Demonstrators, &
Product Promoters, Real Estate Brokers & Sales Agents, Sales Engineers, Telemarketers, Door-To-
Door Sales Workers, News & Street Vendors, & Related Workers, Sales & Related Workers <u>MED</u>:
Chiropractors, Dentists, Dietitians & Nutritionists, Optometrists, Pharmacists, Physicians &
Surgeons, Physician Assistants, Podiatrists, Audiologists, Occupational Therapists, Physical
Therapists, Radiation Therapists, Recreational Therapists, Respiratory Therapists, Speech-Language
Pathologists, Other Therapists, Including Exercise Physiologists, Veterinarians, Registered Nurses,
Nurse Anesthetists, Nurse Practitioners & Nurse Midwives, Health Diagnosing & Treating
Practitioners, Clinical Laboratory Technologists & Technicians, Dental Hygienists, Diagnostic
Related Technologists & Technicians, Emergency Medical Technicians & Paramedics, Health
Practitioner Support Technologists & Technicians, Licensed Practical & Licensed Vocational Nurses,
Medical Records & Health Information Technicians, Opticians, Dispensing, Miscellaneous Health
Technologists & Technicians, Other Healthcare Practitioners & Technical Occupations
Source: Compiled & calculated from PUMS 2013.

Table 3.4 **Occupations and Personal Incomes of the India-born**

Occupational category	Number of workers	Average Personal Income
MED-Physicians and Surgeons	53,746	196,817
MGR-Chief Executives and Legislators	15,341	185,147
MGR-Financial Managers	15,092	114,270
MGR-Computer and Information Systems Managers	35,860	112,590
MGR-Miscellaneous Managers, incl. Postmasters and Mail Superintendents	60,012	110,391
ENG-Electrical and Electronics Engineers	13,110	101,184
ENG-Miscellaneous Engineers, including Nuclear Engineers	19,074	95,146
BUS-Management Analysts	27,315	92,702
MED-Pharmacists	10,642	85,450
CMM-Software Developers, Applications and Systems Software	205,990	85,267
SCI-Physical Scientists	10,925	83,374
CMM-Computer Programmers	35,171	80,227
CMM-Computer Occupations, All Other	19,654	78,909
CMM-Computer Systems Analysts	48,231	77,927
SCI-Medical Scientists, and Life Scientists, All Other	10,553	68,659
MED-Registered Nurses	26,257	68,307
FIN-Accountants and Auditors	40,210	65,172
SAL-First-Line Supervisors Of Retail Sales Workers	38,208	46,500
EDU-Postsecondary Teachers	44,670	45,771
OFF-Secretaries and Administrative Assistants	11,357	45,603
PRD-Inspectors, Testers, Sorters, Samplers, and Weighers	10,475	41,838
TRN-Driver/Sales Workers and Truck Drivers	13,102	38,787
SAL-Retail Salespersons	20,643	34,848
OFF-Customer Service Representatives	13,102	32,433
TRN-Taxi Drivers and Chauffeurs	10,103	32,193

(continued)

Table 3.4 **Continued**

Occupational category	Number of workers	Average Personal Income
HLS-Nursing, Psychiatric, and Home Health Aides	11,322	31,251
EDU-Elementary and Middle School Teachers	13,862	30,116
SAL-Cashiers	54,175	18,934

Notes:

All occupational subcategories with at least 10,000 India-born workers in the U.S. are shown.

The occupational categorical system was changed in 2012 and the category names do not exactly match names in earlier censuses that have been used elsewhere in this chapter.

Source: PUMS 2012.

"computers" category and employed close to 12 percent of all India-born workers. (As we have noted several times, this occupational subcategory was the driver of the new forms of Indian immigration and is key to understanding the rapid changes in the Indian-American population.)

3. "Medical services," a category that employed a little over 9 percent of all India-born workers.

4. "Taxi and limousine service," a subcategory under the category "transportation."

Note from table 3.4 that these latter two groupings—medical services and taxi drivers—were, respectively, the highest- and close to the lowest-paying professions for the India-born.

We chose these categories after careful consideration. We were interested in the leading categories, for sure, but we were also interested in examining some important ideas in the literature on clustering, and in giving due attention to some of the work that tends to get lost in the singular focus on the leading and high-skill, high-technology sectors. The clustering literature suggests that some industries are input-oriented; for example, the information technology industry is more reliant on local inputs like skilled labor, and as a result, is more likely to derive localization economies (i.e., the economic benefits that arise when firms in the same industry are proximate to each other). Therefore, these high-tech industries are more likely to be clustered.

Then, there are other industries that are more market-oriented (rather than labor- or input-oriented); that is, regardless of the spatial distribution of skills, wherever there is a market, the industry will locate there. For example, the health-care industry (like the pizza or personal grooming or taxi

Table 3.5 **Leading Settlements of Selected Occupations of the India-born, 2012**

	All Workers			Computer Systems Design and Related Services	
State	County—Location	Number	State	County—Location	Number
	U.S. Total	1,534,140		U.S. Total	185,591
CA	Alameda—Fremont City (East)	25,974	CA	Santa Clara—Sunnyvale & San Jose (North)	6,797
NJ	Middlesex—Metuchen Borough	23,375	CA	Alameda—Fremont City (East)	5,360
NJ	Middlesex County (Southwest)	19,719	CA	Santa Clara—San Jose (Northwest) & Santa Clara	4,810
CA	Santa Clara—Sunnyvale & San Jose (North)	19,640	WA	King—Greater Bellevue City	4,153
NJ	Hudson—Jersey City (North)	17,832	NJ	Middlesex—Metuchen Borough	4,148
TX	Fort Bend—Sugar Land & Stafford	14,722	TX	Dallas—Irving (Central) & Dallas (Northwest)	3,673
CA	Santa Clara—Cupertino, Saratoga, & Los Gatos	14,659	VA	Fairfax—Reston (North) & Franklin Farm	3,454
WA	King—Greater Bellevue City	13,333	NJ	Middlesex County (Southwest)	3,146
CA	Santa Clara—San Jose (Northwest) & Santa Clara	13,014	CA	Alameda—Union City, Newark & Fremont (West)	2,900
NJ	Middlesex—Carteret Borough	12,808	GA	Fulton—Johns Creek City	2,595
CA	Alameda—Union City, Newark & Fremont (West)	12,038	WA	King—Sammamish, Issaquah, & Newcastle	2,364
NJ	Middlesex—South Plainfield & Middlesex Boroughs	11,975	WA	King—Redmond, Kirkland, Inglewood & Finn Hill	2,322
NY	Queens—Queens Vill, Cambria Hgts & Rosedale	11,446	NJ	Hudson—Jersey City (North)	2,230
VA	Fairfax—Reston (North) & Franklin Farm	10,548	CA	Santa Clara—Milpitas & San Jose (Northeast)	2,138
CA	San Joaquin—Tracy, Manteca & Lathrop	9,672	CA	Santa Clara—Cupertino, Saratoga, & Los Gatos	1,995

State	County—Location	Number	State	County—Location	Number
IL	Will—DuPage & Wheatland	9,416	VA	Loudoun—Ashburn & Dulles Airport	1,973
IL	DuPage—Bloomingdale (South), Wayne & Winfield	9,156	VA	Henrico—Tuckahoe, Short Pump & Wyndham	1,870
PA	Bucks County (Southwest)	9,041	NJ	Somerset County (South)	1,797
NJ	Morris—Lincoln Park Borough	8,837	TX	Dallas—Irving (North), Coppell & Carrollton	1,748
NJ	Somerset County (South)	8,815	CA	Alameda—Livermore, Pleasanton & Dublin	1,722
	Share of total in top-20 PUMAS	18.0		Share of total in top-20 PUMAS	33.0

Medical Services

State	County—Location	Number
	U.S. Total	139,403
TX	Fort Bend—Sugar Land & Stafford	2,327
NY	Nassau—North Hempstead (South)	2,301
NY	Queens—Briarwood, Fresh Meadows & Hillcrest	2,212
IL	Cook—Niles & Evanston	1,845
NY	Queens—Queens Vill, Cambria Hghts & Rosedale	1,533
IL	DuPage—Bloomingdale (South), Wayne & Winfield	1,513
IL	DuPage—York	1,498
TX	Fort Bend County—Missouri City	1,294
MI	Oakland—Troy & Rochester Area	1,179
IL	DuPage—Downers Grove	1,115

Taxi and Limousine Service

State	County—Location	Number
	U.S. Total	10,303
NY	Queens—Queens Vill, Cambria Hghts & Rosedale	2,371
CA	Santa Clara—Sunnyvale & San Jose (North)	789
NY	Queens—Richmond Hill & Woodhaven	695
PA	Delaware—Yeadon, Darby, Lansdowne, Drexel Hill	468
VA	Fairfax—Springfield, West Springfield & Franconia	457
NY	Nassau—Hempstead Town (West Central)	427
NY	Queens—Sunnyside & Woodside	376
WA	King—Kent City	346
NJ	Middlesex—Carteret Borough	305
WA	King—Renton City, Fairwood, Bryn Mawr	298

(continued)

Table 3.5 **Continued**

	All Workers			Computer Systems Design and Related Services	
State	County—Location	Number	State	County—Location	Number
CA	Alameda—Fremont City (East)	1,094	MA	Middlesex—Waertown, Arlington, Belmont	294
CA	Los Angeles—Lakewood, Cerritos, Artesia	1,022	NY	Nassau—Hempstead Town (Northwest)	276
NJ	Middlesex County (Southwest)	995	NY	Queens—Howard Beach & Ozone Park	270
NJ	Middlesex—Metuchen Borough	974	NY	Queens—Jackson Heights & North Corona	263
TX	Brazoria—Alvin City	964	NY	Queens—Jamaica, Hollis & St. Albans	228
MD	Montgomery—Bethesda, Potomac & North Bethesda	959	NY	Queens—Astoria & Long Island City	220
CA	Fresno—Fresno City (North)	946	NY	Niagara—Greater Niagara Falls & N. Tonawanda	215
NJ	Middlesex—South Plainfield & Middlesex Boroughs	913	NY	Queens—Briarwood, Fresh Meadows & Hillcrest	172
VA	Fairfax—Centreville (Southeast) & Lorton	903	CA	Contra Costa—Richmond (Southwest) & San Pablo	172
NY	Westchester—Yonkers City	900	VA	Fairfax—Reston (North) & Franklin Farm	153
	Share of total in top-20 PUMAS	19.0		Share of total in top-20 PUMAS	85.4

Note: Medical services includes home health-care services, hospitals, nursing care facilities, offices of chiropractors, dentists, optometrists, physicians, outpatient care centers, residential care facilities, etc. See note to figure 3.12 for details.

Source: PUMS 2012.

industry), with ubiquitous customers, is likely to be about as concentrated as the general population.[36] That is, wherever there are people, there should be doctors and nurses. Our question was: Were they likely to be Indian doctors and nurses?

Earlier we established the general location characteristics of India-born workers in all occupations and in the largest occupational category ("computers"). Therefore, these localized findings do not offer surprises, but at the same time, they throw up some startling figures on the sheer size of the localized workforce. There were four settlements with around 20,000 or more India-born workers, two each in Silicon Valley, California, and Middlesex County, New Jersey; and twelve more settlements with more than 10,000 workers in each. As expected, the largest settlements were dominated by computer-sector workers, especially the subcategory "computer systems design and related services." Settlements in Silicon Valley were the most important, followed by those in Middlesex County, New Jersey. Also significant were settlements around Seattle (Bellevue, Redmond, Newcastle); Irving in Texas; and Reston, Loudon, and Henrico in Virginia.[37] Note that fully one-third of all India-born workers in "computer systems design and related services" lived in these top twenty settlements (out of about 2,100 settlements in the United States).

As expected from clustering theory, India-born workers in "medical services" were far less concentrated in the top twenty settlements (though they, too, were concentrated, but not as much as in "computer systems design"), and the densest settlements were in different locations from the computer industry. As expected, the concentrations of Indians in "medical services" were in settlements in New York, Illinois, and Texas.

However, clustering theory was turned on its head for the India-born in the "taxi and limousine service" occupation. Fully 85 percent all Indian workers in this occupation were in the top twenty settlements for the occupation. Eight of the top twenty settlements were in Queens, in New York City (which means they could effectively be considered a single settlement), and the largest concentration, in the neighborhoods of Queens Village, Cambria Heights, and Rosedale in Queens, housed almost one-fourth of all India-born taxi drivers in America. In fact, this was the single densest concentration of India-born workers in any occupation.

Half of all India-born workers in the taxi industry were in New York City; the remaining half were spread around the country. It is true that New York City had a disproportionate share of taxis in the United States (because of the uniqueness of its urban formation), but not half the total in the country. The explanation for this extraordinary concentration comes not from clustering theory but from theories on migrant networks and assimilation (more on this follows soon). Those theories also help explain the cluster of India-born "taxi and limousine service" providers in Delaware County, Pennsylvania (ranked fourth in table 3.5), a settlement that includes the low-income communities of Millbourne and Upper Darby, where this chapter began.

We end this section with a few words on the borough of Queens. It is a rather unusual place. We have seen that it was home to the largest number of Indians (close to 5 percent of the national total lived there), and had the largest cluster of low-income India-born families, and had been losing Indian population in the late 2000s; now, we see that it was the location of the largest cluster of India-born taxi drivers, at the same time that it housed two of the top five settlements of the India-born in the medical occupations. In fact, the neighborhoods of Queens Village, Cambria Heights, and Rosedale, where one-fourth of the India-born taxi drivers in the United States lived, was also the fifth-largest settlement of India-born "medical services" workers.[38] Queens is unusual and fascinating, a melting pot of nationalities and languages for sure, but also a wide range of skills and incomes. It is the epitome of diversity in the United States. In fact, the Wikipedia page for Queens County says that it "is the most ethnically diverse urban area in the *world*" (emphasis ours).

The Geographies of Language, Old and New

In chapter 2 we briefly showed that India's linguistic diversity was reflected in the India-born population living in the United States. We identified the languages that were overrepresented—Punjabi and Gujarati, in particular, and to a lesser extent, Telugu, Malayalam, and Tamil, as well as the languages that were underrepresented—Hindi, Bengali, and Marathi, in particular. In this section, we explore the spatial distribution of these languages (at the scales of states and settlements) and identify patterns of the distribution of educational attainment, occupation/industry, and income for the different language groups. The distinctions are stark. The combinations of language-education-occupation-income-place are so marked as to reinforce stereotypes.

We begin with a reminder of the core distinction outlined early in this chapter. In the absence of better terminology, we named the Indian immigrant streams *Settlers 1.0* (made up of the Early Movers and the Families cohorts identified in chapter 2) and *Settlers 2.0* (i.e., the IT Generation). Settlers 1.0 was largely made up of speakers of Punjabi, Gujarati, Urdu, and Malayalam. Settlers 2.0 was largely made up of speakers of Telugu, Tamil, Marathi, Kannada, and Bengali. Hindi speakers were indeterminate; they were equidistant from both categories.[39]

The Indian languages were not evenly distributed inside the United States. Figure 3.13 plots the density of the ten leading languages in the eight leading states. If the distribution of languages had been uniform, all the density figures

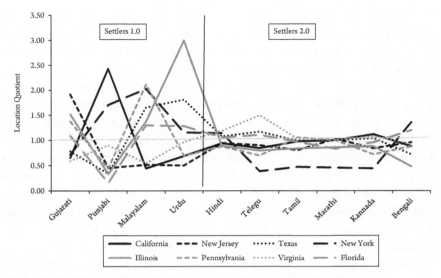

Figure 3.13 Concentration of Indian Language Groups in Leading States.
Note: The Location Quotient is a density measure. It is the ratio of a local value to the average value in all localities. For example, the Location Quotient of Gujarati-speakers in New Jersey is 1.9. This means that in New Jersey there are 1.9 times more Gujarati-speakers than there are in the U.S. as a whole. Location Quotients over 1.0 indicate over-representation (relative to the average). The higher the Location Quotient the denser the over-representation.
Source: Calculated from ACS 2007–11.

(expressed in terms of "location quotients," explained in the notes to figure 3.13) would have been the same—unity. Instead, what we see is considerable variation at the state scale.

The greatest spatial variation—which means there were large concentrations in some states—was among the Settler 1.0 languages: Gujarati, Punjabi, Urdu, Malayalam. The least spatial variation—which means that these language speakers were more evenly distributed among the states—was in the Settler 2.0 languages (Hindi, Telugu, Tamil, Marathi, Kannada, Bengali). This is further evidence of the spatial-temporal narrative we have identified at different points in earlier material. First, the Early Movers and the Families (i.e., Settlers 1.0) located in relatively few states and communities in the United States, following some well-recognized principles of immigration through family networks. These were, more than anything else, primarily Gujaratis and Punjabis, and they settled primarily in New York, California, and Illinois. Then, the IT Generation (i.e., Settlers 2.0) located wherever the IT industry was located; some of it in old Settler 1.0 locations (California, New Jersey) and some in new locations (Texas, Virginia, Washington). These were mainly Telugus and Tamils (plus a significant surge in Hindi speakers). The net result was the formation of a new geography of Indian languages in the United States.

Consider first some specific details of Settlers 1.0. Punjabis were significantly overrepresented in three states—California, New York, and

Washington (the last is not shown in figure 3.13)—and underrepresented almost everywhere else. They made up over one-fourth of all the India-born living in California; to put this in another way, almost half of all Punjabis in the United States lived in California. In New York, they represented almost one-fifth, and in Washington State, they made up over one-fourth of all India-born. Thirteen of the top twenty settlements for Punjabis were in California, most of them in the agricultural belt along Route 99 identified earlier (Bakersfield, Merced, Turlock, Selma, Fresno).[40] Five of the remaining top twenty settlements were in New York, all in Queens County. Gujaratis, on the other hand, were underrepresented in California and New York (the states where Punjabis were overrepresented), but overrepresented in New Jersey and Illinois among the major states, and to a lesser extent in Pennsylvania and Florida. Over one-fifth of all Gujaratis lived in New Jersey, where they made up close to one-third of the state's India-born population; they also made up about one-fourth of Illinois's India-born. Of the top twenty settlements for Gujaratis, New Jersey had nine and Illinois five. Middlesex County in New Jersey (especially Edison and its surrounding settlements) and Schaumberg-Des Plaines in Illinois were the two major regions of Gujarati concentration in the United States.

Settlers 2.0 mapped a different pattern. Speakers of the leading South Indian languages—Telugu and Tamil—who were the leaders of the IT Generation immigrants, were not significantly overrepresented in any of the leading states (with the possible exception of Telugus in Virginia and Texas); on the contrary, both were significantly underrepresented in New York and, to a lesser extent, in Illinois.[41] The states where these two languages were overrepresented were typically smaller ones, in that they were not traditional strongholds of Indians in America (and hence are not shown in figure 3.13): Telugus in Arizona and Minnesota (where they made up over one-fifth of the India-born); Tamils in Massachusetts, Arizona, and Minnesota.

A new geography of settlement was being created by the recent immigrants from India. The oldest settlers, the Punjabis, were clustered in California's farm belt and Queens County, in New York City. The second-oldest settlers, the Gujaratis, were clustered in north-central New Jersey and in and around Chicago. Both languages, however, formed a shrinking share of the India-born population (see chapter 2), Punjabis more so than Gujaratis.[42] The new settlers—especially Telugus and Tamils—were well-represented in California and New Jersey (whose work, as we have seen, was in the new technology sectors) but avoided the old Indian settlements in New York and Illinois (where the high-skilled Indian work force was in medicine, not computers). They were also gravitating toward, indeed forming, the newest hubs of Indian settlement, which were also the newest hubs of information technology, in Texas (especially Irving-Dallas), Virginia (especially Reston-Tyson's Corner), and Arizona (especially Phoenix).

This Is Not India: Polarized by Language

In chapter 2, we showed that the three streams of Indian immigrants were distinguishable by combinations of language and education, and that the older language groups (Punjabis and Gujaratis, in particular) had become less educated over time as family-based migration dominated. We also showed that the newer immigrant language groups (Telugus and Ṭamils, in particular), whose migration was largely skill-based, were more educated and growing more rapidly. Taken together, they tell a story about languages that is persuasive, compelling, and disquieting. At the same time, it is a story that in some key ways is unrepresentative of the situation in India. Our arguments are based on data shown in figures 3.14 through 3.16, the latter showing the simple and clear relationship between language, education, and income of Indians in America (juxtaposed with a selection of other significant immigrant and racial groups).

How different were the two settler cohorts? To begin with, Settlers 1.0 were older and, by definition, had longer tenures in the United States than did Settlers 2.0. When we wrote this book, the youngest Indians were Telugus (average age 35.2) and Tamils (average age 36.6); the oldest were speakers of Urdu, Gujarati, and Punjabi (with average ages of 51.0, 45.9, and 44.2 years, respectively). That is, Telugus and Tamils were younger on average by about ten years than Punjabis and Gujaratis. Now, consider the date of migration. The most recent immigrants were Telugus, Tamils, and Marathis, of whom 71, 65, and 65 percent, respectively, arrived after 2000. The oldest immigrants were, again, speakers of Urdu, Punjabi,

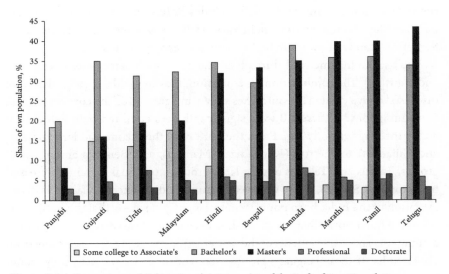

Figure 3.14 Language and Educational Attainment of the India-born Population.
Source: Calculated from ACS 2007–11.

and Gujarati—35, 43, and 44 percent of them, respectively, arrived after 2000.[43] There is no doubt that Settlers 1.0 and 2.0 were demographically distinct groups.

The educational attainment of Settlers 1.0, especially in holding advanced degrees, was significantly lower than that of Settlers 2.0 (see figure 3.14). In general, less than one-fourth of Settlers 1.0 had advanced degrees (despite the fact, explained in chapter 2, that the Early Movers had very high educational attainment levels), whereas more than half of Settlers 2.0 had attained those degrees. The extreme case is a comparison of master's degrees attained by Punjabis (around 8 percent of the language speakers) against Telugus (around 43 percent), a larger than five-fold difference. Similarly, about 1.2 and 1.6 percent of Punjabis and Gujaratis, respectively, had doctoral degrees, compared to over 14 percent of Bengalis (an outlier group on this variable). Some stereotypes are evidence-based.

Comparably distinct patterns could be seen in the distribution of language speakers by industry (see figure 3.15). Settlers 1.0 were least present in the most important industry for the India-born—professional services, which includes computer services—whereas Settlers 2.0 dominated that industry. More than 40 percent of Telugus and Tamils worked in professional services, whereas the share of Punjabis and Gujaratis in that industry was around 8 and 14 percent, respectively. Punjabis tended to work in the retail trade industry (which employed close to one-fourth), and in the transportation and entertainment industries, which provided work for 15 and 10 percent, respectively, of the group. Half of all Punjabis worked in these three industries. Gujaratis had a similar sectoral distribution; one-fifth were in retail trade, about one-sixth were in manufacturing (a surprise for us), and another one-seventh were in the entertainment industry (which includes hotels and restaurants).[44] In general, Settlers 1.0 tended to work in lower-skill, lower-wage industries, whereas Settlers 2.0 tended to work in higher-skill, higher-wage industries.

The path to income runs through education (which determines occupation and industry). The combinations of education/industry with language that were discussed above yielded the outcomes shown in figure 3.16. The core conclusion is unambiguous: Settlers 1.0 were significantly less educated than Settlers 2.0 and earned significantly less. From the bottom of the income ladder (Punjabis and Gujaratis) to the top (Kannadigas, Marathis, and Bengalis among small groups, Tamils and Telugus among large groups), personal incomes increased by factors of 1.5 to 2.5. These were very significant differences. In fact, this disaggregation of the India-born population by language suggests that the outlier status of the India-born (that we established in chapter 2) was driven largely by the attainments and achievements of the Settler 2.0 language groups, especially from South India. If these language groups were considered separately, they would be even more significant outliers than the general India-born population in the

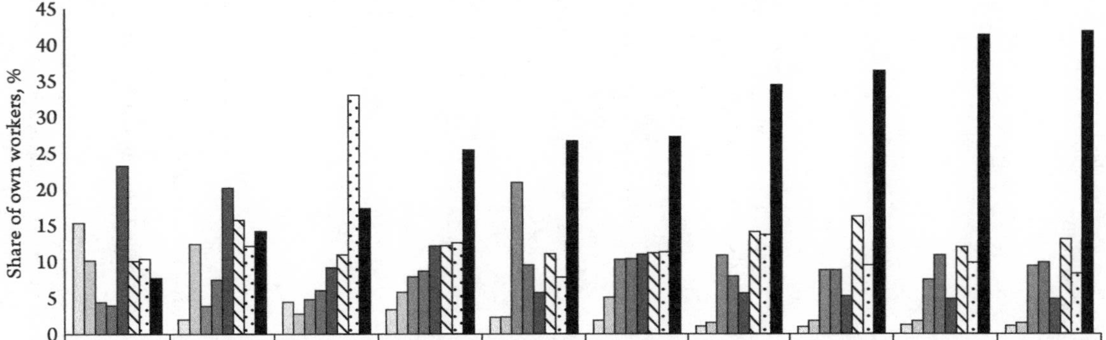

	Punjabi	Gujarati	Malayalam	All India-born	Bengali	Hindi	Kannada	Marathi	Telugu	Tamil
☐ Transportation	15.3	2.0	4.4	3.3	2.3	1.8	1.0	1.0	1.2	1.1
☐ Entertainment	10.1	12.4	2.8	5.7	2.3	5.0	1.5	1.8	1.7	1.5
▨ Education	4.3	3.8	4.7	7.9	20.9	10.3	10.8	8.8	7.5	9.4
▨ Finance	3.9	7.4	6.0	8.6	9.5	10.3	8.0	8.8	10.8	9.8
▨ Retail trade	23.2	20.2	9.1	12.1	5.7	10.9	5.6	5.2	4.8	4.8
▨ Manufacturing	10.0	15.7	10.9	12.1	11.0	11.1	14.1	16.2	11.9	13.0
⊡ Medicine	10.4	12.1	33.0	12.5	7.8	11.3	13.6	9.4	9.8	8.3
■ Professional services	7.7	14.1	17.3	25.4	26.6	27.2	34.4	36.4	41.3	41.8

Figure 3.15 Distribution of Indian Language Groups by Industry.

Notes: Each column represents the share of the language group workers employed in the specific industry. Several industries (Administration, Agriculture, Construction, Military, Social services, Misc. Services, Utilities, and Wholesale trade) are omitted from this graph. Each has less than 2.2% of the working Indian-born.

Source: Compiled and calculated from ACS 2007–11.

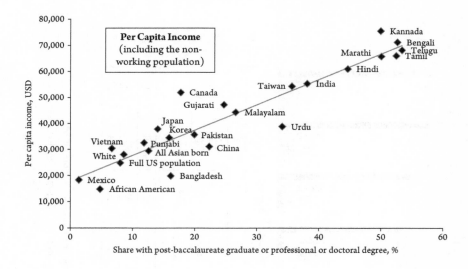

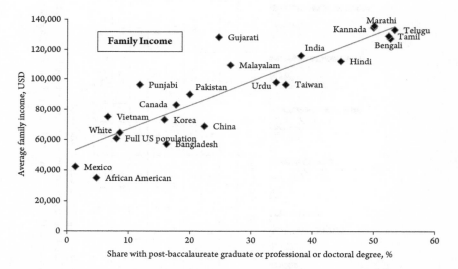

Figure 3.16 Income by Education—Indian Language Groups in Comparison to Other Groups.

Note: This comparison includes Indian-born language groups (Hindi, Gujarati, Punjabi, Urdu, Malayalam, Telugu, Tamil, Kannada, and Bengali), selected foreign-born groups (from China, Taiwan, Korea, Vietnam, Bangladesh, Pakistan, and Mexico), and the major racial groups in the US (White and African American). Source: PUMS 2014.

United States. No group from anywhere with any identity came close to these outliers among the outliers.

The Settler 1.0 language groups also had education and income levels above the U.S. national averages, no doubt, but not by so much as to distinguish them clearly from other immigrant groups from, say, Japan, China, Pakistan, and others not shown in figure 3.16. It is useful to note that as the income-earning unit got larger (from individuals to families), the difference between Settlers 1.0 and 2.0 was mitigated to some degree, especially for the Gujarati population. This feature highlights, again, the importance of family cohesion for economic outcomes for Indian families (a "selection +" feature), but it does not change the core insight of income heterogeneity structured by language and education among Indians. These different language groups were rather distinct populations.

This finding raises some troubling questions. First, does this linguistic cleavage by income and education effectively fragment Indian-American identity? Second, are these cleavages—for example, the polar one between Punjabis and say Telugus—going to widen, both among the first-generation settler cohorts to come and the second-generation America-born Indians? The most careful answer is that we do not know because we do not have the data to answer these questions. But we do know that these language groups reside in different spaces—for example, Punjabis in rural California and inner city New York, Telugus in the suburbs of Silicon Valley and Washington, D.C., and Dallas—so the cleavages are in some important ways more notional than real. That is, the cleavages exist in the form of data (that we, the experts, can see) more than in everyday reality. For that same reason (that the linguistic groups reside in different spaces), it is hard to argue that the Indian-American identity is a particularly cohesive one to begin with.

The core issues here—what constitutes Indian-American identity and how cohesive it is—are taken up seriously in the next chapter and later again in chapters 6 and 7. There, we find considerable evidence of pan-Indian organization and solidarity, but in professional much more than in cultural realms. If we use constructs from sociology like "isolation" and "contact" (devised to examine the interactions between whites and blacks in American cities), we find that these linguistic groups are rather isolated from each other.[45] They live in separate spaces, do different jobs, speak languages that do not even share a script, consume different cultural products, and marry within the community. That they earn different incomes is just one more feature of fragmentation, possibly the one feature that these linguistic communities themselves are least aware of.[46]

This fragmentation is likely to continue, even deepen, as long the new blood keeps getting drawn from the old sources—family and clan networks for Punjabis and Gujaratis versus engineering colleges for Telugus and Tamils. Therefore, we do not expect that these trends will change or the first-generation linguistic cleavages narrow in the foreseeable future. But we are less certain about the second generation. The reasons to think that the gulf will not close easily are many—the very different starting points, the cumulative advantage of the initial pole positions through better schooling in better-off neighborhoods (because public schools in the United States are largely funded through local property taxes), and the increasing skill premium in an increasingly unequal American society. Despite these plausible reasons, we take an agnostic position because (a) we simply do not know enough about the second generation, as it is too young; and (b) we are open to the democratic possibilities of America—not necessarily its mythic rags-to-riches Horatio Alger stories, but its multiple paths to successful lives and careers. We note that there is initial evidence (some from the census on the choice of undergraduate majors and some from anecdotes, personal observations and journalistic accounts, such as in Forbes "30 under 30" discussed in chapter 6) that second-generation Indian Americans are already beginning to choose rather different paths from their parents. Moreover, if the rate of exogamy picks up—and it surely will—then the second generation may indeed see a recalibration of the hierarchy of language and income.

We also note the irony of the contrast of the language-based income ladder in the United States versus India. Punjab was for several decades India's richest state, a position that it lost after the mid-1990s because of a long-term stagnation in agriculture in the state and its failure to industrialize. At this writing, Gujarat is the contemporary model of the "developmental" state in India, which is indus-trializing rapidly and has produced India's latest prime minister (his predecessor was from Punjab). Yet, in the United States, these two language groups, the most established in terms of tenure, are at the bottom of the education and income ladders. The explanation is, of course, not intrinsic. It has nothing to do with any innate quality of being Punjabi or Gujarati. Rather, as detailed in chapter 2, the explanation is extrinsic, specifically the computer-based technological revolu-tion that generated a surge in demand for labor in this new industry and a cor-responding surge in the supply of that labor from South India, enabled by an American immigration system that selected the appropriate labor for entry into its protected labor market. The new work was skilled work, and as a result, there was significant growth in India-born educational attainment. The new work was also well-paid work, and as a result, there was significant growth in incomes for the India-born. Settlers 2.0 were the beneficiaries of this process.

Many Indias, Big and Little

Douglas Massey, a prominent sociologist, summarized the work of a generation of immigration scholars who argued that segregation into "immigrant enclaves" was a "natural" process as a group entered the United States.[47] Chicago-school ecologists like Park, Burgess, and McKenzie identified Little Sicily, Greektown, and Chinatown as "natural" urban (or inner-city) formations.[48] Later, with the arrival of new immigrant groups, scholars identified Koreatowns and Little Havanas as examples of the same process that had produced the first immigrant enclaves. These ethnic communities were often called "ghettos," more in the sense of the original Jewish enclaves of Venice in that they were not necessarily

poor, rather than in the more contemporary sense of "ghettos of despair" of concentrated African-American poverty in inner-city neighborhoods. John Logan
and colleagues write that:

> In the beginning, people's limited market resources and ethnically
> bound cultural and social capital are mutually reinforcing; they work
> in tandem to sustain ethnic neighborhoods. But these are transitional
> neighborhoods—they represent a practical and temporary phase in
> the incorporation of new groups into American society. Their residents
> search for areas with more amenities as soon as their economic situa-
> tions improve, their outlooks broaden, and they learn to navigate daily
> life in a more mainstream setting.[49]

Logan and his colleagues went on to suggest a new terminology—"ethnic
community"—to refer to "ethnic neighborhoods that are selected as living environments by those who have wider options based on their market resources."
Susan Hardwick argued that the United States was moving toward becoming
a "suburban immigrant nation," in which Logan's "ethnic communities" were
"communities of choice" (not absence of choice).[50] Wei Li and others argued
that some such places become "ethnopolises" or "ethnoburbs," where immigrants form visible minorities or even local majorities, whereas others remain
"invisiburbs," where immigrants are too scattered to be distinctly visible.[51]

We suggest that the settlement patterns of the India-born exhibit all these
forms—from the early "ethnic enclaves" in Jackson Heights in New York
City's Queens County and Devon Street in Chicago (and, unusually, Punjabi
enclaves in rural California, such as Yuba City), to "ethnoburbs" like Santa Clara
and Alameda Counties in California and Middlesex County in New Jersey, to
"invisiburbs" in numerous suburbs of American cities. We question, however,
the matter of choice, the assumption that ethnoburbs are, for Indian Americans,
necessarily "communities of choice." If the ethnic enclave of the past existed to
provide social capital and social networks and defensible spaces for low-income
immigrants, leaving little choice for the co-ethnic newcomer to settle elsewhere,
the new ethnoburbs of Silicon Valley or suburban Dallas/Irving in Texas, or
Reston in suburban Washington, D.C., also left little settlement choice for the
India-born. Their choice was limited not by racial discrimination, nor by language barriers, nor by the threat of violence, but by the very nature of the work
they performed. The information technology industry is highly clustered and it
is where it is. The India-born immigrant who was selected and provided a work
permit for that industry had little choice in his settlement location. There is no
doubt that these were not the immigrant enclaves of old, and they did not carry
the pejorative connotations of those old neighborhoods, but they were not

"communities of choice," either. We are not aware of any other immigrant community in the United States that has faced these particular set of circumstances—
that is, *being concentrated in one industry that is also spatially clustered.*

A new terminology is needed to describe these concentrations of skilled and
well-paid labor that nonetheless have limited spatial choice. We suggest, somewhat awkwardly, "ethno-techno-burb." It captures the idea that high-tech work
can severely limit spatial choices for the workers, perhaps as much as resource-
extraction work (such as in the coal and oil industries) or the lack of work (such
as in inner-city America, where the level of unemployment can be as high as
40 percent).[52] The term also captures the notion that these spatially specific
technology clusters are also ethnic clusters. Ethnicity and labor combine to produce the unique geography of the "ethno-techno-burbs" of Indians in the United
States.

We end our analysis in this chapter with a final display of evidence on spatial concentration, shown in figure 3.17. Here are three graphs of the concentration of different populations in the hundred most populous settlements for
those specific populations. The first graph compares the concentration of India-
born to that of six other Asia-born groups. The India-born were the least concentrated, the only nationality that had less than 40 percent of its population
living in the hundred largest settlements (PUMAs); Bangladeshis were the most
concentrated, with over 60 percent of the population concentrated in the hundred largest settlements.

The second graph shows the distribution of the India-born by the five largest
language groups, and we see that every language group (other than Hindi speakers) was significantly more concentrated than the overall Indian population.
Punjabis were the most concentrated, at levels comparable to the Bangladeshis.
Telugus were as concentrated as the Taiwanese, and Gujaratis and Tamils were
as concentrated as the Chinese (and more concentrated than the Filipinos or
Koreans).

The final graph shows the concentration of India-born workers by occupational groups. The highest levels of concentration are seen here. The India-born
engaged in software occupations were more concentrated than any ethnic or language group shown in figure 3.17; they were more concentrated than Punjabis,
more concentrated even than Bangladeshis. For the India-born, the whole computer industry was very concentrated, as were management occupations (which,
when disaggregated, were primarily also in the IT industry). It was no surprise
that these India-born individuals lived close to their jobs.

All these concentrations of occupation and language produced many "Little
Indias." There were big "Little Indias" in places like Queens County and Silicon
Valley and Middlesex County; and there were medium "Little Indias" in places
like Irving, Texas, and Reston, Virginia; with small "Little Indias" in places like

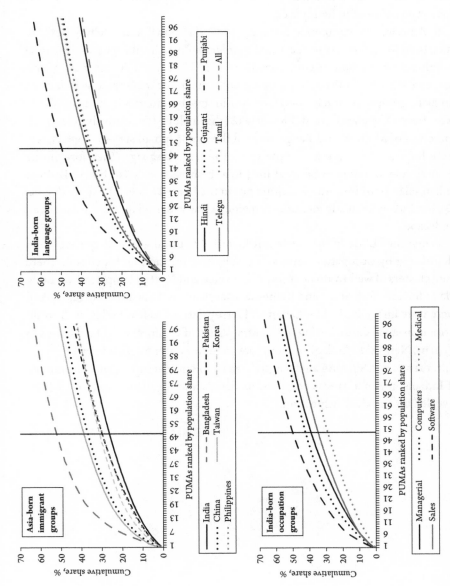

Figure 3.17 Concentrations in Leading Settlements by National Origin, Language, and Occupation.

Source: National-origin and language data calculated from ACS 2007–11; Occupation data calculated from PUMS 2012.

Millbourne, Pennsylvania, and Loudon Valley, Virginia. These "Little Indias" were not necessarily or even usually pan-Indian in composition. There were "Little Ahmedabads" in Edison, New Jersey, and Schaumberg-Des Plaines, Illinois; and "Little Jullundurs" in Yuba City and Bakersfield, California. Was this a replication of Indian space?

In America, the competing metaphors of "salad bowl" and "melting pot" are often used to summarize its racial and immigrant diversity. It is possible to argue that these two metaphors could also be used in India, given its diversity of languages and faith identities, but they are not. One of the main reasons is that the language groups are largely contained within state boundaries in India. With the exceptions of Maharashtra and Karnataka (that include the relatively cosmopolitan cities of Mumbai and Bangalore), all the major Indian states are effectively monolingual—85 percent or more speak the same language. Therefore, if one of these metaphors is to be used for India, it should be "salad bowl." Did the Indian salad bowl turn into a melting pot in the United States? To some degree, yes, but Indian linguistic identities remained clearly identifiable in the American landscape.

When the "Little Indias" were not identifiable by language, they were often identifiable by occupation (and as a result, by education and income). There were clusters of well-to-do doctors in Hicksville and North Hempstead, on Long Island in New York State, and Bethesda, Maryland, and Sugar Land, Texas. And there were financiers in Manhattan and Jersey City, as well as far less well-to-do farmers in small cities dotting the Central Valley of California and taxi drivers in Queens, New York. And, of course, there were computer workers from coders to entrepreneurs in Silicon Valley, central Texas, and northern Virginia. The mosaic of Indians in America was complex, its details and diversities and inequalities revealed only at close inspection.

4

Becoming American

Assimilation in its many avatars—"segmented," "plural," "transculturation," "incorporation," "multicultural"—is the archetypal story of immigrants as they are drawn into the melting pot, or salad bowl, or other metaphors that describe American society. While these benign images of American society give little solace to those who were the original inhabitants or were dragged into the country by force, what constitutes "American" has always been contentious, masked by a perceived political, economic, and cultural hegemony of a white male Anglo-Saxon Protestant (WASP) "establishment." Race, religion, and gender have long been the defining markers of what "American" means, as Irish and Italian, Catholics and Jews, Chinese and Mexican have all learned rather painfully. While the salience of these markers have altered, assimilation— whether a grudging acceptance or an embrace of the mainstream—was often a Hobson's choice if immigrants were to climb the rungs of the social ladder.

But what might have been viewed as a choice upon arrival becomes irreversible as the country of origin quietly slips from sight. The definition of "home" gradually and imperceptibly changes the longer the immigrant stays in his or her adopted country. Over time, for most who choose to stay, home is represented by the present—and future—place of residence instead of the country left behind. At the same time, the predominant culture has become less overpowering, as cumulative waves of immigrants from an ever-widening range of backgrounds have helped redefine what it means to be American.

In this chapter we use *assimilation* in a loose sense, as when an immigrant group's accents, foods and festivals, participation in civic and political life, and portrayal in both elite and popular cultures are taken in stride by the prototypal "mainstream"; and when immigrants are asked with decreasing frequency, ". . . but where are you *really* from?" The assimilation and acculturation of Indian Americans reflects the changes in both the immigrant's economic and social habitus and the society of which the individual is becoming part.

The assimilation patterns of the immigrants that came after 1965 have been somewhat different from those who came a century earlier, for several reasons.[1]

The new immigrants hail from cultures, races, and religions distinct and distant from the European mainstream; communications and transport allow them to keep in touch with the homeland on a real-time basis; the integration of markets means that many markers of a culture—food, music, media—can be sought and consumed almost as easily as if the immigrant had never left. But perhaps most of all, the United States of the twenty-first century is a much more diverse society, where old prejudices and intolerances are more muted, or at least less overt, than the blatant institutionalized racism of a century or more ago. The first wave of immigrants arrived after the passage of the Civil Rights Act of 1964, a new period when race, while important, became a less critical factor in shaping economic outcomes for immigrants, while education, skills, and legal status mattered more.

Despite their professional success, however, the first wave of India-born immigrants paid a high emotional price. In many of the places where they settled, there were few other members of the community, and cultural markers, such as familiar foods or places of worship, were also absent. Communication with family in India was minimal, given India's dismal telephone system at the time. Parents struggled in an unfamiliar environment, not knowing how best to guide their children where Indians were unknown but race was not. Coming from a culture where family and community were so much a part of their daily lives, loneliness took its toll, especially among housewives who were left alone at home while their husbands were at work and their children were at school.[2] The children, especially those who had moved with their parents from India—the 1.5 generation—had to adjust to a completely new system of schooling and face bewilderment from classmates who were familiar with only one kind of "Indian," leading to nicknames such as "Pocahontas." With few other Indian children around, the only way to alleviate the feeling of isolation was to try to blend in. However, the more the children assimilated in school, the greater the stress on their relationships with their parents (and other elders at home), who were fearful of their children losing their cultural heritage.

While Indian Americans gained professional access, many struggled to crack the putative "glass ceiling," because while they were seen as hard working and industrious, they were also thought to lack "leadership material." Even in the late 1990s, when an India-born candidate went to interview at a major Wall Street firm, her interviewer told her, "You have three strikes against you. . . . How can I hire you? You are the wrong gender, wrong color, and wrong country."[3]

Nonetheless, Indian-American immigrants had three distinct advantages over other immigrants that helped them succeed. First, their greater human capital, documented in chapters 2 and 3, provided higher incomes, which meant that they faced less overt racism in housing or in dealing with the government. Money "made white" simply by virtue of where they could afford to live.[4]

Second, they had better English-language skills than many other immigrants, a legacy of British colonialism. And third, they were predominantly from India's upper castes. Apart from the irony of a group whose status at the top of India's social hierarchy had placed it at the giving end of discrimination and was now finding itself at the receiving end (albeit in a much milder way), this group came to the United States equipped with a strong ballast of cultural capital, making them particularly suited to ascend the ladder of American society. When asked about her educational drive, Indra Nooyi, the CEO of PepsiCo, recalled: "[We were] programmed for that. The entire family focused on grades. When parents got together, they only compared the report cards of their kids. Anybody who got together would say, 'so how is your child doing,' 'what rank?' "[5]

The "twice born" (as India's upper castes are termed) were also the "thrice selected," first in India, and then in the United States by immigration officials, and subsequently by educational institutions and labor markets. Selection in India occurred through India's hyper-competitive elite system of higher education, of which the Indian Institutes of Technology, Indian Institutes of Management, and the leading medical schools are the best known. In January 2003, CBS's *60 Minutes* somewhat hyperbolically put it: "The United States imports oil from Saudi Arabia, cars from Japan, TVs from South Korea and whiskey from Scotland. So what do we import from India? We import people, really smart people. And . . . the smartest, most successful, most influential Indians who've migrated to the U.S. seem to share a common credential: They're graduates of the Indian Institute of Technology, better known as IIT."[6]

In 2014, three of the six Indian-American billionaires were alumni of an IIT. A study of venture capital–backed entrepreneurs in the United States in 2014 found that the first non-U.S. university to make the top-five list was the Indian Institutes of Technology, which ranked number four in terms of number of companies (264 founders started 205 companies) and number three in amount of money raised ($3.15 billion).[7]

Under the Kanpur Indo-American program, IIT-Kanpur had received technical assistance from a consortium of nine leading U.S. universities from 1962 to 1972. A decade after its establishment, a fourth of IIT-Kanpur's undergraduates and a fifth of its master's students had gone abroad, mainly to the United States.[8] This points to the second selection mechanism: U.S. universities. Although most Indians who came in the first decade after 1965 were drawn from India's social elites, they were often from middle-class public-sector backgrounds with annual salaries rarely above a few thousand dollars. A sagging economy and severe foreign exchange constraints meant that getting a scholarship to a U.S. university was the surest ticket to a better future. With students from China not yet in competition, and U.S. universities still relatively well funded, research and teaching scholarships were available to well-qualified foreign students.[9]

While India had created a small number of excellent institutions of higher education, it was at the time a very poor country with a per capita income of barely $111 in 1970. Higher education was heavily subsidized and foreign exchange regulations were so severe that students going abroad were allowed a maximum of a few hundred dollars (and often less). Selection by U.S. universities for graduate studies with financial aid was critical (prior to the 1990s, Indian students rarely came for an undergraduate degree). Romesh Wadhwani recalls that he left India in July 1969 "with $300 (max allowed), travelled through Europe with 3 IIT friends for approximately 60 days at $5/day, and arrived in Pittsburgh [to pursue graduate studies at Carnegie Mellon] with $3.48."[10] In 2014, *Forbes* magazine estimated his net worth at $2.5 billion.

In addition, as we explained in chapter 2, in the first decade after the 1965 Immigration Reform Act, it was relatively easy for well-qualified individuals to immigrate. Between 1966 and 1976, "among those immigrants who declared an occupation at their time of arrival, PTKs [professional, technical, and kindred workers] constituted an astonishing 82 percent among Indians, significantly higher than for the Filipinos (62 percent), Chinese (38 percent), or Koreans (52 percent)."[11]

In the rest of this chapter, we examine some of the key measures of assimilation, ranging from naturalization to civic and political participation and the factors shaping them. We further examine three intra-group differences in assimilation: gender differences; intergenerational differences (between the India-born first generation and the U.S.-born second generation); and the specific characteristics of those born in the Indian diaspora and emigrating from Asia, Africa, or Europe.

Naturalization

A critical transition in an immigrant's life is the decision to naturalize and become a U.S. citizen. It signifies an irrevocable resolution of the migration decision, although the decision is perhaps less dichotomous in an era of dual citizenship. More than a mere legal rite of passage, it is a psychological adjustment to a new identity. Furthermore, it is a first step toward having a political voice by gaining the right to vote.

Studies on naturalization in the United States show that the longer the period of eligibility for naturalization, the more likely people are to exercise this option. Naturalization rates increase with the immigrant's level of education, duration in the United States, and proficiency in English. They are also higher when the prospect of returning to the country of origin is more difficult, for political, economic, or geographic reasons. Additionally, if the country of origin permits dual citizenship, the immigrant is likely to naturalize sooner. But the individual's own characteristics are also important determinants of naturalization rates.[12]

Relative to their share of those eligible for naturalization, less educated immigrants from geographically proximate, lower-income countries such as Mexico, El Salvador, and Guatemala are less likely to naturalize, as are more educated immigrants from industrialized countries such as Canada, Japan, and the United Kingdom. On the other hand, more educated immigrants from geographically distant but lower-income countries such as Colombia, India, and Pakistan are more than twice as likely to naturalize relative to each country's proportion in the eligible pool. In 2011, those born in India were 2.8 percent of the naturalization-eligible population, but they made up 6.6 percent of all newly naturalized Americans that year.[13]

Factors influencing the increased naturalization rates of Indian Americans tend to be their higher levels of education, English proficiency, low income in their country of origin, and distance from their country of origin, while they are less affected by the presence of high political liberties and civil rights, since these are also available in India, at least to a considerable degree for the social groups from whom Indian immigrants are drawn. Historically, there were three main reasons immigrants came to the United States of their own volition: to seek freedom from religious persecution, from political oppression, and from economic hardship. Relative to immigrants from many other developing countries, fewer Indians emigrate primarily for religious and political reasons, with refugees and asylum seekers constituting less than 1 percent of all Indian immigrants.[14] Those emigrating to flee economic hardship are also a relatively small fraction since the vast majority hail from relatively better-off households in India. Instead, economic opportunities together with family reunification have been the biggest driving forces. In other words, "pull" factors have been far more important in the migration decision of Indian immigrants compared to "push" factors.

Until the end of the 1990s, the naturalization rates for Indian immigrants was about average, lower than those for migrants from the Philippines and Cuba but higher than those for Mexicans and Canadians (figure 4.1).[15] However, the rates of naturalization declined for immigrants who came after 1995 and were largely holders of H1-B work visas. Of the nearly 1 million H1-B visas issued between 2004 and 2012, about a half-million were issued to Indians (see figure 2.9). Along with dependents, these accounted for more than one-fourth of the Indian-American population in 2014. Given the extremely long waiting times to convert H1-B visas to permanent residency, or green cards (between five and ten years), and another minimum five-year wait to apply for citizenship, relatively few would have been eligible for naturalization at the time of this writing.

Another factor that affected the decision to naturalize was enactment of the 1996 welfare reform, which restricted the entitlements of noncitizens. This policy change increased the incentives to naturalize, but since the economically vulnerable were a smaller fraction of the Indian-American population relative

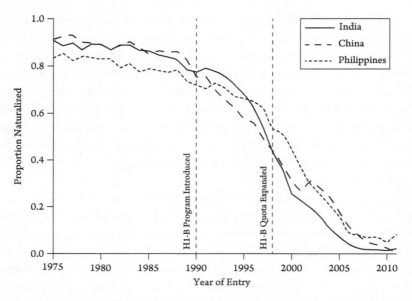

Figure 4.1 Proportion of Selected Asian Immigrants Who Were Naturalized, 1975–2010.
Source: Compiled and Calculated from Department of Homeland Security data, 2014.

to most other immigrant groups, this had less impact on Indian immigrants than on the more vulnerable lower-income immigrants from other countries. Nonetheless, in the years from 2004 to 2013, nearly half a million Indians naturalized (487,162), about 7 percent of the total naturalizations in the decade and the second-highest from any one country after Mexico. These numbers exceeded the total number of naturalizations of Indians in the United States during the entire twentieth century.

Civic Engagement

Writing in 1840 in his classic *Democracy in America*, Alexis de Tocqueville observed that "Americans of all ages, all stations of life, and all types of dispositions are forever forming associations . . . of a thousand different types. . . . Nothing, in my view, deserves more attention."[16] In recent years, however, the alleged decline of civic engagement—and the role of immigration in this decline—has been much debated, particularly since Robert Putnam's *Bowling Alone: The Collapse and Revival of American Community* was published in 2000. Subsequently, a range of studies has shown that notwithstanding Putnam's claims, civic engagement continues to be an important part of immigrant communities. As a form of collective action that entails working with others to solve community problems (beyond those related to personal or family interests), civic engagement not only helps immigrants who have limited recourse to economic and political resources but also facilitates social integration and the practice of citizenship. Greater participation in community organizations helps develop civic skills that in turn lead to greater political engagement.

But what drives civic engagement and what forms does it take? There is strong evidence that for immigrants, organizing locally—that is, within a specific context— is crucial for the degree and form of civic engagement and associational life.[17] As we note later, associational life for Indian Americans varies from membership and participation in functional, nonethnic organizations to pan-Asian ones with a shared regional identity, while others join organizations that reflect India's ethnic and religious diversity. Their purposes vary as well, from those seeking to preserve and celebrate cultural traditions, to those with social and economic networking goals, to others whose activities are transnational, linking to the country of origin.

Indian-American Organizations

Community organizations are a form of collective action, and their numbers, size, and purposes are indicative of the concerns and cleavages in the community. We compiled data on Indian-American organizations from the Guidestar website database on 501(c) (3), (4), (6), and (7) status organizations using India-specific search terms, and we limited our search to organizations with at least $1,000 in reported income in the last year. More details and data limitations can be found in the appendix (section 6). The database includes 966 organizations. This is a lower bound, since there are likely to be many Indian-American organizations that have either not formally incorporated or have incomes less than $1000, or were missed by our search algorithms.

The organizations in the database were categorized based on the community that they target (figure 4.2). The broadest category was "South Asian," and that group was only 7 percent of all organizations. The narrowest category was for caste communities. The database has twenty-four caste-based community organizations, just 2.5 percent of the total. The database also had four organizations that were specific to the Indo-Caribbean community.

Almost half of all Indian-American organizations were religious organizations. This contrasts with Mexican immigrants, whose primary membership organizations were hometown associations (although worker organizations and religious congregations were also important for Mexican immigrants). There were 481 religious organizations in the data set, three-fifths of which were Hindu organizations or Hindu temples, one-fourth related to the Sikh community, and 8 percent were Jain organizations. The percentage of Sikh and Jain organizations

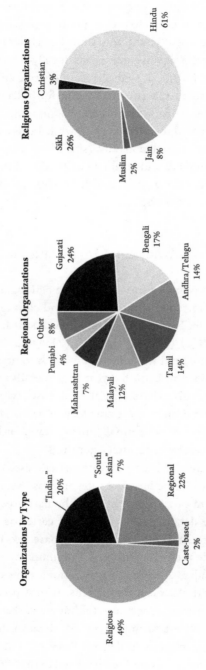

Figure 4.2 Indian-American Community Organizations, by Type.

Source: Compiled and calculated from Guidestar online database, 2014.

Note: N=966 organizations.

was disproportionate to their share of the population, both in India or among Indian Americans. The number of Indian-American organizations for Christians and Muslims was small, at 3 percent and 2 percent, respectively. This is likely because Indian-American Christians and Muslims may join broader religious congregations in the United States that don't specifically serve immigrants from India.

The Gujarati community had the largest share of the regionally specific community organizations (figure 4.2). Twenty-four percent of the 211 regional community organizations were for the Gujarati community. Gujarati Americans also formed the largest number of caste associations in the United States—half of all caste-based organizations were for this community.

The geographical distribution of the civic organizations is given in figure 4.3. The size of the circle in figure 4.3 corresponds to the number of organizations registered in that Zip code. (Alaska has been excluded from the map because there were no Indian-American organizations there.) As expected, Indian-American organizations were in locations with large concentrations of the Indian-American population, with the top four states being California, New York, Texas, and New Jersey. Some states had a disproportionate share of wealthy organizations. For example, while Arizona had only fifteen organizations, three of them were in the top 10 percent of all organizations by income. Among cities, Houston and New York City had by far the largest number of organizations. However, in some metropolitan areas the Indian-American organizations were dispersed into different suburbs and towns. For instance, there were thirty-five organizations in Silicon Valley, including the India Community Center in Milpitas, California (launched in 2002), which was the largest Indian-American community facility in North America.[18]

The average annual income of the organizations was a little over a quarter of a million dollars. About one-fourth of the organizations had an income below $30,000, while the average annual income of organizations in the top decile (90 organizations) was $1.86 million, of which two-thirds were religious organizations. The largest 1 percent of organizations (nine) include five Hindu organizations, an Indian-American Muslim charity organization, Shraman South Asian Museum in Dallas, the American India Foundation (providing social services in India), and the India Community Center.

Aside from serving their specific communities, many of these organizations serve specific functions as professional associations, providing community services (such as immigration services, senior care, and support for domestic violence victims) and promoting Indian or South Asian arts. Others include sports organizations (four of which were for the Punjabi community), literary clubs, language schools, chambers of commerce, and organizations seeking to advance the community's political and civil rights. Occupational organizations tend to

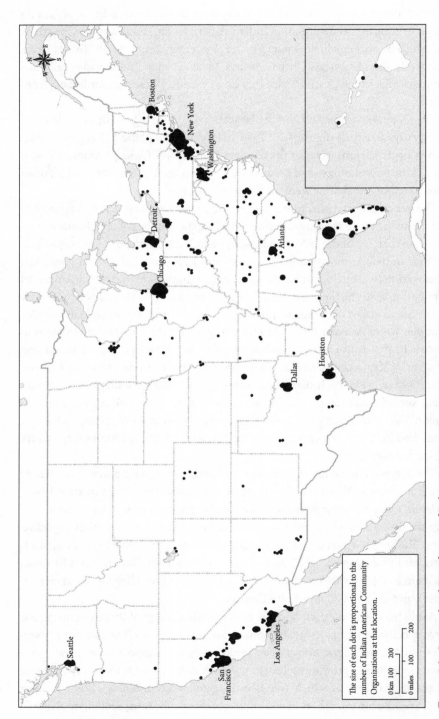

The size of each dot is proportional to the number of Indian American Community Organizations at that location.

Figure 4.3 Geographical Distribution of Indian-American Community Organizations, 2014.

Source: Compiled and calculated from Guidestar online database, 2014.

Note: N = 966 organizations.

be more encompassing and often incorporate a broader South Asia identity, such as the South Asia Journalists Association (SAJA) or the South Asia Bar Association (SABA). And despite its title, the Network of Indian Professionals (NetIP) states its "mission is to serve as the unequivocal voice for the South Asian Diaspora by developing and engaging a cohesive network of professionals to benefit the community."[19] These organizations serve as much of a social function as a means to network. The organization that exemplifies its networking potential—and serves as a marker of the community's success in the technology sector in Silicon Valley—is The Indus Entrepreneurs (TiE), which we discuss in more detail in chapter 6.

It took several decades before these forms of collective action took root. In the early years, the catalyst to organize was often a sense of discrimination. Ironically, it was in a highly skilled white collar profession that the community felt the sting of racism to a degree that compelled it to organize. Many immigrant professionals from non-European countries faced varying degrees of prejudice at the time, and for the Indian-American community, this was manifested in the most successful and affluent group in the first wave of immigrants: physicians emigrating from India.

Organizing Indian-American Physicians

Internationally trained physicians or international medical graduates (IMGs), as they are now often referred to, have been an important part of the American healthcare workforce since the 1960s.[20] In 2010, IMGs accounted for a fourth of all practicing physicians in the United States, and although a majority were foreign born, one-fifth were American citizens who received their medical degrees abroad (mainly in the Caribbean). The largest number of IMGs in the United States are from India. In August 2014, graduates from medical schools in India (nearly 150 different schools) accounted for 5.3 percent (48,086 physicians) of the 899,953 practicing physicians.[21] They were also more likely to be female compared to those trained in the United States: 41.6 percent of all India-educated physicians in the United States were female, compared to the 34.6 percent in the overall physician population.

Physicians trained in India and practicing in the United States are overrepresented as hospital staff (6.5 percent) and underrepresented in research (2.5 percent) and teaching (3.7 percent), as well as in administration (2.1 percent). They are most often found either in states with large Indian-American populations or in states with physician shortages; they constitute a significant portion of the physicians in New Jersey (9.3 percent), Illinois (8.5 percent), Michigan (7.9 percent), and North Dakota (7.9 percent).

IMGs from India began to trickle into the United States for advanced train-ing—and subsequently to practice and settle down—in the 1950s. In 1959, phy-sicians from India accounted for 5.3 percent of that year's physician cohort. Their number was small (only 68), but at the time the training capacity of American medical schools was quite limited—fewer than 2,000 in 1961. Over the next two decades, medical training in the United States expanded rapidly, reaching 10,000 annually in 1972 and 20,000 in 1982, after which the number of graduates began to plateau. The share of Indian IMGs in the physician population of the United States rose steadily over two decades, from the early 1950s to the early 1970s. The share gradually declined over the next decade and a half, and then rose again in the early 2000s. Since then it has been steadily declining (figure 4.4).

In 1970, the number of Indian physicians certified by the American Medical Association (AMA) crossed 1,000 for the first time; that year, 13.4 percent of all physicians certified to practice medicine were from India—the highest ever relative to the year's cohort. With the Vietnam War exacerbating the shortage of skilled workers in the medical profession, the U.S. government responded by welcoming IMGs. To practice medicine in the United States, graduates of foreign medical schools must be certified by the Educational Commission for Foreign Medical Graduates (ECFMG), which was established in 1956 to certify physicians trained outside the United States.[22] Since 1963, the share of those graduating from medical schools in India among all IMGs has varied between 10 and 27 percent. It increased during the 1960s and into the mid-1970s, and sub-sequently declined until the late 1980s, after which there was another increase that lasted until the mid-2000s (figure 4.5).[23]

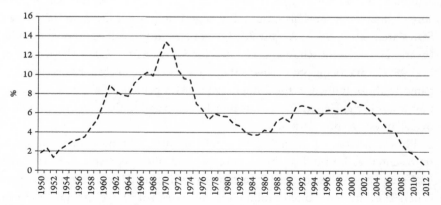

Figure 4.4 Practicing Physicians in the United States Who Are Indian Medical Graduates, 1950–2012.

Source: Compiled and calculated from the American Medical Association Physician Masterfile, 2014.
Note: AMA is the source for the raw physician data; statistics, tables or tabulations were prepared by authors.

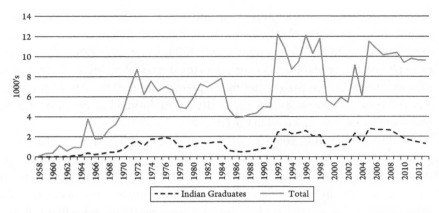

Figure 4.5 Indian Graduate and Total International Medical Graduates Certified to Take Medical Licensing Exam in the United States, 1958–2012.

Source: Compiled and calculated using data from the Educational Commission of Foreign Medical Graduates, 2014.

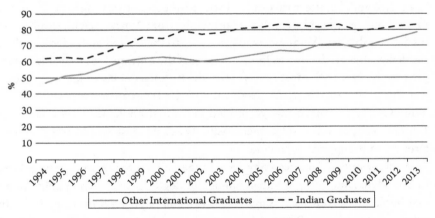

Figure 4.6 U.S. Medical Licensing Exam Step 1 Pass Rates, Indian and Other International Graduates, 1994–2013.

Source: Compiled and calculated using data from the Educational Commission of Foreign Medical Graduates, 2014.

An important factor for the large share of Indian medical graduates among IMGs is their consistently higher performance on the ECFMG certification exams compared to other IMG applicants. Since 1994, Indian graduates had a pass rate averaging 12.8 percent higher than non-Indian graduate doctors on Step 1, and 8.4 percent higher on Step 2 of the certification exam (see figure 4.6).

Over the last decade, four developments have shaped the landscape of IMGs and physicians of Indian origin in the United States. First, since the mid-2000s, there have been more Indian citizens than graduates of Indian medical schools receiving U.S. certification, implying that some Indian citizens are receiving their medical education outside India before applying for certification. Second, with an increasing number of U.S. citizens getting educated in medical schools in the Caribbean, since 2009 this group emerged as the largest share of medical certifications granted to IMGs. Third, the numbers of Indian citizens receiving certification began declining since the early 2000s and in 2013 reached the levels of a half-century ago. This might change as the demand for IMGs is expected to increase in the United States after full implementation of the Affordable Care Act. An aging population, as well as capacity constraints on U.S. medical schools, may likewise increase demand in the future.[24]

Finally, there is an ongoing generational change led by the 1.5 and second-generation Indian Americans who have often followed in their parents' footsteps into this field. In one respect, however, they have gone further by building up a public persona, influencing the understanding of modern medicine, ranging from the physician–patient relationship to differences between healing and curing and health, and well-being more broadly. One trendsetter is Deepak Chopra, who immigrated to the United States in 1970 after getting his medical degree in India. Following a successful career in medicine, he positioned himself as a "New Age guru" in alternative or "holistic" medicine, advocating ideas about the mind–body relationship, combining principles from Ayurveda with mainstream medicine. Abraham Verghese, who also came to the United States for a medical residency after graduating in India, found that the only options available to him (as was the case with most IMGs) were the hospitals in lesser-known places.[25] But those formative experiences of caring for AIDS patients in Johnson City, Tennessee, were transformative and led to his first book, *My Own Country: A Doctor's Story*, as well as subsequent visibility as a novelist, writer, and commentator on contemporary medicine.

Another Indian-American physician in the public eye is Atul Gawande, born in Brooklyn, New York, to Indian immigrant doctor parents, who published his first book, *Complications: A Surgeon's Notes on an Imperfect Science*, in 2002. His subsequent writings—*Better: A Surgeon's Notes on Performance* (which discusses three virtues that Gawande considers to be most important for success in medicine: diligence, doing right, and ingenuity); *The Checklist Manifesto: How to Get Things Right* (which discusses the importance of organization and pre-planning, such as thorough checklists, in both medicine and the larger world); and *Being Mortal: Medicine and What Matters in the End*—have made him one of the most popular writer-physicians in this field. Others include Siddhartha Mukherjee, author of the Pulitzer Prize–winning *The Emperor of All Maladies: A Biography of Cancer* and *The Gene: An Intimate History*, who came to the United States after high school in India; Sandeep Jauhar, author of *Intern: A Doctor's Initiation* and *Doctored: The Disillusionment of an American Physician*, who emigrated from India when he was a child; Sanjay Gupta, born in Michigan, a neurosurgeon and one of the most visible public faces reporting on medicine and health-related issues in his capacity as chief medical correspondent of CNN; and Paul Kalanithi (whose father, a cardiologist, had emigrated from India), whose posthumous *When*

Breath Becomes Air was a hauntingly poignant portrayal about learning how to die and how to live life. And in December 2014, Vivek Murthy—who moved to the United States at the age of three—became the nineteenth Surgeon General of the United States and the country's leading spokesman on matters of public health. His nomination had been hit by headwinds of opposition from the powerful National Rifle Association (NRA), but an important interest group—the American Association of Physicians of Indian Origin (AAPI)—used the techniques it had honed over the previous decades to lobby heavily on his behalf.

AAPI's success came after a protracted struggle. Although foreign medical graduates had to pass tough licensing exams and extra years of residency (irrespective of how many years of prior experience they had) before they were allowed to practice, their competence as physicians was still questioned by the medical establishment, who regarded them as having inferior clinical skills owing to substandard training in their nations of origin and poor language and communication skills to provide quality medical care. A study conducted by the Harvard School of Public Health on the quality of health care provided by physicians, including IMGs, stated that "the degree to which the [I]MG was Americanized" predicted his performance.[26]

At the time there were no systematic studies comparing the performance of IMGs with those trained in U.S. medical schools. Later studies would find that patients of doctors who graduated from international medical schools and were not U.S. citizens at the time they entered medical school had lower mortality rates than patients cared for by doctors who graduated from U.S. medical schools or who were U.S. citizens and received their degrees abroad. The difference between non-U.S.-citizen and U.S.-citizen international graduates was striking, with the former's performance significantly better. But while IMGs who were U.S. citizens performed less well than non-U.S.-citizen IMGs on certifying, training, and specialty board examinations, they had less difficulty in entering the workforce in the United States.[27]

The stigma experienced by IMGs was especially pronounced in the initial years after 1965. A study on Korean immigrant physicians found that "[i]mmigrant status often carries with it connotations of functional defects, cultural differences, or other unsuitable attributes that result in discrimination."[28] Unsurprisingly, studies documented that IMGs tend to practice in physician-shortage areas characterized by high rates of infant mortality and below average physician-to-population ratio; they take care of more minority patients and accept more Medicare and Medicaid patients. In addition, IMGs have tended to work in primary care medical specialties that are less popular with U.S. medical graduates, such as internal medicine, pediatrics, psychiatry, and ob/gyn.[29] The multiple barriers in part reflect a political economy in which the native-born population turned to occupational licensing regulations as protectionist barriers to skilled migrant labor competition. From 1973 to 2010, states with greater physician control over licensure requirements imposed more stringent requirements for migrant physician licensure, and as a consequence, received fewer new migrant physicians.[30]

Frustrated by this state of affairs, in late 1981 a small group of Indian immigrant physicians met at a suburban Detroit home and decided to establish a national organization to represent Indian physicians in the United States and to educate the American medical field and the broader public about what it considered "unfair, unjust, and untrue allegations."[31] Named the American Association of Physicians of Indian Origin (AAPI), it hosted its first convention in the summer of 1982 in Dearborn, Michigan, with the goal of ending what was seen to be a de facto stratification of the U.S. medical system—a two-tiered system that subordinated IMGs to U.S. medical graduates in the physician workforce hierarchy.

Indian IMGs blamed the American Medical Association (AMA) in particular for creating and sustaining a dual labor market. "Despite all these exams, the intention is not to create equality . . . AMA is one of the culprits. . . . The AMA was getting our membership dues but they were not addressing our concern."[32] But as one insightful analysis of their predicament put it, "Despite reaping the benefits of class, caste, and status in their home country, in the U.S. they were unable to escape their background in relation to their nationality, religion, language, and color, and so these products of an Indian caste-based society became, essentially, a lower caste of physicians in their new country of residence."[33]

Identity formation is not just the result of external categorizations but also agency exercised by the group in the face of bias. The initial steps toward collective action among Indian physicians were followed by overtures to other (mainly Asian) IMG ethnic organizations. AAPI was careful in not using the word *discrimination,* since it was conscious that, given the standing of the AMA, it had to try to bring about changes by working with the AMA and not by antagonizing it. However, the AMA proved unresponsive and a resolution introduced by some AAPI members in 1987 to form a section on foreign medical graduates (FMGs) received little support. AAPI was blamed for attempting to splinter the organization along ethnic lines.[34] The defeat in the AMA pushed AAPI's leadership to look for alternative strategies, including approaching the Equal Employment Opportunity Commission (EEOP) and/or filing a class-action lawsuit against the AMA. In the end, however, in conjunction with other IMG communities, it took a more political route: seeking congressional intervention. In the process, AAPI's leadership became familiar with political processes and was the first major Indian-American organization to become politically engaged.

Indian physicians played a particularly important reputational role for the community in the early decades. While there were many engineers, their contacts were largely with other professionals in offices and factories. However, many ordinary citizens first encountered Indian immigrants who were physicians, and at a time when occupations and race were closely interlinked, Indian physician immigrants helped break the mold. But Indian IMG physicians were not the only healthcare workers emigrating from India. Another significant healthcare occupation has been pharmacists, who organized themselves as the American Association of Indian Pharmaceutical Scientists (AAiPS) in 1988. In addition, Indian nurses—primarily from the Kerala Christian community—began to arrive in the United States in the 1970s. Among foreign nurses, those from Canada were the largest number in the United States until the 1970s, but since then nurses from the Philippines have dominated. In the 1980 Census, the share of nurses from India among foreign-educated nurses was 5 percent, behind the Philippines, Canada, and Jamaica. By 2010, the share from India was 7 percent, second after the Philippines.[35] Studies suggest that they have faced discrimination in job assignments and opportunities for promotion, with a combination of race and gender contributing to disempowering them.[36]

A somewhat similar story—of discrimination stoking collective action and civic engagement—led to the formation of another influential Indian-American civic organization. Many Indian immigrants of Gujarati origin who were forced to flee from East Africa in the late 1960s had an entrepreneurial background and entered the hospitality sector in the United States because of its relatively low entry barriers, the ability to employ family labor, its in-built housing situation, and steady cash flows. Since many of them had the last name Patel, their motels gained the sobriquet "potels." However, many of these properties were in the U.S. South, and banks and insurance companies there were disinclined to work with the hoteliers. Mounting frustration with the perceived discriminatory treatment led them to establish the Midsouth Indemnity Association, in Tennessee in 1985, which eventually changed its name to the Indo American Hospitality Association. Meanwhile, another group of hoteliers of Indian origin came together in Atlanta in 1989, with similar goals, and called themselves the Asian American Hotel Owners Association (AAHOA). The two groups merged in 1994, and by the early 2000s, they had emerged as the largest membership-based Indian business organization in the United States. In 2013, AAHOA's 12,500 members owned more than 20,000 hotels, with nearly 2 million rooms and with a market value of $130 billion, employing more than 600,000 full- and part-time workers. While we examine this story in greater detail in chapter 6, it is sufficient to note here that such groups combine two quintessential features of American political life: the ethnic lobby and the business lobby.

Many of these organizations are prone to internecine feuds. Nonetheless, they demonstrate that when facing discrimination, ethnicity can be a salient organizational resource even for skilled immigrants as they move to become part of mainstream civic institutions.[37] In turn, participation in civic organizations tends to increase political participation through sharing of skills and connections and gaining exposure.

Political Participation

On September 28, 2014, nearly 20,000 Indian Americans heard Indian Prime Minister Narendra Modi at Madison Square Garden. The audience treated the Indian prime minster more like a rock star than a politician, and in quintessential American style, a crowd of demonstrators stood outside protesting. With a governor, three senators, and thirty-six representatives (one Republican and the rest Democratic) in attendance, the community-organized event was telling, less for U.S.–India relations or even India's relations with its diaspora (as emphasized by the Indian media) and more as an assertion of the place of Indian Americans in political life in America.[38] In constituencies with less than 0.5 percent Indian-American population, the members of Congress in attendance came to just 2.9 percent. In contrast, in constituencies where the percentage of the Indian-American population was greater than 0.5, the proportion of members in attendance jumped to 12.5 percent of Congress (figure 4.7). Popular commentary in India focused on Prime Minister Modi's popularity among the Indian diaspora

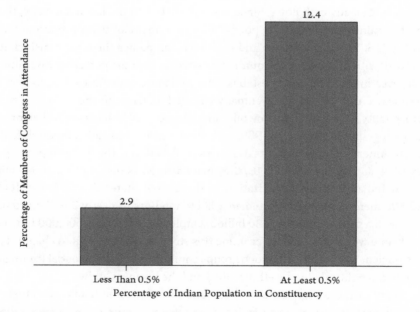

Figure 4.7 Members of Congress with Indian-American Constituents in Attendance at Indian Prime Minister Modi's Madison Square Garden Event in 2014.
Source: Authors' calculations.

and the supposed strong support for his political party, but was oblivious to the other side of the coin. For the planners of the event, the audience was not India or Indian politics per se but a way to signal to American politicians that the community had finally "arrived" politically and needed to be taken seriously by them.

In reality, just two congressional districts (California's 17th District and New Jersey's 6th District) have an Indian-American population greater than 10 percent. Five congressional districts have an Indian-American population between 5 and 10 percent, and another sixteen have between 3 and 5 percent. But even these numbers exaggerate the electoral importance of Indian Americans as voters. In 2004, 49 percent of Indians in the United States were adult citizens and two-thirds of them voted, implying that just one-third of the total adult Indian-American population voted.[39] As discussed earlier, a little less than half of all Indian Americans were naturalized by 2012, and an even smaller fraction were registered and actually voted.

Naturalized citizens tend to vote less than the general population. The other benefits of citizenship are more immediate and tangible relative to those resulting from voting, which might explain why naturalized citizens vote less than other citizens. Broadly, naturalized citizens are statistically less likely than native-born citizens to register (by between one-third and one-half in recent years); and conditional on being registered to vote, naturalized citizens are statistically less likely than native-born citizens to vote (between one-fourth and two-fifths), with the effects being stronger in congressional elections than in presidential elections.

Studies suggest that there are differing effects of country of origin on naturalization and voting, respectively, indicating the distinct natures of these two political processes. An individual's level of political participation in the United States is associated with two key factors: socioeconomic resources, such as time, money, or experience; and rootedness, reflected through indicators such as older age, residential stability, and marriage.[40] While relatively modest socioeconomic indicators might explain lower participation by Latinos, the low turnout of Asian Americans at the polls has posed a bigger puzzle (indeed, Latinos register and vote at higher rates than Asians). Since Asian Americans have higher-than-average resources, and they appear to be strongly rooted, the group context of participation rather than individual-level processes might shed light on this puzzle. Explanations have ranged from community norms to avoid political involvement, experiences of discrimination in the United States, and a lack of political leadership.

But the first two explanations do not easily apply to immigrants from India, given India's strong electoral democracy and its attendant socialization effects on its emigrants, and the relatively lower levels of discrimination faced by the later immigrant cohorts. The relatively recent vintage of these groups is one possible explanation. Since much of the U.S.-born Indian population is young, a significant majority is still not old enough to vote. The remaining are young voters who in general tend to vote less than older native-born voters. Altogether, the share of Indian-American voters is considerably less than even their small share in the population.

Recent work suggests that while resources and rootedness-based models explain the likelihood of political participation, factors such as political representation (the number of candidates from the group) and varying voting rules in different states also matter. An additional reason might be that Indian Americans are strongly partisan supporters of the Democratic Party (for reasons we discuss later), who are also concentrated in reliably blue states in the Northeast and along the West Coast. Unlike, for instance, Cuban Americans who are a swing vote in a swing state like Florida—and are hence courted strongly by both political parties—the votes of Indian Americans do not matter as much, and this realization may dampen voter turnout.

Since most Indian immigrants initially focused on bettering their economic prospects, political involvement was seen as extraneous to their primary goals. They had to learn a new political grammar, since the traditional form for transmitting partisan political preferences—parental socialization—was unavailable. Moreover, most Indians who migrated as adults did not come with the intention of permanent immigration. Their political consciousness gradually awakened as the realization grew that the United States was now "home."

For India-born immigrants, the first structured lesson on U.S. politics and history occurred as they readied themselves for the naturalization process. Another standard source—multiple influences during schooling from peers and pedagogy—was also absent for the majority of Indian Americans who came as adults, although political knowledge imbibed through schooling and college education would influence the 1.5 and second generations, and sometimes reverse the inter-generational transmission of political beliefs from children to parents—a "trickle up" process, as it were.[41]

The standard forms of political participation in the United States range from the directly political—voting, contacting elected representatives, participating in campaigns, funding political parties and candidates, and running for election—to modes more civic in nature, such as attending protests, marches, or demonstrations; working with others to solve community problems; volunteering on local elected and appointed boards; or being active politically through voluntary associations. These multiple pathways to political participation have provided Indian Americans alternative avenues for gaining a political voice other than just through voting. As with other immigrant groups, growth in the Indian-American community, both demographically and financially, has led it to engage more deeply in American political life.

Political participation is not just about beliefs, but also about acting on them, thereby gaining experience in new settings. A traditional pathway to political activism for immigrants is involvement in local communities with a higher concentration of people with shared ethnicity. Owing to their different histories, Indian Americans have fewer spatially concentrated ethnic enclaves, those equivalents of the Chinatowns and Koreatowns. But where they do exist—places such as Edison, Iselin, and Plainsboro in New Jersey; Jackson Heights in Queens, New York; Cupertino, Sunnyvale, and Mountain View in California—they perforce engage in local politics. However, in the absence of neighborhood-centered communities, the family "become[s] almost the sole locus for one's experience of 'Indianness' in America. It is within the family that Indian immigrants and their children determine who they are and where they belong."[42]

A study of an Indian ethnic economy in Chicago (along Gandhi Marg) argued that it represented a space "where Indian American identity has been reterritorialized as Indian Place: . . . a shared history of migration, consumption practices, linguistic affinity, and symbols rooted in an Indian homeland. . . . The India that is showcased on Gandhi Marg, however, is not static, but a dynamic, constantly changing representation of a homeland."[43]

This economic rootedness enabled Indian merchants in the area to develop and situate political power within the ethnic economy. They formed the Devon North Town Business and Professional Association, a not-for-profit organization to serve as a liaison between the city of Chicago and the business community on Devon. Parades organized on India's Independence Day gradually became de rigueur for local politicians to attend, just as the St. Patrick's Day parade had been for many decades. In 2004, Barack Obama, then candidate for U.S. senator, as well as his opponent, walked in the Indian Independence Day Parade, symbolizing the growing political influence of the community in that area.

In the beginning of the twentieth century, as immigrants were surging into the United States, political parties were the critical facilitators in political incorporation. A century later, their role has been substituted by community organizations, even though most do not have explicit political agendas. However, the manner of incorporation depends on political opportunity structures. In communities with a de facto one-party system and a powerful dominant party, marginal political players, such as immigrants, have difficulty breaking into politics, even if they have considerable resources and highly educated members.

The political incorporation of two Asian immigrant communities in Edison, New Jersey, exemplifies this argument. A greater level of civic participation of Indian-American immigrants resulted in their political incorporation, while Chinese immigrants who were less engaged remained marginalized. The differences in political incorporation were rooted in local processes of racialization. In the local context, the Chinese were seen as "successful but conformist model minorities" and the Indians were labeled as "invaders and troublemakers."[44] The racialization of the Indian immigrants led to enhanced political activity and higher levels of political visibility of their organizations.

Politicizing stimuli occur at the individual as well as at the group level. As mentioned earlier, discrimination was the catalyst for organizing AAPI and AAHOA, both eventually emerging as interest groups with the sort of fundraising capabilities that command the attention of politicians of both parties. But as is often the case, grass-roots activism came from younger members of the community who were angered by social injustice. In the mid-1980s, Indian and other South Asian immigrants were subjected to abuse and violent attacks in the New York City and Jersey City region, with groups like the "dotbusters" threatening violence to drive them out. This culminated in a brutal racial attack and murder of Citibank executive Navroze Mody. The apathy of public authorities in prosecuting and preventing further such crimes, and a community wary of getting involved and protesting, led a group of students at Columbia University to establish IYAR (Indian Youth Against Racism, later renamed as YAAR, meaning "friend" in Hindi) to create a greater awareness of civil rights in the community.[45] Activist groups like the South Asian Americans Leading Together (SAALT) are part of the National Coalition of South Asian Organizations (NCSO), a network of forty-nine community-based organizations that focus on social justice; they serve the poorer and marginalized members of the community in areas ranging from housing to racism and discrimination, domestic violence and LGBT rights.[46] At the individual level, the second generation of Indian Americans is more activist oriented, an issue we discuss later.

Funding and Lobbying

Socioeconomic status is a strong predictor of political participation. High socioeconomic status tends to lead individuals to develop a set of civic attitudes, increasing participation in both political and civic life. While it used to be argued that the essence of American democracy lay in Madison's vision of a vibrant pluralism, with faction countering faction, by the late twentieth century, this view had few takers. As Elmer Schattschneider, in his book *The Semi-Sovereign People: A Realists View of Democracy in America in 1960*, wryly put it, "The flaw in the pluralist heaven is that the heavenly chorus sings with a strong upper-class accent."[47] But if participation in politics in the United States began to increasingly tilt in favor of the upper class and corporations—and more broadly toward the preferences of the economically advantaged—then groups with higher incomes, such as Indian Americans, were better placed to leverage these closer links between affluence and influence.[48] The banal reality of money and access is well captured in Indian-American hotelier Sant Singh Chatwal, a fundraiser for the Democratic Party (especially the Clintons), who was quoted in a wiretap explaining, "Without [money] nobody will ever talk to you. That's the only way to buy them, get into the system."[49]

By the end of the 1990s, Indian Americans had become active participants in funding American domestic politics, with estimates of $8 million in individual donations over the three election cycles leading up to 2002. We estimate subsequent contributions of at least $11.1 million, $18.3 million, and $20.6 million in the 2004, 2008, and 2012 presidential election cycles, respectively (table 4.1). Another funding route has been through political action committees (PACs), where the contributions by Indian Americans are not especially noteworthy (figure 4.8). In all, the financial contributions made by Indian Americans to electoral politics in the United States appear to be about average.

In the United States, two approaches to ethnic politics have become particularly noteworthy: the ethnic vote bank and the ethnic lobby. An example of the ethnic vote bank is Tammany Hall, the Democratic Party organization that dominated New York City politics from the 1790s to the 1960s. The ethnic lobby, on the other hand, is exemplified by the Jewish community in the United States. Though demographically localized and nationally small in size, the Jewish community in the United States has long had a reputation for leveraging its economic clout and its organizational ability to galvanize support for issues related to concerns of the Jewish community, ranging from anti-Semitism, to the plight of Soviet Jews during the cold war, to support for Israel.

Table 4.1 **Electoral Financial Contributions of Indian Americans**

Year		Total Amount ($ million)	Mean ($)	Median ($)	No. of Donors
2004	Indian American	11.1	1,270	500	8,703
	All Americans	2,156.5	1,284	500	1,680,175
2008	Indian American	18.3	1,586	500	11,513
	All Americans	3,007.0	1,582	500	1,900,888
2012	Indian American	20.6	1,744	500	11,817
	All Americans	4,019.9	2,279	500	1,763,833

Note: The data are drawn from the FEC's individual contributions file, which contains each contribution of at least $200 from an individual to a federal committee. If a donor made multiple donations, the donor average and median above is aggregated across all FEC-reported donations that a donor made in each election cycle.

Source: Compiled and calculated from the online Federal Election Commission (FEC) data, 2014.

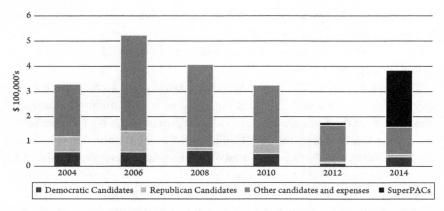

Figure 4.8 Donations Made by Indian Americans to Political Campaigns, 2004–2014.
Source: Compiled and calculated using data available on Opensecrets.org, 2014.

Through ethnic lobbies, small demographic groups can exert considerable influence over U.S. foreign policy, since only a small fraction (surveys suggest around 5 percent) of the American public is active on issues of foreign policy, leaving space for motivated interest groups. The success of an ethnic lobby is based on the organizational strength of the community, its cohesiveness and electoral turnout, the force and framing of its message, and the degree to which political leaders are predisposed to engage with the lobby. Indian Americans have created an ethnic lobby by building upon these tenets, although its scope and clout are still fairly modest.

The earliest Indian lobby was formed around the issue of advocating for citizenship rights for East Indians, which was later followed by pro-independence advocacy. During the 1970s, groups such as the Association of Indians in America (AIA) and the National Association of Americans of Asian Indian Descent (NAAAID) successfully lobbied to add an "Asian Indian" category to the 1980 Census.[50] It was not until after the end of the cold war, in the 1990s, with a substantial Indian-American population, that Indian-American political strength began to coalesce.

In 1993, the Congressional Caucus on India and Indian Americans was formed. The origins of the establishment of the India Caucus lay in growing attacks on small Indian businesses (especially grocery stores) in the 1980s. These stores were often located in poor neighborhoods and were important centers of cultural life for communities resident in those neighborhoods. As Indian owners moved in, they rarely recruited staff from the community nor tried to integrate in other ways, and resentments simmered over. The model of the India Caucus was the Black Caucus, and initially its goals were to address challenges facing the Indian-American community and, to a lesser extent, India–U.S. relations. Over time, however, its focus shifted primarily to the latter.[51]

As late as 2001, a paper on Indian-American political organization contended that the community was "seen, rich, but unheard."[52] The change coincided with U.S. governmental interest in India. Though relations began to warm following the end of the cold war, the level of engagement between India and the United States was quite limited. The landmark March 2000 presidential visit by Bill Clinton to the subcontinent got little coverage in the American press. At a time when India was entering the global discourse as an emerging power, one congressional aide pithily summed up the general knowledge of most members of Congress on South Asia as follows: [they] "wouldn't know India or Pakistan if they came up and bit them on the ass."[53]

The roots of Indian-American political organization extend to ethnic, professional organizations such as AAPI and AAHOA, which fostered ethnic activism along economic agendas, creating Indian-American solidarity across professional lines. These professional developments were accompanied by the rise of Indian-American news outlets, notably the well-regarded publication *India Abroad* (published since 1970 in New York), which was an important community forum on questions of Indian-American identity.[54] These were followed by groups that sought to engage the community in electoral politics, including the Indian American Forum for Political Education (IAFPE) established in 1982, the Indian-American Leadership Initiative (IALI) which has focused on developing leadership among Indian American Democrats, and the first major Indian-American political action committee, the U.S. India Political Action Committee (USINPAC), which like many other ethnic lobby organizations tried to model itself after the American Israel Public Affairs Committee (AIPAC), the powerful pro-Israel lobby group of the Jewish community.

In the aftermath of 9/11, hate crimes against the Indian American community, and South Asians in general, increased sharply. Civil rights groups like SAALT and the Sikh Coalition lobbied to raise public awareness and political consciousness against the spate of racist attacks. After more than a decade of lobbying (and the killing of six worshipers at the Sikh gurdwara in Oak Creek, Wisconsin, in August 2012), their efforts finally persuaded the FBI to start tracking hate crimes against Hindus and Sikhs (and Arabs) beginning in 2015.[55]

Candidates and Voting Behavior: Indian-American Political Preferences

Though Dalip Singh Saund was elected to Congress in the 1950s, in the mid-1990s, after a long hiatus, Indian Americans began running for elected office at local, state, and national levels. In 2004, Piyush "Bobby" Jindal became the first person of Indian origin to be elected to the House of Representatives in half a century. Ami Bera, a second-generation Indian American, was elected to the House in 2012 (and reelected in 2014) as a Democrat in a close election in which crucial financial support from Indian Americans pushed him over the top.

Two of the three Indian Americans elected to Congress have been Democrats (Rep. Dalip Singh Saund and Rep. Ami Bera) and one a Republican (Bobby Jindal, before he became Louisiana's governor). While most Indian-American state legislators have been Democrats, at the time of this writing the two most prominent Indian-American politicians on the national scene are Republicans: Louisiana Governor Bobby Jindal and South Carolina Governor Nimrata "Nikki" Randhawa Haley, a remarkable achievement given how minis-cule the Indian-American community is in these two states.

The political contributions of Indian Americans have been increasing at the level of state and local government. During the entire 1990s, three Indian Americans were elected to state legislatures. Kumar Barve was the first Indian American to be elected to a state legislature (Maryland) in the United States in 1991, eventually reaching the position of majority leader. The second, Nirmala Swamidoss McConigley, served in the Wyoming State Legislature from 1994 until 1996. McConigley, who was born in Madras, was also the first woman and first India-born person to serve in any state legislature. Satveer Chaudhary was elected in 1996 as a representative in the Minnesota House of Representatives, and in 2000, to the state's Senate, making him the first known person with Indian ancestry to be elected to a state Senate seat.

Not surprisingly, the ethnicity of many Indian-American candidates has been an issue in their election campaigns. When Swati Dandekar was campaigning for state office in Iowa, her opponent stated in a campaign email that "[w]hile I was growing up in Iowa, learning and reciting the Pledge of Allegiance to the Flag, Swati was growing up in India, under the still existent caste system. How can that prepare her for leading Iowa or any other part of our great United States?"[56] Such concerns about the fitness of Indian Americans for political office have stretched back as far as Dalip Singh Saund's campaigns for public office in the 1950s.

Yet, in spite of the prevalence of such views, the number of Indian Americans running for public office has continued to increase. In 2010, shortly before the congressional mid-term elections, National Public Radio ran a feature entitled "South Asia Americans Discover Political Clout" and argued that the "trick for these candidates is to never let voters forget you are running to represent Sacramento, or Wichita . . . not Bangalore."[57]

In the 2014 elections, ten Indian Americans were elected to state legisla-tures: six men and four women—six Democrats and four Republicans. However, this constituted barely 0.14 percent of the total elected state legislators, and in Congress, it was approximately one in 535 (0.19 percent). There are other elected offices where Indian Americans have had modest success, however. For instance, Kamala Harris (whose mother is Indian and father is Jamaican) was elected as the attorney general of California (and who, at the time of this writing, had declared her intention to run for the Senate in 2016); and Kshama Sawant, who immigrated after completing her undergraduate degree in India, was elected to the Seattle City Council on a Socialist ticket, becoming the first socialist to win a city-wide election in Seattle over nearly a century. Still, these are few and far between, and they are a stark contrast to the economic success of the community, underscoring the diverse patterns of immigrant groups in American politics. The Cubans, for instance, have been much more active than the equally numerous Salvadorans.

Two characteristics of Indian Americans—higher income and social conservativeness—should at first glance make the community lean toward the Republican Party. Calling it a "group of American superachievers," conservative columnist Jay Nordlinger asserted,

> Republicans think—and hope—that this group is ripe for their party. The thinking goes like this: "Indian Americans are entrepreneurial, hard-working, striving, traditionalist, family-oriented, religious, assimilationist, patriotic–what could be better?" And what are their "issues"? Tax reform and regulation, particularly as they affect small businesses; free trade, which includes a robust defense of outsourcing; and perhaps more than anything else, tort reform. Indian-Americans are a community of doctors, not plaintiffs' attorneys, and their political activity has been fueled by a desire to rein in medical liability. . . . [M]any Indian Americans had nasty experiences with preferential policy back in their homeland. This community as a whole—to indulge in some (further) stereotyping—is exceptionally merit-minded.[58]

At the time that Nordlinger was writing, a nationally representative survey of the Indian-American population found that 46.4 percent identified themselves as Democrats, 8.7 percent as Republicans, 23.3 percent as independents, and the rest responded "don't know."[59] In the 2008 presidential elections, over 90 percent of Indian Americans reported voting for Barack Obama. In a 2012 nationally representative survey of Asian Americans, half of Indian Americans identified themselves as "Democrat," just 3 percent as "Republican," and the remainder as "Independent/Non-Partisan."[60] In the 2012 presidential election, 84 percent of the Indian-American population voted for President Barack Obama while just 14 percent voted for Mitt Romney, a level of partisan support higher than the Asian-American average and significantly higher than traditional Democratic Party bastions such as the Jewish and Latino communities.[61] And a Pew survey of the largest Asian-American groups in 2012 found that "Indian Americans are the most Democratic-leaning of the six U.S. Asian groups. Nearly 65 percent of Indian Americans identify with or lean to the Democrats, while 18 percent identify with or lean to the Republicans."[62]

Historically, there were good reasons for Indian Americans to favor the Democrats. After all, it was the Democrats who were responsible for passage of the historic 1965 immigration law, which made it possible for them to come to the country in the first place. Subsequently, when President Nixon tilted U.S. policy toward Pakistan in 1971 during the India-Pakistan war that led to the creation of Bangladesh, it turned a generation of educated Indians who emigrated to the United States against the Republican party.[63] By the 1990s, however, incessant pressure on India by Democratic-led administrations on issues ranging from financial-sector liberalization, to human rights in Kashmir, to an insistence that India sign the Comprehensive Test Ban Treaty (CTBT), led to disenchantment with the Democrats. Although President Clinton's historic visit to India in March 2000 was met with approval, it was Republican President George W. Bush who pushed through the historic U.S.–India nuclear agreement in 2005 that shattered long-held dogmas isolating India in the global nuclear order for over three decades (we discuss this in more detail in the last chapter). This breakthrough was heralded by the Indian-American community—and should have yielded domestic political benefits for the Republican Party, but, if anything, the opposite happened.

There appear to be three reasons Indian Americans do not support the Republican Party, despite a greater congruence with its more conservative economic message. The first is that the Democratic Party has, at least over the past half-century, had a more "big tent" approach toward racial minorities than have had Republicans. Second, the anti-immigrant message of the Republican Party, even though in principle aimed mainly at illegal immigrants (and hence, with less impact on Indian Americans), has led virtually all recent immigrant communities, whether Asian American (with the exception of Vietnamese American) or Latino, to be more supportive of the Democrats. Finally, there has been a growing unease in the community, whose members are Hindu, Sikh, Muslim, Christian, Buddhist, and Jain, of the influence of evangelical Christians in the Republican Party.[64] Indeed, one analysis finds that "religion appears to be one of the strongest factors driving Indian Americans' unexpected affiliation with the Democratic Party."[65] That may seem surprising, given that the most prominent Indian-American politicians—Louisiana Governor Bobby Jindal and South Carolina Governor Nikki Haley—are from the Republican Party. But it is less so when one realizes that both converted to Christianity, and their faith has been an important part of their political campaigns. The counterfactual—that they could have been nominated by the Republican Party, let alone won, if they had not converted—strains credulity given the nature of the Republican Party base in Louisiana and South Carolina.

As this book was going to press, a representative survey of the political behavior and beliefs of the six main Asian-American groups in the United States (Chinese, Indian, Filipino, Japanese, Korean, and Vietnamese) was released in May 2016. Responses from that survey, comparing Indian Americans with Chinese Americans as well as Asian Americans more broadly, is provided in table 4.2.

Table 4.2 **Asian-American Voter Survey, Spring 2016**

	Indian	Chinese	Total
In the last 12 months, have you (% answering Yes)			
- worked for a candidate, political party, or some other campaign organization?	5	18	8
- contributed money to a candidate, political party, or some other campaign organization?	16	23	17
- worked with others in your community to solve a problem?	37	17	25
- donated money to a religious organization?	56	42	55
- donated money to any other charitable cause?	70	49	60
% with a very favorable impression of:			
- The Republican Party	6	6	8
- The Democratic Party	31	22	27
- Barak Obama	56	18	36
% with a very favorable impression of Donald Trump	10	4	8
% with a very unfavorable impression of Donald Trump	53	29	47
Do you support or oppose banning people who are Muslim from entering the United States? (% Oppose)	70	53	58
Do you favor or oppose affirmative action programs designed to help blacks, women, and other minorities get better access to higher education? (% Favor)	68	41	64
% Strongly or somewhat agree that undocumented immigrants should have the opportunity to eventually become U.S. citizens	59	45	58
If a political candidate expressed strong anti-Muslim views, and you agreed with him or her on other issues, would you still vote for that candidate, or would you vote for someone else?			
-Still vote for candidate	24	47	35
-Someone else	59	24	44

Source: Inclusion, Not Exclusion. Spring 2016 Asia American Voter Survey. At: APIA Vote/AAJC/ AAPI Data.

Three findings of this survey are worth noting. One, it appears that despite coming from a country with robust electoral democratic politics, Indians do not seem to be more involved, on average, in the formal political process. Whether it comes to working on campaigns or contributing money, they are less engaged than the Chinese community. However, they are quite engaged—more than average and more than Chinese Americans—when it comes to a general sense of civic participation (working with the community, charity, etc). Two, with regard to political preferences, the contrast in the community's support for Democrats (compared to Republicans) is stark. The favorable ratings of Obama were notably higher compared to other Asian Americans. And three, despite much simplistic and empirically untethered commentary about the community's alleged anti-Muslim and upper-caste prejudices, compared to other Asian Americans they are less inclined to support hot button issues such as banning Muslim immigrants, supporting candidates with anti-Muslim views, or supporting Trump. Furthermore, their views were also relatively pro-affirmative action and in favor of citizenship pathways for undocumented immigrants compared to other Asian Americans.

The coexistence of "prejudice" and moderation perhaps reflects the paradox of modern India itself. Since Muslims are a live political reality for Indians, as opposed to Chinese, it could be that Indians are careful about expressing political preferences on this issue; that is, they are just more attuned to "political correctness" and also have a more realistic live-and-let-lie attitude than others. Similarly, on affirmative action, while most Indian Americans are upper caste, they have also grown up in a milieu where they instinctively know that excluding others is inviting a political storm. Indians have a greater exposure to these issues than, for instance, Chinese Americans, which could result in more muted opinions. Another possibility is that Chinese Americans do actually think affirmative action reduces places for them (as evidenced by contentious debates on this issue in California).

Intra-group Variation in Assimilation: Gender

Immigrants "carry" with them the cultural mores and behavioral norms of the country of their origin. This includes gender roles, which for immigrants from poor countries often means a subordinate status for women in the household and large gender gaps in education and labor force participation.[66] But the evidence suggests that on some gender-related indicators there is rapid assimilation with the second generation's fertility and education levels, as well as labor supply, converging toward those of native-born women.[67] However, this research assumes that those who emigrate have gender-related preferences (for instance,

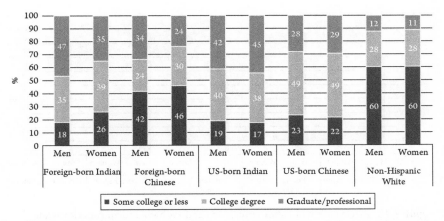

Figure 4.9 Educational Attainment of Indian Americans, Men and Women, Compared to Other Groups, 2007–2011.
Source: Compiled and calculated from ACS 2007–11.

on fertility and labor force participation) that reflect the national average in their country of origin. In the Indian-American case this is a strong assumption, given the significant selection of who emigrates.

As we have seen in chapter 2, the India-born Indian-American population has significantly higher education levels, for both men and women, than the non-Hispanic white population. However, as with other foreign-born Asian groups, Indian women have less education than their male counterparts. But by the second generation, this gap vanishes, in line with the national trends of higher college enrollment and completion for women compared to men.[68] U.S.-born Indian women have slightly more graduate or professional degrees than their male counterparts (figure 4.9), although the gender gap is small relative to the Hispanic or black community.[69] However, as with other groups in the United States, the education "advantage" for women has not resulted in equality in wages.

A report from the U.S. Department of Labor in 2014 found that Asian Indians have higher labor force participation rates and lower unemployment rates when compared to most other Asian groups and non-Hispanic whites.[70] However, while India-born women are highly qualified, their labor force participation rates are relatively low—indeed, the lowest rates of all subgroups compared, including black, white, Hispanic, and all other Asian populations. Figure 4.10 illustrates how labor force participation rates compare among non-Hispanic white, Indian, and Chinese communities in the American Community Survey data. Although the data do not control for age (and therefore also reflect retirees as nonpartici-pants), it is apparent that the India-born women—a fairly young cohort—have the lowest labor participation rates. Only about 59 percent of those with college

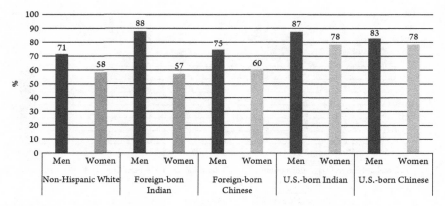

Figure 4.10 Participation in Labor Force, Men and Women, Indian Americans and Other Groups, 2007–2011 for 25+ Population.
Source: Compiled and calculated from ACS 2007–11.

degrees and 68 percent of those with graduate degrees are in the labor force—significantly lower than other Asian populations, as well as non-Hispanic whites. However, by the second generation, U.S.-born Indian women have one of the highest labor force participation rates—even higher than white males. This is an apparent jump of over 20 percent in participation in one generation; however, it needs to be qualified, since the India-born figures come from different cohorts of immigrants. Nonetheless, there appears to be a considerable difference between the labor force participation of first- and second-generation Indian-American women, which may be either due to social norms (of the first generation) and greater assimilation (of the second)—or due to some other factor.

One reason many India-born women do not work is because they cannot work. As we have seen in chapter 2, a key driver of the post-1995 jump in the Indian-American population was the H1-B visa. Dependents of H1-B visa holders, who are disproportionately women and who move to the United States to follow their husbands, receive H-4 visas.[71] This visa does not allow them to have a Social Security number or to work in the country. The visa has been dubbed the "depression visa" and the "prisoner visa," since the women, who are often highly qualified and have work experience, become depressed and frustrated in the traditional "housewife" role that U.S. immigration policy forces on them. Ironically, instead of escaping patriarchy by leaving, they find it reinforced, since they are completely dependent on their husbands.[72]

The ACS data also suggest that this nonparticipation in the labor force is not by choice. The labor force participation rate of naturalized Indian-American women above twenty-five years old is significantly higher than that for noncitizens (65.3 percent compared to 49 percent). Thus, a change in legal status results in a 16.3 percent increase in labor force participation (in the same generation), while there is a 20 percent increase from one generation to the next.[73]

It is also possible that the presence of multiple generations in Indian-American households affects female labor force participation. Families with three or more generations in the household often have grandparents who may be able to provide free childcare, freeing the wife to work outside the home. The data from ACS do not support this hypothesis, however. Indian-American women (both India-born and U.S.-born) are actually less likely to work the more generations there are in their households. This could be because traditional gender roles dominate in families practicing a "joint-family" system or because the additional generations have added to the workload of the women in the households (elder care, etc.).

With their higher educational qualifications, it is not surprising that Indian-American women have a higher median individual income than do non-Hispanic white women. However, the median income gap in the India-born between men and women is large—over $30,000 annually (figure 4.11). Owing to the large number of tech-sector immigrant workers, as well as their older average age,[74] the India-born have higher median *individual* income than the U.S.-born, but because of higher rates of female participation in the labor force, *household* median income of the U.S.-born is greater.

There have been fears whether the troublingly adverse (and increasing) gender ratios—the result of a strong cultural preference for sons in India, particularly in North-West India—are carried over by immigrants. Before we present the results, a word of caution. We have to be careful in interpreting population estimates, since these data are based on a sample from ACS and thus are subject to sampling variability, which is important considering the small sample sizes at specific ages. We have used two different methods to estimate population counts

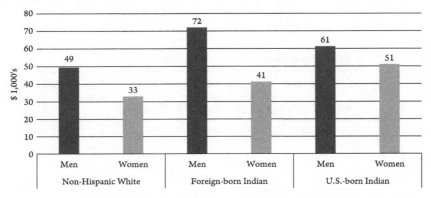

Figure 4.11 Median Individual Income by Race and Gender for Indian Americans and Non-Hispanic Whites, 2007–2011.

Source: Compiled and calculated from ACS 2007–11.

at each age: first, simply using sampling weights provided by ACS (method 1); and second, using statistical smoothing techniques, which assume that sampling weights are independent of gender after controlling for age (method 2). The results using both methods were comparable.

In examining the data, we found it necessary to keep two demographic realities in mind. First, the overall sex ratio in any population is usually skewed in the favor of women, owing to higher male mortality at older ages. Second, the natural sex ratio at birth skews the other way, ranging from about 102 to 106 boys born per 100 girls. As we see in table 4.3, the overall sex ratio among the India-born population in the United States was 112, while in the U.S.-born population it was 105, compared with 97 among non-Hispanic whites. However, given that the ratio among the India-born may simply reflect the gender selection in emigration (more males leave India), rather than a bias against the girl child per se, we present gender ratios at five-year age intervals (owing to sample size constraints). Taking the NHW (non-Hispanic white) ratio as the yardstick, there does not appear to be a preference for sons at birth (or in the age group 0–4) for U.S.-born Indians. The India-born group has sample sizes of less than 1,000 in that first age interval, so the results should be interpreted with caution. In the age group 5–9, the ratio appears more or less in the normal range.

However, a study based on data from the 2000 Census found a male-biased sex ratio for births to Indian, Korean, and Chinese Americans. The ratio of the oldest child was within the normal range; however, if there was no previous son in the family, then the ratios became increasingly adverse at higher birth orders. The third child of a woman had 50 percent higher odds of being male if the two previous children were female. That means that the ratio was 151 for third births to women who already had two daughters. The study found that these results were robust regardless of the citizenship status of the mother, suggesting that assimilation may not have a dampening effect on preference for sons

Table 4.3 **Sex Ratio among Indian Americans**

Age	India-born		U.S.-born Indian		Non-Hispanic Whites
	Method 1	Method 2	Method 1	Method 2	
0 to 4	97	98	102	103	105
5 to 9	102	101	100	102	105
Overall	112	108	105	104	97

Method 1: Based on sampling weights provided by American Community Survey.
Method 2: Statistical smoothing techniques which assume that sampling weights are independent of sex after controlling for age.

for Indian Americans.[75] The two findings are not necessarily contradictory. As we have noted earlier, since 2000 the composition of Indian immigrants has shifted considerably, with more coming from South India where son-preference is less marked than in North India. International immigration tends to systematically alter gender dynamics within the household. This may not necessarily be a positive outcome for women, as new opportunities can also come with new burdens.[76] There are many reasons immigration alters gender dynamics, ranging from nuclear families, to changes in employment opportunities available to women, to exposure to different norms of gender relations, especially greater sharing of household responsibilities between men and women.

In addition to juxtaposing these multiple roles, another challenge faced by immigrant women is the burden of expectations that they should be repositories of the culture of the home country. This means women have a harder time negotiating their life in a new culture, given that they are required to balance old and new ways of life. The influence of the outside culture often places more responsibility on Indian-American women to be the "main symbols of cultural continuity."[77] The expanded identity as "cultural custodians" can be empowering, but it can also be limiting in its conception of women as mothers and wives.[78]

These dilemmas suggest that perhaps the most transformative dimension of the female immigrant experience is in her sense of personal autonomy.[79] The increase in personal autonomy is most palpable among first-generation female immigrants, who experience the biggest change in their lives. The sources of this increased autonomy might include moving away from parents and, for married women, from in-laws; having more physical mobility as a result of fewer concerns about safety and more ease in personal travel; less direct interference from family members in making big and small decisions; fewer dress-code restrictions; fewer expectations regarding appropriate behavior for females; more financial independence (though this depends on whether the women are legally allowed to and can find work); and generally a more liberal culture.

Autonomy, however, has been a mixed blessing. In the early decades of immigration, when the community was small, leaving existing support networks in India meant psychological isolation. For second-generation women, on the other hand, the Indian provenance has been sometimes viewed as a source of diminished autonomy and increased cultural conflict. This is because they are more likely to use their American peers' lives as reference points, rather than the lives of women in India. A major factor triggering intergenerational conflict, especially for daughters, is dating. Indian-American parents police their daughters more than their sons, wanting them to conform to the values and expectations of traditional Indian culture.[80] One of these traditions, "arranged" marriages, has been another source of stress as Indian traditions clash with pervasive American ones. However, as attitudes toward arranged marriages among educated urban Indians (the principal source of immigration from India to the United States) have eased in recent years, these tensions are also perhaps less intense in more recent immigrant cohorts.

Several studies suggest that women play an important role in buttressing the myth of Asians as the "model minority"; they do so by upholding two key American values—family and hard work. To live up to the high standard of family values that the Indian-American community has set for itself, they must "deny . . . or make . . . invisible any issue that is perceived as eroding that image."[81] However, much of this analysis is based on unrepresentative small samples, and it is hard to say how valid the data are for the community at large. It is quite likely that actual gender outcomes are mediated by class, education, visa status, and employment options.

External factors like U.S. immigration policy also play a role in the gendered experience of Indian immigrants. The Immigration Marriage Fraud Act in 1986 exacerbated the problem by requiring that newlyweds enter on "conditional" visas until the legitimacy of their marriage could be proven through two years of living together. The unintended consequence of this law was that women who had followed their husbands to the United States were not able to leave an abusive husband without being deported. In 1990, this problem was recognized and an amendment was added that removed some of the obstacles that abused dependents faced in seeking protection from their abusers. The Violence Against Women Act (VAWA) of 1994 created a process by which women could self-petition for immigrant status and seek protection both from their abuser and from deportation. However, seeking protection is arduous and few women take that formal route. The isolation from their familial support system, as well as the unequal relationship as a visa dependent, inevitably skews the power relationship within immigrant families against women.[82]

The immigration experience also places new pressures on women and familial bonds that can lead to domestic abuse, owing to the uniquely vulnerable position of immigrant women and to the patriarchal culture they have often brought with them. The "theme of deep shame, failure, and disgrace is echoed repeatedly in the voices of battered South Asian women," who often face a host of barriers in accessing services, including legal and police protections, from their abusers, racial stereotyping, and language problems.[83] The literature on domestic violence in the Indian-American community emphasizes the "invisibility" of this problem, owing to an attempt by the community to hide issues that would tarnish its image as a "model minority." Data inadequacies make it difficult to gauge how the incidence of gender violence in the Indian-American community compares with that of other immigrant groups or to its incidence in India. Since the 1980s, a number of community-based organizations have sprung up to meet the needs of battered women from the subcontinent and provide culturally relevant services.[84]

Intra-group Variation in Assimilation:
The Second Generation

Assimilation and acculturation are intergenerational processes. Second-generation Americans usually outpace their immigrant parents in key socioeconomic indicators such as levels of education, English-language skills, and occupational status.[85] Studies have highlighted the different processes of acculturation that occur in the second generation of immigrant families: dissonant (when children assimilate faster than parents), consonant (when both generations adapt to the new culture at the same time), and selective (or "segmented") acculturation (when the acculturation process is incomplete and slow). Within this framework, through both dissonant and consonant acculturation, the immigrant group's native language and many (or even most) traditions are soon abandoned.[86]

Whether the second generation assimilates in some sort of straight-line fashion or in a segmented way has been the subject of much debate. The second generation has to inevitably find its ways between two competing forces—that of the parents' culture and social norms and the dominant societal culture. It could also potentially enjoy the "best of both worlds," accessing both cultural systems (those of the parents' ethnic group and those of American society). Unsurprisingly, the fortunes of the second generation depend on their parents' history: their educational and ethnic backgrounds, when they immigrated, where they settled, and the reason for their arrival (i.e., whether as students, family reunification, illegal, refugee, etc.). All of these factors affect the social mobility of the second generation.[87]

Our analysis of the second generation of Indian Americans is based on data from the ACS.[88] The median age of the first generation is significantly older than the second generation (39.5 compared to 13.4), and hence we focus on the 25+ age population for both generations.

Given the already high levels of education that Indian immigrants come with, it is not surprising to find that their children, the second generation, are also highly educated and more likely to have a college education. In the data, just 3.1 percent had only a high school diploma or less, compared to 7.9 percent of the first generation (figure 4.12).

First-generation Indian Americans had a slightly higher median individual income when compared to their second-generation counterparts. The data, however, are skewed because of more years of work experience in the first generation compared to the second generation (which is much younger, even among those who are more than 24 years old). Second-generation households, on the other hand, had a higher median household income than the first-generation households, likely because of greater female labor force participation rates.

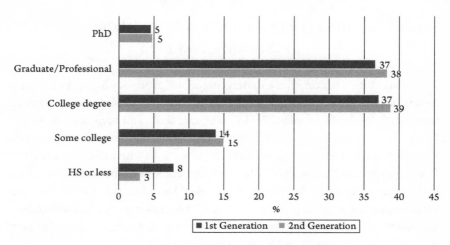

Figure 4.12 Educational Attainment of First- and Second-Generation Indian American Population, 2007–2011.
Source: Compiled and calculated from ACS 2007–11.

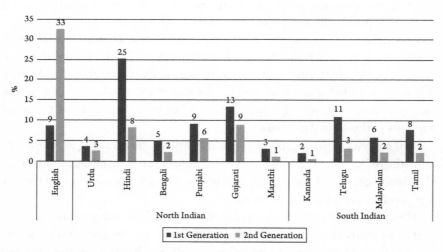

Figure 4.13 Languages Spoken at Home by First- and Second-Generation Indian Americans, 2007–2011.
Source: Compiled and calculated from ACS 2007–11.

Language has been known to play an important role in assimilation and has been found to be correlated with attitudes on a range of issues. While less than one-tenth of first-generation Indian-American households spoke English at home, a third of the second generation did, which is lower than what one might expect given the higher levels of English proficiency of the first generation. The linguistic assimilation seems highest among Hindi speakers and least among Gujarati speakers (figure 4.13).

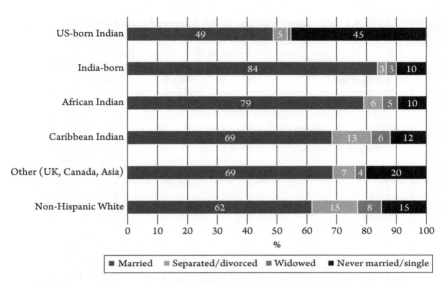

Figure 4.14 Marital Status of Selected Indian Americans and Non-Hispanic Whites, 2007–2011.

Source: Compiled and calculated from ACS 2007–11.

Two characteristics of Indian Americans stand out as regards their marital behavior. First, they have very high rates of marriage and low rates of divorce (figure 4.14). And second, among major Asian-American communities, Indian Americans—both men and women—had the highest rate of endogamy in both the first and second generations (table 4.4). Nonetheless, there was a noticeable increase in out-marriage in the second generation (among women more than men). However, among Asian Americans, Indian Americans are least likely to marry other Asian Americans who are not of Indian origin.

Historically, the second generation of immigrants does not necessarily climb the social ladder relative to the first. It may actually experience downward economic mobility resulting from a "reactive ethnicity" and a rejection of mainstream institutions.[89] This does not appear to have been the case with the Indian-American community, however. In part this could be because voluntary and higher-income immigrant groups are better able to "resist mainstream American culture while not embracing an oppositional minority culture."[90] A study of a low-income Indian-American community—Punjabi agricultural immigrants—found that they did not have the same degree of "rejection" of mainstream institutions as some other lower-income immigrant communities.[91] This was corroborated by another study that observed that a move toward Hindutva, or "reactive ethnic" association within some sections of the Indian-American community, did not correspond to a move away from mainstream institutions.[92] This is not surprising. Immigrants strive for success through both mainstream American institutions and association with "ethnic" or religious associations that celebrate their unique identity.

Table 4.4 **Marriage Patterns for Six Largest Asian-American Ethnic Groups (2011)**

Racial Categories	Gender	All Spouses (%)	USR + USR or FR (%)	USR + USR only (%)
Indian	Men	92.5	76.9	62.4
	Women	92.9	70.6	52.0
Chinese	Men	88.8	63.9	53.6
	Women	79.9	52.4	46.1
Filipino	Men	85.1	54.2	42.1
	Women	61.6	36.7	29.1
Japanese	Men	62.8	54.5	53.8
	Women	44.4	48.9	49.3
Korean	Men	90.4	61.1	44.8
	Women	68.1	35.4	24.1
Vietnamese	Men	92.6	71.0	59.0
	Women	84.6	56.3	40.6

Note: USR = U.S.-raised (1.5 generation or higher); FR = foreign-raised (first generation); "USR + USR or FR" = spouse 1 is USR while spouse 2 can be USR or FR; "USR + USR Only" = both spouses are USR

Source: C. N Le. *Asian Nation. Asian American History, Demographics, & Issues.* At www.asian-nation.org/interracial2.shtml.

A range of studies in the 1990s suggested that second-generation Indian immigrants, especially girls, lived "fractured" lives, trying to fit into two often-conflicting cultures, and were often constrained by Old World gender roles. The resulting inter-generational conflicts have been found to be correlated with higher depressive symptoms and lower self-esteem.[93] These characterizations have been changing because India itself has not been static, making the attitudes of more recent cohorts of immigrants less socially conservative.

Second-generation Indian Americans deviate noticeably from their parents' generation in their career choices. While 25.9 percent of the first generation (over 24 years of age) is in STEM (science, technology, engineering, and mathematics) occupations, only 13.4 percent of the next generations is. The second generation is more likely to work in STEM-related occupations than directly in STEM (17.3 percent). As illustrated in table 4.5, the most popular occupations for the second generation are in the healthcare industry. Indeed, almost 20 percent of all second-generation Indian Americans are in the health field—more

Table 4.5 **Occupations of First- and Second-Generation Indian Americans**

Occupation Categories	Non-Hispanic White	1st Generation (India-born)	2nd Generation (U.S.-born)	Generational difference
Computer and Mathematical	3	24	8	−17
Production	6	3	1	−2
Architecture and Engineering	2	6	4	−2
Transportation and Material Moving	5	3	2	−2
Sales and Related	11	10	9	−2
Education, Training, and Library	7	5	6	1
Arts, Design, Entertainment, Sports, and Media	2	1	2	1
Office and Administrative Support	14	7	8	1
Business Operations Specialists	3	3	6	2
Financial Specialists	3	3	7	3
Legal	2	0	5	4
Healthcare Practitioners and Technical	6	10	19	9

Note: Occupation categories in which the generational difference was less than 1 were excluded from the table. All figures are percentages.

Source: Compiled and calculated from ACS 2007–11.

than double that of the first generation. Other popular industries for second-generation Indian Americans are finance (6.8 percent) and legal services (4.6 percent). The generational difference is greatest in computer and mathematical careers. There is a drop of over 16 percent in participation in that industry within one generation. Three examples illustrate the greater diversity in occupational choices of the second generation relative to the narrower choice set of their parents, although that apparent choice set was distorted by the selection mechanism favoring IT workers.

One occupation that was rare in the first generation but more prevalent in the second, albeit at still low levels, is service in the U.S. military.[94] There are multiple pathways to integration, and one of those leads through military service. While there are no explicit data from the armed forces themselves, according to data from the 2013 PUMS, the India-born have virtually no presence in the armed forces (0.04 percent of the labor force, compared to 0.28 percent for all foreign-born). Although U.S.-born Indian Americans are an order of magnitude more likely to join the armed forces compared to the India-born, it is still half as likely as the general population (0.36 percent of the labor force compared with 0.68 percent). The low representation of first-generation immigrants is likely because most Indian immigrants are on average older and more educated, with better labor market prospects when they arrive in the United States, making a military career less attractive.

The reasons for joining the army stem more from a sense of service (duty) rather than need (jobs or immigration-related), although there are some who have benefited from the Military Accessions Vital to the National Interest (MAVNI) program that grants citizenship, and others who may have joined to avail medical school tuition benefits from the military. Many of those serving came from army or air force families in India, and hence there was already a military tradition in their families. Indeed, the so-called army brats from India—children of Indian army officers—have in general done quite well in the United States (children of enlisted men in the Indian armed forces rarely make it to the United States, another indication of the selectivity in emigration from India). There is a greater likelihood of Indian Americans to be in the officer corps—again reflecting their above-average educational attainments compared to the general U.S. population.

While the U.S. Army was the principal choice of service for the first generation (especially in the medical corps), the second generation has shown a preference for the Marines. The first and only Indian-American general, Brigadier General Balan Ayyar, served in the U.S. Air Force. There have been relatively few Indian-American women in the military. Sunita Williams was the first Indian-American female to graduate from the U.S. Naval Academy and also the first Indian-American military officer to be selected as an astronaut. While Sikhs serve in disproportionately large numbers in the Indian army, they have faced major hurdles in joining the U.S. Army since the 1980s, when it banned the wearing of "conspicuous" articles of faith. Although in 2009 three service members were granted "waivers" to this policy—one of whom was awarded the Bronze Star and another the NATO medal—there was no official policy change, resulting in multiple legal challenges to nudge the Defense Department to allow Sikhs to serve their country without being forced to compromise their religious beliefs. Finally, on March 31, 2016, the U.S. Army granted a permanent accommodation to Captain Simratpal Singh (who had filed a legal challenge) to continue to serve while retaining the articles of his Sikh faith.[95] For some time, the Air Force Academy was also seen as unwelcoming to other religious faiths.[96]

The contributions of Indian Americans to the U.S. military have been more indirect, with thousands of engineers employed through the principal defense contractors and in defense-related research and development. As relations between the United States and India began to warm, the United States has leveraged the presence of Indian-American personnel for training and liaison with the Indian military.

Another example of differences in the second generation comes from the activist community. By and large, the activism of the first generation was confined to issues of concern to the community. The second generation has been more comfortable in its American identity and its activism has also been less community specific. Bhairavi Desai's family had emigrated from Gujarat to Harrison, New Jersey, when she was six years old. Her father, who had been a lawyer in India, had trouble finding work and started a grocery store. She faced hostility and racist attacks in the neighborhood where she grew up. The experience politicized her, and soon after graduating college she began working with a South Asian community organization that provides social services to taxi drivers. She began to organize them into a union, and as executive director of the New York Taxi Workers Alliance (a rare woman in an overwhelmingly male industry), she came to prominence in 1998 when she led a strike to protest new rules imposed by then New York City Mayor Rudolph Giuliani.

Urvashi Vaid saw herself as an outsider as a child because of her ethnicity, accent, and intellectual interests. Despite growing up in a socially conservative community where homosexuality was a taboo subject, in 1989 she became Executive Director of the National Gay and Lesbian Task Force. Surveys suggest that while more Indian Americans accept homosexuality than discourage it (49 percent versus 38 percent), the numbers are lower than those for the general U.S. population (56 percent versus 32 percent).[97]

The third example of occupational changes has been in the legal field. While barely 0.4 percent of the first generation was in this field, 4.6 percent of the second generation is—an order of magnitude increase. This is not surprising since among the professions the one that is most country-specific is law. Between 1990 and 2013/14, data from three elite law schools—Harvard, Stanford, and Yale—showed a tripling of Indian-American students (albeit still small in absolute numbers). While the consequences have been more visible in law firms, its longer-term impact is being felt in appointments as judges (Judge Sri Srinivasan on the U.S. Court of Appeals for the D.C. Circuit) and prosecutors

(U.S. Attorney Preet Bharara for the Southern District of New York), as well as staff positions in the executive and legislative branches of government (Vanita Gupta, U.S. Assistant Attorney General for the Civil Rights Division at the Department of Justice). These positions often serve as a launchpad for entry into elected office, and it is in this area that this occupational shift will most likely be felt in the long run.

An analysis of nationwide scholastic awards in high school and college, ranging from the Scripps National Spelling Bee to the Intel Science Talent Search, the Rhodes Scholarship or the Harry S. Truman Scholarship, shows the types of academic success of the second generation of Indian Americans (table 4.6). It is interesting to note the fields in which the community demonstrates talent and where it does not. For instance, in music, in the 2013 All-National Honor Ensemble, 45 percent of the musicians in orchestra and 13 percent in band were Asian Americans, but just 2 percent and 1 percent, respectively, were Indian American. They are similarly poorly represented in math competitions. In both areas children of immigrants from East Asia (especially of Chinese and Korean backgrounds) excel. Similarly, in athletics and team sports, while they may actively participate in high school, they are virtually absent at the college level and in professional sports, where communities such as African Americans excel.

Table 4.6 **Indian-American Scholastic Achievements (High School and College)**

	1985–1994 (%)	1995–2004 (%)	2005–2014 (%)
Scripps Spelling Bee	20	30	81.8
National Geographic Bee	(Began in 1989)	0	60
Siemens Science Competition Gold Medal Winner	(Began in 1999)	5.3	11.4
Intel Science Talent Search (percent of Top Ten)	5	10	12
Mathcounts	0	0	10
U.S. Presidential Scholars	2.4	3.7	7.3
Rhodes Scholars	2.2	4.7	7.2
Truman Scholars	1.4	3.4	3.7
Churchill Scholars	1	4.6	8.4
Marshall Scholars	NA	4.6	6.6

Source: Authors' estimates.

There is a range of plausible reasons why talent in some communities gets directed into some channels and not into others, but in the case of second-generation Indian Americans, the pathways of the parents who immigrated to the United States is perhaps the most important factor in determining their choices.

A Minority within a Minority: Indian Immigrants Born in the Diaspora

There has been a long history of migration from the Indian subcontinent. In the colonial era its onset can be traced back to the end of slavery in the British Empire, in the 1830s. In the nineteenth century, most migrants from the subcontinent went to South or Southeast Asia, and the rest to Africa, the Caribbean, and the Pacific, with the vast majority going as indentured labor.

International migration from independent India was initially driven by the large demand for unskilled and semi-skilled workers in the United Kingdom following the end of the Second World War. Subsequently, two distinct streams of international migrants from India evolved from the late 1960s onward. One stream resulted from the economic boom that followed the sharp increase in oil prices in 1973, which created a large demand for less skilled labor in the Middle East. However, because the policies of the Middle East countries have made permanent settlement extremely rare, Indian migration to this region has been inherently temporary. The onset of the second stream followed the liberalization of restrictive "white only" immigration laws in Anglo-Saxon countries (especially Australia, Canada, New Zealand, the United Kingdom, and the United States), resulting in higher-skilled migrants moving to these countries.

About one-tenth of the Indian-American sample in ACS consisted of people of Indian origin who were born neither in India nor in the United States. About one-third of the born-elsewhere group were born in Bangladesh and Pakistan. The others were mostly born in South America and the Caribbean (especially Guyana and Trinidad), Africa, and other parts of Asia (see chapter 2). Unlike their India-born counterparts who are more likely to have emigrated directly from India to the United States, this population may have spent much of their lives elsewhere. This group exemplifies the complexities of global migration today, where national origin, race, and ancestry are less coterminous. While simplified classifications can be analytically hazardous, this group self-reports race as "Indian" (in the U.S. Census) and place of birth that is neither India nor the United States. In analyzing the characteristics of this subgroup, we focus on those age twenty-five and older.

For nearly half of this population, English was the primary language spoken at home—more than even the second generation of Indian Americans. Of the

Indian languages, Hindi and Gujarati were the most commonly spoken by this population (10.7 percent and 11.3 percent, respectively). Relative to the dominant Indian-American population, this group had a larger female population (54.6 percent of the Caribbean Indians and 52.2 percent among those born in the United Kingdom, Canada, and Asia). This group was also less likely to be married and more likely to live in multi-generational homes and be naturalized U.S. citizens.

People of Indian origin who have immigrated to the United States from Africa are the most similar to the India-born group, perhaps because their move from India to East Africa, in particular, had been only a couple of generations earlier. They had a high rate of marriage and low rate of divorce or separation (79.1 percent and 6.2 percent, respectively; see figure 4.14).[98] Like their India-born counterparts, they sometimes lived in multi-generational homes (13.2 percent with three or more generations). They had the lowest female labor force participation rate of all diasporic-Indian groups. They were the oldest group, with an average age of 47.7 years, and had been in the United States longer than any other Indian-American group, with an average of 21.9 years. Many members of this group are likely to have arrived in the United States after they were pushed out of East Africa in the late 1960s–early 1970s.

Caribbeans of Indian origin who settled in the United States were also an older population who had been in the country for an average of 21.5 years. As a group, their characteristics least resembled the India-born population. Their ancestors had left India primarily between 1838 and 1917, and they had weaker direct links to contemporary India and Indian culture than had their African-Indian counterparts. They often lived with other Caribbean Americans in places such as New York City (with 62 percent living in the Northeast). They had a divorce or separation rate similar to the non-Hispanic white population (13.1 percent). Although nearly three-fourths were naturalized citizens, they were the poorest Indian-American group.

Diasporic-Indian immigrant communities in the United States had significantly lower education levels when compared to their India-born counterparts. Whereas 78.3 percent of India-born Indian Americans had at least a college degree, only 50.3 percent of diasporic Indians did (although this was still higher than the 39.8 percent of non-Hispanic whites who had college degrees). Approximately 16.5 percent of all diasporic Indians in the United States had a high school degree or less. Most of those with a high school diploma or less were from the Caribbean-Indian group, which had lower education levels (table 4.7).

Caribbean Indians were also the only group of Indian origin that had a lower median individual and household income ($32,866) than non-Hispanic whites. They were also almost twice as likely as whites to receive food stamps. The Caribbean-Indian population was also much less likely to participate in STEM

Table 4.7 **Summary of ACS Data on Various Indian-American Groups**

	Education: Less than HS (%)	Education: Graduate/ Professional (%)	Female (%)	Female LFP (%)	Male LFP (%)	Naturalized citizens (%)	Mean years in the US
Diasporic Indian (non-U.S., non-India born) Other (UK, Canada, Asia)			52.2	66.2	85.3	56.0	18
Caribbean Indian	23.6	7.7	54.6	66.8	78.7	72.6	22
African Indian	9.4	25.0	49.9	64.5	84.3	71.7	22
Total Diasporic Indian			47.3	66.2	82.7	65.0	20
India-born	7.9	41.2	47.2	57.1	87.8	48.1	15
2nd Generation	3.1	43.1	47.5	78.3	87.4		
Non-Hispanic White	9.2	11.8	51.7	58.2	71.4		

Note: LFP = Labor force participation

Source: Compiled and calculated from ACS 2007–11.

professions (only 3.7 percent had STEM jobs). In economic terms, this group was quite dissimilar from the other Indian-American groups and more similar to the Caribbean-American community. In terms of cultural identity, Warikoo explains that second-generation Caribbean-Indian youths navigate their complex identity by selective association with either their religious, national, ethnic, or ancestral identity.[99] Since many Caribbean Indians live in spatially concentrated geographies (especially in and around New York City), they are also able to maintain a unique "Indo-Caribbean" culture in their community.

While other diasporic-Indian groups in the United States were more likely to work in STEM fields than the Caribbean and the non-Hispanic white populations, they were still significantly less likely to work in this industry than were the India-born group. Few in this group were likely to be on H-1B visas or were recruited to work specifically in the technology sector. The occupational sectors that the diasporic-Indian populations work in tend to mirror the non-Hispanic white population in its diversity. They do, however, have a much higher participation rate in the healthcare sector than non-Hispanic whites (10.1 percent, compared to 6.1 percent) and were almost twice as likely as the India-born and second-generation Indian Americans to work in administrative or office work jobs, with 12.9 percent (the largest share) working in those occupations.

Race and Identity

More than a century ago, when Indians first began coming to the United States, their racial identity posed a conundrum. That conundrum persists, albeit in less virulent ways, having taken many twists and turns from Hindoo to Asian to South Asian to Asian Indian to Indian American; from "ABCDs" (American-Born Confused Desis), to "dotheads," to "model minority."

On January 2015, in an address to the Henry Jackson Society in London, Governor Bobby Jindal emphatically declared, "I do not believe in hyphenated Americans. . . . My parents came in search of the American Dream, and they caught it. To them, America was not so much a place, it was an idea. My dad and mom told my brother and me that we came to America to be Americans. Not Indian-Americans, simply Americans."[100] This transubstantiation was perhaps necessary for the governor's political ambitions, just as a month earlier Miss America 2014, Nina Davuluri, emphasized, "The fact that I am rooted in Indian culture helped me win [the] Miss America pageant."[101] She said this while visiting India, and like Governor Jindal, she too probably had her audience in mind. When she won the pageant, her perceived identity earned her a barrage of racist comments suggesting she was a foreigner, Miss 7-Eleven, an Arab, and even a terrorist with ties to Al Qaeda. Meanwhile, a debate erupted in India suggesting that her dark complexion meant that she was unlikely to win a beauty pageant in India, a society obsessed with fairness as a standard of beauty.

Race and identity involve both ascription and agency within a specific context of reception, often in unanticipated ways. Since 1980, the U.S. Census has categorized Indians as "Asian Indian," a subset of the "Asian" racial category, suggesting that Indians are officially Asian. It is well known that racial categories are not innate but constructed. The U.S. government's Office of Management and Budget, which issued "Directive 15: Race and Ethnic Standards for Federal Statistics and Administrative Reporting," has a pointed caveat: "The categories in this classification are social-political constructs and should not be interpreted as being scientific or anthropological in nature." Hence there is no categorical logic why West Asia is always excluded from any construction of "Asian American," and it is unsurprising that Indians and other South Asians fit uneasily into that category as well. They are "a part, yet apart, admitted, but not acknowledged" among Asian Americans, for whom the most apt characterization might be "ambiguously nonwhite."[102]

Generally, when immigrants arrive they are more likely to identify with their national-origin group, but as they adjust to life in the United States, they become more likely to identify pan-ethnically. A study based on the 1990 Census data found that more assimilated Indian Americans were more likely to identify as white or black as opposed to Asian, suggesting that for Indian Americans, exposure to the U.S. racial system may actually suppress pan-ethnic identification.[103]

More integrated Indian immigrants—who have longer experience with American racial boundaries—appeared less likely to identify pan-ethnically, rather than more, perhaps stemming from a racialization process that includes learning that Indians are considered racially different from other Asians. However, more recent survey data suggest that, despite their outsider status among immigrants from Asia, Indian Americans generally do not have markedly lower rates of pan-ethnic identification compared to more traditional groups from East Asia: in the 2008 National Asian American Survey (NAAS), 33 percent of Indian respondents identified as "Asian" or "Asian American," compared to 37 percent of Chinese respondents and 30 percent of Filipino respondents.

The more interesting question perhaps is not whether Indian Americans are more or less "pan-ethnic" compared to these other groups, but whether Indian immigrants choose a pan-ethnic identification for reasons that are distinct from other Asian subgroups.[104] While "model minority" experiences may be shared across Asian ethnic groups, discrimination based on post-9/11 racial profiling has impacted the racialization and politicization of Indian Americans as they also have become targets of anti-Muslim/anti-Arab discrimination, irrespective of their actual religious beliefs. Incidents of violence against South Asian minority communities surged after 9/11. Investigative reports have documented that

Muslims bore the brunt of violence, and the killing of six people at a Sikh gurd-wara in Oak Creek, Wisconsin, in 2012 was a tragic reminder of the racializa-tion of religion and violence in the United States.[105] Pan-ethnic identities emerge out of shared histories and struggles that define who is and who is not a mem-ber of the group, and are not just convenient racial or political labels, or based on myths of shared racial or geographic origins. It has been suggested that the lukewarm response of pan-ethnic Asian organizations in defending South Asian hate-crime victims after 9/11, likely attenuated pan-Asian ethnic identification among Indian Americans.[106] While this experience led some to activate a South Asian identity in solidarity, for others the association of Pakistan with South Asia and its embroilment in terrorism was a reason to decouple from that identity.

The evidence regarding the degree of discrimination against Indian Americans is mixed. Wong et al. found that Indians (both foreign and native born) report higher levels of race- and immigrant-based discrimination than any other major Asian group, suggesting that Indians experience racial dis-crimination in different ways and/or at a higher frequency than other Asian subgroups.[107] Brettell found that Indian respondents are more likely to report individual experiences of discrimination than they are to say that Indians as a group are discriminated against, which she posits may be driven by Indians' high socioeconomic status.[108] However, these claims are not supported by the Pew survey of Asian Americans, which found that the percentage of Indian Americans reporting that discrimination against their group is "a major problem" was 10 percent—considerably below that reported by Koreans (24 percent), Chinese (16 percent), and Vietnamese (13 percent), but more than that reported by Filipino and Japanese (8 and 6 percent, respectively).[109] Similarly, when asked whether they had personally experienced discrimination in the past year, 18 percent of Indian Americans answered affirmatively—slightly less than did Chinese, Koreans, and Filipinos. Data from the Pennsylvania Human Relations Commission, a government agency that tracks illegal dis-crimination, found that between 2006 and 2010, 16,101 complaints were filed in the state, but just 74 were by Indian Americans.[110]

An interesting aspect of the construction of identity is the term "South Asian." In multiple surveys, Indian Americans identify themselves in different ways, but few do so as South Asian. A small section of academics and activist groups, however, are as committed to the term as the population in question appears not to be. In 2012, the U.S. Supreme Court heard an affirmative action case: *Fisher v. University of Texas*.[111] Three Indian-American groups joined an amicus brief opposing race-conscious admissions policies at the University of Texas at Austin. They argued that "Asian Americans are the new Jews," because policies to promote diversity through race-conscious admissions in college admissions in effect discriminated against them, drawing a parallel with past discriminatory policies that excluded Jews from many universities. Conversely, several South Asian organizations signed on to an amicus brief in *Fisher* supporting race-conscious policies, arguing that "Asian-Americans continue to face racial discrimination and benefit from race-conscious policies, which help to break down racial stereotypes by facilitating interactions between students of diverse groups." The three organizations that signed on to the anti-affirmative action brief all emphasized "Indian" identity, while those that supported race-conscious policies preferred the "South Asian" designation.

Conclusion

Identity issues facing the Indian-American community are not just about being a particular category of hyphenated American. Living as an Indian American is to experience both the "Indian" and the "American" complexities of the identity—and everything in between. In the intermixing of two societies that are among the world's most heterogeneous, the cleavages of caste and class, region and religion are carried over from one society to the other—where they encounter the new variable of race.

As DiPietro and Bursik argue, while many contemporary "race/ethnicity-oriented social scientists have questioned the relevance of the specific country of origin in the contemporary United States, suggesting that a focus on global, pan-ethnic categories is now substantively warranted," the empirical reality is rather different.[112] A majority of Hispanics (51 percent) identify themselves by their family's country of origin, while just 24 percent say they prefer a pan-ethnic label.[113] Based on a representative survey carried out in 2012, less than one-fifth (19 percent) of people of Asian origin living in the United States appear to view themselves as Asian American. A majority (62 percent) described themselves by their country of origin, while just 14 percent most often simply call themselves American (the percentage doubles among U.S.-born Asians). The data for U.S. residents of Indian origin is pretty similar: 20 percent describe themselves as Asian American or Asian, 61 percent describe themselves as Indian or Indian American, while 17 percent say they most often simply call themselves American.[114]

But identity is of course not just about what an individual wants it to be; it is also about how society, governments, and, yes, even academics perceive it to suit their specific agendas. When emigrants left Italy in the late-nineteenth century, their loyalties were particularist, rooted in the regions that constitute Italy. "Many became 'Italian' only when they left home; when they returned, neighbors called them 'germanesi' or 'americani.'"[115] The nature of the boundary and the context—temporal, spatial, occupational—shapes the nature of the identity. It does not matter whether academics and activists insist on the moniker "South Asian" or whether others see them as "Asian." The fact is that whether it is a Rajat Gupta or Fareed Zakaria or a Satya Nadella, or the character of Apu in "The Simpsons" or of Raj in "The Big Bang Theory," or Kal Penn's Kumar in "Harold and Kumar," in popular discourse they are all (for now at least) seen to be largely either Indian Americans or Americans of Indian origin, and not as solely "American," as Bobby Jindal insists they are. While the community's subregional or ethnic identities within India or supranational "South Asian" or "Asian" identities or religious identities undoubtedly exist, not least in the self-construction by individual members of the community, this is not (at least as yet) the case either with self-identification as reported in surveys or in the popular discourse within their country of adoption.

But this self-identification is hardly static. On the one hand, even among descendants of European immigrants, "symbolic ethnic" identification continues to be surprisingly resilient, perhaps because ethnic identities allow people to navigate contradictory American values of choice, individuality, and community.[116] However, recent empirical evidence suggests that ethnic attrition can be quite rapid over generations—more in some than others. By the second generation, overall rates of ethnic identification drop to below 84 percent for Chinese, Koreans, and Filipinos; 76 percent for Indians; and 68 percent for Japanese. For third-generation Asian children, the corresponding rates vary from 48 percent to 66 percent, but are just 36 percent for Indians.[117] Whether the former or the latter trend prevails is likely to be shaped as much by domestic trends within the United States as by the patterns of future immigration from India.

5

Entrepreneurship by The Numbers

Earlier chapters have detailed the historical and geographical patterns of the presence of Indian Americans in their new country, as well as the processes of adapting and making new lives. A classic view of immigrant socioeconomic mobility includes making a transition from marginal to mainstream occupations, also encapsulating shifts from ethnic enterprise to well-paid, high-status professions. Of course, some entrepreneurs, immigrants or not, have always become very wealthy in ways that pursuing professional occupations does not typically support, but even those newly rich may have struggled for social status.

The Indian-American case is somewhat different from past immigrant stories, though, because of who came and when. As has been laid out in the preceding chapters, this was and is, on the whole, an exceptionally educated population, and it came at a time (and partly because) of a major technological change in the U.S. economy, the information technology boom.[1] These circumstances have given the entrepreneurial activities of Indian Americans a special place in their story, accelerating their rise in an America that has itself been undergoing rapid economic change. For example, of eighty-one U.S. startup companies valued at $1 billion or more, but not publicly traded as of January 1, 2016, just over half (44) had at least one immigrant founder. Of sixty-one such immigrant founders or co-founders, fourteen were of Indian origin.[2]

Entrepreneurship has iconic status in the United States. It more than simply signifies jobs or wealth; it has a deep cultural resonance, since it reflects the individualism that has been the hallmark of this country's self-image. Entrepreneurship is a pathway to assimilation, one that (as this chapter and the next will show) Indian Americans have trodden especially well. Indeed, the importance of enterprise is a longstanding aspect of thought and action in America. Writing as long ago as the first half of the nineteenth century, Alexis de Tocqueville opined, "It may be said that, in the United States, there is no limit to the inventiveness of man to discover the ways of increasing wealth and to satisfy the public's needs. The most enlightened inhabitants of each district constantly use their knowledge to make new discoveries to increase the general prosperity, which, when made, they pass eagerly to the mass of the people."[3] He further argued that "the primary reason for [the country's] rapid progress, their strength and greatness is their bold approach to industrial undertakings" and that what astonished him was "not so much the marvelous grandeur of some undertaking as the innumerable multitude of small ones."

De Tocqueville's favorable view of American enterprise has been widely shared by Americans. A serial entrepreneur, writing in *Forbes* magazine, offers the reasons for "Why Americans Make the Best Entrepreneurs" as "a confluence of money, empathy and culture."[4] Culture in this telling includes embracing risk-taking, celebrating the underdog, and utilizing a high degree of connectedness.

If we return to purely economic impacts, we see recent empirical research as confirming the importance of small enterprise in the country's job creation overall,[5] as well as in the obvious case of fast-growing firms.[6] And the "United States of Entrepreneurs" has been estimated to create innovative entrepreneurial firms at more than double the rate of Germany or Japan.[7,8] Economic theorists, too, have increasingly focused on Joseph Schumpeter's ideas of "creative destruction" and the role of innovation in economic growth.[9] In this context of entrepreneurship being important for economic growth, the role of immigrant entrepreneurship has particular salience. For example, in the face of evidence that business dynamism in the United States has been undergoing a broad-based secular decline (exacerbated by the financial crisis of 2007–2009), the authors of a Brookings Institution study highlight "liberalized entry of high-skilled immigrants" as a possible policy response for enhancing entrepreneurship.[10]

The decline of new business formation after the financial crisis also hit Silicon Valley startups. A study undertaken for the Kauffman Foundation on entrepreneurship reported that immigrants were founding fewer companies, with the striking exception being Indian Americans.[11] These Indian Americans include representatives of all three waves of immigration identified in chapter 2, but their ranks have been particularly swelled by the third wave, the IT Generation; that group will be most important for the future. In short, Indian-American entrepreneurship will continue to grab headlines.[12]

This chapter and the next examine the entrepreneurial experience of Indian Americans in the context of the important ongoing national debates about economic growth, job creation, and immigration. The initial focus is on the data, starting with information that can be gleaned from the U.S. Census. Insight into national patterns of business ownership and performance complements the analysis of the Indian-American presence discussed in chapters 2 and 3. But there is more to what makes Indian-American entrepreneurs tick than what can be found in government data files. This chapter also presents results from a unique survey of Indian-American entrepreneurs, conducted by the authors, that asked questions about motivations, entrepreneurial experience, perceptions of the drivers of success, and cultural values, in addition to basic demographics.[13] The survey also included nonentrepreneurs, allowing for comparisons between them and entrepreneurs. Questions explored with the survey data include what the differences are between men and women entrepreneurs, the differences across age groups, sources of finance, and the possible impacts of life experiences on entrepreneurship decisions. The survey allows us to identify some distinctive features of the Indian-American entrepreneurial experience (see appendix 2).

Numbers can only reveal so much about Indian-American entrepreneurs. Like other immigrant groups, Indian Americans have long sought whatever avenues have been open to them for getting ahead, economically and socially. A hundred years ago, a handful of people from India made their livings in America as itinerant spiritual teachers, in an early type of entrepreneurial endeavor.[14] Others started out as agricultural laborers until they could buy and run their own farms.[15] As immigration and citizenship laws eased, they found ways to own gas stations, convenience stores, and motels. Many of these stories have been told, in individual interviews or in books about groups such as the Patels of Gujarat, who came to dominate the American motel industry.[16] Some of these stories will be revisited in the next chapter, adding depth and nuance to the patterns revealed in the data.

We next draw on a rich literature on immigrant and ethnic entrepreneurship to summarize some of the key concepts and results from past analyses. This provides a foundation for analyzing national census data on business ownership, which is also connected back to the findings of chapters 2 and 3. Finally, the results of the survey round out this chapter.

Immigrant and Ethnic Entrepreneurship

The 1965 Immigration Act, described in chapter 2, not only had major consequences for levels and patterns of entry into the United States, but it also spurred renewed scholarly interest in ethnic entrepreneurship by these new entrants. Earlier studies had looked at the experiences of previous immigrant ethnic groups, such as Jews in New York City,[17] but the post-1965 world of immigrant entrepreneurship has been marked by greater diversity and complexity, more detailed data, and more sophisticated conceptual frameworks. Understanding this broader context helps frame the specific story of Indian-American entrepreneurship.

Studies of immigrant and ethnic entrepreneurs over the past few decades have shared an important common theme with earlier work on previous immigrant experiences—namely, the role of entrepreneurship as an avenue for economic mobility. This is a more fundamental question than the headline issues

of the impacts of immigrant entrepreneurs on aggregate job creation and economic growth, briefly mentioned in the beginning of this chapter. In fact, the
two kinds of outcomes are not necessarily tightly connected.[18] If a few members
of an ethnic group are very successful entrepreneurs with significant positive
impacts on the economy, that may not be a general description of outcomes for
the group as a whole. In fact, there may be nothing particularly ethnic about a
highly educated immigrant succeeding in building a high-tech enterprise.[19]

What matters, then, for thinking about ethnic entrepreneurship, especially
by, but not restricted to, immigrants? One conceptual distinction is based on
the nature of economic interactions with the "nonethnic" mainstream or with
other ethnic groups. So-called *middleman minority entrepreneurs* primarily serve
customers outside their own group, as in the examples of Korean grocery stores
in black neighborhoods of Los Angeles, or Gujarati motel owners in Middle
America. By contrast, *enclave entrepreneurs* serve their own communities, typically within a circumscribed geographic area, such as Chinatown in San Francisco
or any number of the Little Indias described in chapter 3. In practice, these types
may overlap, so that there is a more general concept of an ethnic economy.[20]
Indeed, enclaves may be centered on noneconomic activities, including social-
izing and other shared leisure pursuits, without constituting economic enclaves
such as a traditional Chinatown; many of the Indian-American clusters mentioned in chapter 3 might fit this description. Another consideration, related to
the earlier point about possible irrelevance, or at least lack of salience, of ethnic
identity, is that several other group characteristics might come into play in determining the nature of entrepreneurship and its outcomes, including gender, class,
and educational background.[21]

Going beyond the basic classification of ethnic enterprise to considering
its determinants and outcomes, the standard approach identifies three dimensions of interest: access to opportunities, group characteristics, and emergent
strategies.[22] Opportunity structures include market conditions such as the nature of the product or service, economies of scale, and degree of uncertainty.
Opportunities also depend on access to ownership, which is shaped by factors
such as government policies and interethnic competition. Group characteristics
are determined by selection and settlement patterns—the subject of chapters 2
and 3—and the more amorphous variable of "culture," including aspirations
and other social norms. This last variable also enters considerations of resources
available to the ethnic group, including financial, human, and social capital. In
particular, a major issue in analyses of ethnic entrepreneurship has been the relative roles of these different kinds of potential resources.

Early national-level data on ethnic enterprises is sparse. From 1972 to 1986,
a period covering parts of the first two phases of Indian-American immigration
post-1965, the national self-employment rate increased slightly from 6.9 percent

to 7.4 percent, with a slightly larger increase for Whites only. Nonwhite self-employment rates during this period stayed at around 4 percent. However, 9.2 percent of the foreign-born population in the country's 272 largest urban areas (Census SMSAs) was self-employed in 1980, versus 7.1 percent of the native-born. This difference was somewhat larger for both Whites (11.3 percent vs. 7.9 percent) and Asians (8.4 percent vs. 5.3 percent).[23] While changes in economic structure might have been buoying self-employment rates (services replacing manufacturing, but being less subject to economies of scale), immigrants seemed to be filling the new business niches created by these structural changes.

Other data from the 1980 Census on business participation rates by self-reported national ancestry, which did not distinguish between immigrants and nonimmigrants, indicated that Indian Americans were not exceptionally entrepreneurial by that measure, but they did well when they chose that route, consistent with the selection story of chapter 2.[24] On the other hand, the top four national-origin groups[25] all had participation rates more than double the national average. The business participation rate for those of Korean, Chinese, and Japanese ancestry were also higher than the national average. On the other hand, the average (mean) income of self-employed Indian Americans was $29,800—third in the national rankings and well above the national average of $18,630—while the self-employed of Korean, Chinese, and Japanese ancestry had mean incomes close to the national average. Other 1980s data provide a slightly different picture, however: Indian-American rates of business ownership were estimated to be more similar to the other three Asian groups,[26] while average sales per firm for Indian Americans were reported at $65,000, as against $84,200, $55,600, and $115,000, respectively, for the other three Asian groups.

For the first two decades after the liberalization of immigration policy, there was little quantitative analysis beyond documenting self-employment rates and incomes. Can one draw any conclusions about the interplay of opportunity structures and immigrant characteristics? A reasonable inference from the observations made in chapter 2 is that Indian Americans' greater levels of education contributed to their higher self-employment incomes. There is also evidence, based on 1980 Census data for 272 SMSAs, that immigrants contributed to the trends in self-employment beyond what an equivalent native-born population would have done.[27] Another study uses data from the General Social Survey, 1983–1987,[28] which includes information on national origin, but also, exceptionally, information on whether respondents were Jewish. Jewish Americans were more likely to become entrepreneurs, whereas the self-employment rate for Asian Americans was not significantly different from the national average. Self-employment rates were also higher for men, married people, older people, and those with a self-employed father. On the other hand, being foreign born did not increase the rate of self-employment in this data set. The result for Jewish Americans can be taken as indirect evidence for the notion of middleman minority enterprise, but Asian Americans in this sample do not fit that classification; indeed, when self-employment rates are estimated only for those who had self-employed fathers, the rate for Asian Americans was significantly lower than the average. Self-employed Asian Americans in this data also had lower incomes than their non-self-employed ethnic counterparts.

A major step forward in understanding the determinants of entrepreneurial success was a study by Robert Fairlie and Alicia Robb, comparing White, African-American, and Asian-owned businesses.[29] Most of their detailed analysis, however, used 1992 data, before the third wave of Indian immigration identified in chapter 2. Some basic trends were reported up to 2006; for example, in that year, the Asian-American rate of self-employment was 11.8 percent, slightly higher than for Non-Hispanic Whites.[30] The 1992 data reveal that Asian-American firms did not do as well as White-owned firms overall, but did better than African-American or Hispanic-American firms. They also did better than White-owned firms for some kinds of firms. Entrepreneurship decisions were strongly influenced by previous family enterprise, and prior work experience in that enterprise improved later business performance.

Prior work experience in a similar industry, education, and startup capital all had positive impacts on entrepreneurial outcomes, and helped explain the strong performance of Asian-American firms.[31] There were differences in the characteristics of foreign-born and U.S.-born Asian Americans, but they did not lead to significant differences in business performance. Other analysis with this data set has interpreted variables such as being married and receiving startup funds from family members as social capital, and has argued that social capital facilitated entrepreneurial entry, but that post-entry success depended more on human and financial capital.[32]

As the foregoing indicates, Indian-American entrepreneurs had not made much of an impression on official data collection or empirical researchers until quite recently. Quantitative studies of ethnic entrepreneurship tended to analyze Asian Americans as an aggregate, or focus on Korean Americans, or even on longer-present groups such as Chinese Americans and Japanese Americans. However, this view began to change with the acceleration of Silicon Valley's growth in the 1990s. A study using the Dun and Bradstreet database estimated that 9 percent of Silicon Valley high-technology startups founded between 1995 and 1998 were run by an Indian American.[33] Almost certainly, these were not from the IT Generation of Indian-American immigrants, but had come in the first two waves, almost always as graduate students. For example, Kanwal Rekhi arrived in the United States as a graduate student in the 1960s, and in the early 1980s he became one of the first Indian-American entrepreneurs in Silicon

Valley.[34] Indian Americans might have been successful entrepreneurs in mid-dleman minority roles, or in ethnic enclaves, but the stereotype was that while they made good engineers, they were not cut out to be mainstream entrepre-neurs or corporate leaders.[35]

Recent surveys have continued to update the importance of Indian-American entrepreneurs in technology startups. Vivek Wadhwa and his coauthors estimated that 15.5 percent (up from the earlier 9 percent) of all Silicon Valley startups founded between 1995 and 2005 had Indian Americans as key founders, with a nationwide estimate of almost 7 percent (about seven times the population proportion of Indian Americans) of all high-technology startups having founders of Indian origin.[36] A study with a more inclusive sample than Wadhwa's, focusing on the years 2002 to 2006, estimated that 16 percent of high-technology, "high-impact" companies had foreign-born founders, and 40 percent of those founders were from India.[37] Assuming an even distribution of founders across companies, this would imply that 6.4 percent of such companies had India-born founders, similar to Wadhwa's figure. Finally, Wadhwa and his co-authors further updated their earlier estimates to cover 2006 to 2012, and reported figures of 8 percent na-tionally, and 14 percent for Silicon Valley, for Indian-American founders of high-tech startups.[38] This latest period, of course, begins to include the post-1995 IT Generation of immigrants among those founding companies.

Most recently, Robert Fairlie and several co-authors have examined entrepre-neurship by immigrants from India, in comparison to several other Asian groups, as well as across three countries (the United States, Canada, and the United Kingdom).[39] They used 2000 Census data for the United States, so the period covered predated the main effects of the IT revolution on Indian-American en-trepreneurship. Indian-American immigrants had self-employment rates similar to the national average, whereas Korean-American immigrants had much higher rates, and Pakistani-American immigrants were also more likely than the average to be self-employed. However, less-educated India-born immigrants were more likely to be self-employed, fitting older models of ethnic entrepreneurship. For the United States, greater education explained half of the business-earnings ad-vantage of Indian Americans over Whites, with industry choice and other factors explaining a further one-fourth. Importantly, well-educated Indian-American immigrants had higher business incomes than the average, but their less edu-cated compatriots did not.[40]

Building on the data in chapter 2, all these studies suggest that Indian Americans have followed two distinct paths of entrepreneurship. The less ed-ucated have self-employment propensities and outcomes that fit traditional models of ethnic entrepreneurship, choosing that path in the face of structural constraints, while the more educated (who are exceptionally so, compared to most other groups) most likely pursue entrepreneurship with much more freedom, with attractive professional opportunities as an alternative. This narrative will be developed further in the next chapter.

Nationwide Patterns

This section uses two U.S. Census data sources: the American Community Survey (ACS) and the Survey of Business Owners (SBO), which provide complementary perspectives on entrepreneurship. The ACS was discussed in chapter 2, and as a household-level survey, it picks up part-time and smaller entrepreneurs, whereas the SBO directly collects data from businesses identified as such by tax records.[41] The ACS data used in this chapter cover the period 2006 to 2010, and yielded about 13.4 million business owners, of whom about 135,000 were identified as Indian American. The SBO data are from 2007, the latest available at the time of this analysis, and had about 26.3 million firms whose owners' ethnicity was identifiable;[42] about 308,000 of these were Indian Americans. The SBO data can be split further into firms with and without employees. For all firms with owners whose ethnicity was identifiable, about 5.3 million (about 20 percent) had employees, with the rest having no employees other than the owner. For Indian-American firms, the proportion with employees was somewhat higher than the national average, at over one-third (about 109,000 firms).

Size and Economic Importance

According to the SBO data, in 2007 (table 5.1), Indian-American-owned firms had about $151.8 billion in sales, 844,000 employees, and total annual payrolls of over $26.8 billion. The totals for all firms classifiable by ethnicity of owners were almost $11 trillion in sales,[43] 56.6 million employees, and aggregate annual payrolls of $1.9 trillion. As an initial measure of the contribution of these Indian-American-owned businesses, note that the ratio of number of businesses, sales, employees, and payrolls for the group to the respective national totals exceeds the Indian-American population proportion of about 1 percent; this disproportionate contribution is true of the average figures as well.[44] As noted earlier in the chapter, the rate of business ownership for Indian Americans is not the highest among immigrant groups—in particular, Korean Americans have considerably higher entrepreneurship rates.

How do firms run by Indian Americans compare with those in the mainstream and those run by members of other ethnic groups? The basic story is that Indian-American firms are smaller, but they do better once size is controlled for; this is consistent with being a recently arrived but high-human-capital immigrant group. Table 5.1 has numbers on average sales, employees, and payroll per

Table 5.1 **Sales, Employees, and Payrolls**

	All Firms	All Firms Classifiable	White, Non-Hispanic	Indian	Japanese	Korean	Chinese
Total number of firms with and without employees	27,092,908	26,294,860	20,334,877	308,491	108,338	192,509	423,650
Total number of firms with employees	5,735,562	5,189,968	4,390,891	109,151	22,820	71,411	109,653
Total number of firms without employees	21,357,346	21,104,892	15,943,986	199,340	85,518	121,098	313,997
Average sales and receipts, all firms ($1,000's)	1,108	416	486	492	363	407	336
Average sales and receipts, firms with employees ($1,000's)	5,066	1,930	2,079	1,285	1,573	1,007	1,165
Average sales and receipts, firms without employees ($1,000's)	46	44	48	58	40	53	47
Average annual payroll ($1,000's) per employer firm	841	374	403	244	314	141	189
Average number of employees per employer firm	20.45	10.91	11.53	7.73	9.17	5.93	7.13
Average number of employees per firm (all firms)	4.33	2.15	2.49	2.74	1.93	2.20	1.84

Source: Authors' calculations from Survey of Business Owners, 2007.

firm for Indian Americans and several other Asian ethnic groups. By these average measures, Indian-American firms overall are comparable to Non-Hispanic
White firms in sales per firm and employees per firm, and do somewhat better
than firms of the other Asian ethnic groups. Separating firms with and without
employees reveals that Indian-American firms' sales advantage is restricted to
those without employees, which overall also have quite low per-firm sales in
the aggregate (less than one-third of the total sales of all firms with employees).
Among employer firms, Non-Hispanic White firms are considerably larger in
sales, payrolls, and employees per firm—well ahead of the other ethnic groups
(including Indian Americans), with Japanese-American firms a partial exception. This differential is persistent from earlier data, possibly reflecting the age of
firms and the durability of older firms' reputational capital and customer bases.

The sales advantage of Indian-American-run firms vis-à-vis the other Asian
ethnic groups can be broken down by size categories (figure 5.1). For the two
highest sales-level categories, Indian-American-run businesses have proportions
higher than those of any of the other comparison groups, and higher even than in
the overall distribution (excluding publicly held firms). This fact, combined with
the average figures, is indicative of a size distribution of Indian-American firms
with fewer extremely large firms, but a healthy number of sizable companies.
Similarly, for the next two size categories, the percentages of Indian-American
firms are mostly higher than for the other three Asian-American groups.

Figure 5.2 further uncovers the source of differences in average size by showing employee size distributions of employer firms. Comparing the distribution
of employee numbers of Indian-American and Non-Hispanic White firms,
Indian-American firms have slightly higher percentages in the lower four size
categories, and correspondingly lower percentages in the higher four size categories. At the upper end, the percentage point differences are small, but they
represent considerable proportionate differences; for example, the percentage
of firms with more than 500 employees is almost three times as great for Non-
Hispanic White firms as for Indian-American firms.

Industry Patterns

Indian-American business owners were quite distinct in the pattern of industries in which they operated in 2007, in comparison to the mainstream (Non-
Hispanic Whites), as well as the Asian groups used as comparators. Some of
these differences are also distinct from the overall occupational patterns of the
community (see chapter 3), and are indicative of ethnic niches in entrepreneurship, discussed earlier in this chapter.[45] In particular, Indian-American firms
were more concentrated in Professional and Technical Services, Retail Trade,
Health Care, Accommodation and Food Services, and Transportation and

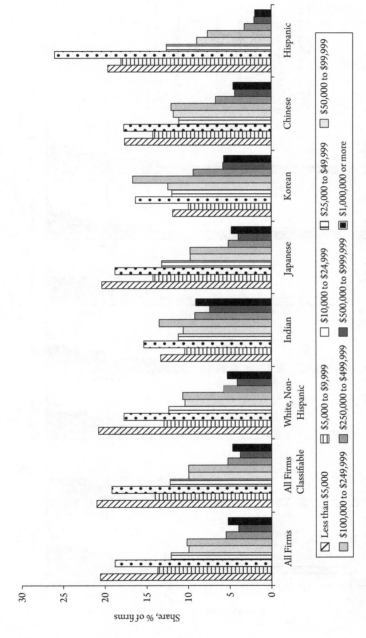

Figure 5.1 Annual Sales for Businesses Owned by Indian Americans and Selected Other Groups, 2007.

Source: Survey of Business Owners, 2007.

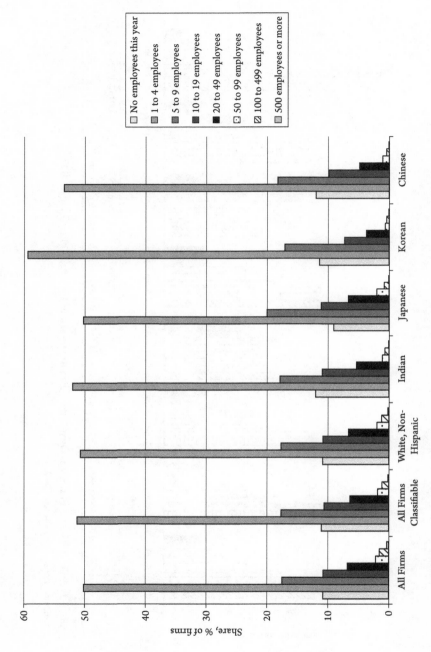

Figure 5.2 Numbers of Employees for Businesses Owned by Indian American and Selected Other Groups, 2007.

Source: Survey of Business Owners, 2007.

Warehousing. There were strong differences in industry patterns for firms with employees and those without employees (figures 5.3 and 5.4).

Figure 5.3, for firms with employees, shows an industry distribution that was heavily concentrated (much more so than for other ethnic or mainstream groups) with just two industries, Retail Trade and Accommodation and Food Services, accounting for more than half of Indian-American firms.[46] The industries in this figure are ordered by the percentage of all Indian-American firms that are in the industry. The next two most popular industries were Health Care and Social Assistance, and Professional, Scientific, and Technical Services, which accounted for another 31 percent of Indian-American firms.[47] Another notable feature in comparing Indian-American firms to the mainstream was their relative absence from Construction, which accounted for the largest number of firms owned by Non-Hispanic Whites, at over 15 percent.[48]

For firms without employees (figure 5.4), one striking difference is that the percentage in Accommodation and Food Services was substantially lower. Professional, Scientific, and Technical Services, Transportation, Health Care and Retail had the largest percentages, in that order. These four industries accounted for close to 56 percent of all Indian-American firms without employees—higher than the four-industry concentration ratio for other groups in the study, but much less (in absolute and relative terms) than the concentration for firms with employees. For firms without employees, there were differences again in industry presence of Indian-American business owners versus the Asian-American comparison groups, but also similarities (for example, Professional, Scientific, and Technical Services was the most common industry for both Chinese-American and Japanese-American firms). The high percentage of Indian-American firms without employees that were in the Transportation and Warehousing sector was somewhat distinctive, perhaps indicating a high presence in specific occupations such as taxi driving (see also chapter 3).

The ACS data broadly confirms industry patterns in the SBO data (figure 5.5). Recall that the ACS data are at the household level, so they exclude larger enterprises, but can still include smaller incorporated businesses, as well as unincorporated self-employment. One important advantage of the ACS data is that they include information on whether business owners were born in the United States or not, enabling examination of differences in industry presence between immigrant and nonimmigrant business owners. Compared to all business owners, Indian Americans were more concentrated in Retail, Health Care, Accommodation Services, and Transportation. For each of these four industries, the proportion of Indian Americans was more than double the national rate. Professional Services was the third most popular sector for Indian-American businesses, but the proportion was less than that for the nation as a whole. In the Wholesale sector also, the proportion of Indian-American businesses was higher

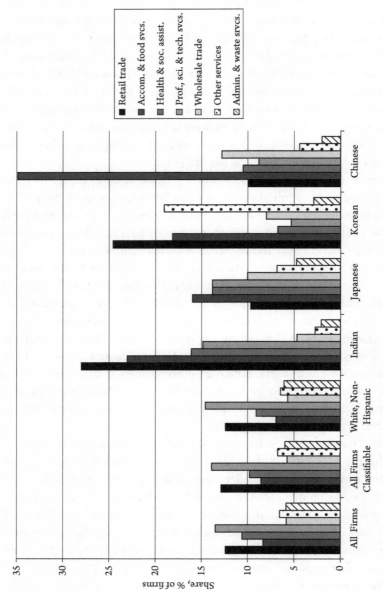

Figure 5.3 Industry Distribution for Businesses with Employees, Indian American and Selected Other Groups, 2007.

Source: Survey of Business Owners, 2007.

Note: Top 7 sectors based on Indian-American shares.

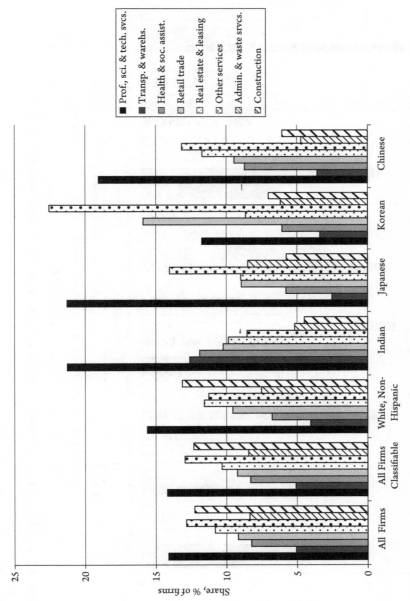

Figure 5.4 Industry Distribution for Businesses without Employees, Indian American and Selected Other Groups, 2007.

Source: Survey of Business Owners, 2007.

Note: Top 8 sectors based on Indian-American firms.

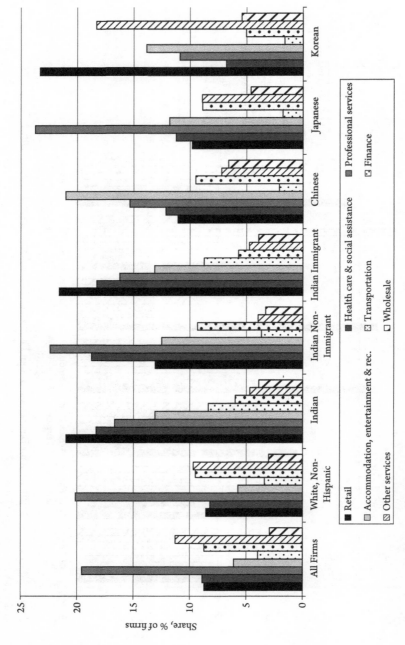

Figure 5.5 Distribution of Businesses by Industry, Indian American and Selected Other Groups, 2006–2010.

Source: American Community Survey, 2006–2010.

Note: Top 8 sectors for Indian-American firms.

than the national figure. On the other hand, the proportion of Indian-American business owners was lower than the national figure in the Information industry as well, though the percentages were quite small.[49]

Figure 5.5 also reveals interesting differences between immigrants and U.S.-born Indian Americans. The latter group was less likely to be in Retail Trade or in Transportation, but more likely to be in Finance, Information, Professional Services, and Educational Services. There was not any apparent shift of this group out of Health Care and Social Assistance, or out of Accommodation. In those two cases, it is possible that changes within sectors are masked in the overall percentages, since these two sectors are quite broadly defined and likely to be more diverse than, say, Retail or Wholesale. For example, second-generation Indian-American motel owners may have larger or higher quality properties.[50]

Sales/Earnings and Industry Patterns

The distributions of sales by industries can be used to explore to what extent differences in average performance across ethnic groups may be attributed to differences in industry choices versus other factors. Of course, those other factors might have played a role in the industry choices themselves. The following analysis will show that differences in average performance across groups were largely *not* due to differences in industry choices.

Figures 5.6 and 5.7 show SBO data on average sales, disaggregated by industry, for firms with employees and without employees, respectively. In each figure, the industries are listed by sales rank per firm for Indian-American firms. For firms with employees, there were few industries where Indian Americans did better than the national averages, with Professional, Scientific, and Technical Services standing out in this respect. In several industries, Indian-American firms had higher average sales than all or some of the three other Asian-American comparison groups, with the most significant cases being Professional, Scientific, and Technical Services (once more), as well as Health Care. For firms without employees (figure 5.7), Indian-American firms did better than the national average and firms of other ethnic groups in industries where they had a strong relative presence, such as Retail Trade, Wholesale Trade, Health Care, and Accommodation and Food Services, suggesting benefits from occupational clustering.

ACS data on earnings of business owners by industry are in figure 5.8. Consistent with the SBO data of table 5.1, earnings for Indian-American business owners are considerably higher than the national average, and higher than the three other Asian-American groups considered here. In addition, average earnings for Indian U.S.-born or nonimmigrants are similar to those for Indian immigrants. However, the distribution of earnings across industries shows some

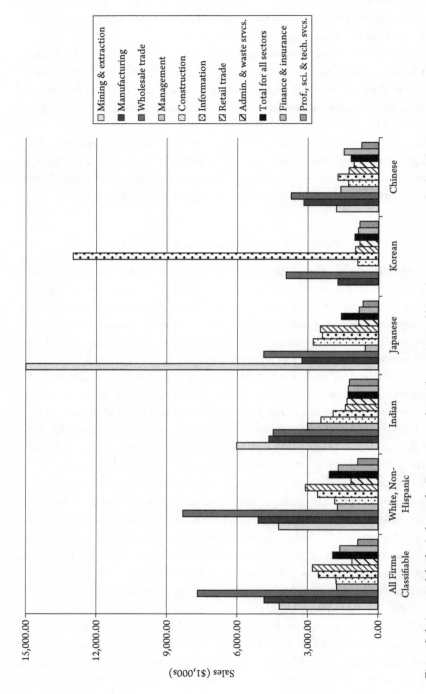

Figure 5.6 Average Sales by Industry for Businesses with Employees, Owned by Indian Americans and Selected Other Groups, 2007.

Source: Survey of Business Owners, 2007.

Note: Japanese-American data for mining/extraction is 20,715. It has been cut off for better visual representation. Top 11 sectors for Indian-American firms.

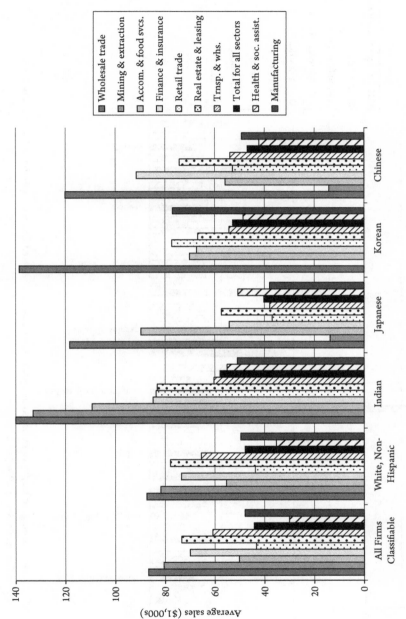

Figure 5.7 Average Sales by Industry for Businesses without Employees, Owned by Indian Americans and Selected Other Groups, 2007.

Source: Survey of Business Owners, 2007.

Note: Top 11 sectors for Indian-American firms.

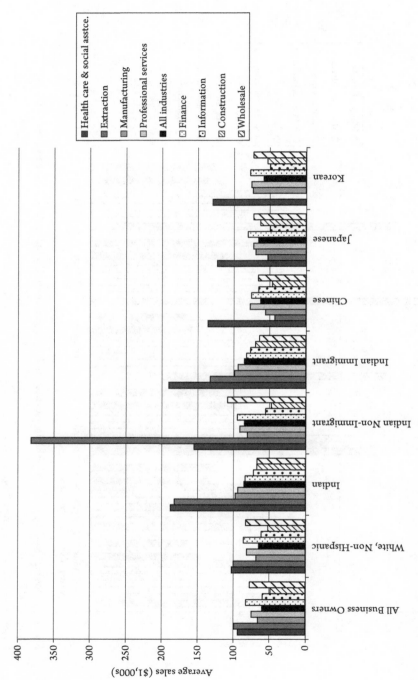

Figure 5.8 Average Earnings of Businesses Owned by Indian Americans and Selected Other Groups, by Industry, 2006–2010.

Source: American Community Survey, 2006–2010.

Note: Top 9 sectors for Indian-American firms.

significant differences between Indian immigrants and nonimmigrants, with particularly striking divergence in Wholesale Trade.[51]

Next, the SBO data is used to decompose sales or earnings differences into those that can be attributed to different industry choices and a residual, which would be a purer "group effect." This group effect might be further traced to education or other characteristics, but those connections cannot be directly identified. The methodology used for this decomposition, known as "shift-share analysis" is described in this chapter's appendix. The results for firms with and without employees are in tables 5.2 and 5.3, respectively. For firms with employees, Indian-American firms on average had sales almost $800,000 less than Non-Hispanic White firms, with less than one-third of this sales gap being attributable to the difference in distribution across industries. Compared to Japanese-American firms, Indian-American firms again had a sales gap, almost $300,000 in this case, but with almost two-thirds of this difference potentially explained by differences in industry choices. On the other hand, Indian-American firms had higher average sales than Chinese-American and Korean-American firms, but lagged with respect to the industry composition effects.

Comparisons for firms without employees are more uniform across different groups. Compared to the mainstream and to other Asian-American groups, Indian-American firms had higher average sales, the difference ranging from

Table 5.2 **Group-Industry Sales Decomposition ($1000s), Firms with Employees**

Comparison Group	White, Non-Hispanic	Japanese	Korean	Chinese
Total Difference in Average Sales	(794.18)	(287.62)	279.13	120.21
Indian Sales Advantage	(561.95)	(109.56)	337.56	319.36
Indian Industry Composition Advantage	(232.23)	(178.06)	(58.43)	(199.15)

Source: Survey of Business Owners, 2007.

Table 5.3 **Group-Industry Sales Decomposition ($1000s), Firms without Employees**

Comparison Group	White, Non-Hispanic	Japanese	Korean	Chinese
Total Difference in Average Sales	9.98	17.63	5.17	11.09
Indian Sales Advantage	6.64	11.83	4.07	11.19
Indian Industry Composition Advantage	3.34	5.80	1.10	(0.10)

Source: Survey of Business Owners, 2007.

about $5,000 to $18,000 a year, and most or all of this difference is attributable to the group effect, with a small positive difference due to the industry composition effect. Hence, unlike firms with employees, Indian-American firms without employees were not disproportionately in industries where average sales tended to be lower. The difference between Indian-American success in firms with and without employees may be an indicator of barriers to transitioning from independent entrepreneurship to larger enterprises, or may be the result of culturally related preferences, but both possibilities are somewhat conjectural.

The ACS data is based on earnings rather than sales, but it allows comparisons between immigrant and U.S.-born Indian Americans, so the shift-share analysis is repeated with this data. Business owners in the ACS data would be most similar to firms without employees in the SBO data. The overall average difference in earnings between Indian-American immigrant and Non-Hispanic White business owners was about $20,500 (table 5.4). The shift-share decomposition implies that this aggregate average difference can be broken down into a group effect of $15,100 and an industry distribution effect of $5,400. These numbers are broadly similar to calculations from the SBO data on sales for all Indian-American businesses without employees. Compared to the other three Asian-American groups, Indian-American firms had average earnings advantages ranging from $19,400 to $26,500, and except in the case of Korean-American firms, this is mostly attributable to a group effect rather than an industry-composition effect. For U.S.-born Indian Americans (table 5.5), there are two clear patterns. First, the differences in average earnings compared to the mainstream or other Asian-American groups were almost identical in magnitude to those for immigrant Indian Americans. However, in all four comparisons, a larger fraction of this difference is attributable to an industry-composition effect rather than to a group effect. For example, the industry effect accounts for about half the difference between U.S.-born Indian Americans and Non-Hispanic Whites, but a quarter of the difference for Indian-American immigrants. Qualitatively, for U.S.-born Indian-American business owners versus their immigrant counterparts, the

Table 5.4 **Group-Industry Earnings Decomposition ($1000s), Indian Immigrants**

Comparison Group	*White, Non-Hispanic*	*Japanese*	*Korean*	*Chinese*
Total Difference in Average Earnings	20.47	19.41	26.54	22.32
Indian Earnings Advantage	15.06	17.10	11.69	17.44
Indian Industry Composition Advantage	5.41	2.32	14.85	4.88

Source: American Community Survey, 2006–2010.

Table 5.5 **Group-Industry Earnings Decomposition ($1000s), U.S.-born Indian Americans**

Comparison Group	White, Non-Hispanic	Japanese	Korean	Chinese
Total Difference in Average Earnings	20.34	19.29	26.41	22.19
Indian Earnings Advantage	10.25	12.84	8.02	13.31
Indian Industry Composition Advantage	10.10	6.45	18.39	8.89

Source: American Community Survey, 2006–2010.

earnings advantage over the mainstream comes more from industry choice than being based on unidentified group characteristics.

Education Matters

Can the data tell us more about the sources of earnings differences for business owners? As for the general population, education matters for business owners, too. The ACS data confirm that Indian-American business owners are more educated than mainstream business owners (figure 5.9): the proportions are similar to those presented in chapter 2, for the general population. Business owners from the comparison Asian groups also have more education on average, but Indian Americans include a much higher proportion with graduate education, again similar to the comparison for the general population. The ACS also has data on fields of undergraduate education (figure 5.10). Compared to the general population of business owners, Indian-American business owners' educational achievements are more heavily weighted toward the natural sciences, engineering and computer science, and medical and health services; they are comparable in business and management; and they are lower in the social sciences and in the arts and humanities. Examining the relatively small number of nonimmigrant Indian-American business owners, there is a tendency for the choice of degree fields to converge toward the national pattern among this group.

To sort out the effect of education on the earnings of business owners, one has to allow for other differences across groups. For example, Indian-American business owners include a higher percentage of males (71.7 percent) than the national average for business owners. On the other hand, the proportion of women business owners is higher than the national average for Chinese-American, Japanese-American, Korean-American, and Hispanic-American businesses. The ACS data show that business owners had a considerably higher rate of homeownership than the national average. Indeed, the homeownership rate is one characteristic for which Indian-American business owners are not

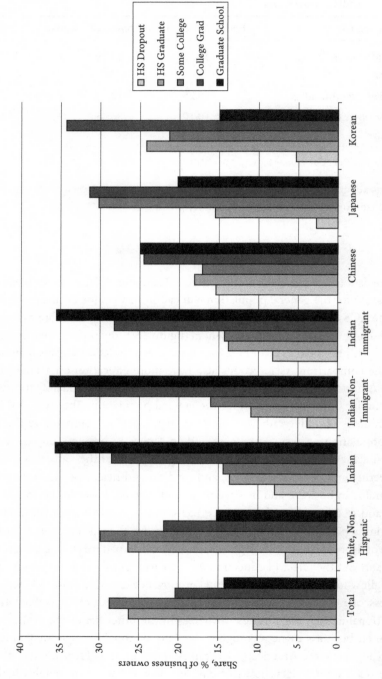

Figure 5.9 Education Levels for Business Owners, 2006–2010.

Source: American Community Survey, 2006–2010.

Note: N's: Total: 13,385,469; White non-Hispanic: 10,360,215; Indian: 135,269; Indian non-Immigrant: 9,962; Indian Immigrant: 125,307; Chinese: 171,285; Japanese: 52,885; Korean: 130,305.

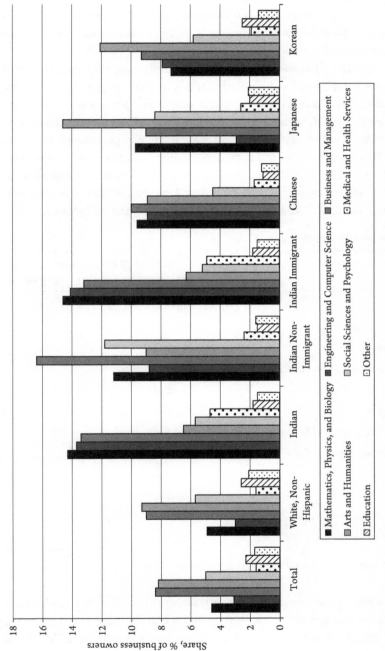

Figure 5.10 Field of College Degrees of Indian American Business Owners and Selected Other Groups, 2010.

Source: American Community Survey, 2010.

Note: Less than bachelor's degree (%): Total: 64.9; White non-Hispanic: 61.9; Indian: 38.4; Indian non-Immigrant: 37.4; Indian Immigrant: 38.5; Chinese: 54.0; Japanese: 48.6; Korean: 51.7.

different from the national average, although they have a slightly lower rate than Non-Hispanic White American business owners. On the other hand, Indian-American business owners had homeownership rates higher than Japanese-American and Korean-American business owners, and similar to those of Chinese-American business owners.

To control for all these varied factors in explaining differences in self-employment earnings across households and across ethnic groups, among the total set of business owners, the ACS data were used to run a series of multi-variate regressions. The variable to be explained was self-employment earnings. Characteristics used to explain this outcome included age, immigrant status, gender, ethnicity, education, industry, and location. Homeownership (or alternatively, home value) was also included as a proxy for wealth.[52] When all these other factors were accounted for, being Indian American did not matter for self-employment earnings.[53] The qualitative results are summarized below.

Influences on Self-Employment Earnings

Variable/Characteristic	Impact on Self-Employment Earnings (Measured by Statistical Significance)
Indian	None
Chinese, Japanese, Korean	None
Other Asian	None
African American, Latino, Native American	Negative
High School	Positive
College Degree	Positive*
Graduate, Professional, PhD Degree	Positive*
Homeownership/Home Value	Positive
Female	Negative
Immigrant	Positive
Immigrant Professional Degree	None*
Indian Immigrant Professional Degree	Positive*

Note: * denotes effect measured relative to next highest education level.

The self-employment earnings equation was also estimated including additional interaction terms, where the characteristic of being Indian American was interacted with age, immigrant status, gender, English use, and education level. With one exception, none of these interaction terms was statistically significant, implying that how these characteristics affected self-employment earnings was not different for Indian Americans than for the average business owner. The exception was for

Indian-American immigrants with graduate or professional degrees: the education premium for this group of Indian Americans was greater than the average. Overall, there is no evidence of any "secret sauce" for the higher self-employment earnings of Indian Americans. In particular, more education and greater familiarity with English[54] are plausible explanations for their relative success.

The pervasiveness of the education factor is important for understanding Indian-American entrepreneurship. In the past, the professions might have been seen as a path out of the social limitations of entrepreneurship, particularly where that enterprise was confined to ethnic enclaves or particular niches. However, the national numbers suggest that more recent entrepreneurs are leveraging their education to move beyond traditional professional routes, taking a chance on getting the big prizes in a winner-take-all economy. Education plays a larger role as the economy becomes more complex and technology driven, while these same factors also increase the social acceptance of being a business person versus being a professional.[55] The next section analyzes the upper end of the Indian-American population so as to understand its entrepreneurship in the context of these broader forces.

An Emerging Elite?

The findings in this section come from a survey of Indian-American business persons conducted between May and November 2013.[56] The sample composition differs from the studies of high-tech entrepreneurs described earlier in this chapter, where sample selection was based on success, entrepreneurship, being an immigrant, and technology focus. This survey is unique in picking up characteristics and performance of nonentrepreneurial professionals as well as entrepreneurs, and the U.S.-born as well as immigrants, across a wide range of industries and locations. On the other hand, the focus here is on Indian Americans only, not immigrants in general.

The survey demographics reveal a highly educated, very successful group of individuals. There were a large number of entrepreneurs in the sample, and their answers indicated a depth and breadth of entrepreneurial experience that would stand out next to most comparison groups. While a third of the group was in information technology or professional and technical services, the distribution of respondents across sectors was quite broad. The overall picture that emerged from the survey responses was of a group with global experiences and outlooks, driven to succeed, and with the skills and backgrounds to achieve their ambitions. At the same time, many of the entrepreneurs in the sample had started out with modest amounts of financial capital, and all of the entrepreneurial respondents implied that a combination of several factors had contributed to their success.

Demographics

The survey yielded 629 responses from business people of Indian origin. Of these, 450, or close to 70 percent, were men, matching the national percentage of males among Indian-American business owners. There were 432 U.S. citizens, with 164 born in the United States. Among the foreign-born, over 90 percent (431) were born in India. The dispersion of the sample across the United States was quite close to the overall geographic distribution of Indian Americans analyzed in chapter 3.[57]

While all the respondents were business professionals, not all were business owners or entrepreneurs (as before, using the two terms interchangeably). The survey asked questions that allowed categorizing the respondents into four groups (table 5.6), as follows. Seventy had been entrepreneurs in the past, but were not currently running their own company. A large proportion, 283, or close to 45 percent, were current entrepreneurs, including those who had also previously founded or co-founded other companies. The first two categories combined, constituting 353 respondents, are referred to collectively as *experienced entrepreneurs*. This proportion is obviously much higher than the rate of entrepreneurship in the overall Indian-American population. Of the nonentrepreneurs, 123 answered affirmatively to a question asking if they planned to start a company in the next twelve months, earning the label *aspiring entrepreneurs* and leaving 153 *nonentrepreneurs*. The large proportion of aspiring entrepreneurs is also noteworthy among a group of professionals that was already relatively successful.

There were only slight differences among the entrepreneurial groups in terms of the proportion born in America.[58] The average age of the sample was 37.8 years, and they had lived in the United States for 18.5 years, on average. Aspiring entrepreneurs were slightly younger on average (34.8 years) and had been living in the United States for slightly less time (15.4 years). The figures for the other three groups were more similar to each other.

In a familiar story, the respondents were mostly extremely well educated (figure 5.11). Over 70 percent of experienced and aspiring entrepreneurs had graduate

Table 5.6 **Entrepreneurship Categories**

	Number	Percent
Past	70	11.13
Current	283	44.99
Aspiring	123	19.55
Not entrepreneur	153	24.32
Total	629	100

Source: Authors' Survey.

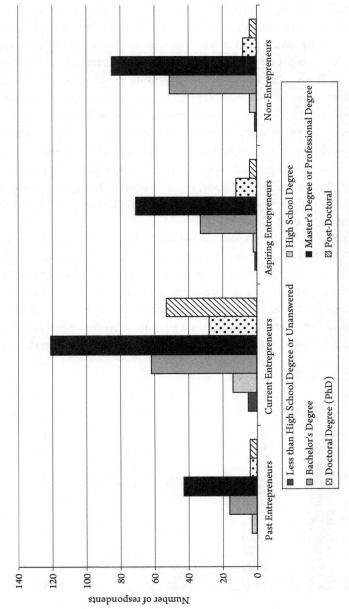

Figure 5.11 Highest Education Completed for Entrepreneurs (Past, Current, Aspiring) and Nonentrepreneurs.

Source: Authors' Survey.

Note: Total Indian-origin entrepreneurs: Less than High School Degree or Unanswered-7; High School Degree-23; Bachelor's Degree-162; Master's Degree or Professional Degree-320; Doctoral Degree (PhD)-52; Post-Doctoral-65.

degrees, comparable to the most highly educated geographic clusters observed in chapter 3, and almost all the others had bachelor's degrees. The percentage of those with college degrees was similar among the nonentrepreneur respondents, but the fraction with graduate qualifications was slightly lower (about 63 percent). Nevertheless, the entire survey sample was distinguished even from the highly educated Indian-American population by its high average level of education.

The survey also asked where respondents had obtained their education (figure 5.12). There were 484 responses regarding the location of undergraduate education: among those who responded, aspiring entrepreneurs and nonentrepreneurs were most likely to have received their first degree only in India (58.6 percent and 56 percent, respectively). Current entrepreneurs were most likely to have obtained their undergraduate degree in the United States (50.7 percent) and to have undergraduate degrees from U.S. as well as from Indian institutions (6.8 percent). Unsurprisingly, in all categories, the percentage of those who had obtained their graduate degrees in the United States was higher than for obtaining undergraduate degrees.

What subjects had the respondents studied? Unsurprisingly, in the light of the data in chapters 2 and 3, and the SBO data earlier in this chapter, engineering and computer science and business and commerce were the top two clusters of undergraduate specialization. Some respondents had combined these two, having studied business/commerce and engineering together. In some cases, respondents reported having studied three or more subjects. Overall, the patterns of undergraduate field choices were suggestive of a conclusion that those in the

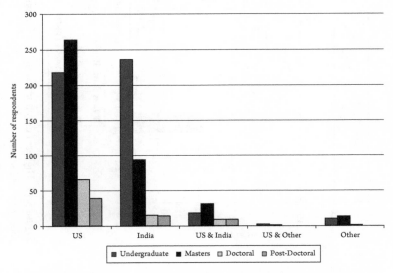

Figure 5.12 Location of Undergraduate, Master's, Doctoral, and Post-doctoral Education Achieved by Survey Respondents.
Source: Authors' Survey.

entrepreneurial category were more diverse in their choices and somewhat more likely to have training across more than one field at the undergraduate level.

At the master's or professional-degree level, the MBA and MS or MTech were by far the most common degree types in any of the four categories of entrepreneurial experience. Current entrepreneurs were somewhat *less* likely to have MBAs. Entrepreneurs were also somewhat more likely to have a combination of graduate qualifications, mirroring the pattern found at the undergraduate level.

Backgrounds

The sample respondents came from highly educated families, on average, and parental entrepreneurship was an important part of the background of the entrepreneurs in the survey. Their motives for coming to the United States, and the regions of India they came from, however, were similar to the broader population of Indian Americans described in chapters 2 and 3. Asked about parents' education and entrepreneurial background, a high 70 percent of respondents reported that their father had a bachelor's degree or better in terms of educational level; this sample was not only highly educated on average, but its members were typically born into relatively well-educated families. There were differences across entrepreneurial categories, with proportions ranging from 60 percent for past entrepreneurs to 78 percent for nonentrepreneurs. The respondents' mothers were also relatively well educated. About 55 percent reported that their mother had a bachelor's degree or better, ranging from 44 percent for past entrepreneurs to 57 percent for nonentrepreneurs.

Answers to a question about parental entrepreneurship (either parent or both) revealed (table 5.7) that almost 35 percent of the sample had a parent who had been an entrepreneur. This proportion was as high as 44.5 percent for current entrepreneurs and 32.9 percent for past entrepreneurs. Even for aspiring entrepreneurs, the proportion who had a parent with entrepreneurship experience was 31.7 percent. In the nonentrepreneur category, however, only 19.6 percent reported a parent with an entrepreneurial background, indicating a clear difference between this group and the others.[59]

The India-born were asked the state in which they were born, eliciting 424 definite responses. The responses indicated some urban bias in the selection of Indians who immigrate to the United States, at least within the sample. For example, 12 percent named Delhi as their place of birth, whereas Delhi has only 1.4 percent of India's population. Maharashtra (12.5 percent of the sample, 9.3 percent of India's population) and Tamil Nadu (12.7 percent of sample, 6 percent of population) were also common birth states, containing two of the other three big metropolitan cities of India (Mumbai and Chennai, respectively). In Tamil Nadu's case, the fact that it and other southern states have

Table 5.7 **Parental Entrepreneurship**

| | Respondents of Indian Origin | | | |
	Yes	No	No response	Total
Entire Sample	218	402	9	629
Percent	34.7	63.9	1.4	100.0
Past Entrepreneurs	23	46	1	70
Percent	32.9	65.7	1.4	100.0
Current Entrepreneurs	126	152	5	283
Percent	44.5	53.7	1.8	100.0
Aspiring Entrepreneurs	39	82	2	123
Percent	31.7	66.7	1.6	100.0
Nonentrepreneurs	30	122	1	153
Percent	19.6	79.7	0.7	100.0

Source: Authors' Survey.

disproportionately provided skilled workers for the U.S. IT sector no doubt plays a role, as discussed in chapter 2. For Andhra Pradesh (which included the major city and Indian IT hub of Hyderabad), the corresponding figures are 13.4 percent of respondents versus 7 percent of India's population, while the figures for Kerala are 5 percent of the sample and 2.8 percent of India's population.[60] The states of Gujarat and Punjab, with disproportionate numbers of U.S. immigrants (see chapter 2), bear that out in the sample, especially when Chandigarh (the shared capital with Haryana) is combined with Punjab. On the other hand, Bihar, Chhattisgarh, Jharkhand, Madhya Pradesh, Odisha, Rajasthan, and especially population-giant Uttar Pradesh all appeared much less frequently as birthplaces in the sample, as compared to their population percentages in India. Overall, the geographic selection of this sample vis-à-vis India as a whole was fairly similar to that of the entire Indian-American population.

If we look at the different categories of entrepreneurial experience or aspirations, we see the numbers are quite small, reducing the reliability of possible conclusions. However, Andhra Pradesh and Tamil Nadu seemed to have relatively higher percentages in the nonentrepreneur category, perhaps reflecting peculiarities of migration from those states into the IT sector, which provides opportunities for rapid advancement and wealth accumulation through stock options without being an entrepreneur. On the other hand, Gujarat and Punjab were birth states where the percentages in the three entrepreneurial categories combined were higher than for nonentrepreneurs from these states. While the numbers are small, these patterns do fit with prior knowledge about propensities for entrepreneurship across different Indian ethnic groups in the United States.[61]

The survey also asked for the number of different countries, U.S. states, and Indian states lived in by the respondents. The responses suggest that entrepreneurs in the sample had a greater diversity of experience compared to nonentrepreneurs, with respect to different countries and Indian states, but not with respect to U.S. states. This finding is consistent with the hypothesis that experiencing diversity goes hand in hand with entrepreneurship, since there is much greater heterogeneity across countries or Indian states, as compared to states in the United States. This experience of diversity can plausibly lead to greater tolerance of ambiguity and risk.[62]

The immigrants in the sample were asked their main motive for coming to the United States. Of those who responded (381 of 464), 42.3 percent gave "education" as their main motive, closely followed by 37.3 percent who reported "employment." The other options of "joining or accompanying family" and "to start a business" were a distant third and fourth frequent as responses. For current entrepreneurs, however, "education" was twice as common as "employment" as the main motive. This group, unsurprisingly, was also much more likely to have come specifically to start a business. Interestingly, in a probable reflection of the H-1 visa program and IT Generation discussed in chapter 2, the proportions and ranking of "education" and "employment" were reversed among aspiring entrepreneurs as compared to the current entrepreneurs.

Characteristics of Entrepreneurship

The survey respondents included a relatively large number of experienced entrepreneurs, but unlike previous surveys, they had not been selected on the basis of leading successful high-tech companies. This provides a broader picture of Indian-American entrepreneurship than previous surveys. What did emerge was a picture of individuals who had combined their education with substantial experience in their relevant industry (a decade, on average) to start out on their own, and had relied on significant, but usually not large amounts of financial capital to make these starts. The responses suggested persistence, vision, global outlooks, and an ability to combine a range of positive personal and societal factors into eventual success.

The survey asked respondents to choose from a menu of options describing the industry or sector of their current work (table 5.8). The most common chosen sector was Information, with 17 percent of respondents. This is much higher than the percentage for the overall population of Indian-American business owners as gleaned from the SBO data. There was no strong difference between the proportions for experienced versus aspiring entrepreneurs or nonentrepreneurs.

Table 5.8 **Sector of Employment (Percentages)**

	All	Past Entrepreneurs	Current Entrepreneurs	Aspiring Entrepreneurs	Non-Entrepreneurs
Agriculture, Forestry, Fishing & Hunting	1.7	0.0	3.2	0.8	0.7
Mining, Quarrying, and Oil & Gas Extraction	1.0	1.4	0.4	2.4	0.7
Utilities	1.4	4.3	0.7	0.8	2.0
Construction	4.5	8.6	4.9	3.3	2.6
Wholesale Trade	6.5	2.9	8.1	9.8	2.6
Information	17.0	20.0	15.9	19.5	15.7
Finance and Insurance	8.1	7.1	5.3	11.4	11.1
Real Estate and Rental & Leasing	1.7	0.0	2.5	2.4	0.7
Professional, Scientific, and Technical Services	16.7	15.7	13.8	18.7	20.9
Management of Cos. & Enterprises	4.3	2.9	4.9	4.9	3.3
Admin. & Support and Waste Mgt. & Remed. Svces.	0.5	0.0	1.1	0.0	0.0

Educational Services	3.3	2.9	2.1	4.9	4.6
Health Care & Social Assistance	5.6	5.7	6.4	7.3	2.6
Arts, Entertainment, & Rec.	3.2	1.4	5.7	0.8	1.3
Accomm. & Food Svces.	2.7	1.4	4.6	1.6	0.7
Public Administration	2.5	2.9	3.2	1.6	2.0
Other Svces. (except Pub. Admin.)	1.0	1.4	0.4	0.8	2.0
Other	18.1	21.4	16.6	8.9	26.8
No response/ N.A.	0.2	0.0	0.4	0.0	0.0
Total	100.0	100.0	100.0	100.0	100.0

Note: auto repair, software, architecture, advertising, online marketing, consulting, pharmaceutical, nonprofit, food manufacturing and restaurants, and transportation were among many listed under "other."

Source: Authors' Survey.

The next most common sector was Professional, Scientific, and Technical Services, with 16.7 percent of respondents. Here, the percentages for both experienced entrepreneur categories were lower than for nonentrepreneurs or aspiring entrepreneurs. The third most common sector was Finance and Insurance, and here as well, experienced entrepreneurs were less common (7.1 percent and 5.3 percent) than their counterparts in the other two subgroups (over 11 percent), though the absolute numbers in such cases start to become quite small.

Overall, the distribution across sectors did not show strong differences between experienced entrepreneurs and other categories, nor between aspiring entrepreneurs and those who expressed no such wish, with one exception in the latter case being Wholesale Trade, with a much higher proportion among aspiring entrepreneurs versus nonentrepreneurs. Finally, there were no dramatic differences between the sectoral distribution of sample respondents and the national census figures for Indian-American business owners.

Asked about the revenue of their companies (table 5.9), about 90 percent responded. Almost one-fourth worked for large firms, with over $50 million in revenue. As one would expect, this fraction was only about 10 percent for current entrepreneurs, and the percentages were correspondingly higher for the other three categories. The smallest two categories in the survey covered annual revenue amounts up to $1 million. About one-third of the sample was in these lowest revenue categories, while for current entrepreneurs it was about 42 percent and for nonentrepreneurs it was dramatically lower. Interestingly, for aspiring entrepreneurs, the entire revenue size distribution of the firms they worked for was lower than for past entrepreneurs or nonentrepreneurs, suggesting they

Table 5.9 **Revenue Range for Current Company, 2011 and 2012**

	2011	2012
	Percent	*Percent*
Between 0 and $250,000	16.7	13.2
Between $250,000 and $1 million	17.8	16.7
Between $1 million and $5 million	14.8	14.3
Between $5 million and $25 million	12.4	11.6
Between $25 million and $50 million	9.7	11.0
More than $50 million	20.0	24.2
Don't Know	6.4	5.4
Do not wish to disclose/Not Applicable	2.2	3.7
Total	100.0	100.0

Source: Authors' Survey.

might be working in smaller, more entrepreneurial firms than other nonentrepreneurs. Overall, the survey sample was skewed toward individuals working for larger firms, as compared to Indian-American-owned firms with employees in the SBO data.

The responses about numbers of employees across locations suggested that the Indian Americans in the sample tended to work for companies with deeper connections to India than the typical U.S. multinational. Three location options were given: the United States, India, and other countries. For example, 5.7 percent of current entrepreneurs reported having no U.S.-based employees, while 60.8 percent of them reported having employees in India. The latter figure was even higher for aspiring entrepreneurs: 73.1 percent worked for a company with employees in India. The responses were consistent with a picture of larger firms being more globalized, which is unsurprising, but a striking feature was that the percentages of firms with employees in India were close to those having employees in the entire rest of the world.

Given prior conceptual discussions of possible drivers of entrepreneurship, including opportunities and resources, a critical question concerned entrepreneurs' motivations for choosing that path. Respondents were given seven different choices, and asked to rank each one on a scale from 1 (Not a Motivator) to 5 (Extremely Important Motivator) (figure 5.13). Among the experienced entrepreneurs, on average the strongest reason for choosing entrepreneurship was "Independence and 'to be my own boss'" (mean score 3.74), very closely followed by "To pursue something new" (mean 3.65). Not far behind was a third reason, "To solve a problem to benefit society" (mean 3.61). These entrepreneurs were avowedly driven by "pull" motives that fit with the image of enterprise that de Tocqueville described so long ago, as well as more recent psychological characterizations of entrepreneurs.[63] The other reasons that respondents ranked were "Money" (average score 3.27), "Influence of peers" (2.71), "Fame" (2.66), and the most negative one, "Laid off or difficulty finding work" (2.41). The low importance given to the last reason probably reflects the selection of the sample, which would not include those who might be struggling to find work or make careers.[64]

The survey also asked about financing of entrepreneurial ventures (figure 5.14); their last such effort for past entrepreneurs, their ongoing venture for current entrepreneurs, and anticipated needs and sources for aspiring entrepreneurs. Almost one-fourth of the experienced entrepreneurs reported raising $50,000 or less for their venture. On the other hand, only 13 percent of aspiring entrepreneurs anticipated that this amount would be enough for them. Among past entrepreneurs, the most common range of financing reported was the next lowest category, from $50,000 to $250,000, with 32.9 percent. For current entrepreneurs, the percentage in this range was much lower, at 18.4 percent, with higher percentages than past entrepreneurs in all the higher financing ranges.

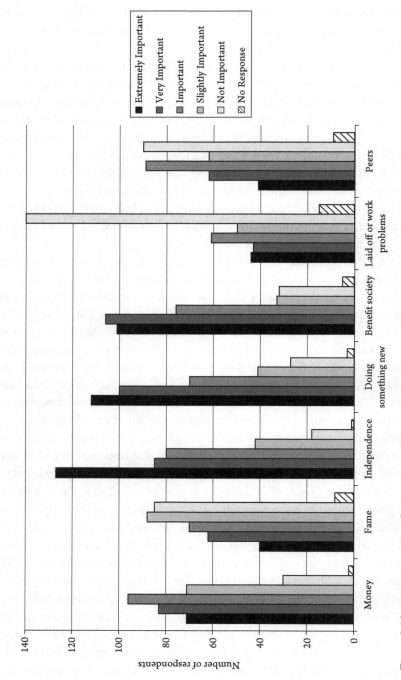

Figure 5.13 Motivations Given by Experienced Entrepreneurs for Founding a Venture.
Source: Authors' Survey.

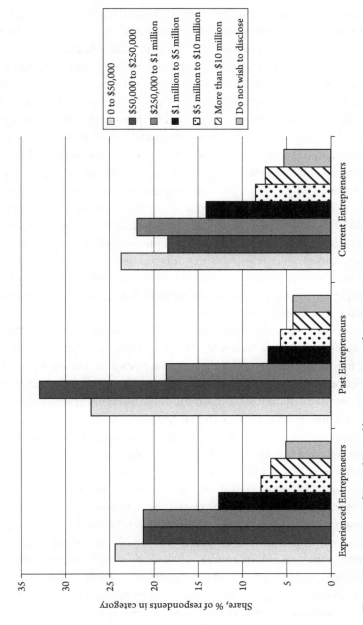

Figure 5.14 Amount of Capital Raised by Entrepreneurs for Current Venture.
Source: Authors' Survey.

Aspiring entrepreneurs, on the other hand, aside from the lowest category, had conservative estimates of how much funding they expected they would need, with 35 percent choosing the second lowest funding range.

Also, aspiring entrepreneurs were more optimistic about receiving institutional funding than their experienced counterparts (figure 5.15). When asked about the main source of financing, 48.4 percent of experienced entrepreneurs reported personal or family savings, whereas only 22.9 percent reported using a business loan or line of credit from a financial institution as the main source of financing. Aspiring entrepreneurs, however, anticipated using this latter option 38.2 percent of the time versus 33.1 percent for personal or family savings.

To round out the picture of financing, the survey asked about how much personal capital had been, or was expected to be put, into the individual's venture. Of experienced entrepreneurs, 28.6 percent reported investing $50,000 or less of their own money, whereas 14.6 percent of aspiring entrepreneurs expected to put in so little. Whereas 20 percent of current entrepreneurs reported putting in over $1 million of their personal capital, only 12.2 percent of aspiring entrepreneurs expected to do so. Whether this represents undue optimism or changing circumstances (e.g., differences in the industries or technologies of future versus current startups) is a matter of conjecture. The fact that one-fifth of current entrepreneurs in the sample had the capacity to invest over $1 million of personal capital further indicates the elite nature of this sample.

Entrepreneurial strategies have also been the concern of much of the prior analysis of ethnic entrepreneurship. About two-thirds of past entrepreneurs and over four-fifths of current entrepreneurs reported having experience in the industry or sector of their past or current venture. The average amount of experience was just over a decade for each group. These numbers fit with other studies of entrepreneurship: whiz kids are the exception rather than the rule. The aspiring entrepreneurs were quite similar to their experienced counterparts: over 70 percent reported experience in the industry or sector of their future venture, and the average number of years of experience was only one year less.

Various questions were asked about the number of companies founded or co-founded by the entrepreneurs in the sample: about 40 percent reported founding one company, one-fourth reported founding two, and about 12 percent reported founding or co-founding three companies. Over 20 percent reported starting four or more companies in their careers. Asked about the number of companies still operational, only 6.5 percent of the respondents reported that none of their startups were still in operation; 46.7 percent reported one, 19.8 percent reported two, and 8.2 percent reported three, while 18 percent reported having four or more of their founded companies still operational. Patterns of success and failure were very similar to those implied by the distribution of survivorship. Hence the sample included many successful serial entrepreneurs.

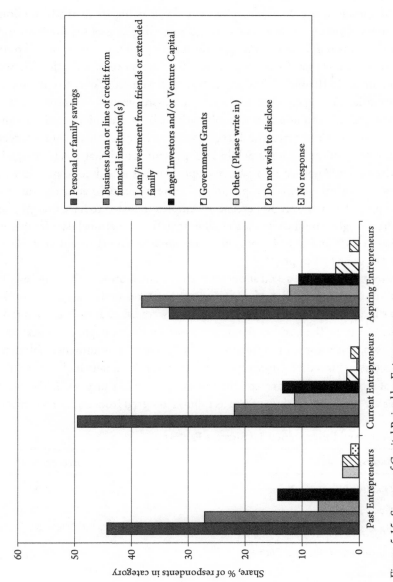

Figure 5.15 Sources of Capital Raised by Entrepreneurs.

Source: Authors' Survey.

What was "success" for these entrepreneurs? It was measured indirectly, through questions about value and outcomes. Past entrepreneurs were asked about the value of their most recent venture, and 35.7 percent reported that this was less than $1 million. Another 32.9 percent reported a value of between $1 and $10 million, and 25.7 percent reported values higher than $10 million: a high proportion of significant success, although one cannot say how this translated into personal wealth. Among current entrepreneurs, one-fourth reported valuations of less than $1 million, while 30.4 percent reported values between $1 million and $10 million. The percentage with valuations over $10 million was a substantial 35.7, again indicating a very successful group of entrepreneurs.

Experienced entrepreneurs were also asked about the outcome of their most recent venture. Almost two-thirds (63.5 percent) reported that their most recent venture was still operational, while 19.3 percent stated that it had merged or been acquired. Another 11.3 percent reported that it had gone public, which represents an exceptional proportion of entrepreneurial ventures. The combined proportion of over 30 percent of ventures reported to have merged, been acquired, or gone public was much higher than that in national data for venture-funded firms,[65] and only 4.8 percent of respondents' most recent ventures had closed or gone bankrupt.

Entrepreneurs were asked about the factors contributing to their success. This question gets to the heart of opportunity structures and strategies, discussed earlier in the chapter. Nine different options were offered, each to be rated on a scale of 1 to 5. The number of nonresponses for each category was very small. Therefore, this sample of entrepreneurs had a clear, multidimensional view of the factors behind their success. The averages were generally higher than in the case of motivational factors, and the responses were less dispersed. The average scores are reported in tabular form as follows, ordered from highest to lowest.

Perceived Entrepreneurial Success Factors

Success Factor	Average Score
Quality of Founding Team	4.00
Good Timing	3.82
Professional and Social Networks	3.82
Learning from Previous Failures	3.73
Education	3.73
Financial and Non-Financial Support from Family and Friends	3.51
Personal Capital	3.46
External Capital: Debt and Equity	3.44
Technology Developed or Obtained	3.39

In some respects, the responses bear out conventional wisdom, with the quality of the founding team, good timing, and professional and social networks taking precedence over other factors. Education was not ignored by this highly educated group. The dimension of financing considered most important was one that was intertwined with nonfinancial support, providing an indicator of the importance of social capital. Technology comes in last, but it was still considered important on average, and again this reflects the special nature of the sample, which is of highly educated entrepreneurs, with relatively large proportions in technology or skill-intensive sectors.

Ties to India

The survey sought to document perceived and tangible links to India among the respondents. To elicit how the respondents viewed themselves in terms of what might be labeled "Indian" characteristics, they were asked if they identified with Indian values. Response rates were close to 100 percent, and over 85 percent in all categories answered yes. These affirmative respondents were given eight different "Indian values" and asked whether each had had a positive, negative or no impact for them. Nonresponse rates for each value were low. Overall, "Strong family ties" was viewed as most positive, with 77.1 percent of respondents judging their impact to be positive. The other values, in order, were "Respect for elders" (73.8 percent), "Comfort with social diversity" (70.7 percent), "Group harmony and co-operation" (68.7 percent), "Spirituality" (61.4 percent), "Thrift" (55.3 percent), and "Comfort with uncertainty" (55 percent). "Argumentativeness" (playing off Amartya Sen's work[66]) came in a distant last, with 30 percent viewing it as having a positive impact versus 27.7 percent viewing its impact as negative. For other values, percentages viewing them as having negative impacts were higher than those judging no impact, with the difference ranging from small (comfort with uncertainty) to considerable (spirituality).

Importantly, both nonentrepreneurs and aspiring entrepreneurs were much less positive about thrift as an Indian value, as opposed to experienced entrepreneurs. They were also less positive about comfort with uncertainty, as compared to entrepreneurs. Interestingly, they were significantly less positive about argumentativeness as well, compared to entrepreneurs.[67] Differences across the groups were smaller in terms of judgments on positive impacts of the other values, indicating that experienced entrepreneurs seemed to differ from their nonentrepreneurial counterparts in certain aspects of their worldviews while being similar in terms of their overall identification with perceived Indian values. The importance of family ties, across all categories, fits well with the demographic analysis of chapters 2 and 3, while there are also suggestions in these responses of what makes entrepreneurs different from their professional counterparts.

The survey also explored business, financial, political, and personal ties, and found very high levels of such linkages. Over 70 percent reported that their firm had a strategic relationship in India (R&D or an offshore unit, major suppliers, key partners, major customers, and merger and acquisition activities being the options). For each of the five types of strategic relationships, respondents with current ties reported similar plans for the following twelve months, indicating continuity of engagement. These ongoing strategic relationships existed at roughly similar levels across all four categories of respondents: India was clearly in the sights of these business people and the firms they worked for, more so than the typical U.S. firm.[68]

A further set of questions explored financial links with India. For the entire sample of respondents of Indian origin, 52.3 percent said they had sent personal capital to India in the past twelve months, with current and aspiring entrepreneurs having higher percentages, and nonentrepreneurs and past entrepreneurs lower ones. When asked if their current company had received capital from India in the past twelve months, 37 percent of the sample responded affirmatively, with the percentages being higher (41 percent and 45 percent, respectively) for current and aspiring entrepreneurs, and below 30 percent for nonentrepreneurs and past entrepreneurs.

Response rates to a question about the amount of personal capital sent to India in the past twelve months were 50 percent or lower, but of those who responded, about 40 percent of past entrepreneurs sent from $500,000 to over $5 million. For current entrepreneurs, about 20 percent of respondents sent over $5 million of personal capital to India. When asked about the uses of personal capital, respondents could choose multiple options. Across all four categories, the most common choice was for family and friends, with over 70 percent of those who answered affirmatively reporting this purpose.

Investments in real estate were the second most common purpose, with proportions over one-half. Investments in stocks or mutual funds was the third most common purpose across all groups, though the proportions dropped off considerably for nonentrepreneurs (29 percent) and past entrepreneurs (40 percent), remaining high for aspiring (50.7 percent) and current (58.4 percent) entrepreneurs. The difference across groups was most striking for the choice of sending personal capital to India to invest in other companies. Half of current entrepreneurs reported this purpose, compared to one-third of aspiring entrepreneurs, 30 percent of past entrepreneurs, and 20 percent of nonentrepreneurs.

Turning to political and business links, respondents were asked about their political activity in India and the United States. Current entrepreneurs were by far the most politically active, with 58 percent reporting such activity (27.6 percent in both India and the United States, 26.1 percent only in India, and 4.2 percent only in the United States). This indicates a very high level of engagement with Indian politics, presumably because Indian policies are more of a constraint on business, especially when involving foreign participation. Past entrepreneurs were next in the level of political engagement, followed by aspiring entrepreneurs, and nonentrepreneurs far behind, with only 22.9 percent reporting political activity. Aspiring entrepreneurs were somewhat more likely to be engaged in political activity in the United States only, as compared to the other three groups.

Asked about the importance of U.S.–India relationships for their business activities, there was greater similarity across groups, with around three-fourths reporting that such relationships were somewhat or very important. There was a slightly greater difference across groups when asked a similar question about the importance of U.S.–India relationships for their political activities, with over two-thirds of current and aspiring entrepreneurs judging them to be somewhat or very important, versus less than 60 percent for past entrepreneurs and nonentrepreneurs.

Patterns of Difference: Immigrant Status, Gender, Age, and Experience

Four important dimensions of difference were also analyzed with the survey responses: between immigrants and U.S.-born, between men and women, between younger and older respondents, and between first-time and seasoned entrepreneurs. In all cases, differences in patterns were statistically tested using chi-square tests of association. Immigrants in the sample were clearly still adapting to their new country: they had lower financial resources, were more likely to have changed industries, and were less likely to be entrepreneurs or have corporate leadership positions. The women in the sample were younger, and again less likely to be in C-level positions, but were just as likely as the men to be entrepreneurs versus nonentrepreneurs. They had somewhat different educational backgrounds and occupational choices, but for this selected group, were close to the men in achievement. The younger respondents were more educated, and the younger entrepreneurs gave hints of changing patterns of entrepreneurship: more attempts, more failures, but also more successes. Finally, the first-time entrepreneurs were slightly older than their experienced counterparts, more likely to be women, had more diverse educational backgrounds, and worked for smaller companies on average. These last findings all fit with a pattern of a community diversifying its entrepreneurial base, beyond the stereotypical man with a strong technical education and industry experience.

Immigrants and U.S.-born

The immigrants in the sample were older (five years, on average), consisted of more men, had mostly not grown up in the United States, and had lived in more countries. Their education levels were more concentrated at the master's level and in technical fields or professional degrees such as MBAs. There were significant differences in the occupational sectors of immigrants and U.S.-born respondents. Immigrants were more concentrated in a few sectors, such as finance, health care, and professional, scientific and technical services. They were also less likely to hold titles such as CEO, CTO, and CFO, and more likely to have titles such as manager, director, and VP. Immigrants in the sample were more likely to be working for larger firms and less likely to be current entrepreneurs.

Among entrepreneurs, immigrants reported smaller amounts of personal capital and total capital raised for their ventures. They were less likely to have had an exit through merger or acquisition or going public, versus continuing to run their company. With respect to motivations, there was not much difference between average responses for the different motivations, but there were significant differences in detailed patterns. For example, immigrants were more likely than U.S.-born respondents to say that fame was not a motivator at all, the U.S.-born had more diverse responses than immigrants with respect to the importance of money as a motivator, and immigrants were *less* likely than the U.S.-born to report being laid off or looking for work as a motivator.

Interestingly, immigrants were more likely than the U.S.-born to be entrepreneurs in a different sector than where they had gained experience,[69] but at the same time they had much more experience than their U.S.-born counterparts. Immigrant entrepreneurs in the sample had founded fewer companies, and also had fewer successes and fewer operational companies. However, they reported fewer failures before their first success. Responding about factors leading to success in entrepreneurship, immigrants rated education, good timing, and the quality of the team somewhat higher than the U.S.-born, and external capital as less important.

Surprisingly, U.S.-born respondents were more likely than immigrants to report strategic relationships with suppliers and customers in India, as well as various financial ties to India. However, immigrants were more likely than their U.S.-born counterparts to invest in Indian real estate. The U.S.-born were more likely than immigrants to discuss U.S. business opportunities with Indian contacts, though there were no differences in their view of the importance of the U.S.–India relationship for their business activities. Finally, the U.S.-born were more politically active in both countries, and viewed the U.S.–India relationship as more important for these activities.

Men and Women

The women in the sample were about four years younger than the men, on average. They were more likely than the men to have been born and grown up in the United States, and were less likely to have studied engineering or computer science, versus business, commerce, or humanities subjects. Occupations reflected these educational choices, with women less likely than men to be in the

IT sector. They were also less likely to be in real estate, but more likely to be in finance or the arts and entertainment. Women in the sample were less likely to be CEOs, and more likely to hold designations such as manager. Women were also more likely to work in smaller firms.

In contrast to national patterns, the rate of entrepreneurship among women in the sample was not significantly lower than for men. Women entrepreneurs were also much more likely than men to have parents who were entrepreneurs. With respect to motivators for becoming an entrepreneur, women reported being laid off or having difficulty finding work, and the example of peers as stronger reasons than did their male counterparts. Consistent with their relative youth, women entrepreneurs in the sample had two and a half years less experience than their male counterparts. Interestingly, they reported having founded more companies on average, and having more operational and successful companies, than the male entrepreneurs, but also more failures before their first success. Compared to the men, the women entrepreneurs viewed financial support from family and friends as more important, and the quality of the founding team as less important.[70]

Our results with respect to gender lie somewhere in the middle of the range of previous studies, which either found significant differences or very minor ones. The latter depended on choosing only successful entrepreneurs,[71] and observed almost no difference between men and women in characteristics beyond a finding that the successful women were more likely than men to have received encouragement and funding from a business partner. The present results are not restricted to successful entrepreneurs, though the sample is weighted toward more educated, successful professionals, but they are specifically for Indian Americans, unlike the other studies. Our findings do hint at some leveling of the entrepreneurship playing field across genders, at the upper end.

Young and Old

To analyze the variation of entrepreneur characteristics with age, the sample was divided into five-year ranges, except at the ends of the distribution (below 25 and above 50). Those born in India were more concentrated in the higher age groups, while younger respondents were more likely to have grown up in the United States. Those who had been in the United States the longest reported having come for education, while more recent immigrants most often reported coming for specific work. The younger cohorts in the sample had slightly higher education levels on average. Respondents' mothers also had significantly less education among the older cohorts.

Among entrepreneurs, older age cohorts more often reported personal savings as the main source of finance, and having companies that were still operational, versus younger entrepreneurs who more often reported exits such as going public. Older entrepreneurs rated money and being laid off as less important motivators for entrepreneurship than younger cohorts. Interestingly, younger entrepreneurs reported, on average, more ventures, more successful ventures, more operational ventures, and also more failures before their first success. All of this suggests a different approach to entrepreneurship, which could reflect a combination of a changing entrepreneurial environment and changing characteristics of the entrepreneurs themselves. Interestingly, there was no major difference in how different age cohorts viewed the various possible success factors.

For several dimensions of business relationships with India, younger entrepreneurs were more likely to give them strategic importance. Younger entrepreneurs were also more likely to send capital to India, particularly for investment in stocks and in other companies. They were more likely to be engaged in discussions of cross-border business opportunities between the United States and India. Finally, younger respondents tended to report political activity, both in India and in the United States, more often than their older counterparts, and more often reported the U.S.–India relationship as important for their business activities.

Experience

The survey also allowed a comparison of first-time and experienced entrepreneurs. First-time entrepreneurs were slightly older, by an average of 1.5 years. The proportion of women was higher, by over 10 percentage points. They were less likely to have a PhD or postdoctoral experience, and more likely to have studied business or commerce versus experienced entrepreneurs who were more likely to have studied engineering. Interestingly, first-time entrepreneurs were more likely to have highly educated parents, but less likely to have a parent who had been an entrepreneur.

The first-time entrepreneurs were less likely to be in the professional and technical services sector, and tended to work for smaller firms on average than those who were on their second or later venture. They had raised less overall capital and less personal capital, were less likely to have majority ownership, and more likely to have a venture that was still operational, versus having been sold or merged. Interestingly, the first-time entrepreneurs rated fame, peer influence, and difficulty in looking for a job as greater motivators for entrepreneurship, as compared to those who were on their second or later venture. On the other hand, there was no significant difference between the two groups in their ratings of success factors for entrepreneurship.

When comparing links to India, the first-time entrepreneurs were quite different from those with more experience. They were less likely to view strategic links to India as important, to have capital from India, or to be sending personal capital to India, with the exception of money for family and friends. They discussed cross-border business opportunities less often, and were also slightly less likely to identify with Indian values (though the percentage remained high). Finally, first-time entrepreneurs gave less importance to U.S.–India ties in business and politics, and they engaged in political activity in either country much less often.

Some Lessons

The mythology of the United States includes its characterization as a land of opportunity and enterprise. At the same time, it is a land of immigrants, and waves of immigrants have pursued enterprise in myriad ways, creating rich case studies of ethnic entrepreneurship. Indian Americans are no exception to this pattern, but as explained in earlier chapters, they have come to the United States with exceptional characteristics and in exceptional circumstances. This chapter's tour through some of the numbers that characterize Indian-American entrepreneurship suggests that this group's education and skills are starting to translate into significant impacts on the American economy. There is a case to be made that entrepreneurs have strong multiplier effects on economic activity, and while the national census data only show glimmers of these possible effects, surveys, including a unique new one with results described in this chapter, hint at a larger economic role for Indian Americans in the future. The next chapter will flesh out the numbers with individual narratives, and further illustrate the diversity and evolution of Indian-American entrepreneurship.

Appendix to Chapter 5
Shift-Share Analysis
Definitions of a, b, c, d—each is a vector

a = % of Indian-American firms in each industry
b = % of other group firms in each industry
c = average sales for Indian-American firms in each industry
d = average sales for other group firms in each industry
(e.g., "other" can be Japanese, White Non-Hispanic, etc.)

Decomposition

Average sales of Indian firms across industries are ac, the product of the two numbers

Average sales of other firms across industries are bd

Hence, $ac - bd$ reflects two effects

1. Difference in Indian and other firms within industries
2. Difference in distribution of Indian and other firms across industries

Decomposition Method 1

$$ac - bd = \{a(c-d) + d(a-b)\}$$

The first term is the Indian earnings advantage controlling for differences in the distribution across industries. The second term is the effect of different distribution of Indian and other firms across industries.

Decomposition Method 2

$$ac - bd = \{b(c-d) + c(a-b)\}$$

The first term is the Indian sales advantage controlling for differences in distribution across industries. The second term is the effect of different distribution of Indian and other firms across industries.

The difference between methods 1 and 2 is in the weights used: method 1 uses the distribution of proportions of Indian firms across industries and the distribution of sales of other firms across industries as weights, while method 2 uses the distribution of proportions of other firms across industries and the distribution of sales of Indian firms across industries.

Decomposition Method 3

This method averages the weights of the two methods, using the formula

$$\{[(a+b)/2]*(c-d) + [(c+d)/2]*(a-b)\}$$

Since method 3 averages across the two other decompositions, results from this calculation are reported in the chapter.

‖ 6 ‖

Entrepreneurial Narratives, Niches, and Networks

Several themes have run through the earlier chapters of this book. Indian Americans have been shown to have a complex but understandable history that has shaped a specific presence in their country of residence. Three waves of immigration after the 1965 liberalization of entry rules have culminated in a large and increasing number of highly skilled and educated Indian Americans. They have spread across the country, but also have remained in ethnic enclaves, where they are in some ways most visible. Their education has contributed to incomes much higher than the national average, but there is considerable variation across different regional language groups and geographic and occupational clusters.

Indian Americans have, in some respects, followed traditional paths of immigrant upward mobility, but their experience has also been shaped by the circumstances of time and place: their migration has been at a time of a new version of globalization (unlike that of a century ago) and of technological change. Indeed, as demonstrated in chapter 2, the IT revolution has had a major impact on the characteristics of Indian-American migration from the mid-1990s onward. The particulars of the current wave of globalization, and America's own increasing pluralism and multiculturalism, have allowed Indian Americans to assimilate or acculturate in ways that would not have been possible a few decades earlier. They have gone into professions such as law, politics, and the media, with lower degrees of forced adaptation of heritage or culture: retaining "foreign" last names, and even turbans, in settings that would not have permitted their preservation even very recently.

In the last chapter, the quantitative role of Indian-American entrepreneurship was examined through national census data and a unique survey. The national data provided further evidence of the income advantages gained through exceptional levels of higher education, as established in chapters 2 and 3 for the overall population of the community, but as extended in chapter 5 to the specific case of entrepreneurs. Entrepreneurial occupational niches were clearly visible in the national data through concentration of certain kinds of enterprise in a few sectors of the economy. Overall entrepreneurship rates were not exceptionally high for Indian Americans compared to other groups, but their enterprise seemed to translate into greater success, more because of observable characteristics such as education or strong family structures than because of any "secret sauce" of cultural traits. However, focusing on the upper end of entrepreneurship—that is, successful newer companies—Indian Americans are present in numbers far greater than their population proportion. The survey data in the last chapter provided specific insights into the upper end of this emerging entrepreneurial class, and painted a picture of a successful, self-confident group with a clear sense of what had made it successful and that is ambitious to achieve even more.

But numbers do not capture completely the intricacies and variety of entrepreneurial challenges that Indian-American entrepreneurs have experienced—whether headlining high-tech entrepreneurs or those who run small businesses, from gas stations and convenience stores to restaurants and a variety of professional services firms. This chapter tells some of those individual stories. Several themes from earlier chapters are treated in greater depth through narratives drawn from a combination of brief and detailed interviews, previous research, and reporting by journalists increasingly drawn to the topic by the richness of the community's experience and its expanding presence in American life.

One important narrative is that of Indian Americans in Silicon Valley, which combines themes of adaptation, occupational niches, and ethnic networks in a setting that probably has no precedent. Much has already been written about this unique place, but this chapter adds a range of new personal insights. The story of IT is significant because it is tied closely to the latest and largest wave of Indian-American immigration. There are threads that go beyond Silicon Valley to the nation's capital, as well as back to India. There are generational differences in addition to changes in entrepreneurship driven by technological change itself, with the younger generation expanding into new forms of enterprise, as well as new professions. The high-tech pioneers have also been important in trying to translate their success into benefits for their land of birth, using their "doing well" to try to "do good." And Indian Americans have become important shapers of the evolution of the United States' innovation system, including but going beyond the ecosystem of Silicon Valley.

As has been emphasized and illustrated in the preceding chapters, however, the Indian-American experience, including that of entrepreneurs, has not been uniform; not every member of the community is a highly educated, wealthy technology company founder. It is important to understand the full range of entrepreneurial experiences and outcomes for the different components of the larger community. Chapters 2 and 3 identified the differing histories, characteristics, and outcomes of Gujarati and Punjabi speakers, in comparison to the newer IT generation, and this chapter provides insights into ethnic entrepreneurial networks for each of these two communities, building on some of the discussion in chapter 4. These communities illustrate how Indian-American entrepreneurship has dealt with constraints, and sometimes has transcended them, creating new opportunity structures in processes that parallel those of Silicon Valley, but in accommodation, food services, and other sectors.

Furthermore, this chapter once again recognizes that not all Indian-American entrepreneurs fit the mold of the "model minority" stereotype. The community has its share of low-end workers and entrepreneurs, trapped by their immigration status, lack of education, or absent family support structures. The range of outcomes for the Indian-American self-employed clearly illustrates many of the themes of ethnic entrepreneurship that are woven into U.S. history, including the challenges of "fitting in" to the dominant culture.

The chapter begins with the core story of Indian-American entrepreneurs in Silicon Valley, centered on the workings of The Indus Entrepreneurs, the community's powerful networking and mentoring organization. It then provides variations on this basic theme through a range of in-depth interviews that illustrate geographical variations, different gender experiences, and versions of ethnic clustering. The next major part traces the generational shifts, but also the continuities, illustrated through interviews and case studies. Aspects of assimilation and acculturation, discussed more broadly in chapter 4, emerge in these narratives as well.

Then, the chapter takes on some aspects of the stories of Gujaratis and Punjabis. The Gujarati story focuses on their evolving dominance in the hotel and motel industry, providing a new context and integration of various parts of their experience, which was introduced in chapter 4 in the context of organization building. The Punjabi story is variegated, incorporating the older rural communities of orchard farming in California, taxi drivers, and gas station owners, and various waves of newer professional immigrants; the story is complicated by the religious dimension, since most Punjabi immigrants from India are Sikhs. Again, themes of assimilation and adaptation are entwined with human and social capital as the drivers of these outcomes. The chapter then turns to other examples of geographic and occupational clustering, further illustrating the diversity of Indian-American entrepreneurial experiences, as well as the importance of niches and networks.

Another theme explored in this chapter is an offshoot of the Silicon Valley story—that of social entrepreneurship. The case studies here illustrate a transition or broadening from a traditional model of sharing the fruits of immigrant success with those "left behind," to more local efforts; and a reversal of the flow between "doing good" and "doing well," with social entrepreneurship becoming an aspect of personal brand building in a quintessentially American manner.

Finally, the chapter closes by returning to chapter 4's theme of "fitting in," through organization building and social participation in the context of these various strands of Indian-American entrepreneurship.

The Silicon Valley Ecosystem

If the hallmarks of American industrial might in the twentieth century were the steel mills of Pittsburgh and the automobile plants of Detroit, the emblem of American economic innovation in the twenty-first century is undoubtedly California's Silicon Valley. And while many in the labor force that powered Ford's factories and Carnegie's mills were immigrants from Europe, the IT specialists and tech entrepreneurs of Silicon Valley are a vivid cross-section of American ethnic diversity, including many immigrants, but this time from Asia. "Ajay," a successful entrepreneur, whose interview is summarized later in this chapter, offered a succinct analysis that captures the essence of why Silicon Valley is so innovative: "You have to be in an immersive state of mind and you have to be amongst people who are thinking the same way, because it is not something you can do in isolation. Yes, there are certain types of innovation you can do by yourself, but by and large this is a team sport, where you have to bounce off ideas with other people. Every time you come up with ideas, some new ideas emerge." But it is also vital that this critical mass of innovative minds exists in a supporting environment of flexible labor markets and dense professional networks.[1]

By 2000, 29 percent of Silicon Valley's technology businesses were run by Indian- and Chinese-American engineers,[2] a figure that has increased over the past decade: 43 percent of Silicon Valley tech businesses founded between 2006 and 2012 had at least one foreign-born founder and one-third of these were India-born—more than the next nine countries combined.[3] But this development did not happen automatically. Chapter 5 first mentioned Kanwal Rekhi and his observations on the glass ceiling in Silicon Valley. Obstacles existed within corporate hierarchies, as well as for those who might seek to escape the glass ceiling by striking out on their own. Rekhi and several of his compatriots overcame the obstacles to entrepreneurship, but later changed the game as well for those who followed them by founding The Indus Entrepreneurs. In the process, they changed the Valley's business ecosystem.

The Indus Entrepreneurs

The Indus Entrepreneurs, now typically known as TiE, was founded in Silicon Valley in 1992, at a time when engineers from India were just beginning to enter the American IT industry in large numbers. By 2000, there were over 200,000

India-born workers in the Bay Area in the IT sector alone. Indian Americans were particularly valued as engineers and technicians, many rising to become CTOs (chief technology officers) and IT development managers in their firms; yet, the share of Indian-American technology entrepreneurs was low at the time that TiE was founded. Most Indian Americans in Silicon Valley were employed strictly in technical positions, because they were viewed as unsafe choices for managerial positions. John Dougery, managing director of Inventus Capital, recalls, "Back then, Indians weren't perceived as winning CEOs. We didn't know if people would trust them as managers."[4] Venture capitalists were hesitant to fund Indian-American entrepreneurial ventures, often insisting that Indian-American firms bring in non-Indian CEOs before they received investments.

The difficulty for Indian-American entrepreneurs was compounded by the fact that there was no Indian-American networking association to help guide them through the intricacies of venture funding. The well-honed business structure of Silicon Valley requires capital-seeking entrepreneurs to pitch their products flawlessly and slickly, particularly in a place where innovation seems endless but money is limited. This is where TiE stepped into the picture in 1992, providing the first network for Indian-American entrepreneurs to meet in a social setting and discuss ideas.[5]

TiE co-founder Kanwal Rekhi was described, tongue-in-cheek, by *Forbes* magazine in 2000 as the undisputed godfather of the Silicon Valley "Indian Mafia," an acknowledgment of the incredibly dense network that TiE represents and that Rekhi helped to develop. Kanwal Rekhi can be termed a "mentor entrepreneur"; that is, he succeeded in his own IT business and he now helps budding Indian-American entrepreneurs develop their own strategies and marketing pitches. This was TiE's initial model: setting up forums, whether formal marketing symposiums or informal conversations over *biryani*, which would enable new entrepreneurs to gain advice and augment their professional connections.

TiE started off slowly, but began to pay real dividends as venture capitalists reassessed their views of Indian-American entrepreneurship. It became apparent that not only did Indian Americans make equally good managers and businesspeople, but they also excelled in attracting technical talent to their firms. In an industry where innovation is key and advanced technical knowledge is the most precious resource, TiE's networking enabled Indian-American entrepreneurs to recruit IT engineers at rates far faster than could most other Silicon Valley firms. Furthermore, as Valley firms began to consider the economic benefits of globalized outsourcing, Indian-American entrepreneurs took the lead, developing sister firms or business branches in India, where the labor force for basic technical support was not only numerous but also substantially cheaper than in the United States. In its first ten years, TiE opened twenty-five chapters, mainly in the United States and India. By 2016, some twenty-four years after it was founded, TiE comprises sixty-one chapters in eighteen countries, counting over 13,000 members. Moreover, TiE estimates that, in its twenty-four years of existence, it has fostered a staggering $200 billion of wealth creation through its members and their firms.

One of the distinguishing features of TiE, illustrated in the use of "Indus" in its name, was its aim to transcend not only regional distinctions within the complex mosaic of India (brought out very clearly in the story told in chapters 2 and 3) but also the national divisions created when the British gave up the jewel in their imperial crown. One of TiE's proudest achievements has been the creation of chapters in Pakistan. Most important, however, TiE has created an ethnic network not bound by traditional regional, caste, or linguistic bonds but, rather, something as innovative as the region it started in.

Today, TiE continues to serve the South Asian entrepreneurial community in Silicon Valley; however, it has also gained a reputation as a leading angel investor association, providing capital for small firms or promising startups around the globe. Its latest and boldest initiative, the Billion Dollar Babies Program, began in 2014; this is a competition among startups originating in and based in India, in which three finalists are sponsored by TiE to temporarily transplant their operations to Silicon Valley, where they will be introduced to leading venture capitalists, legal consultants, and mentors. The hope is that by exposing more Indian startups to the intense environment of Silicon Valley, these firms will begin to develop the skills and marketing acumen needed to transform themselves into billion-dollar enterprises.

What TiE has achieved has also transformed California's Silicon Valley. The Valley was growing and diversifying in any case, as the digital revolution encompassed the Internet and its associated innovations, but TiE formalized, expanded, and deepened the nature of professional networks, promoting knowledge sharing and linkages in ways that had hitherto not been thought of. For example, its annual worldwide conference, TiEcon, has become a focal point for entrepreneurs and investors from around the globe, and the initial Silicon Valley version has spawned similar events worldwide.

Vignettes from TiEcon Silicon Valley

TiEcon Silicon Valley remains the largest of the gatherings among all of TiE's chapters. It provided the location for a series of brief interviews we conducted in 2011, yielding vignettes about high-tech entrepreneurship and innovation taking place in the region and radiating out from it. On-the-spot interviewers asked questions about motivation, success factors, and the entrepreneurial ecosystem, touching on some of the topics explored in the survey described in chapter 5. Pioneers and legends of Indian-American entrepreneurship rubbed shoulders with aspiring and striving ones in TiEcon's innovator exhibit area. The leaders of the Indian-American community of technology entrepreneurs readily shared their views on their own experiences, and were living lessons for others seeking to follow in their footsteps.

Kanwal Rekhi spoke about becoming an entrepreneur in the 1980s, after seeing his friends taking that route and saying "Why not me?" Exhibiting an attitude that has become emblematic of the message of TiE to Indian Americans, he encouraged those thinking of becoming entrepreneurs to go out and try it, not just think about it. Suhas Patil, another pioneering Indian-American entrepreneur, co-founder of TiE and its first president, implicitly extolled the organization when he spoke of the many facets of entrepreneurship, the benefits of learning from experienced entrepreneurs and their mistakes, and the value of advice from someone not immersed in the day-to-day details of a startup. Patil described growing up in India in a town built by an entrepreneur and having a dream of doing something new. In a story not uncommon in Silicon Valley, but once unheard of in India or among Indian Americans, he had been a professor, working with advanced technology, and left academia to start a company (Cirrus Logic) that would make the technology useful. Like Rekhi, he had become a serial entrepreneur, mentor, and prolific angel investor.

Naren Bakshi, founder of Versata, a successful serial entrepreneur and active TiE member, described how he became an entrepreneur to have the satisfaction of creating jobs rather than seeking a job. He emphasized the importance of an entrepreneur's having a passion for the subject of his efforts and of a willingness to take risks. Kumar Mallavalli, co-founder of Brocade Communications, spoke of needing to believe in what one is doing as an entrepreneur, having a good idea, being able to communicate it, staying focused, and having a good team, as well as good timing. He became an entrepreneur because he had a clear idea of what was missing in the space of IT-based storage; for him, wealth was a by-product of being able to fill an important market need.

Shailesh Mehta, who succeeded at the intersection of finance and technology, said he became an entrepreneur to be able to control his own life. He was passionate about this, and was willing to take the risk of setting out on his own. He emphasized the importance of following through on one's decisions, and on not second-guessing one's choices. Gunjan Sinha, founder of WhoWhere, eGain, and MetricStream, spoke of his motivation to become an entrepreneur as having come from deep within and from wanting to make a difference. He described the initial challenges, in raising money, bootstrapping his first company, and doing whatever it took to succeed. Vish Mishra, an early partner of Rekhi, now a venture capitalist and TiE leader, emphasized wanting to document and explain the success of the Indian-American entrepreneurship community in the United

States, to provide role models for aspiring Indian-American entrepreneurs, as well as budding entrepreneurs in India.

Many younger entrepreneurs also described their efforts and challenges. One, just starting out and seeking first-round venture capital funding, was motivated by a motto from his alma mater, Stanford University: "Building organizations, changing lives." His startup was inherently global, based in the United States and South Korea, doing product development in the latter and seeking to expand into India. His greatest challenge was getting funding for the company. Another entrepreneur spoke of being his own boss and wanting to "do the right thing" as his motivations, and of the challenges of building an entrepreneurial organization that respected his own values. Yet another described his motivation as wanting to fill a gap in his wife's profession; the result was a company to create a technology platform for services related to special education. He emphasized building a good team and having access to capital as his key success factors, as well as his greatest challenges. Another entrepreneur had started out in India, moving from financial services to IT infrastructure outsourcing after eight years. For him, being focused and pursuing one's dreams were the keys to successful entrepreneurship.

A serial entrepreneur based in Dallas, Texas, had two previous startups and two current ones involving tech staffing and mobile software. He spoke of optimism and self-belief as crucial for success, as well as the need to be prepared for the worst. He discussed the importance of having a high-quality team, frankly attributing previous failures to the absence of such a team. He had self-funded his ventures, reinvesting his earnings to sustain them.

One young entrepreneur making mobile cameras for security saw meeting an unfilled need as the genesis of technology entrepreneurship, and he thought that entrepreneurial networks can be built as needed. Another described how his first and only venture had been motivated by a desire to create a social networking site appropriate for young children, including his own three children. He had been successful and sold his startup to a major media company.

Two women entrepreneurs displayed somewhat differing views of entrepreneurial goals. One had founded a business in India, coordinating all the components of the value chain involved in building lower-middle-income housing, viewing this as an underserved but potentially very large market. The other had started a software services firm in Silicon Valley, with the vision of creating a company where everyone would work collaboratively, including the clients. She described creating the organization itself as a major challenge because of its innovative nature.

What emerged from these interviews was an infectious sense of energy and optimism, but also a display of the diversity of Indian-American entrepreneurship in a world where the vast majority of such enterprises do not succeed.

Hearing what the interviewees had to say, one could understand the human factors that stood behind the success catalogued in the survey responses described in chapter 5.

The Valley and Beyond

From the 1960s to the 1980s, Indian immigrants who came to Silicon Valley were highly selected—their route was mostly higher education, typically in engineering or computer science (still a fledgling field in the 1980s). Many on this path became academics, others obtained business degrees and went into corporate management. Many of those who found jobs in the Valley were either motivated by entrepreneurial visions or embraced the region's culture. Some are well-known names, like co-founder of Sun Microsystems, Vinod Khosla.[6] Many are less well known but still exceptionally successful. The initial generation were pioneers in every sense of the word, but later waves of immigrants have pioneered in their own ways, both by branching out in their entrepreneurial choices and in their global reach. The interviews and stories in this section provide a sense of the depth and breadth of the Indian-American entrepreneurial presence. The examples also illustrate the expanding boundaries of the high-tech presence, including a Pakistani immigrant and a technology pioneer based near the nation's capital, Washington, D.C.

The Model Minority

"Ajay" is an exceptionally successful Silicon Valley entrepreneur. He has sold one software company, taken another public, and currently has yet another active company. His background certainly contributed to this success. His father was an engineering professor, and he received his bachelor's degree from one of the elite IITs. He came to the United States for a master's in computer science and later obtained a second master's in engineering management. In the interview, though, he described being bitten by the entrepreneurial bug as an undergraduate, and therefore he chose the location of his master's to be close to Silicon Valley. He failed with his first two ventures, including one as an undergraduate at IIT, before succeeding with his third. Ajay contrasted the intense competition for grades at IIT with the opportunity to be creative in the United States.

Ajay went into more detail about his motivation and experience with entrepreneurship. He had been fascinated by technology early on, but his first successful company, an online community, was inspired by volunteer work with the Red Cross. The experience with that first success taught him about the importance of online customer service, and it gave him the idea for his second company. He talked about enjoying video games when he was growing up, and he spoke of his entrepreneurial experiences in terms of "playing the game." For Ajay, the process of entrepreneurship, the act of creation, and the creativity of being an entrepreneur are what matters.

Discussing the drivers of success as an entrepreneur, Ajay implicitly noted the importance of timing, since when he began thinking of creating online connections the first Internet browser had just become available, providing the platform for his venture. He explicitly emphasized the importance of Silicon Valley as a place for entrepreneurship because it allows for immersion, and Ajay stated that "innovation requires immersion." He expressed views that capture some of the basic worldview of an entrepreneur, looking at risk as a positive rather than as a barrier: "People had this notion that entrepreneurship is a risky thing; I felt the other way around. I think you are taking way too big of a risk for not trying it out, especially when you are young since there is not much to lose. I see that happening way more now than . . . in 1992."

On the theme of encouraging entrepreneurship, Ajay noted that he was serving on a collaborative U.S.–India effort to fund innovation and entrepreneurship between the two countries. He observed that entrepreneurship requires some fundamental skills and capabilities, irrespective of location, but he emphasized the differences in the two countries and the need to tailor one's efforts to a specific market and customer base, rather than seek generic or global approaches. He emphasized the barriers both to starting and closing companies in India, and suggested that public policy in India has an important role to play in fixing this. Other factors he mentioned included the need to train a skilled workforce, the importance of incentives such as favorable tax treatment of capital gains, and the overall treatment of investment and small businesses.

Asked about how the younger generation of Indian-American entrepreneurs might be different from earlier generations, Ajay noted that there is now greater acceptance of entrepreneurship and a stronger business ecosystem, including mentors and funders, but also that the pressure to succeed is greater now than before.[7] In this context, he returned to the theme of creativity and innovation as more important than monetary success: "I think the focus ought to be very much 'How do I innovate? How do I create? How do I build something nice and beautiful and how does it get better and better every day?' That's all you can do. It's a very private journey at some level."

In many ways, Ajay epitomizes the marketing ideal of the Indian-American entrepreneur in Silicon Valley: smart and thoughtful, repeatedly successful, socially engaged, and transnational in experience and outlook. His narrative provides an anchor for an exploration of the many variations on this story.

Builders

"Dilip" was in the early wave of Indian students who settled in the Bay Area. He graduated from an IIT, got a Ph.D. from the University of California, Berkeley in the late 1960s, and joined what was essentially a startup—not the kind that now flourishes but a company that helped design nuclear power plants around the country. It was quintessentially a business requiring specialized human capital, but it was also in an area where computing knowledge was necessary, and Dilip described writing their own programs for power plant engineering design. The company was sold, and Dilip co-founded a company to provide similar kinds of structural engineering services more broadly. This startup was successful, and it was also sold, providing the seed capital for him to create, with his co-founder, a venture fund investing in early-stage companies.

Asked about the drivers of entrepreneurial success, Dilip emphasized the need to stay focused and not try to please too broad a range of customers. He suggested that venture capitalists might not always be beneficial for a startup, and that bootstrapping might be better as a startup strategy. He discussed the difficulties of managing multiple rounds of venture funding. When asked about skills needed as a venture capitalist, he stressed the importance of understanding the market and customer needs, of knowing the competitive landscape, and having a strong network to support the companies that were funded. His own fund specializes in IT, investing in the range of $100,000 to $500,000 for very early-stage companies. He noted that he had not made a large amount of money investing, but had better than average returns, and viewed his efforts as an opportunity to help the community more broadly. Asked about what advice he would give an entrepreneur starting out, Dilip said that the most important thing is to have a passion for and knowledge of the product. This, in his view, is more important than just financial or market calculations.

Asked about his associational experience with India, Dilip described being a limited partner in a larger fund that invests in India and, in that role, inspecting companies in that country. He thought that there were some extremely good entrepreneurs in India, but viewed the country's infrastructure as a major limitation on sustainable growth for startups there; additionally, many skills are in short supply. He spoke about how the entrepreneurial landscape had changed in India. Before the financial crisis, money had been pouring into India at unsustainable levels. However, there were not enough people who understood the Indian market well enough to provide useful advice to its entrepreneurs. Dilip also emphasized the need for better execution, rather than cutting-edge innovation, in the Indian context. On possible lessons India could learn from Silicon Valley, he emphasized the attitude toward risk—that is, understanding, targeting, and accepting risks, including possible failure. He also described the cultural and intellectual fertilization and cross-pollination possible because of the great universities in the Bay Area as a model for India.

Asked about whether specific Indian values had helped him, Dilip gave the example of cultural networks of Indian Americans that had provided corresponding professional networks; hence, the commonality of being Indian and sharing a heritage helped him become successful, and actual "Indian" values had been only an indirectly influence.

Dilip offered an analysis similar to Ajay's of the intensity of information flows in Silicon Valley, including the key role played by TiE. He described being involved in TiE Silicon Valley from its early days, and how that involvement simultaneously gave him opportunities to help budding entrepreneurs, but also to stay abreast of technology trends. For him, TiE was an entry point and offered an organizing structure for the Silicon Valley business ecosystem. He emphasized the richness of this business and technology ecosystem and the intensity of learning in the Valley. The challenge of achieving entrepreneurial success in Silicon Valley was one of handling the speed of industry innovation.

Anil Godhwani and his younger brother Gautam, along with two other co-founders, were among the earliest Indian-American entrepreneurs to succeed with an Internet startup, founding AtWeb—which specialized in website maintenance tools for small businesses—in 1996 and selling it to Netscape in 1998.[8] Anil described his desire to be an entrepreneur to achieve financial independence, and to be able to pursue his fundamental life goals (his "list of dreams").[9] Anil and Gautam each went on to found other companies, and were active in mentoring and funding other entrepreneurs, but they may be best known for another joint creation, the India Community Center (ICC) of Milpitas, California.

The Godhwani brothers were the moving spirits and co-founders of ICC in 2001. Community leaders and successful entrepreneurs soon stepped in to help with advice and funding; they included Kanwal Rekhi, angel investor Prabhu Goel, Shailesh Mehta, and Naren Bakshi. The ICC was not the first Indian-American community center, however. A pioneering effort had been launched in Cleveland, Ohio, in 1976, and Bakshi had been a co-founder there. Even in Santa Clara, in the heart of Silicon Valley, an Indo-American Community Service Center (ICSC) had been in operation since 1992. But the Godhwani brothers envisaged something on a much larger scale, professionally run, and carefully designed to serve a range of community needs. They looked to the established nationwide model of Jewish community centers, and sought scale and financial sustainability by merging with the ICSC. Bakshi described the Godhwanis' approach: "I have never seen such a professional and organized approach. They are (proceeding) like the business world would do it. 'This is our vision. Let's do the market research with different focus groups and decide what our community really needs.'"[10] The ICC has expanded dramatically since its inception, met challenges head-on, and continued to attract members and supporters, realizing one item on Anil Godhwani's "list of dreams."

Power Couples

"Chetan" and "Nina" are a couple who now are partners in their own venture capital firm, investing in early-stage Silicon Valley companies and in later-stage companies in India, the latter more akin to private equity funding. They are somewhat of a rarity, but not the only Silicon Valley professional couple who are both engaged in the entrepreneurial ecosystem.

Asked about why Indians had been successful in the United States, and Silicon Valley more specifically, Nina emphasized the high education levels of Indian immigrants, their fluency in English, and their ability to adapt culturally to the United States. She viewed the United States as meritocratic, suggesting that the absence of caste and class barriers was a big plus for Indian immigrants. Chetan emphasized the high value placed on education in India and immigrants' strong motivation to succeed, combined with the urge to work very hard. Nina noted the large population of India and its very limited opportunities, which leads to intense competition for academic success; the top group who succeeded in India were acutely selected to come to the United States.

Chetan thought there was a glass ceiling in major corporations for earlier immigrants from India, which was strong motivation for them to move into entrepreneurship. According to him, this glass ceiling was no longer the main motive for newer Indian-American entrepreneurs. Nina noted that she had started her first company while she was very young, having left a large multinational corporation because she was unable to do anything creative and exciting within it, but before she hit a glass ceiling there.

Asked about trends in entrepreneurship in the United States and in India, Chetan observed that young people in both countries were flocking to entrepreneurship. They were coming up with simple ideas, leveraging the Internet and World Wide Web to target large markets very quickly. He saw entrepreneurship going well beyond narrow high-technology applications to services such as health care, media, education, and law. He noted that the amount of capital required for many such startups had gone down, since they do not need extensive equipment or facilities. Globalization was also a factor, leveling the playing field and allowing a greater reach for customers. He also highlighted the move of both Indian and Indian-American entrepreneurs into social entrepreneurship (startups with a social good component), citing examples such as solar lighting for villagers not on the power grid and low-cost medical devices for the poor, and noting that for-profit startups in India were developing hybrid models to include social components as well.

"Vijay" and "Meera" are another successful entrepreneurial couple. They have advised and supported each other in separate ventures. Vijay could not be interviewed, but his trajectory is well known: an IIT degree and a doctorate from Stanford University, followed by taking his first technology startup public, subsequently leading a succession of successful enterprises, and finally founding a prominent venture capital firm that invests in both the United States and in India. In published interviews, Vijay has described his motivations for entrepreneurship as the enjoyment of and desire to be his own boss.[11] He has acknowledged his wife for mentoring his efforts.

Meera, like Vijay, was one of the early Indian-American technology entrepreneurs. She also has an IIT undergraduate degree, followed by a master's from UCLA, and had chalked up considerable experience working in engineering management positions in the industry for ten years. Meera described how she had learned from this corporate experience, including developing ideas for product innovation, but the learning curve flattened out, leading to dissatisfaction and a desire to set out on her own, following her husband's earlier path in entrepreneurship. She made a clean break and commited to something new. Her motivation was the desire to do something exciting and to test herself, rather than independence or money. Being in Silicon Valley showed her that entrepreneurship was also possible for a woman, though uncommon at that time. She described the generous mentoring and advice she received from more experienced people in the Valley, highlighting the value of this kind of support.

Asked about the challenges of being a woman entrepreneur, Meera said she never allowed her gender to limit her thinking or to define her. Being of Indian origin was a greater challenge than being a woman in the 1980s, because of ignorance of her community among Americans at the time, while she had received some degree of admiration for being a woman entrepreneur.[12]

Meera encountered an important set of entrepreneurial challenges in building and managing teams, something that had not been part of her experience as a technologist or engineer. She also noted challenges with respect to knowing what "makes people tick," especially in regard to attracting investors. Her initial partnership with a co-founder had not worked out well, but she held on, noting that she managed tasks well enough so that the venture capitalists funding her operations had never tried to oust her from her CEO position.

On changes in the entrepreneurial landscape, Meera said that VC funding at an early stage, and even angel funding, was nonexistent when she started out, and developing prototypes in the case of electronics, or even new software, were greater challenges than today's world of software apps.[13] Business failure is now more acceptable, and business models are more flexible, making entrepreneurial risk-taking somewhat easier. But product cycles are shorter, reducing the room for making mistakes and requiring faster execution of ideas.

Comparing the United States and India as environments for entrepreneurship, Meera suggested that technology entrepreneurship is quite recent in India, spurred on by the confidence that came after Y2K. She suggested that India is catching up with the United States in some aspects of innovation and entrepreneurship, adding that the best new entrepreneurs in India are impressive. However, she felt that the United States still leads in creativity, noting the limitations imposed by class hierarchies and elitism in India; indeed, Indian entrepreneurs could learn from their U.S.-based counterparts in this social dimension.[14]

The Maverick

"Bhaskar" is the youngest son of a judge who was earlier a freedom fighter, and the first in his family to go into business. He trained in the hospitality industry in Mumbai, went to Europe to study advanced hotel management along with wines, and then went to northern California to earn an MBA. His first startup was in organic food, in the early 1990s, but it did not succeed; he feels he was ahead of his time with that effort. He emphasized the learning and experience gained from that failure, and noted the acceptance of failure in Silicon Valley, as well as the encouragement he received to keep trying.

A passion for food and thinking about opportunities in that area led Bhaskar to create a restaurant that served quality authentic Indian food to a burgeoning diverse population of those in the high-tech boom. He had a vision for introducing the Silicon Valley population to such food, where there was really nothing else of that nature. He emphasized that he was able to take advantage of the U.S. visa structure to bring highly skilled Indian chefs to his restaurants, and that this program was central to implementing his vision.

Bhaskar described the innovative culture of Silicon Valley as crucial for motivating him to set out on his own as an entrepreneur, and he highlighted the region's overall interest in innovation, even in dining experiences. From his initial failure he learned about negotiating business leases, pricing, and marketing. The first location for his business was not right for his high-quality offerings, and his second venture, his first restaurant, was instead in the heart of Silicon Valley. He financed his venture by using his credit card and obtaining loans from friends, since his personal capital had been depleted by the previous attempt. An initial very favorable restaurant review led to further good reviews, and to quickly achieving a reputation in its field and ultimate financial success. His restaurant developed such strong customer loyalty that they lobbied for including his restaurant in the *San Francisco Chronicle*'s list of 100 Best Bay Area Restaurants. The freshness of the food and the quality of service were key to his inclusion in the listing. He noted that the local Indian-American community was very

supportive, bringing their non-Indian friends to the restaurant; the establishment gained popularity with Valley entrepreneurs to the extent that it became a
place to discuss business and do deals.

With respect to the entrepreneurial ecosystem of Silicon Valley, Bhaskar
emphasized its openness to innovation and the completeness of its infrastructure. When a new mixed development was planned for San Jose, the project
developers, who were customers of the restaurant, approached Bhaskar to open
a second location in that new development. He noted the high quality and pro-
fessionalism of all involved in the project, and their offering help and advice
in a range of areas. Bhaskar explained how increased costs associated with the
industry's regulations, wages, insurance, and raw materials were significant challenges for his business. He also noted that visa regulations tightened over time;
he successfully sought support from local congressional representatives, particularly in making the case that chefs with advanced degrees were needed for his
restaurants.

Bhaskar was not the first to open an Indian restaurant in the San Francisco
Bay Area. Previous attempts had included a few upscale efforts aimed at the
mainstream population, as well as lower-end ones serving students, seekers
of ethnic food, and a growing immigrant population. Ethnic food has always
been an important field of cultural engagement, beyond being the foundation of a business, and Bhaskar epitomizes the successful entrepreneur who
combines an understanding of the market, creative vision, and excellent timing. The Indian-American presence in Silicon Valley created a supporting
infrastructure of Indian grocery, video rental, and clothing stores, as well as
restaurants, each with its own story. It is over a hundred years since the first
Indian restaurant opened in the United States, in New York City, but Bhaskar's
efforts perhaps best matched the ethos of a particularly entrepreneurial time
and place.[15]

Rags to Riches

The entrepreneur interviews featured so far have involved Indian Americans
from middle-class or even elite backgrounds in India, but there are also stories of
greater upward mobility, two of which follow. The experiences of Frank Fakhrul
Islam and Anila Jyothi Reddy, both tech entrepreneurs but in different ways,
span the main period of Indian immigration to the United States and illustrate
its evolution.

Fakhrul Islam grew up in a village in Uttar Pradesh, attended Aligarh Muslim
University, and then went to the University of Colorado, Boulder, in 1969, where
he obtained bachelor's and master's degrees in computer science.[16] He went to
work for IT companies, but says he had always wanted to be an entrepreneur. He

launched his company with $500 and no employees, but built it up in thirteen years to the point where he could sell it for several hundred million dollars.

Islam operated far from Silicon Valley, in a place that shaped his business and subsequent activities—Washington, D.C. The federal government was his main client, and Islam benefited from the efforts of another Indian-American entrepreneur, Sharad Tak, who helped secure minority status for Indian Americans in federal contracting decisions.[17] After his company's sale, Islam became involved in politics and philanthropy, contributing to Barack Obama's presidential campaign, and sitting on boards such as those of the John F. Kennedy Center for the Performing Arts and government and university advisory councils.

This pattern of engagement could be that of any successful American entrepreneur, Indian or not, immigrant or not. But Islam's story stands out because he is a Muslim from India. Muslims in India are, on average, less well educated and less well off than other religious groups, and Islam's philanthropy has included creating educational pathways for young Muslims like himself from the area where he grew up, so as to follow in his footsteps.

However, Islam's direct engagement with India is limited to some money, some personal encouragement, and some mentoring. Frank Islam's life remains focused on America. His wife grew up in Canada, his house is a stately mansion on the Potomac River, and he heads an investment firm that seeks to invest in U.S. startups. Islam does promote political and business ties between India and the United States. As Silicon Valley technology titans have deepened their engagement with policymakers in the nation's capital, Indian-American entrepreneurs from the West Coast have followed suit, and their approach and interests align with leaders like Islam, who have always been near the government. Returning the favor, entrepreneurs like Islam are members of TiE-Washington, DC, one of many regional organizations that copied the template of the first TiE in Silicon Valley. In December 2014, TiE DC honored Islam, Sharad Tak, and another entrepreneur, Ken Bajaj, with TiE Legends awards.[18]

Frank Islam's first step out of poverty was the significant one of graduating from Aligarh Muslim University, having obtained a publicly funded college education like so many of his somewhat better-off Indian contemporaries. The path followed by Anila Jyothi Reddy was more tortuous.[19] She grew up in poverty in a village in Telangana, was forcibly married to a farmer at the age of sixteen, became a mother at seventeen, and worked as a farm laborer. In 1990, while in her early twenties, she got a government job teaching stitching to rural women and children. She completed a vocational degree from Ambedkar Open University; then a cousin who had immigrated to the United States encouraged her to study computer science and try to come to the United States as well. Once she got her H1 visa in 2000 and moved (leaving her husband and teenage daughters behind), she took a series of temporary jobs until she got one as a software

recruiter. Anila built on this experience to start her own successful IT outsourcing company, Key Software Solutions, located in Phoenix, Arizona.

Reddy took a path that would not have been available to Islam's generation,
when poor women could not seek careers on their own, immigration to the
United States was primarily through relatively elite channels of higher education, and networks of Indian Americans were tightly knit but small. Instead, she
was able to ride the IT boom of the 1990s, which particularly benefited the region she had grown up in. She succeeded as an entrepreneur in a global context
that did not exist when Islam was pursuing his success. Illustrating the generational impact of this evolution, Reddy's two daughters, who followed later with
her husband, are both software engineers in the United States.

Global Impact

"Farhad," another interviewee, illustrates the impact of TiE, since he is not
technically "Indian American," but finds a place in the same entrepreneurial
space. He grew up in Pakistan and came to the United States for his undergraduate degree, then went on to get an MBA from the Wharton School. He
worked for a big-four consulting firm, then for tech giants in Silicon Valley.
Farhad's choice of whether or not to work for a big company was constrained
by his need to be sponsored for a work visa. Once his visa status was secured,
he grew frustrated with the slow pace of innovation and execution in big companies. His chance to break away came when he was asked to be CEO of a
Turkish social media company, appointed to lead a turnaround in response to
Facebook's competitive onslaught. He went on to become the U.S. president
of a company founded in India (but funded by U.S. venture capital, with a
parent company incorporated in Delaware) that provides customer help desk
solutions worldwide.

Farhad emphasized the desire to have a societal impact as a driving force for
his entrepreneurial efforts. He wanted to build and change things. He noted the
advantages of his cross-cultural, global background, which positioned him well
for the kinds of ventures in which he became involved and gave him an edge. He
was categorical that passion and a desire to have an impact are keys to entrepreneurial success. Asked about Silicon Valley's role, Farhad emphasized the value
of the business ecosystem in providing access to talent and networks, though
he saw the Valley as increasingly having a virtual existence, not just a specific
geographic location. He described himself as politically active and engaged,
including mentoring entrepreneurs, advocating for civic causes, and serving on
a presidential advisory commission on Asian Americans. His political engagement seems consistent with his views on having a global impact through the
global nature of his business.

Concerning challenges for immigrant entrepreneurs, Farhad noted the constraints imposed by the high-risk nature of entrepreneurship, especially for new immigrants who might have social or family obligations to send money home, and who lack capital or networks, though he suggested that the situation has improved for more recent immigrants. Asked about the challenges facing entrepreneurship in India, he suggested that business relationships there are more transactional and lack enough trust, whereas Silicon Valley has a culture of paying forward, of helping others without considering an immediate quid pro quo. On South Asian values, he believed there is a culture of hard work, vital to entrepreneurial success, as well as a hunger for success that drives immigrants in the United States, as well as Indian workers in places like Chennai.

The New Generation

The lives of younger Indian Americans reveal more varied paths to entrepreneurship than those taken by the previous generation. Some of these younger entrepreneurs were born or grew up in the United States, and they are shaped as much by that experience as by their Indian heritage. An entrepreneur like Gurbaksh Chahal, who dropped out of high school to pursue his entrepreneurial dream, took a path that was obviously not available to the Indians who came to the United States as graduate (and later, undergraduate) students. But some younger Indian Americans have continued to follow that traditional route.

Comic Book Heroes

Dinesh Shamdasani was born in Dubai and moved to Hong Kong when he was four years old.[20] There, he became friends with Jason Kothari, and they shared a passion for the world of Valiant comics. Valiant, a latecomer to a comic universe dominated by DC and Marvel, featured a complex array of flawed heroes and ambiguous villains, as well as the racial diversity missing from the big two comics. The company was bought by the video game company Acclaim Entertainment, which focused on games and folded the comic book series. But Acclaim went bankrupt in 2004, putting the Valiant universe of characters up for grabs.

Meanwhile, Kothari and Shamdasani, like so many other Indians, had come to the United States for college, pursuing degrees in business and film, respectively. Their teenage passion for Valiant comics had been reignited by nostalgia and the Internet, and they joined forces to purchase Valiant as Acclaim's assets were liquidated. After a series of setbacks and legal battles, the childhood friends obtained their prize and they have relaunched the comic books, as well as introducing digital versions and signing a multi-movie deal with Sony Pictures.

The story of Kothari and Shamdasani epitomizes the globalization of Indian entrepreneurship and its "normalization." When Kanwal Rekhi was starting out as an entrepreneur, it was not expected that someone from India could lead a sophisticated, highly successful company.[21] Only two decades later, though, two young men could find backing from investors and become leaders of a high-risk enterprise involving creativity, multiple media channels, and a complex value chain. The fact that they were of Indian origin either did not matter or it was viewed as a positive by those putting up the money. Another interesting aspect of their story is the global diasporic element—their exposure to Valiant comics might not have occurred in the same way if they had grown up in India.

Plus Ça Change

If Kothari and Shamdasani illustrate how things have changed for diasporic Indian entrepreneurs, the case of "Hari" shows how the traditional Silicon Valley story of technology entrepreneurship still holds, albeit within an environment that allows more and easier access, thanks to social as well as technological change. Hari was a star student at IIT Bombay, working closely with a key faculty member to write and publish technical computer science papers while still an undergraduate. This helped him gain admission to Stanford University, where he began a Ph.D. program in computer science. But, much like Larry Page and Sergei Brin of Google, the research led to a business idea, and he quit with a master's degree, to start a software company along with another Indian American who was his classmate.

Hari emphasizes the entrepreneurial culture of Silicon Valley, and of Stanford in particular, describing deep ties between faculty and industry. He had taken some entrepreneurship courses at Stanford, and assessed them frankly, saying that he had not expected them to be of value at all, and that on a scale of 0 to 100 measuring a successful entrepreneurial journey, they got one as far, perhaps, as 10. Asked about the environment for entrepreneurship in India, Hari was detailed and forthright, taking the position that government controls and restrictions act as barriers to innovation and entrepreneurship. He himself did not come from an entrepreneurial family, even in his extended family circle, although his co-founder did. One interesting aspect of his upbringing, reminiscent of the survey responses given in chapter 5, was that he had lived in several different cities in India when growing up, and this seemed to be reflected in his attitude toward risk and innovation—he accepted change as natural.

Hari's story is, perhaps, a generic one of immigrant selection based on skill or talent, mediated by the top end of the American university system, and tempered in the crucible of entrepreneurship that grew around Stanford. Being Indian was less important than being at the top of his field, in an entrepreneurial ecosystem geared toward turning science into successful businesses. Like Google, Hari's company is a pure software venture, its existence completely driven by the opportunities created by the Internet and the World Wide Web. His relatively easy entry into the world of entrepreneurship was determined as much, if not more, by the groundwork done by companies such as Google, as opposed to ethnic forebears such as Kanwal Rekhi, Vinod Khosla, or Kumar Mallavalli. Hari did not need TiE to get started, but he may soon become someone whom TiE draws on as mentor and role model for those who do not have access to the same exceptional and favorable initial conditions.

Dreams and Darkness

Gurbaksh Chahal was not interviewed for our study, but he was a presenter at TiEcon 2011, where the interviews described earlier in this chapter were conducted. His session at TiEcon was geared specifically to young, aspiring entrepreneurs, and Chahal was the ideal example—a man who dropped out of high school and became extremely successful at a very young age, having a net worth over $100 million well before he was thirty. Chahal had come to the United States with his parents, as a toddler, and had grown up in a family with strong Indian values.

Before his TiEcon presentation Chahal had appeared on *Oprah* and on *The Secret Millionaire* TV shows, and had been photographed with President Obama.[22] He had written a popular book describing his path to entrepreneurial success.[23] Clearly, he is driven and focused, and timed his startup well, pursuing an idea related to Internet advertising back in the late 1990s. His subsequent ventures have also been in the same space. He relished the fame that came with early success and the things that wealth could buy him.

At TiEcon, Chahal emphasized family values and the important role his grandmother played in bringing him up. His parents attended his talk and spoke with pride of his accomplishments. According to Chahal, his success was not defined by wealth and successful exits, but by family relationships, being creative, and working on what he was passionate about. Some of this persona exhibited at TiEcon seemed inconsistent with the TV celebrity aspect of his recent past, his tendency to emphasize the importance of perceptions over reality and of selling oneself hard, and perhaps his comments about mentoring, which made it clear the thought he had neither the skill nor the time to mentor or advise budding entrepreneurs (beyond what was in his book).

The paradoxes of this one-time teen entrepreneur came to the fore in 2013, when Chahal was charged with multiple felony counts of domestic violence against his girlfriend. By May 2014, he had pled guilty to a much-reduced single misdemeanor charge, paid a $500 fine, and been put on three years' probation. But his initial response to the charges, which was dismissive and defensive, including impugning his victim, had earned him opprobrium, and he was forced by his board to resign as CEO of his third startup, which was about to go public (his first two had been acquired, making his fortune).[24] By July 2014, however, Chahal was back heading his fourth startup, once again related to Internet advertising.[25] The website promoting his achievements and his book was replaced by a blog and a nonprofit foundation page that sought to remake his image, but in yet another chapter of the story, darkness defeated the dream of success when Chahal committed another domestic violence offense and was sent to jail in August 2016.

Bright Young Stars

If Hari epitomizes the "new traditional" Indian-American entrepreneur—bright, highly educated in India, entering seamlessly into Silicon Valley—the recent *Forbes* "30 under 30" lists[26] provide insight into a broader set of Indian-American entrepreneurial stories that range beyond even the Valiant comics champions. In its first year, 2014, the *Forbes* list had about 450 names, with 30 in each of 15 different fields. In 2015, the list was expanded to 20 fields and about 600 names. In 2014, 19 of these bright young stars were of Indian origin, many with global life narratives, with about half who might fit the entrepreneur label. The corresponding number for 2015 was 37, with about half of them again entrepreneurs; while in 2016, the total increased to 47, but without an increase in the number of entrepreneurs. Therefore, Indian Americans made up over 5 percent of this list of young stars, or five times their proportion in the population.

By 2016, this prominence was receiving mainstream media attention.[27] The *Forbes* list obviously pushes the American dream of self-made success based on talent and hard work, but it has a strong immigrant component (36 percent on the list in 2016). While the stories of these young Indian Americans further illustrate the increasingly diverse pathways to prominence, education remains an important common factor.

Over all three years, the fields of Finance and Venture Capital tended to lead in terms of Indian-American names, with technology-related categories not far behind. The only Indian American in Technology in 2014 fit a very different profile from the more common earlier type illustrated by Hari. Instead, Sahil Lavingia is more in the mold of Bill Gates or Mark Zuckerberg, having dropped out of college to found an e-commerce software company. Lavingia, twenty-one, the son of investment bankers, grew up in Singapore, Hong Kong, London, and New York, and came to Silicon Valley at the age of seventeen. He tried only one semester in college, became a key designer for Pinterest, and then struck out on his own.

The 2015 *Forbes* list featured five Indian-American entrepreneurs in Enterprise and Consumer Tech: a Harvard Business School dropout and son of a senior Indian civil servant; the son of a successful Indian-American technology entrepreneur; a Harvard graduate who founded his first company in high school; a Thiel Fellow[28] and MIT dropout; and a graduate from a college in southern India who became an entrepreneur there, then moved to the United States while working for Amazon, thence returning to India to found companies. The half-dozen entrepreneurs on the 2016 list also came mostly from elite universities, with software businesses dominating their ventures.

The category of Games is essentially an offshoot of Technology, and it featured another variant on Indian-American entrepreneurship. Amir Rao, on the 2014 list, is a successful game designer and co-founder of a game design company initially headquartered in the Silicon Valley house where he grew up. But Rao majored in English before coming to work at Electronic Arts as a prelude to his entrepreneurial venture. As in the case of high school or college dropouts, this reflects a combination of trends. That is, innovation has expanded beyond areas requiring a deep science or engineering background, and simultaneously, second-generation Indian Americans are widening their educational choices.

The Social Entrepreneurship category on the *Forbes* 2014 list included several Indian names, with two based in India. Kavita Shukla best fits the "Indian-American" label, having invented and patented food packaging made of edible organic ingredients: her inspiration came during a visit to India via a home remedy given to her by her grandmother—illustrating once more the influence of global lives. The 2015 social entrepreneurs included a Harvard undergraduate and MPA and Stanford MBA working to replace dirt floors with more hygienic alternatives; and a Dartmouth graduate from Mauritius innovating in social funding institutions. In 2016, Indian Americans in this category on the list tackled education in Southeast Asia and sanitation in India.[29]

The Science and Health care categories featured two Indian-American entrepreneurs in 2014. Divya Nag, in biotechnology, and Surbhi Sarna, in medical devices, both founded companies in the San Francisco Bay Area. Sarna went to the University of California Berkeley, while Nag dropped out of Stanford University, where she was already publishing research papers as an undergraduate. Sarna's father and husband both work in Silicon Valley, illustrating the path dependence that characterizes much Indian-American success. The *Forbes* category was split in 2015, and included one entrepreneur in Health Care, a graduate of Stony Brook in New York, who created a social network to support patients with various illnesses. In 2016, two Indian-American entrepreneurs were working on sensors and wearable electronic records, respectively.

The three annual lists featured Indian-American entrepreneurs in the Education, Media, Law, Marketing and Advertising, and Food categories, again often in technology-related ventures. The exception was the Food category on the 2014 list: Aditi Malhotra sells artisan chocolate in New York, having studied at the Glion Institute in Switzerland. Her father and grandfather have run successful Indian restaurants in New York City since the 1970s—a far cry from the Ceylon India Inn of 1913—and a Parisian chocolatier was a family friend.[30] In the subsequent Food category lists we find Apoorva Mehta (2015), a tech entrepreneur who offers an app-based online grocery delivery service (after multiple previous efforts), as well as Anjali and Nikhil Kundra (2016), who are developing software for managing inventory in bars.

The lists have featured Indian-American representatives of other industries as well. For instance, the co-founder of a menswear company; the founder of a company that makes ultra-functional purses; a technologist getting an MD at Brown University while running an innovative mattress company; a founder of a company that makes and sells solar lanterns in the developing world; and a biomedical engineering graduate whose startup is making a more comfortable crutch.

Reflecting the broadening educational backgrounds and interests of the new generation of Indian Americans, as well as the expanding scope of digital technologies, these entrepreneurs can be found in fields as diverse as Law, Food and Marketing, and the more "traditional" high-tech areas. Is anything uniquely Indian about these bright young stars of Indian origin? Perhaps the only common feature is an emphasis on education. Even the college dropouts appear to have had the benefit of growing up in highly educated homes, with rich opportunities for personally directed learning. Several of the young stars have global life narratives, and even those who have grown up only in the United States appear to have been influenced by their global backgrounds and travel. But these are some of the most important characteristics of Indian-American entrepreneurs in general, not just the young stars.

Minorities Within

Chapters 2 and 3 highlighted many of the heterogeneities among Indian Americans as a broad category. Two of the largest groups of Indian Americans are Gujaratis and Punjabis, the latter mostly but not exclusively Sikhs. It was pointed out in chapter 3 that these two groups are less highly educated than other linguistic groups, particularly the new arrivals of the IT generation from southern India. Nevertheless, each group has managed to make its mark in different ways, particularly in entrepreneurship.

The Largest Ethnic Network

America's Gujarati motel owners have garnered increasing attention, fueled most recently by a sympathetic account of their lives and their evolving place in America's economy and society, as portrayed in Pawan Dhingra's *Life Behind the Lobby*. There is much other research on this group, and they constitute an important story of Indian-American entrepreneurship that is older and broader than that of the high-profile Silicon Valley entrepreneurs—indeed, it is part of a global narrative.[31]

In one way, the presence of Gujaratis in the American motel industry was an accident; such an industry did not previously exist elsewhere to serve as a training ground for Gujarati motel owners, and the initial entrants did not have experience in any related industry. On the other hand, what the Gujarati community in America brought to their new country was a tradition of enterprise in a range of areas, including trading and shopkeeping. Indeed, some of the Gujaratis came to the United States via East Africa or Britain, where they gained experience as immigrant entrepreneurs and businesspeople.[32]

While the first Gujarati in the American hotel business can be traced back to the 1940s, the real takeoff came in the 1960s and 1970s.[33] This was when the first generation of American motel owners was retiring, and their children or grandchildren no longer wanted to be part of a lifestyle that meant being stuck in small towns and wayside locations across America. At the same time, U.S. immigration laws had recently been liberalized and more Gujaratis were entering the country. For these recent immigrants, the benefit of running motels at the low end of the market was a viable business opportunity that also provided housing. The properties were in large supply and were inexpensive, located in cities as well as rural areas. The hours were long but also flexible, and the work was more intermittent than running a convenience store.[34] Rural locations, while isolated from ethnic kin, were also safer for families than living in possibly high-crime urban areas.

Initially, Gujarati motel owners were stereotyped and disparaged, with their properties sometimes characterized as unclean or shabby. They suffered discrimination from neighbors and from potential guests, and often resorted to staying in the back, behind the lobby, and using white Americans as front desk staff.[35] However, as Dhingra and earlier writers highlight, their story went beyond being stuck in this situation; it has been one of squeezing costs to earn money, either for reinvestment in more upscale businesses such as brand-name franchise hotels, or for children's education as the younger generation moved to professions such as finance, law, or real estate. Interestingly, many of the first generation of Gujarati motel owners did not have experience in the industry, but might themselves have been from professions or been white collar workers.[36] Owning and operating a motel gave them an entry point into the American economy, providing a stable island for the whole family or, indeed, part of an archipelago of Indian-owned motels.

One of the distinctive features of the Gujarati motel owners is its ethnic network based on kinship and trust. New arrivals were sponsored for immigration by extended family, and then helped financially to enter the motel business by others already in the network.[37] In fact, research has shown that smaller, unbranded Gujarati motels did better when located near a branded property owned by someone in the same ethnic network.[38] In fact, the informal network of motel owners was quickly transformed into a formal institution, the Asian American Hotel Owners Association (AAHOA), which today has over 12,000 members, almost all of whom are Gujarati.

As described in chapter 4, AAHOA has played a critical role in consolidating and enhancing the presence of Indian Americans in the hospitality industry. As early as the 1970s, Indian-American motel owners faced discrimination from insurance companies, and xenophobic views about them were openly expressed.[39] A precursor of AAHOA was formed in 1985 to fight such discrimination on multiple fronts, and AAHOA itself came into being in 1989, with the two organizations merging in 1994. In the past two decades, AAHOA has worked to smooth the path of Indian-American motel owners into benefiting from franchising opportunities, giving them access to training, know-how, and economies of scale. AAHOA holds annual conferences to promote information sharing,[40] acts as a collective voice for the interests of franchisees, and works to improve the image of Indian Americans in the industry.[41]

Pawan Dhingra, building on the work of earlier writers, has rescued the image of those Gujarati motel owners from its stereotype by showing them as successful in participating in the American dream, taking on entrepreneurial activities that were considered undesirable or unattractive, and turning them through thrift and hard work into solid, lasting ventures. He emphasizes their cultural resilience and strategic adaptation, but what stands out most in their story is the size and strength of their ethnic network. As it has grown, the network has broadened in scope, and there are now a nontrivial number of non-Gujarati Indian Americans in the industry as well. That is, the success of this group has attracted completely new players. In particular, after the last recession and the severe downturn in the travel industry, entrepreneurs from India began to look for bargain U.S. properties to buy up, finding them cheaper than comparable hotels in major Indian cities.[42] The next chapter in the story may well be one of transnational capital, rather than the small-scale, individual and family enterprise that started it all.

The Visible Minority

Sikhs in America represent a special case of Indian Americans. They are only 2 percent of India's population, but they are close to 10 percent of the Indian-American population. Unlike language categories such as Gujarati or Telugu,

"Sikh" is a religious category. Nevertheless, Sikhs are mostly of Punjabi heritage (though they may have come to the United States via East Africa or Britain), and they speak Punjabi, so there are nonreligious markers as well for this community.

Two factors distinguish Punjabi-speaking Sikhs. One is that they were some of the earliest Indian immigrants to the United States, and were therefore positioned to bring over relatives under the new family preference rules when immigration laws were overhauled in 1965. The implication of this is that many Sikhs in the United States have come from rural Punjab, with somewhat different socioeconomic profiles than most Indian Americans. In particular, Punjabi speakers were seen in chapter 2 to be prominent in the Families cohort (1980–1994), even more than in the Early Movers cohort (1965–1979); but with diminishing educational attainment of more recent arrivals (see figure 2.15) and the lowest income of all Indian language groups (figures 3.16 and 3.17).

An important example of these earlier Sikh immigrants bears out the significance of ethnic networks and geographic clustering. There have been Sikh farmers in California's Central Valley for many decades, and family reunification efforts have led to expanding and interlocking kinship networks, fed by new immigrants from rural Punjab. Whereas the earlier settlers had been able to purchase land, and some became among the largest orchard farmers in the state, the later immigrants could not afford this route and did not have the education or skills to move up the occupational ladder; if they moved out of farm labor, they went into factory work or trades, or at best, into small family businesses.[43]

A second, and most important, distinguishing factor is that orthodox Sikhs do not cut their hair, and men and boys are most noticeable because of their turbans.[44] The turban is now charged with negative symbolism in the United States, conflated at first with the Iranian hostage crisis of 1980, but even more so with terrorism after 9/11. The first American post-9/11 casualty was a Sikh gas station owner in Arizona, Balbir Singh Sodhi, who was shot and killed for looking—in the mind of the shooter—like the mastermind behind 9/11.[45] Even before these events, though, the turban had signaled for many white Americans that Sikhs were foreign, exotic, or the quintessential Other. In recent decades, the Sikh sense of separation has been heightened by events in India, where political turmoil in their "homeland" of Punjab led to brutal government repression—to the point where many Sikhs in the United States do not see themselves as part of a broader Indian-American category. This alienation has created a distinct minority within the Indian-American minority.

It should be acknowledged that there is tremendous variation in practice as well as in attitudes among the Sikh community in the United States. Gurbaksh Chahal comes from a Sikh family and views himself as practicing the religion at some level, but he chose to abandon his beard and turban when he set out on his own as a teenaged entrepreneur, while his parents maintain their long hair.

Many Sikhs choose a more assimilative look, but others maintain their traditional appearance,[46] even while engaged in visible occupations such as driving taxis or running convenience stores or gas stations.

To get a sense of the experiences of Sikh entrepreneurs, we interviewed several Sikh men who are entrepreneurs in Silicon Valley and who maintain their beards and turbans. Our questions focused on their understanding of their identity as Sikhs and how that translated to their lives as entrepreneurs. The interviewees represented a wide range of ages and levels of success. They were highly selected, in that they tended to be well-educated, mostly with technology backgrounds, and were more like the general Indian-American entrepreneurial population in that sense.

These entrepreneurs suggested that their distinctive identity was not always a negative in the circles in which they moved. Several said that their standing out, as well as the precepts of their faith, caused them to have higher standards of action in business and served a positive signaling function. Several also acknowledged challenges, and explained how they overcame them by being open and willing to talk about themselves and their backgrounds in their business interactions, so as to put their counterparts at ease. In a way, this reflects a general opening up of American business to a more diverse set of participants, even in traditionally closed professions such as investment banking.

Undoubtedly, Sikhs have benefited from the changes in attitudes and awareness sometimes brought about by civil rights legislation. On the other hand, as the case of Balbir Singh Sodhi and events like the mass shooting at a Wisconsin gurdwara in 2012 illustrate, positive attitudes are not universal, and there can be circumstances in which the turban and beard elicit hostility. One Sikh woman entrepreneur who left a managerial position in Silicon Valley to open an Indian restaurant described responses to her turbaned teenage son when he happened to be at the order counter; these responses ranged from admiring his appearance to negative online reviews about the food (linked to his presence, she suggested).

Several of the entrepreneurs referred to the three-part summary of Sikh practice, which for many Sikhs encapsulates the rules of living: meditating on the Divine, working hard and honestly, and sharing with others. They described their engagement with Sikh teachings on an active, daily basis (reciting daily prayers, for example) and of being conscious both of the need to share the fruits of their success and the limitations of material wealth as defining success or creating happiness. At the same time, several of them emphasized how much of their entrepreneurial motivation and experience was not tied to their faith but, rather, was driven by curiosity, independence, and a willingness to experiment and take risks—exactly the characteristics identified in chapter 5.

No sense of a Sikh ethnic network emerged from the interviews. Several had partnered with other Indian Americans, and one interviewee was very active in

TiE, which aims to transcend regional or religious ties. Unsurprisingly, several interviewees spoke of family support of their entrepreneurial ventures, though the support was indirect, rather than direct. There is evidence for ethnic entrepreneurial networks among Sikh or Punjabi taxi drivers and gas station owners, as described later in the chapter, but these networks are not as strong or as extensive as for Gujaratis, and the Patels, in particular, among them. There are differences in business traditions in their specific, traditional Indian contexts, as well as in the tightness of ethnic networks, which explain the greater business success of Gujaratis in America. Education differentials and initial access to capital may also be factors in explaining the different economic performance of the two groups.[47]

Niches and Clusters

Entrepreneurship represents a significant aspect of the geographical clustering analyzed in chapter 3. A good example of the interaction of entrepreneurial niches and geographical clustering is that of restaurant and food store franchise owners. Indian Americans have had enough capital to enter into franchising arrangements, and changes in franchise organizations have coincided with greater immigration, thus permitting significant entry into this business type. Indeed, a study on Indian-American franchises argues that the structures of ethnic Indian networks and families have facilitated the extension of franchising in ways that would not have otherwise been possible.[48]

Two examples that particularly illustrate the complementarity of ethnic entrepreneurial niches and regional clustering are Punjabis in Subway and 7-Eleven outlets in the Los Angeles area, and Gujaratis in Dunkin' Donuts restaurants in the greater New York and Philadelphia regions. Both these could be characterized as middleman minority business types (see chapter 5) and are not dissimilar to motels or gas stations in requiring long and inconvenient hours. Important, however, is that the franchise model permits an expanded ability to support extended families. The franchise operations have been characterized by trust, information sharing, and cooperation, all easier to maintain with the growing opportunity created by corporate expansion. Kinship networks have also been an important source for the capital required for franchise entry. Interestingly, the family structures and higher education levels of Indian Americans have provided more flexible sources of labor to cover gaps in the external labor market—for example, retired parents might help with supervision or financial recordkeeping at work, as well as handle family-related tasks at home.

Franchises represent a different form of clustering from the traditional ethnic enclave, which also becomes a basis for middleman minority businesses. For example, Houston's Little India evolved from a sweet shop that opened in 1985.[49]

The Hillcroft district of Houston now has dozens of restaurants and stores, and serves an Indian-American population from several surrounding states in addition to local Indian Americans (highly educated and with higher than average incomes), as well as people of other ethnicities in Houston. The Punjabi family that opened this sweet shop tells of long hours, re-investment and expansion, incorporation of additional family members, and a sharing of knowledge, expertise, and short-term capital for bridging emergencies.

An important variant on the benefits of geographical and ethnic clustering is found in the town of Edison, New Jersey, which has its own Little India. Several of the wealthiest Indian-American business owners in Edison own multiple franchises or their own small regional store chains. They are almost all Gujarati, with names like Patel and Shah. And these businesses led the way in creating what is essentially an enterprise fund for all the other, smaller Indian-American business owners in the area.[50] In some cases, the trust prevalent in these ethnic networks fosters the funding of businesses as far away as Missouri and Tennessee. As with the other two examples, Edison illustrates the combinations of available human, family, social, and financial capital that have enabled Indian Americans to create vibrant business clusters and occupy significant entrepreneurial niches.

Doing Well, Doing Good

"Doing good by doing well" is one way to think of social entrepreneurship, which employs business techniques and the private sector to address social, economic, and environmental problems. It emphasizes commercial viability to distinguish it from philanthropy. Social entrepreneurship features prominently in the *Forbes* "30 under 30" list. Additionally, The Indus Entrepreneurs recognized the importance of social entrepreneurship in its annual conference, TiEcon, as early as 2005. Silicon Valley and TiE luminaries such as Vinod Khosla, Kumar Mallavalli, Anil Godhwani, and Talat Hasan extolled the value of social entrepreneurship, recognizing it as part of the evolution of the Indian-American community. According to Hasan,

> When people came in the 1960s and 1970s, they were more focused on putting roots down, making a career, and gaining acceptance in the community. Only when that is taken care of, is there time to turn around and think of giving back. That is what is happening now. This is not just happening within the Indian community, but also other communities. The only difference may be that since Indians were better educated when they arrived, it may seem like things were done in a more compressed time frame.[51]

Hasan and Godhwani both highlighted the ICC as an example of social enterprise, or using commercial strategies to create something of value for their own community.

Perhaps the most high profile example of an Indian-American social entrepreneur, with major impacts on India, is Vikram Akula.[52] Akula was born in India but immigrated to America with his parents at the age of three. He grew up in Schenectady, New York, and obtained a Ph.D. from the University of Chicago. In 1990, he began serving as a community organizer of women's self-help groups for a nonprofit organization in rural Andhra Pradesh, India. His career then spanned the United States and India, until he founded SKS Microfinance as a nonprofit lender to poor women in Andhra Pradesh. He led SKS, and expanded it, until 2004, when he spent a year with consulting giant McKinsey in the United States. Akula returned to India in 2005, eventually taking SKS public as a for-profit company serving 7 million borrowers across India by 2010. But that rapid expansion came with a deterioration in borrower selection and collection practices. There followed severe new regulations imposed by the state government and a near collapse of micro-finance, including SKS's market.[53] Akula was forced out in November 2011, and he has since focused on writing and speaking about his experiences. He advises budding social entrepreneurs, works with another social enterprise called AgSri,[54] and engages in philanthropic efforts spun off from SKS.[55] He divides his time equally between India and the United States. Meanwhile, struggles continue over control of SKS, now renamed Bharat Financial Inclusion.[56]

A more traditional story than Akula's is that of B. P. Agrawal,[57] who grew up in a village in Rajasthan, received his undergraduate degree from the Birla Institute of Technology and Science, and obtained a Ph.D. in engineering science from the University of South Florida. After a long stint in corporate R&D positions and an executive education program at MIT, Agrawal founded a couple of technology companies in telecommunications and health informatics.

In 2003, Agrawal began to develop a rainwater collection system, called Aakash Ganga, which won a World Bank award in 2006 and then a Lemelson-MIT award for Sustainability. The rainwater collection system has been successfully installed in several villages in Rajasthan and Gujarat and serves over 10,000 villagers. It may yet spur larger-scale efforts along the same lines, though that may be more in the nature of a public-good investment by the Indian government. Some of the collected rainwater is used for revenue-generating horticulture, which helps to cover the system's operating costs. Agrawal himself has gone on to found Sustainable Innovations (SI), a nonprofit dedicated to building sustainable enterprises, and engages young entrepreneurs in culturally and economically viable ventures.

If B. P. Agrawal embodies the older generation of social entrepreneurship, focusing on giving back to India after having a successful career in America, the story of Priya Haji, who died suddenly in 2014 at just forty-four, captures the spirit of the new generation.[58] Haji grew up in Texas, but settled in the San Francisco Bay Area, earning an undergraduate degree from Stanford University and an MBA from the University of California at Berkeley. However, her first effort at social enterprise was to start a free clinic with her father in Texas when she was sixteen. Then, as an undergraduate, she created Free at Last in working-class East Palo Alto, an agency that provides mobile health clinics, affordable housing, and economic development and counseling to thousands of people. Haji went on to co-found World of Good, a fair-trade and sustainable goods online marketplace that was acquired by eBay; and SaveUp, a personal financial savings app that uses built-in incentives to help low-income individuals save money. These were venture-backed enterprises, unlike the publicly funded efforts of Agrawal.

Unlike Akula and Agrawal, Priya Haji's social efforts were either local or global, with no India-specific component. As the Forbes "30 under 30" examples illustrate, the younger generation of Indian-American social entrepreneurs may still engage with India, but they are just as likely to try to solve U.S. domestic or global problems. In some cases, these new social enterprise efforts are firmly mainstream—mixed with profit motives and celebrity culture. Indian-American actor Ravi Patel, a former investment banker, sells granola bars for profit, but like Newman's Own, he uses some of the profits for social good. For every bar sold, a partner produces a nutritional packet that is distributed where needed to combat malnutrition.[59] This approach is global, eclectic, and lifestyle-focused, in contrast to the technology-based, India-focused efforts of the older generation.

Fitting In

Stories of Indian-American entrepreneurship inevitably lean toward successes because the successful have the time and inclination to tell their stories. While Indian Americans on average are far better educated and earn substantially more than the national average, there is a significant Indian-American population that struggles at the lower end of the income distribution, as detailed in chapter 3. This population can include entrepreneurs or business owners, as well as employees.[60] In many respects, stories of these Indian Americans are no different from other immigrant narratives, past and present. Indeed, rants posted on Internet sites about the large and visible presence of Indian Americans driving taxis or running convenience stores, gas stations, and motels are reflective of more generalized racism.

Of the various entrepreneurial activities in this category, motels have been discussed in this chapter, and they lie at the upper end of the economic ladder in terms of capital required, possibilities for economic advancement, and size and strength of an underlying ethnic network. Toward the bottom of the ladder, perhaps, are found the taxi drivers. This profession draws on the widest range of immigrant groups, simply because entry barriers are low. While owning a taxi and the medallion that allows one to work in a city like New York may require a half-million dollar entry fee, an individual taxi driver may pay $100 to $200 to rent a taxi for a twelve-hour shift. Along with gasoline costs, he (drivers are almost all male) may have to collect $250 in fares and tips during the whole shift to break even, and average yearly earnings may be $19,000[61] to $32,000 (table 3.4)—it's among the lowest paid jobs for Indian Americans. Many of those taxi drivers may have come to the United States with unrealistic expectations of obtaining middle-class jobs, but without the education to realize those goals. Some turn to taxi driving almost as a last resort, and many move out of it as soon as they can.[62] Racial discrimination—extending to violence—from passengers and police, low social status, and asymmetric economic power all work to place this job at the bottom of the pyramid of self-employment, bearing none of the typical connotation of the word *entrepreneurship*. Being on the margins of the U.S. economy compounds the challenges of "fitting in," as illustrated by ethnographic studies of Punjabi (Sikh) taxi drivers, though groups like this still seek to build social capital through their ethnic networks, hoping to improve their economic situation.[63]

Owning convenience stores and gas stations sits somewhere between taxi driving and running a motel as entrepreneurial businesses. In many respects they are like motel ownership, since they involve physical assets, fixed locations, and possibilities for upgrading (especially in the broader category of retailing) and expansion. On the other hand, convenience stores and gas stations (which overlap to an increasing degree) are also more vulnerable than motels to violence, including robbery and murder, as well as discrimination, including satirical spoofing (the fictional character Apu in *The Simpsons* TV show).[64]

Convenience stores and gas stations are included in more general studies of immigrant networks and ethnic specialization.[65] These networks may be local and path dependent. For example, unlike the national success of Gujaratis in the motel and hotel industry, while Punjabi Sikhs dominate owning and operating gas stations in and around New York City, gas stations in Los Angeles are mostly run by Korean immigrants.[66] Donatella Lorch emphasizes the "road to riches" story for such ethnic entrepreneurs, focusing on examples such as that of Parmjit Singh, who went from mechanic on a Greek ship in 1981 to busboy and cook in New York City, before working for a fellow Punjabi who owned a gas station in the city. After learning the business, Singh went on to own thirteen stations himself by 1992, employing mostly fellow Sikhs, who have repeated the pattern of working long hours and saving as much as they can.

Some of the evolutionary patterns that emerged in the hospitality industry are repeated in small retailing. Regional ethnic chains of independent store owners, such as the Virginia Asian American Store Owners Association, Florida Asian American Store Owners Association, and Asian American Retailers Association (AARA, serving New Jersey businesses) were formed after 2005 to give their members greater buying power in competing with large chain stores. The AARA now organizes trade shows, again paralleling the path taken by AAHOA, and all the associations have annual conventions for members to share information and experiences. A national organization, the Asian American Convenience Store Association (AACSA), actually pre-dates these regional groups, modeled on AAHOA when it was founded in 2004. AACSA now has members with over 80,000 stores, representing over half of the independently owned and run convenience stores in the country; it partners with the mainstream National Association of Convenience Stores (NACS) on issues such as trying to reduce the debit card swipe fees charged by banks.[67]

While taxi drivers remain on the margins of American society and experience limited economic success, and retailers and gas station owners are working their way up the ladder and into the mainstream, it would seem that those highly educated professionals and entrepreneurs who are keenest to tell their stories have certainly arrived at their destination. But this is not always the case.[68] Consider Badal Shah. With his brother Aakash, he runs Aakash Chemicals in Glendale Heights, Illinois. The company was founded by their father Satish, in 1977;[69] it remains family owned, and produces several types of specialized products, with annual revenues estimated at $50 million.

Badal Shah was roused to action by a survey of members of the Young Presidents Organization (YPO), a global networking group of business leaders. According to the survey, a majority of respondents thought that Indian Americans "are lacking in trust, leadership and teamwork capabilities."[70] Shah agreed with this assessment, based on his own experiences and observations that Indian Americans are steered away from team sports when growing up and more toward games like tennis and golf—characteristics that were touched upon in chapter 4 as well. Shah found evidence to back up this negative perception in U.S. Census data that purportedly showed Indian Americans as holding "the smallest proportion of executive management positions (leading teams of 20 people or more)."[71] After researching existing options, Badal Shah launched the Dream India Academy,[72] a twelve-week program to teach young Indian-American children basketball as a way to develop teamwork abilities. The program, subsidized by his family, began in 2013 with fifty children enrolled; but there is no evidence of growth from this starting point.

Shah sees his effort as crucial to leadership development, and he is clearly attempting to level the playing field for his Indian-American community in this regard. But of course, establishing a level playing field in business is much more complicated. Teamwork and leadership also depend on mutual respect and acceptance, and it is entirely possible that attitudes are shaped by stereotypes on all sides. Stereotypes are what Silicon Valley's Indian-American entrepreneurs had to overcome, but many of them did so without necessarily adopting traditional American models of social networking.

Indeed, it is not clear that bonding over sports have been a central part of corporate leadership or even entrepreneurship in the Valley.[73,74] By establishing his academy, Shah has implicitly acknowledged that Indian-American children needed their own sandbox to learn teamwork, but it is not obvious how this will translate into managing cross-cultural work teams.[75] It is also not clear that the low proportion of Indian Americans in certain managerial positions is not a result of history and bias, unconscious or conscious,[76] or that there might be other reasons for the choices Indian Americans make. Indeed, running one's own practice as a doctor or an engineer might be more lucrative than being in one of a shrinking number of lower-level executive management positions as organizational hierarchies flatten. Nevertheless, the Dream India Academy, in the country's heartland where many Indian Americans have made their home, illustrates the challenges faced by even the "successful" in adapting to their new country. In this, they are not that different from their brothers and sisters who drive taxis and run convenience stores, gas stations, and motels.

7

Host and Home

The civil rights movement in the United States and the rhetorical and ideological imperatives of the cold war together led to passage of the historic Immigration Act of 1965. The Act's supporters believed it would not increase overall levels of immigration and would change its composition only marginally. Secretary of State Dean Rusk, when queried by the Senate Subcommittee on Immigration and Naturalization about the number of people from India who would want to immigrate to the United States, responded: "The present estimate, based upon the best information we can get, is that there might be, say, 8,000 immigrants from India in the next five years."[1] The quotas put in place exempted family reunification, with the understanding that this would ensure that immigrants were predominantly from Europe (or, less politely, would not upset the racial balance). Half a century later, we know just how erroneous those assumptions were. While the United States has always been a nation of immigrants, the Act refashioned the country with colors and cultures that were distinct from those of its founding fathers. It also had significant effects—political, social, and economic—on the countries of origin.[2]

While international migration's principal impacts are on the migrants themselves, it can also significantly affect the country of origin and the destination country, as well as relations between them. The precise effects depend on who leaves, how many leave, where they go, why they go, and when. While this book's principal focus has been on Indian immigrants in the United States, in this concluding chapter we focus briefly on some broader implications of a half-century of emigration to the United States.

We begin with the transnationalism of Indian Americans and how immigrants negotiate overlapping attachments to their country of birth and their country of settlement. We subsequently examine some consequences of Indian Americans on India and the response of the Indian State—in particular, the growth of dual citizenship. Diasporas, with their complex sense of belonging to both source and destination country, have emerged as important actors in international politics.[3] What role are Indian Americans playing in the U.S–India relationship? We then discuss some implications for U.S. immigration policy and conclude with some informed speculation on how this community might demographically evolve in the future.

Transnationalism

Even as immigrants settle down and take root in their new country, many of them maintain ties with their country of origin. Immigrants are also emigrants, and this duality underpins the desire to be connected to people and places they left behind.[4] These ties may be entirely personal, rooted in familial concerns and anchored by sending financial remittances. Alternatively, they can be broader, ranging from international business transactions to collecting funds to support civic, political and even sectarian organizations.

For many immigrants, the cognitive maps of their decision-making encompass both the country of origin and of destination, a phenomenon known as "transnationalism." The term was coined in 1916 by a journalist arguing against the dominant "melting pot" metaphor of assimilation.[5] While the term fell out of favor, it resurfaced a couple of decades ago, coinciding with changes in immigrant experiences and assimilation pathways. The term transnationalism has served as a framework for understanding the ways in which immigrant communities, particularly in developed countries like the United States, maintain links with their places of origin.[6]

While immigrants—and especially first-generation arrivals—have always tended to maintain some ties to their country of origin, transnationalism is distinctive for its critical mass of people regularly and routinely engaging in economic, political, and communicative activities with the country of origin.[7] For recent immigrants, cross-border ties have been facilitated by technological changes that have made travel easier and communications almost costless. Nonetheless, most lives are rooted in the local. A study of Salvadoran, Dominican, and Colombian immigrants in the United States found that only a fraction of them (less than one-fifth) could be classified as "transnational."[8] Moreover, the degree to which transnationalism persists over an immigrant's life and its inter-generational transmission are open questions.

Nonetheless, it is certainly true that many recent immigrants maintain close ties with their communities of origin, and this affects modes of cultural reproduction and identities that have been variously termed "liminal," "hybrid," "syncretic," and the like. Moreover, these recent immigrants often leverage political, economic, and social power in their country of origin. In a country the size of India, this is typically less the case at the national level and more prevalent at local and community levels.[9]

One area where transnationalism manifests itself is in regard to philanthropy and (more recently) social entrepreneurship. The motivations for this "civic bi-nationality" are complex and may involve integrating the "giving norms" of the country of residence with the "giving norms" that come from faith and cultural heritage. Philanthropy offers individuals an opportunity to both network and raise their status within the community. The latter could be defined broadly, as in Indian-American immigrants, or narrowly, with regard to an ethnicity or a sect within a religious group. But philanthropic activities in the country, and more specifically, in the community of origin, are also a means to anchor or resist a possible drift in ethnic identity. For instance, the engagement of Mexican immigrants has been driven as much by a desire to create cohesive communities in their adopted country as to improve conditions in their hometowns in Mexico. In a similar way, inviting the second generation to trace its ancestral roots appears to be an important motivator for the leadership roles taken by many Indian-American organizations engaged in philanthropic activities in India.[10]

It is important to emphasize that the Indian-American community is very heterogeneous along ethnic, linguistic, and religious lines, and its philanthropy has been largely personal rather than institutional, although it has been shifting towards the latter. As immigrants integrate in their new country, those who are older and with high net worth create the institutional mechanisms for funding, while the next generation turns its interests toward volunteering and other forms of social work (especially in education and health-related endeavors) in the country of their heritage. Several examples of social entrepreneurship cited in chapter 6 illustrate these trends.

Like other diasporas, Indian Americans engage in civic nationalism, such as sending funds to India in the aftermath of a natural calamity or for development activities directed toward raising the living standards of the poor. Some of the more prominent examples of this civic nationalism are patterned after American philanthropic traditions, establishing organizations with professional staff and chapters. For example, the American India Foundation (AIF) was established in the aftermath of a massive earthquake in Gujarat in 2001, and it raised more than $100 million in the following decade and a half. Another group, Indiaspora, was set up as a collective action mechanism to involve influential community members on a platform to help strengthen U.S.–India relations, create networks to support members of the community running for political office, and encourage philanthropy.[11] Indian NGOs also look to the community for fundraising. For Pratham, India's largest nongovernmental educational movement, fundraising in the United States is a critical lifeline that is undertaken by volunteers in chapters in fourteen cities across the United States.[12]

However, more contentiously, Indian Americans also fund ethnic nationalism—for instance, by supporting a variety of ethnic nationalist groups in

India. A survey of Indian-American transnational organizations found that religious groups represent the largest category (30 percent) of such organizations, with almost equiproportional shares among Christian, Hindu, and Sikh groups, which is substantially different from their shares of the Indian or U.S. population as well as the number of faith-based organizations of these communities (discussed previously in chapter 4).[13] Indian-Muslim organizations in the United States were just 2.5 percent of the total number of transnational organizations, which is very likely less than their share of the Indian-American population and considerably less than their share of the Indian population.

There have been concerns that conflict-generated, minority, and faith-based diasporas can be deeply partisan, selectively supporting communities and causes in their countries of origin. In the wake of the 2002 riots in Gujarat, concerns were raised about the role of some Hindu charitable organizations in the United States that are associated with the Hindutva (Hindu nationalist) movement in fanning sectarian strife. Financially at least, these charges are much exaggerated, since any self-respecting politician in India can easily raise the resources domestically to foment riots.[14] However, the long-term effects in India of ideological support from abroad could well have more pernicious consequences.

A recent analysis of Indian-American philanthropic organizations found that in fact most of them push for secularism and religious freedom in India, or at least overtly espouse it, and education appears to be a major focus.[15] Christian organizations in the United States, for example, have called attention to anti-Christian violence in India and pressed the U.S. State Department, and in conjunction with other groups highlighted issues of religious freedom in India. Muslim organizations also advocate for secularism in India, but they have done so by working with their counterparts in India to reframe the anti-Muslim rhetoric from identity and religion to class.[16] Interestingly, all these groups in India portray themselves as "minorities under threat." Although Hindus are the majority religion in India, they see themselves under attack by the global religions of Islam and Christianity; Christians feel their co-religionists are under pressure in India because of the rise of Hindu fundamentalism; Sikhs find themselves under attack in the United States on the one hand (by being mistaken as Muslims) and in India as victims of egregious miscarriages of justice, traced back to the massacre of several thousand Sikhs after the assassination of the Indian prime minister in 1984 and suppression of the Khalistan movement. And Indian Muslims in the United States see themselves as threatened by the war on terror in both their country of origin and the country of settlement.

However, attention to transnational philanthropic and political activity obscures the reality that, as Indian Americans grow deeper roots in the United States, their priorities have been veering as well. The community's philanthropic activities within the United States have been growing, with higher education a key focus given its crucial role in ensuring the social mobility of this community. Starting with six-figure gifts to support academic chairs and programs in the languages, cultures, and religions of India (from Sanskrit to Sikh studies), it has grown to seven- and eight-figure gifts to various U.S. universities for centers and schools, with the corresponding naming rights that have so long been an academic tradition in the United States.[17] And three Indian-American entrepreneurs recently agreed to become part of the Bill Gates and Warren Buffet-led Giving Pledge initiative, which requires them to pledge the majority of their wealth to philanthropy—indicative of the socialization effects of American society.[18] There are clear generational divides emerging in the community's political priorities, as well, with the first generation more focused on strengthening U.S.–India relations, while for the second generation domestic issues like Indian-American political candidates and racial identity are more important.

The transnational practices of Indian Americans range from diasporic and medical tourism to India to retirees who spend the winter in India and the summer in the United States. Many H1-B visa holders tired of waiting for their green cards return to India, and sometimes circle back to the United States. And even as the second generation of Indian Americans assimilates, it deploys ethnicity strategically, when it is a useful economic resource to realize economic opportunities in India.

While what constitutes "assimilation" has been changing, just as what constitutes "American" is contested (and contentious), the overall trend is unambiguous: the United States is home now and ethnic identities are giving way to broader national ones. There is no inherent contradiction between the persistence of ethnicity and Americanization—indeed, that may well be what constitutes being American. But these waves of ethnic reinforcement and Americanization have also impacted the country of origin, India. We now turn to these effects.

Effects on India

If Indian immigrants have been positively selected (on education) relative to the resident U.S. population, they have been much more so compared to the resident population in India. While their absolute numbers are small compared to the entire U.S. population, and even smaller compared to the Indian population, their share is much more substantial at the upper tail of the human capital distribution. The consequences of this selection on India have been manifold. Politically, the dominance of upper-caste elites in the first few decades of the post-1965 migration from India to the United States made India's polity less contentious.[19] Elite "exit" through emigration ensured that their economic interests were unimpaired (indeed, as the book has documented, they improved manifold). External opportunities, notably in the United States, further reduced the insecurity of India's upper-caste elites, thereby making them less implacably opposed to the political ascendancy of hitherto marginalized social groups. Thus, elite emigration lubricated the political ascendancy of India's numerically dominant lower castes, resulting in greater political stability than might have been the case if this option had not been available.[20]

Other political effects have been less salubrious, arising from support for extremist nationalist and separatist groups. Nonetheless, the evidence suggests that the degree of involvement of Indian Americans and the systemic effect of their support is relatively modest compared to domestic variables in India and much less important than vociferous critics insist.[21] However, this large elite exit arguably reduced incentives to exercise voice, particularly for human capital-creating public goods such as health and education, which have been the very basis for the mobility of Indian elites. One wonders, if the option of higher education in the United States had not been available for the Indian elite, would they have voiced a stronger demand for better higher education in India?

The economic effects of Indian emigration to the United States have worked through three pathways: ideational effects, principally by influencing policy preferences in India; economic effects via financial flows; and cognitive effects, especially as reputational intermediaries. The U.S.–India migration corridor has channeled "social remittances" that have reshaped political understandings and policy preferences. While for a long time the emigrants' broad social networks gave them access to national political elites, a gradual expansion of the social base in India has opened up networks to certain regional elites in high-emigration states such as Andhra Pradesh and Gujarat.

The distinctively "elite" character of Indian emigration to the United States (in the sense that it is drawn disproportionately from the upper tail of India's human capital distribution) has amplified these "social remittance" effects, both because of the reputational effects of this diaspora's overseas success and its access to influential institutional channels to transmit these ideas. As India's former finance minister, P. Chidambaram, explained, "First, the phenomenal success achieved by Indians abroad by practicing free enterprise meant that if Indians were allowed to function in an open market, they could replicate some of that success here. Secondly, by 1991, [the] sons and daughters of political leaders and senior civil servants were all going abroad. . . . I think they played a great part in influencing the thinking of their parents."[22]

Direct economic effects have come through financial remittances, foreign direct investment, and portfolio flows. As the world's largest recipient of financial remittances ($71 billion in 2014), with the second largest share coming from the United States (after the UAE), India has benefited in multiple ways, ranging from increased consumption levels to provisions for social insurance at both the household and national levels, thereby mitigating the effects of external shocks.

The contribution of Indian Americans to capital flows through foreign direct investment (FDI) to India (and of the Indian diaspora in general) has been much less compared to the Chinese diaspora. While the overseas Chinese played a key role in FDI into China, propelling that country into becoming the word's factory, the Indian diaspora's role has been more indirect, catalyzing Western FDI into India and helping build the country as a powerhouse in software services.[23] The emergence of the United States as India's largest trade and investment partner is in part due to the network effects of Indian Americans as successful entrepreneurs as well as their rise to senior positions at U.S. corporations, both of which facilitated FDI into India with concomitant positive effects on employment and exports.[24] While there is anecdotal evidence that the presence of Indian Americans, both as direct investors and in decision-making roles in U.S. firms and funds, has enhanced private equity and portfolio flows (or through funds in Mauritius), it is analytically difficult to distinguish Indian-American investors from other American investors. It should be noted, however, that compared to the substantial presence and success of Indian-American entrepreneurs documented in this book, few have established greenfield investments in India, perhaps because of weaknesses in the country's investment environment.[25]

The third mechanism, that of cognitive effects, has resulted from the visible success of Indian Americans. The extreme selectivity of this emigration from India and its success in the United States transformed the "brain drain" into a latent "brain bank" with spillover effects for India. In particular, the economic success of Indian Americans has parlayed into large reputational influence simply because it has come in the world's systemically most important country. And this success extends beyond the entrepreneurs chronicled in the previous chapter. The emergence of Indian Americans in the top management ranks of corporate America—a hidebound group not known for its openness to gender and racial diversity—exemplifies this. The first sector to see this was the airline industry in the late 1990s, when Rakesh Gangwal became CEO of US Airways and Rono Dutta was president of United Airlines. In the next decade, it was in the chemicals industry, with Raj Gupta at Rohm and Haas, and in food and beverages (Indra Nooyi, CEO of PepsiCo), followed by finance (Citigroup CEO Vikram Pandit and Ajay Banga, CEO of MasterCard) and consulting (Rajat Gupta at McKinsey). In this decade, technology firms with CEOs like Shantanu Narayen (Adobe Systems), Satya Nadella (Microsoft), and Sundar Pichai (Google) have greater visibility, given the iconic status of these firms.[26]

The visibility of these corporate leaders has positive cognitive externalities on global perceptions of India, including improved perceptions of Indian technology businesses. As reputational intermediaries and as credibility-enhancing mechanisms, Indian Americans have favorably influenced India's image world-wide. However, this reputational role of Indian Americans was more important when information about India was still meagre; it is much less now, as investors and markets have greater knowledge of India.

But there are negative effects as well. Concerns about immigration's adverse effects on inequality in the destination country have overshadowed its possible effects on inequality in the source country. When skilled emigrants move from a country with limited human capital to one where it is plentiful, the price of human capital will likely be bid up in the former and bid down in the latter, reflecting the relative scarcity and abundance in the two countries.[27] If this is so, international emigration from India to the United States will have had adverse effects on inequality in India.[28] But that will be even more the case if the canvas is expanded from a territorially bounded India to the territorially unbounded Indian nation, now including Indians in the United States whose average incomes are ten to forty times those in India (depending if measured in PPP terms or on an exchange rate basis); then, Indian Americans are the 1 percent of the Indian nation.

Dual Citizenship

In the new millennium, there has been greater acknowledgment on the part of the Indian state that Indian Americans are important sources and transmitters of ideas and practices, especially the more tacit elements of knowledge and financial flows. Like many other countries attempting to leverage their diasporas, India has sought to strengthen its relationship with its diaspora by instituting a form of dual citizenship, albeit in a severely constrained way.

The acquisition of citizenship in the destination country has implications for one's rights and entitlements, socioeconomic integration, and prospects for family members. It also affects the links that immigrants have with their countries of origin. When the countries of origin and destination do not allow dual citizenship, migrants are compelled to make a choice regarding citizenship.

In recent years, the large number of international migrants has (among other reasons) forced countries to grapple with their formerly settled assumptions about national identity. In 1930, the League of Nations proclaimed that "All persons are entitled to possess one nationality but one nationality only." Today, dual citizenship has grown substantially as countries seek to maintain their ties with their former residents, presumably to reap economic and political benefits.[29] In a survey of worldwide citizenship practices in 2011, the United Nations found that 53 percent (of 195 countries) allowed their nationals to retain their original citizenship when naturalizing in another country, 19 percent recognized dual citizenship for their emigrants but with certain restrictions, and 28 percent did not allow dual citizenship for their expatriate nationals.[30]

Underlying the growth of dual citizenship (with varying degrees of restrictions) is the idea that a new legal status can result in a stronger identification with (and attachment to) the country of origin, and thereby increase economic engagement and rates of naturalization and circulatory migration. In one sense, dual citizenship is a recognition that a country's diaspora is not simply a bounded and precisely defined group. It is also a form of identity and solidarity, with its own claims on the country of origin. States use symbols and ideologies to construct peoplehood, and dual citizenship is one way to ensure continued membership in a cultural community, with presumably reciprocal and symbiotic benefits to foster attachments.[31]

Official Indian government policy has taken note of changes in citizenship laws occurring worldwide. Until the 1980s, the Indian government and its diaspora shared mutual apathy and even disdain for one another. The Indian government did little to press for better treatment of its diaspora when it faced expulsion or discrimination (as occurred in Uganda in the late 1960s and Fiji in the 1980s). Following independence, India's fears of interference from the outside world were reflected not only in its policies toward international trade and foreign investments but also in an indifference bordering on resentment toward its more successful diaspora.[32] In the 1990s, the ideological climate changed in India and the success of its diaspora, especially in the United States, instilled greater self-confidence in both, leading to a strengthening of bonds that have transformed their relations. In 2003, the BJP-led NDA government organized the first Pravasi Bharatiya Divas (Overseas Indians Day), officially sealing India's recognition of its diaspora. In 2005, the Congress-led UPA government amended the Citizenship Act of 1955 to allow for registration of persons of Indian origin holding foreign citizenship as "Overseas Citizens of India" (OCI).

While this status provides certain privileges, such as the right to live and work and buy property (other than agricultural land) in India, the nomenclature is misleading since it does not confer any political rights, such as the ability to vote or run for office, or be eligible for government jobs, or, conversely, demand any obligations of citizenship, such as taxation. When the OCI scheme was launched in late 2005, it was hoped that this status would help overseas Indians "to travel to their motherland, bring economic value and benefits to Indian economy and contribute to the development process."[33]

Between December 2005, when applications began to be accepted, and February 2015, 1.72 million Overseas Citizens of India (OCI) cards were issued, of which about one-third were from the United States (see figure 7.1). Since only about half the India-origin population in the United States was naturalized by the end of 2014, this indicated that around one-third of those eligible

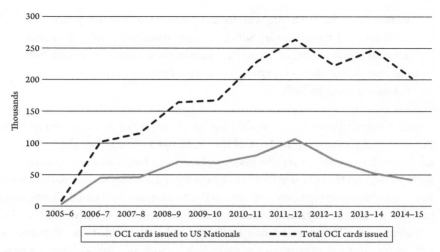

Figure 7.1 OCI Cards Issued to U.S. Nationals, 2005–2015.
Note: Fiscal year begins in April and ends in March of the following year. For 2005–2006, the data is from December 2005 to April 2006 only and the 2014–2015 data ends in February of 2015.
Source: Government of India.

had acquired an OCI card by this time. While the impact of this new legal status on the relationship of Indian Americans with India remains to be seen, it appears to have had a mildly positive effect on their propensity to naturalize (which has been observed in other settings as well).[34]

U.S.–India Relations

Historically, as long as the British flag flew over the Indian subcontinent, U.S. engagement with the region—whether in government, academia, or civil society— was much weaker compared to its intense focus on East Asia, whether that was because of the enormous pouring of American blood and treasure in wars in that part of the world (China, Japan, Korea, and Vietnam) or the relatively weaker presence of other major European powers.[35] While almost a quarter million U.S. troops were exposed to India during World War II as part of the Burma campaign, they represented barely 2 percent of all U.S. troops deployed.

In the waning years of World War II, as the outlines of a new world order began to emerge, the United States began to take notice of India. Thus, the official 1945 U.S. Army guide prepared for American troops posted in Calcutta stated:

> You already know that India is one of the main arsenals as well as principal bases for the war against Japan. What you may not have stopped

to realize is that after the war, in any permanent plan for peace that includes (and must include) Southeast Asia, India must and will assume a prominent role. You are a practical person from a practical nation. You can see that it makes common sense for anyone to cultivate a lasting friendship with India.[36]

But relations between the world's largest democracies would be fraught for the next half-century. At the root of the "Estranged Democracies" (as the title of Dennis Kux's comprehensive history of relations between the two countries aptly put it) was the cold war that overwhelmingly dominated U.S. relations with the newly decolonizing countries. Indian Prime Minister Jawaharlal Nehru, who laid the foundations for independent India's engagement with the world, felt that nonalignment allowed an economically and militarily weak India to pursue a policy of "engagement without entanglement," and hence India's interests were served best by keeping out of formal alliances. In the "for or against us" charged atmosphere of the early years of the cold war, this was viewed by the United States as "irritating and pretentious," a sign of "moral confusion," or simply a camouflage for anti-Americanism.[37] Simply put, despite sharing common values, the two countries had different interests.

But some crucial similarities accentuated the differences. Both countries professed high idealism, but their actual behavior was a far cry from their high-minded rhetoric. The iron fist of realism cloaked in the velvet glove of idealism reeked of hypocrisy to both sides. It was not until the 2000s, as the global order and domestic politics changed, and the Indian economic and military heft matched more closely to the country's size, that a deeper relationship began to be forged—one that was at least partly lubricated by the Indian diaspora in the United States.

Unlike most countries, in the United States the legislative branch of government is an important actor in the formulation of its foreign policy. This relative porosity has led immigrant communities to lobby individual members of Congress, especially congressional committees and their staffs on various causes related to their places of origin. Recognizing the importance of Congress, activists in the Indian-American community began searching for ways in the early 1990s to inform and educate congressional lawmakers for better U.S. relations with India. During Bill Clinton's first term as president, a new Bureau for South Asia Affairs was created in August 1992 (the lateness of the date being a reflection of the region's relative unimportance in U.S. strategic thinking until then). At the time, India faced a serious insurgency in Kashmir, and while the roots of the unrest were domestic, it was fueled by infiltration from Pakistan. The new assistant secretary of state for South Asia Affairs, Robin Raphael, in her congressional testimonies and functioning had been critical of India.[38] Indian-American community activists saw Raphael as an example of what they regarded as American apathy and ignorance about India and its domestic and foreign policy challenges, which eventually led them to organize and launch a lobby group in Congress.

The idea was simple: members of Congress responded to their constituents' concerns to gain their electoral support and in turn could question the administration and thereby influence policy. Community activists targeted representatives with large Indian-origin populations in their constituencies. Representatives from New Jersey (all Democrats) were targeted and the Congressional Caucus on India and Indian Americans was formed in 1993.[38a]

By the end of the 1990s, Indian Americans had become active participants in American domestic politics, making financial contributions in proportion to their share of the population, with an estimated $8 million in donations over the three election cycles leading up to 2002 (detailed in chapter 4). The U.S. sanctions on India in the aftermath of India's nuclear tests in 1998, and Pakistan's military incursion in Kargil the following year, galvanized the community into lobbying Congress and thereby put pressure on the White House.[39]

The acid test of the community's lobbying power was the Indo-U.S. Nuclear Agreement. In this case, the principal proponent of the deal was U.S. President George W. Bush, who saw it as the key to unlocking the door to building a long-term strategic partnership with India. For the Indian government, led by Prime Minister Manmohan Singh, it symbolized how far the United States was willing to trust India and view it as a long-term partner. The deal hinged on the United States lifting its moratorium on nuclear trade with India, technically circumventing aspects of the Nuclear Non-Proliferation Treaty, which India had not signed. Although the deal required India to put in place a long list of safeguards, the anti-proliferation lobby staunchly opposed the deal, arguing that it would allow India to enhance not only its civilian nuclear industry but also its military nuclear complex. In 2005, when the deal was conceived, hopes for congressional approval were slim.

The nuclear deal became a cause célèbre for the Indian-American community, which saw it as a pivotal moment with the possibility of fundamentally transforming U.S.–India relations, as indeed did its Indian and U.S. progenitors. To ensure passage of the agreement, they organized a major campaign urging community members to petition their individual representatives. Working with the executive branch, leading congressmen who were part of the India Caucus were nudged to issue supportive statements. If the Indo-U.S. nuclear agreement was a clear marker of the deepening relationship between the two countries, it also signaled the political maturing of the Indian-American community as a lobbying group, which brought together an alphabet soup of community organizations including the AAPI, AAHOA, the Indian American Friendship Council, the Indian American Forum for Political Education, the Global Organization of People of Indian Origin, the National Federation of Indian-American Associations, the United States-India Business Council, and the U.S. India Political Action Committee, as well as high-net-worth influential Indian Americans. The community invested heavily in the political instruments long honed by other immigrant groups in the United States, spending heavily on lobbying, organizing fundraisers and campaign contributions, inundating Capitol Hill with briefings, emails, petitions, phone calls—all part of a campaign to persuade Congress to approve the deal. The breadth of this activism was such that the *New York Times* ran a front-page article on the lobbying efforts of the Indian-American community in which the House Chair of the India Caucus, Gary Ackerman, noted that Indian Americans were "tripping all over each other to get behind this. . . . On a scale of 10, this is probably a 15 for them."[40]

The Nuclear Agreement was passed by overwhelming margins in both the U.S. House of Representatives and the Senate in 2006, and was signed into law on December 18, 2006 (The House vote was 298–117 and the Senate vote was 86–13). The bipartisan approval of this agreement was a major victory for the community and its activists who had shepherded the bill through stiff opposition. It not only demonstrated the effectiveness of their lobbying prowess in U.S. politics but also epitomized the newfound confidence and strength of Indian Americans with regard to their involvement in the country's political life. Nicholas Burns, an under-secretary of state in the Bush administration, declared that the campaign for the Indo–U.S. Nuclear Agreement "has been your coming out party in our country."[41]

During this period, Indian Americans were beginning to ascend to senior positions in the U.S. government, which would sometimes become a source of confusion in both countries. At a congressional hearing in July 2014, Congressman Curt Clawson repeatedly mistook two senior U.S. officials—both Indian Americans—for representatives of the Indian government. In an awkward exchange, the Florida Republican boasted of attending school in India and his love of Indian films to Nisha Biswal, the assistant secretary for the Bureau of South and Central Asian Affairs at the State Department, and Arun Kumar, the director general of the U.S. and Foreign Commercial Service and assistant secretary at the U.S. Department of Commerce. "I am familiar with your country," Clawson told the two assistant secretaries. "I love your country." He then went on to request that India open itself to increased U.S. investment. "I ask co-operation and commitment and priority from your government in so doing," he said. "Can I have that?"[42]

The incident reflected, as *The Atlantic's* Peter Beinart noted, the continued difficulties of acknowledging the American-ness of nonwhites: "It's worth noting how unlikely it is that he would have mistaken an Irish-American for a representative of the government of Ireland or a German-American for a representative of the government of Germany."[43] However, just a few weeks earlier, while visiting India, Ms. Biswal was told by a retired senior Indian official at a meeting, "It is a bad idea for the U.S. to send Indian-American diplomats here; they end up having to prove their loyalty to the U.S. more than others, and it doesn't help us."[44]

Edward R. Murrow, the prominent American broadcaster who ran the U.S. Information Agency during the Kennedy administration, once said to a group of young diplomats that the most important link in the international communications chain is the last three feet—one person talking to another.[45] Although that might matter less in the digital age, physical presence continues to matter in diplomacy, and while the presence of Indian Americans appears, on balance, to have contributed to weaving a stronger fabric of U.S.–India relations, it has also provided a few speedbumps, with fresh sources of contentiousness and misunderstandings.

In March 2005, the United States denied a visa to Narendra Modi (then chief minister of the state of Gujarat who became Prime Minister in 2014) because of the 2002 riots in Gujarat that left more than 1,000 people dead (the large majority of whom were Muslim), while he was in office. It was pushed through by "a highly unusual coalition made up of India-born activists [in the United States], evangelical Christians, Jewish leaders and Republican members of Congress concerned about religious freedom around the globe."[46] And when Indian diplomat Devyani Khobragade was arrested by U.S. authorities in New York in December 2013 for allegedly making false statements on a visa application for her housekeeper, one reason the incident drew outrage in India was that many of the U.S. officials connected to the case, from Nisha Biswal, to New York State Attorney Preet Bharara, to the State Department official for Labor and Human Rights Uzra Zeya, were of Indian origin.

And at the time of writing, urged by Indian-American parents, among others, on the abduction of their children to India by their estranged spouses, congressional legislation led the U.S. State department to prepare annual reports on International Parental Child Abduction. (The issue is much larger, involving cross-border marriages more generally). International migration has many unanticipated cross-border effects, and with India not being a signatory to the 1980 Hague Convention on International Child Abduction, and the absence of any protocol with the United States to "resolve abductions," this exemplifies the sorts of issues that will continue to crop up in the relations between the two countries precisely because of the multiple webs of ties between them resulting from the migration of Indians to the United States. While it remains to be seen whether these are simply bumps on a long road or they presage further complications, it is also the case that the selection effects of this immigration has meant that elites from many different ethnicities and social groups in India are all deeply invested in the United States through familial and social networks.

Immigration Policy

Immigration was America's historical raison d'être.[47] As the historian Oscar Handlin famously put it, "Once I thought to write a history of the immigrants in America. Then I discovered that the immigrants were American history."[48] But the past is not the future, and in the United States as in many other countries around the world, immigration is a hotly contested terrain. The who, when, why, how, and how many of immigration not only has major economic consequences for any country but also affects its self-conception as a political community.

The economic success of Indian Americans naturally raises the question of its causes—and possible implications for immigration policy. Historically, how well immigrants do depends not only on individual characteristics but also on the contexts of their exit from their homeland and their reception in their host country.[49] Certainly, there is a markedly different context for their reception in the post–Civil Rights Act America, but that has been true of most immigrants in general, at least those who come legally. But the context of exit for Indian emigrants differs considerably from those for several other immigrant groups, such as Cubans or Vietnamese, though not markedly different from groups such as Filipinos or Brazilians.

Where Indian immigrants differ from other immigrants is on their individual characteristics—in particular, their level of education. The evidence presented in earlier chapters of this book is compelling: the economic success of Indian Americans is primarily due to selection effects within India (itself the result of privileges in caste and class) and the selection mechanisms in the United States that favor highly educated immigrants. To be sure, there might be additional group attributes, such as thrift and pooling of savings, ease with the English language, established social networks and trust, and cohesive families. It is also possible that the social heterogeneity within India makes immigrants from there more adaptable, an important attribute for individuals, firms, and countries alike. However, these possibilities are necessarily speculative, since we do not have independent evidence to evaluate them.

This book has argued that the success of Indian Americans is at its core a selection story. Figure 7.2 is a schematic illustration of the Indian-American "selection premium" that has been the prime cause of this economic success. The average human capital of India's residents is substantially less than the average human capital of U.S. residents. However, the average human capital of Indian

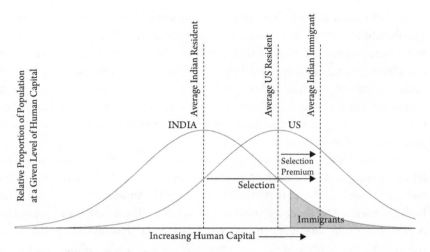

Figure 7.2 The Immigration Selection Premium and Economic Outcomes for India and United States.

immigrants is considerably more than the average human capital of U.S. residents. In part this has been because of the four principal pathways for immigrating to the United States—family reunification, family sponsorship, refugee and asylum, and work-related visas, the last has been relatively much more important for Indian immigrants, especially since the mid-1990s. *How* one enters the United States matters critically for immigrants' economic outcomes, a factor that has received less attention than it deserves.

At one level, all societies—especially fiscally stressed ones—want high-skilled immigrants—the "best and brightest" who will contribute to innovation and entrepreneurship, as well as those who are likely to be "net fiscal contributors" because their higher incomes mean they will pay more taxes and make lower claims on the government's welfare programs.[50] This explains why countries like Australia and Canada have moved to a points system that favors the educated and those whose "assimilability" is deemed higher.

Indeed, when possible, that has been the rationale behind U.S. immigration policy. Examining a century of Chinese immigration demonstrates how the earlier selection process allowed scholars and businessmen to come while excluding everyone else. As a result, as one study has argued, fears of the "yellow peril" a century ago were overturned and the community is being celebrated today as a "model minority." The screening processes have had two primary goals: enhancing American economic competitiveness and extending America's influence in China, a pattern that still shapes immigration and assimilation today, with nearly one-third of all student visas and asylum admissions and 80 percent of the investment visas going to Chinese nationals in 2013.

And of course it is not just who comes to the United States but how many. The debate between nationalists (who emphasize the priority of co-nationals) and cosmopolitans (who emphasize universal concern) has long animated political philosophers, and now environmentalists have joined the fray, arguing that current levels of immigration are undermining efforts to achieve a more economically just and ecologically sustainable society.[49] But curbing immigration may simply result in economically unjust and environmentally unsustainable societies, albeit elsewhere.

If the Iron Curtain in Europe reflected the Soviet Union's intrinsic disbelief in its own propaganda, the new iron curtain is militarized border fences and controls. The harsh reality is that while welcoming the tired and the poor and the huddled masses was an aspirational self-image of a self-confident and expanding America in the nineteenth century, it is a vision that has few adherents today, not just in the United States but anywhere in the world. While the United States keeps its doors open to political refugees and asylum seekers—albeit, it is a modest opening—those doors are essentially shut to poor and low-skilled immigrants unless they have family members willing to sponsor them.

This policy is evident in the way the United States has used disincentives to discourage low-skilled immigrants. The weakness of public assistance and social protection programs for immigrants has checked some of the anti-immigration anger, arising against a seemingly disproportionate use of scarce public resources. There has been a massive increase in the imprisonment and deportation of immigrants who have committed even only minor infractions, which has ended up targeting largely poor immigrants, who are also disproportionately illegal. Claims of a "criminalization of immigration policy" reflect the reality that between 1998 and 2010, "growth in the number of immigrant offenders accounted for 56 percent of the rise in federal prison admissions. . . . As of 2013, nearly 11 percent of the inmates in federal prisons were serving time for immigration-related offences."[52]

But the fiscal and economic story captures only one aspect of a deeper struggle to shape and manage the political community that constitutes the United States. Immigration, assimilation, and acculturation have profound effects on the meaning of a political community—an issue that many European countries are painfully grappling with as well. In the United States, the changing cultural mix of immigrants has meant that the traditional black-white binary has blurred into more variegated colors. Yet, this appears to have simply shifted the locus of schisms in American society. Whereas the "central cleavage in American life was once clearly between whites and nonwhites, now there is mounting evidence that it is between blacks and non-blacks."[53]

But if race has been the leitmotif of American society, the arrival of immigrants with religious backgrounds outside Judeo-Christian traditions has caused a new fault line to form. Contrast the welcome accorded to Irish illegal immigrants by white politicians in the 1980s and 1990s with the fear and disdain shown to Latino and Muslim immigrants; both race and religion continue to matter, with the racialization of religion emerging as a new fault line.[54]

Perhaps more than any other policy issue, immigration captures the contradictions and tensions of liberal, capitalist democracies as they simultaneously pursue policies of openness and building walls. As one observer noted, "The liberal state has a Janus face with regard to immigration policy. While representative politics and nationhood drive a restrictive approach, capitalism and constitutionalism tend to reverse these pressures. The intractable nature of immigration policy is not a failure of governance, but rather a reflection of contradictory imperatives of the state."[55]

Sweden grants its immigrants equal rights and treats them far more fairly than Saudi Arabia. But as a result, it allows only a tiny fraction of poor Bangladeshis to come and work in the country, compared to Saudi Arabia. Which policy contributes more to the welfare of Bangladesh? Family sponsorship—an important component of U.S. immigration policy—might seem humanitarian, but in the immigration lottery it hugely favors the incumbents, as if to confirm the maxim, "He that hath shall be given." It is now well recognized that greater cross-border labor mobility would do more for the world's poor than almost any other development policy.[56] But that is the one policy change least likely to occur in U.S. immigration reforms. And policies instituted in a different era, as with Cuban refugees, have remained steadfast even as circumstances have drastically changed.

At the time of this writing, the United States had been struggling to pass a new immigration reform act (the last one was passed in 1986). The issue had emerged as a third rail of U.S. politics, which means that what happens is likely to occur more by default than by design. While American public opinion favors reducing the levels of immigration, economists believe that even larger numbers of low-skilled migrants would benefit the average U.S. citizen.[57] Studies show that immigration has had "very small impacts on wage inequality among natives" in the United States[58] and that "net growth of immigrant labor has a zero to positive correlation with changes in native wages and native employment, in aggregate and by skill group."[59]

There is more consensus in public opinion about who should be admitted into the country. Broadly, "Americans view educated immigrants in high-status jobs favorably, whereas they view those who lack plans to work, entered without authorization, are Iraqi, or do not speak English unfavorably."[60] These views are unaffected by the respondent's education, labor market position, or even political beliefs. The portents point to favoring immigrants with higher human capital, but how many and from where they will come is an open question. What might the future hold for the Indian-American community?

Looking Ahead

This book was completed amid an extraordinary presidential campaign unfolding in the United States and global upheavals caused by the "Brexit," the referendum in the United Kingdom to leave the European Union. Observers have been surprised by the degree of popular support for anti-establishment and populist candidates and for a retreat from globalization in many Western democracies. Even if economists are sanguine about the aggregate effects of immigration, its impact on politics has been deeply pernicious. There is strong evidence that fears about immigration are having a significant impact on white Americans' political identities, policy preferences, and electoral choices.[61] This is driving a widening racial chasm in politics, with racial divisions in partisanship and voting exceeding demographic divisions such as class, age, and gender.

A century after the first "golden age of globalization" ended, there appears to be a growing backlash in the United States, as well as Europe, against the key drivers of globalization—trade and immigration. There has been much debate about whether the recent decades of stagnating living standards for middle-class Americans are due to trade, immigration, technological change, or a political economy that has undermined government and fostered "winner-take-all" policies.[62] In the quarter-century between 1990 and 2014, the share of immigrants in the U.S. population increased by nearly 60 percent (from 9.2 to 14.5 percent). This rapid increase, coupled with the Republican Party's attempts to sharpen social cleavages, has intensified the salience of racial and cultural factors and has fanned anti-immigrant sentiments. As one observer put it, "[if] rights of abode, still more of citizenship, are not protected, this dangerous resentment will grow. Indeed, it already has in too many places."[63]

Whether the aftermath of the 2016 presidential election will be as critical a juncture in Indian immigration to the United States as were the immigration policy changes in 1965 or the post-1995 increase in the flow of technology workers is hard to tell. But the present moment does provide a vantage point to look back and reflect on the road that has been traveled, and to peer ahead toward what might come in future decades. As long as predictions are based on projections of the past, they are relatively straightforward. It is far more difficult to anticipate the unexpected, the twists and turns of a narrative with many actors, where the only certainty is uncertainty.

Consider projections about the long term. In general, we know that domestic and international demographic forces will be important in influencing immigrant flows to the United States. The U.S. Census Bureau projects that between 2014 and 2060, the country's population will increase by nearly 100 million (from 319 million to 417 million), assuming net international migration during this period of about 64 million.[64] If this were to occur, the United States will be racially and ethnically a very different country, one unimaginable when the 1965 Immigration Reform Act was passed.[65] The Non-Hispanic white population is projected to drop to 44 percent, while the share of the Hispanic population will climb to 29 percent (from 17 percent in 2014). And the Asian population is projected to nearly double from 5.4 to 9.3 percent of the total population by 2060.[66] The fastest-growing group is expected to be "mixed race," whose share of the total population is projected to increase from 2.5 percent in 2014 to 6.2 percent by 2060 (and many of whom may well regard themselves as "sociologically white").

What major immigration flows might one expect? The second "great migration" in the second half of the twentieth century was dominated by immigrants from across the country's southern border—from Cuba, the Caribbean, and Central America, but above all from Mexico (whose emigrants made up more than one-fourth of the 41.3 million foreign-born population in the United States in 2013). By 2014 the number of new permanent residents from Asia exceeded those from Latin America, with Mexico (13 percent), India (7.7 percent), and China (7.5 percent) the leading countries of birth.[67]

The dramatic decline of immigrants from Mexico—from 369,000 in 2005 to 125,000 in 2013, a fall of two-thirds in just eight years—was driven primarily by a steep decline in illegal immigration, itself the result of changes occurring on both sides of the border. In 1960, the Mexican fertility rate was 7.3 children per woman. By the end of the 2010s, it is likely to drop below replacement level (2.1) and shrink the pool of potential immigrants (albeit with a lag). Concurrently, economic growth in Mexico and a more robust border control and immigration system (with more forceful practices on deporting unauthorized immigrants) are making the United States relatively less attractive for Mexicans.

The other big source of immigrants—China—has had fertility rates well below its replacements levels because of its "one child policy" enacted in 1980 and the preferences of young, urban, and affluent Chinese for small families, notwithstanding the recent relaxation in the policy. This could attenuate emigration pressures from China, but its sheer size and the relatively low number of emigrants compared to its population may make this unlikely. There are other factors to consider, too. Chinese immigrant flow into the United States is channeled along two distinct pathways—skills-based (like Indians, through student and employment-based visas) and asylum seekers.[68] How will these flows change? If China's economy continues its extraordinary performance, more Chinese students may return to China and fewer workers may want to come to the United States. On the other hand, a more authoritarian turn of government may well increase the number of asylum seekers.

With India's population expected to grow by another 400-odd million people by 2050, demographic pressures there will continue to drive international emigration from India.[69] If Indians continue to come into the United States at the rate they have in recent years (about 10 percent of international migrants in 2012 and 2013), another 6 million-plus immigrants could enter by 2060. But we certainly cannot project that far with any confidence—about India, or for that matter, about China or Mexico. There are too many uncertainties.

It is difficult enough to project into the near future, given the volume of Indians coming to the United States on employment-related visas (H1-B and L-1) and their susceptibility to the vicissitudes of economic cycles and political pressures (with denunciations that they are "stealing" American jobs). The politically contentious immigration reform bill of 2013 (Senate Bill S-744), if passed in its current form, will have ambiguous effects on Indian immigrants. While it is likely to ease entry for individuals to access the U.S. labor market, it will also make it harder for Indian IT firms to operate in the United States by constraining their ability to bring in skilled workers from India.[70]

If there are no major changes in the short term—that is, the current inflows continue without significant increase or decline—some projections are possible. For one, the linguistic composition of this population will be significantly different, along the lines we identified earlier. Gujarati and Punjabi, the languages that defined Indian Americans until the IT generation, are falling rapidly behind Hindi, Telugu, and Tamil. If this trend continues, in the next fifteen years, Hindi will strengthen its position as the leading language of Indian Americans, and Telugu and Tamil will become the dominant regional languages, with concomitant changes in the definition of Indian Americans and the visible markers of these linguistic cultures—cuisine, places of worship, cultural performances, and so on.

But the precise composition will also be determined by another selection: who returns to India and in what numbers. At the individual level, among students at least, there continue to be significant selection effects, with the stronger students more likely to emigrate and less likely to return. There appears to be negative selection in return migration manifest in multiple dimensions—including ability, postmigration human capital investment, and income.[71] Furthermore, economic and social changes within India will affect the social composition of Indians coming to the United States. The selection effects of the upper and dominant castes will attenuate, with greater numbers coming from hitherto socially marginalized groups as their gradual social mobility within India equips them with the human capital to make it over the selection hurdles that have been highlighted in this book.

The settlement patterns of these newest arrivals are likely to be tied to their workplaces in the IT economy, continuing to weaken the significance of New York City while strengthening even more some established centers like Silicon Valley and Middlesex County, New Jersey, but newer IT centers in Texas and Virginia will grow in significance as well. In fact, if the spatial distribution of new arrivals mirrors that of the established Indian Americans, there will be some remarkable local concentrations of the community in places like Middlesex County, New Jersey, and Santa Clara County, California. These regions will almost certainly see the community organizing politically and beginning to elect members at local, state, and national levels.

These projections are based on the assumption of continuity and the absence of exogenous shocks like Y2K and another "great recession." But, there is an arena that will be immune to such shocks: the second generation of Indian Americans, the children who have been born in the United States of India-born parents. In 2030, over 300,000 America-born Indians that now are ten to twenty-five years old will turn twenty-five to forty years old, more than doubling the size of the economically active second-generation cohort. Based on our initial analysis, this increasingly large second generation is likely to be different from its parents, not only in its professional and occupational choices but also in marriage, fertility, location, and participation in the political and cultural life of the country (although perhaps not in sports). To the extent that their parents' selection mechanisms are reinforced by the structural advantages of relative privilege, it seems reasonable to guess that Indian-American representation in various elite achievement groups will continue to be amplified.

These projections are tenuous because the second-generation cohort is currently small. As the cohort grows significantly larger, though, we will have more definitive evidence on the varieties of assimilation. Of this we are reasonably sure: given that the recent cohorts of Indian immigrants are a young population in the prime of fertility and reproduction—two-thirds were between twenty and thirty-five years in age—the combination of recent immigrants and the youth and reproduction of the second (and gradually third) generations may well make the title of this book only half as accurate within a couple of decades. While the Indian-origin population could well double (from a little over 3 million to more than 6 million) and the "other one percent" will perhaps become the "other two percent", identity attrition might reduce the officially recorded numbers as future generations gradually fuse into an ever-evolving American mainstream. If that comes to pass, this book will need to be rewritten, and its new authors will perhaps be the children of the first generation. But that is some time away. These are anxious times and, more than at any time in recent memory, the future of immigration policy in the United States is fraught. Whether and how this will affect Indians in America remains to be seen.

Appendix

DATA USED AND EXPLANATIONS

This is a data-driven study. Our claims and arguments are based on data that are either publicly available or have been generated by us for the purposes of this study. This appendix summarizes the different data sets used in the book: their sources, strengths and drawbacks, and a clear rationale for using what we have used. This discussion should be useful for most readers, including expert data users who may not be as familiar with data involving small populations.

Broadly, there are three primary data sources:

- By far the largest and most important source is the U.S. Census Bureau (USCB) and the varieties of data it collects on a range of subjects. The USCB collects "facts"—about identity, origin, family structure, income, education, employment, housing, immigration, transportation, business ownership, etc.
- Our second significant data source is the Pew Research Center, a nonpartisan fact tank that conducts public opinion polling, demographic research, media content analysis, and other empirical social science research. Pew collects data that the USCB does not—opinions and attitudes. We make extensive use of a major survey of Asian Americans conducted by Pew in 2012.
- The third significant data source is a survey of Indian-American entrepreneurs conducted in 2013 by the Center for the Advanced Study of India at the University of Pennsylvania. This survey was undertaken for the specific purpose of this book project.
- In addition, we use other data as available, from special groups such as professional, linguistic, and religious associations.

We discuss the details of the three significant data sets we have used in the remainder of this appendix.

1. Data from the U.S. Census Bureau

This section on the USCB data is the most detailed and complex, not least because of the range of issues that need to be covered, including samples and sample sizes, timings, geographies, unit-level vs. summarized data, and special-purpose censuses (such as on business owners). The U.S. Constitution requires the USCB to conduct a national census of the population. Recent censuses up to 2000 took place every ten years (called the decennial census). It consisted of a "short form," which included basic questions about age, gender, race, household relationship, and owner/renter status, and a "long form" used for only a sample of households (about one-sixth of the total households) that included not only the basic "short-form" questions but also detailed questions about socioeconomic and housing characteristics. The short form was used to provide basic counts by basic categories (gender, age, race, etc.), and the long form was used to provide counts by subcategories (for example, national origin, occupation, education, etc.) and critical details of social and economic conditions.

However, after the 2000 Census, the long form was discarded, and in 2005 the Census Bureau began administering the American Community Survey (ACS), which is considered the most substantial change in the decennial census in more than 60 years. To emphasize, the decennial census that is a full count of the population still takes place (and last took place in 2010), but with only the short form, which does not allow the data to be reported along our key categories of interest. The ACS has replaced the decennial census long form and now collects similar information annually rather than only once every ten years.

The ACS is a nationwide, continuous survey designed to provide reliable and timely demographic, housing, social, and economic data every year. The ACS samples nearly 3 million addresses each year, which leads to about 2 million final interviews. The annual ACS sample is much smaller than the Census 2000 long form sample, which included about 18 million housing units, but the five-year summary ACS (discussed below) has a sample of about the same size.

This is an important point. The ACS is not a census because not every individual is counted and queried. Rather, a sample of the population is counted and queried every year, and detailed tallies of the population and its characteristics are created based on the sample. The smaller the base population—that is, the smaller the geographical area (say, a rural county) or population subgroup (say, the Indian-American population)—the smaller is the sample size and the less reliable is the information in a given year. As a result, the annual ACS does not provide reliable information at all spatial scales or for small subgroups every year; instead, it combines data from multiple years to produce more reliable data for small areas and small, subgroup populations that are scattered over large areas. To provide information for communities each year, the ACS provides one-, three-, and five-year estimates. Table A.1 provides information on the various spatial scales at which different forms of census data are released.

Therefore, two types of data are available from the USCB: the unit-level sample data itself (that is, the raw data collected by the USCB at the household level) and various summaries or aggregates of these unit-level data tallied for different time periods (1-year, 3-year, and 5-year summaries) at different spatial scales and for subgroups of the population. We have used both data types in the analysis. We begin with a discussion of summary/aggregate data from the census that is based on a complex census geography.

Aggregated Census Data

Census geography and data quality

From the largest to the smallest spatial units, the census geography of the United States follows this hierarchy: state level—51 units; county level—3,141 units;

Appendix Table A.1 **U.S. Census Geography and the ACS**

Type of area	Number of areas	Percent of areas receiving		
		1, 3, & 5 yr estimates	1 & 3 yr	5 yr only
States and District of Columbia	51	100.0	0.0	0.0
Congressional districts	435	100.0	0.0	0.0
Public Use Microdata Areas	2,071	99.9	0.1	0.0
Metropolitan statistical areas	363	99.4	0.6	0.0
Micropolitan statistical areas	576	24.3	71.2	4.5
Counties and county equivalents	3,141	25.0	32.8	42.2
Urban areas	3,607	10.4	12.9	76.7
Townships and villages (minor civil divisions)	21,171	0.9	3.8	95.3
ZIP code tabulation areas	32,154	0.0	0.0	100.0
Census tracts	65,442	0.0	0.0	100.0
Census block groups	208,801	0.0	0.0	100.0

Source: A Compass for Understanding and Using American Community Survey Data. Available at www.census.gov/content/dam/Census/library/publications/2008/acs/ACSGeneralHandbook.pdf

minor civil division level—21,171 units; ZIP code level—32,154 units; census tract level—65,442 units; and census block group level—208,801 units. The smaller units (such as block groups and census tracts) can be added up to create other, larger geographical units, such as metropolitan statistical areas (which is the Census Bureau's terminology for what, in India, would be considered metropolitan cities or urban agglomerations—that is, large, continuously urbanized areas that can cut across county and state boundaries). The larger a geographical unit, the more readily available its data, but the more aggregated it is; the smaller a geographical unit, the less readily available its data, but the more disaggregated it is.[1] Therefore, if we are interested in any scale smaller than a U.S. state or metropolitan statistical area—say, a county—we have to use the five-year ACS estimate. No one-year or three-year estimate can provide information on all counties (or subcounty units such as minor civil divisions, or MCDs) of the United States.

This conclusion is reinforced by the Census Bureau's caution that mean values for small subgroups of the population should be interpreted carefully because the mean is influenced strongly by extreme values in the distribution and susceptible to the effects of sampling variability, misreporting, and processing errors. Not only should mean values be carefully interpreted, but also simple counts should be subject to the same cautions. It goes without saying that the larger the ACS sample, the more reliable the counts of our populations of interest. Since we are interested in small population data (because we know that Indian Americans make up about 1 percent of the U.S. population), we generally have to rely on three- or five-year ACS estimates. This does not provide the most current information, but for small populations this is often the only statistically reliable information. Hence, though the one-year 2012 ACS estimate provides the most current information, it cannot be used for some of the analysis because (a) it is not available at scales smaller than U.S. states; and (b) it is not reliable, even at the state level, for small populations.

The approach we have taken is to give careful attention to the standard errors (SE) of the estimates. The smaller the SE, the more reliable is an estimate. Consider, for example, the data in appendix table A.2. Here we show estimates for the headcount of the India-born population and its per capita income for the entire United States and two states—California, which had the largest number of India-born, and Florida, which was ranked sixth for the India-born—from two sources: the latest ACS, from the single year 2012, and the latest three-year summary ACS from 2010–2012.[2] The main features of the variation are immediately obvious: (1) the latest single-year estimate yielded higher population numbers (at the national and state scales); this was very likely because of the continued year-on-year rapid growth of India-born population; (2) the three-year estimates had significantly lower standard errors, which means that these estimates were closer to the real numbers; (3) the larger the base population, the smaller the standard error.

Appendix Table A.2 **Examples of Variations Introduced by Sample Size**

	Population of India-born		Per Capita Income	
	Estimate	Standard Error	Estimate ($)	Standard Error
USA 2012 ACS	1,967,998	± 31,113 (1.6%)	53,936	± 1,175 (2.2%)
USA 2010-12 ACS	1,881,130	± 19,145 (1.0%)	52,521	± 471 (0.9%)
California 2012 ACS	382,852	± 15,788 (4.1%)	58,036	± 2,065 (3.6%)
California 2010-12 ACS	364,307	± 7,805 (2.1%)	56,506	± 1,142 (2.0%)
Florida 2012 ACS	64,692	± 6,249 (9.7%)	50,635	± 6,642 (13.1%)
Florida 2010-12 ACS	64,492	± 3,842 (5.6%)	48,698	± 4,079 (8.4%)

Note that for Florida (which had a substantial number of India-born), the standard errors of the single year estimates were 10 to 13 percent of the base population. In states with smaller India-born populations (that is, the remaining 44 states), the standard errors were much larger. This was so much so that state-level comparisons were not possible with the 2012 ACS because the India-born population was reported only for the top eight states (the sample size was too small in the remaining states for the USCB to calculate reliable estimates).

Which estimate to use? In general we use the following method: (1) Find the most recent estimate; (2) examine its coverage with three critical questions: Are all needed geographies covered? Are all needed subpopulations covered? Are all needed categories and subcategories covered?; (3) interpret the reliability of the data with careful consideration of the standard errors, rejecting some data if necessary.

The Public Use Microdata Sample

The problem of obtaining data for small groups (like the India-born) becomes even more acute when the analysis needs to be carried out for subcategories or at local scales. An example of the former is the occupational category "computers," which employed around 350,000 India-born—easily the largest occupational category for the group. It was necessary, therefore, to analyze this occupational category in detail with India-born data. For that, we needed occupational data that could be disaggregated by subcategory (say, "computers" or "medicine") and by subpopulation (the India-born). At the same time, the local scale issue was important because we knew that the India-born population was concentrated in a small number of counties in a handful of states; close to half the India-born lived in about 32 of the 3,141 counties in the United States. Not only that, but even within these counties, the India-born were concentrated in a handful of localities. Therefore, any analysis of subcategories (that are important for the India-born community) or microgeographies (that contain very large numbers of India-born) requires the use of data that are available for subcategories and at the subcounty scale for the India-born population.

The only reliable and disaggregated estimate of socioeconomic characteristics of small populations is the Public Use Microdata Sample (PUMS), which is collected at a "made-up scale" called Public Use Microdata Area (PUMA). A PUMA is a statistical geographic area defined specifically for the tabulation and dissemination of the U.S. Census. PUMAs are nested within states, and in urban areas, within counties, and are typically aggregated from census tracts. Each PUMA is supposed to have a population of around 100,000, but there is significant variation whereby the population can range from 50,000 to 200,000. There were 2,071 PUMAs nationwide in the period under study (see appendix table A.1). They are very useful for disaggregating small populations to small geographical scales. In urban areas, they are smaller than counties, and hence it is possible to undertake analysis at the subcounty scale. They are larger than census tracts, hence the estimates have smaller standard errors and therefore are more reliable.[3]

Nonetheless, there is great variation in the reliability of PUMS data, as illustrated in appendix table A.3. Here, we show average household income of

Appendix Table A.3 **Variations at the PUMA Scale for India-born Household Income**

PUMA, state	Locality	# India-born	Avg. household income	Std Error
Highest Household Incomes (all population sizes)				
03801, TX	Waco	14	726,100	699,687
03300, TX	Odessa/West Odessa	70	595,857	390,635
00700, KY	Bell/Harlan/Whitley Counties	93	524,290	333,529
04800, OH	Ironton	62	519,710	346,106
03701, CA	Atascadero/Baywood-Los Osos	98	509,037	340,789
Highest Household Incomes (minimum 1,000 India-born)				
04202, NY	Glen Cove/Jericho/Syosset	1,679	285,210	32,943
01705, MO	Clayton/Creve/Coeur	1,458	229,248	47,278
01903, NJ	Berkeley Hghts/New Providence/Plainfield	1,428	215,992	30,872
02707, CA	Cupertino/Los Gatos/Saratoga	10,813	211,585	11,680
02505, MI	Beverly Hills/Birmingham/Bloomfield	2,844	208,876	21,633

the India-born population at the PUMA scale. The five highest average household income PUMAs are listed using two ranking methods: one list shows the highest-income PUMAs regardless of the number of India-born in them; the second list shows the highest income PUMAs with at least 1,000 India-born in each. It was obvious that unusable income figures are generated by the Census Bureau's sampling method when there were few India-born in a PUMA. The top five were all in isolated rural/small town areas that had fewer than 100 India-born in each. The standard errors were so large as to make these data meaningless. On the other hand, when there were at least 1,000 India-born in a PUMA, the income estimates were more reliable. They were not precise (a sample can never yield precise counts or means), but they were usable.

We make extensive use of PUMS data to analyze categories like income, education, occupation, industry, employment, language, housing, and immigration. We also use PUMS data to undertake microgeographic analysis and mapping of some key variables, such as income and industry.[4]

2. Survey of Business Owners, 2007

The Survey of Business Owners (SBO) collects demographic and economic data on all nonfarm businesses filing Internal Revenue Service tax forms as individual proprietorships, partnerships, or any type of corporation with annual receipts of $ 1,000 or more. This survey has been conducted every five years, since 1972. The aggregate data are public records and can be retrieved at the U.S. Census Bureau's website. We use the 2007 SBO data, which was the most recent available at the time of the analysis. Approximately 2.3 million businesses received the 2007 SBO questionnaire.

The sampling frame for the SBO captures all large firms with certainty. There are nine frames for sampling, mostly based on ethnic groups, but also including women-owned businesses. The SBO universe is stratified by state, industry, frame, and whether the company has paid employees. Sampling from each of these strata includes large companies with certainty (but with the cutoff for "large" depending on the stratum), and with systematic random sampling for the rest of each stratum. Hence, all reported aggregate numbers are essentially estimates of the true national values.

3. Unit-Level American Community Survey Data

The 2007–2011 American Community Survey (ACS) five-year pooled sample is used for unit-level analysis, in order to obtain an adequately large analytic sample size for our subpopulations of interest: foreign-born Indians (born in India), and U.S.-born Indians of Indian parentage. We identified Indian-origin individuals based on self-report of race. For foreign-born Indians, this means identifying those individuals who claim "Asian Indian" as their race and India as their place of birth. For U.S.-born Indians, the same racial identification holds true, with the sample restricted to those born in the United States. There is a third Indian-origin group that we include in certain portions of the analysis. These are individuals who report "Asian Indian" as race, but are not born in India or the United States ("born-elsewhere"). About 56 percent of this group trace their birthplace to Africa or South America/Caribbean, while 22 percent are born in various Asian countries. Since these individuals are heterogeneous with respect to birthplace, reasons for immigration, and occupational categories, we focus on the Africa and South America/Caribbean contingent in the analysis of the "born-elsewhere" group.

While self-reported ancestry is another indicator of heritage, this variable includes ambiguous responses with individuals claiming "Bengali" or "Punjabi" ancestry, thus they could be Bangladeshi or Pakistani, respectively, rather than Indian. Our aim is not to study Indian Americans in isolation, but as a comparison with the dominant group in the country: Non-Hispanic whites and other Asians, specifically Chinese, Korean, Japanese, Vietnamese, and Filipinos. We restrict all these samples to those above age 25 in order to approximate completed education, as some of our main outcomes of interest are group differences in income and occupation. Our final sample sizes for the Indian analytic groups are 66,968 India-born, 5,639 U.S.-born, and 9,883 born-elsewhere (South America, Caribbean, or other parts of Asia).

The sampling design of the ACS includes an over- or under-sampling of certain subgroups in various geographic areas across the country and varying degrees of nonresponse, all of which can have an impact on standard errors, as described above. To obtain estimates that accurately represent subgroups of interest, we use sampling weights provided by the ACS—"perwt" for person-level analysis and "hhwt" for household-level analysis. As discussed in appendix table A.1, there are various levels of geographic stratification in the ACS. There are additional sampling specifications at the household level for variance and standard-error estimation. We include ACS-provided technical variables "strata" and "cluster" to account for the impact of complex sample design stratification at the unit level.

4. The Pew Survey of Asian Americans, 2012

The Pew survey sample design takes into account the relatively low proportions of Asian population spread across the country, with specific clusters in certain states like California. It is thus a probability-based sample with various sampling instruments like phone landlines, cell phone random digit dial, and list samples from a commercial database of households with common Asian names, with interviews in English and Cantonese, Hindi, Japanese, Korean, Mandarin, Tagalog, and Vietnamese.

The final sample size is 3,511 Asian individuals, including 580 Indian Americans. Of these, 439 (76 percent) were born in India and 61 (11 percent) in the United States. For analysis, we do not disaggregate the Indian groups owing to the small sample size of the latter group, and we use the 580 as the Indian-origin sample. One note of caution in interpreting these results: they are likely to represent the views of India-born Indian Americans, rather than that of U.S.-born. Given the complex sample design, we use the appropriate PEW-provided sampling weight to adjust for probability of selection, coverage of households using landlines and cell phones, and balancing population totals with the Asian-American adult population in the ACS. We use the Pew survey to identify Indian-American political behavior (party, ideology) and social behavior (education, income, religiosity, views on intermarriage, etc.).

5. The CASI Survey of Indian-American Entrepreneurs

The survey was titled the Indian-American Business Leaders Survey, and was conducted by Princeton Survey Research Associates International (PSRAI), from May 14, 2013, to November 4, 2013, using a questionnaire developed by project researchers at the Center for the Advanced Study of India (CASI) at the University of Pennsylvania and the University of California, Santa Cruz. Two data sources were used for sampling. First, a sample was purchased and supplied by the University of Pennsylvania and the University of California, Santa Cruz to PSRAI (listed sample). The second source of data was an online panel sample from Universal Survey. A total of 649 respondents were interviewed via phone ($n = 6$) and online ($n = 643$). A copy of the questionnaire and a description of the survey methodology follow.

Contact procedures and outcomes were as follows.

Listed Sample

An initial pilot batch of 1,500 names was selected. This pilot batch did not have email addresses, so they were sent an initial advance letter and then phone call follow-ups were made to obtain an interview via phone or online. Phone calls were halted after one week owing to extremely low response. The University of Pennsylvania undertook the task of attempting to obtain email addresses for the initial pilot sample, and an additional sample was released in an effort to obtain email addresses. The email invitations were sent out mid-July 2013 through mid-September 2013. Each selected respondent received three emails in an attempt to secure a completed interview. For the listed sample portion, 96 completes were received out of 5,668 requests for participation. This translates to a 2 percent participation rate.

Panel Sample

Data collection from the panel sample began October 9, 2013, with email invitations to potential eligible respondents. A total of 552 responses were collected from the panel sample. Email invitations went out on a rolling basis until the desired number of completes was achieved. For the panel sample, 553 out of 24,093 initial invitations participated in the survey. This represents a 2 percent participation rate.

Sample Composition

The sample was more educated than the population of Indian-American business owners, or Indian Americans in general. The survey sample contained both business owners and other professionals. The occupational distribution was also somewhat skewed compared to the general population, having participants who were more successful on average than the general population. The proportion of women respondents was similar to the proportion of women business owners among Indian Americans. The proportion of U.S.-born Indian Americans in the sample was higher than for Indian-American business owners.

Questionnaire

The questionnaire promised anonymity and explained the purpose of the study: "The project aims to understand the motivations, determinants of success, and economic and social impacts of entrepreneurs. In addition, the survey hopes to understand the channels that link the U.S. and India together through flow of investment, ideas, and business relationships and thereby contribute to policy debates in the U.S. and India on these issues."

The first set of questions asked about the respondent's company size (revenue and employees), industry or sector, location, and the respondent's position within the company. Then questions were asked about whether the respondent had founded his or her current company, founded a company in the past, or planned to found a company in the next 12 months. Current, past, and planned founders were asked questions specific to entrepreneurship. These included sources and levels of initial funding for their companies, motivations, experience, outcomes, and success factors. Then a series of questions was asked about company and personal links to India, including financial transfers in either direction, purposes of the transfers, strategic business relationships, political links and activities, and perceptions of preselected Indian values. The survey finished with demographic questions about age, gender, education, place of birth, citizenship, and immigration history.

As with any survey, there is no independent way of checking the accuracy of responses in any category. One can guess at possible directions of bias in responses relating to achievements or attitudes, but these issues would be present in any survey of this nature.

6. Indian-American Organizations

Data on Indian-American organizations was compiled from the Guidestar website database on 501 (c) 3, 4, 6, and 7 status organizations using India-specific search terms. The data analyzed was limited to organizations which reported an income of at least $1,000 in the last year that was reported. This was done to avoid counting organizations which were nonfunctioning "shell" organizations. Two key categories were excluded from analysis: (1) missionary organizations and (2) organizations which have a primary focus of doing development work in India unless they appear to be run entirely by Indian Americans and have a social component in the United States (e.g., American India Foundation). Organizations based on broad pan-Asian identity were also excluded from the dataset because it was discovered that many organizations for the Asian community primarily catered to East Asians. Foundations were also excluded because they usually do not serve as a community organization. The database includes 966 organizations. There are likely to be many Indian-American organizations not included in the database because they may not have official status or an income of over $1000 or they may have been missed in the data collection process.

Limitations of the Data

The data contains organizations which were collected using search terms, so one limitation of the dataset was the scope of the searches. Search terms that were used included but were not limited to: India, Indo-, South Asia, South Asian, Samaj, Mandal, Sangam, Koota, Sabha, Sangh, Sikh, Jain, Bohra, Pradesh, Hindi, Hindu, Sanskrit, Sanskriti, Arya Samaj, India(n) Muslim, India(n) Christian,

Sindhi, Dalit, Brahmin, Rajput, Chinmaya, Ramakrishna, Krishna, Parivar, caste, jati, and regionally specific terms for each state such as Malayalee, Malayali, and Kerala for Kerala. It is possible that, using these search terms, certain organizations were missed. All organizations listed under the NTEE classification X70 (Hindu) religious organizations were included, which may have inflated the numbers for Hindu organizations, given that Indian-Muslim and Christian groups may have fallen through the cracks of the search terms since they were more difficult to distinguish from general Muslim and Christian groups. Another limitation is the fact that not every organization has data for the same year. The data is generated from the last year's tax documents submitted by the organization; however, some had not submitted in a few years. For this reason, it is not possible to make any claims about in- and out-flows in any given year for Indian-American organizations.

NOTES

Preface

1. Anita Raghavan, *The Billionaire's Apprentice. The Rise of the Indian-American Elite and the Fall of the Galleon Hedge Fund* (New York: Business Plus, 2013), 416.
2. Maritsa V. Poros, *Modern Migration. Gujarati Indian Networks in New York and London* (Stanford, CA: Stanford University Press, 2011).
3. For a recent summary, see Ariela Schachter, "Finding Common Ground? Indian Immigrants and Asian American Panethnicity," *Social Forces* 92 (2014): 1487–512. doi: 10.1093/sf/sou019; and for a well-cited example of writing in this vein, see Vijay Prashad, *The Karma of Brown Folk* (Minneapolis: University of Minnesota Press, 2000).
4. The only comparable case we can think of is the migration of about a million Russian Jews to Israel after the collapse of the Soviet Union; 60 percent had a college degree, which was double the rate prevailing in Israel at the time.
5. The literature on social capital—that is, the positive externalities of cooperation based on a shared attribute—is vast, including contributions from seminal figures, from Alexis de Tocqueville through Jane Jacobs, to James Coleman and Robert Putnam and Hillary Clinton.
6. Perhaps TiE (The Indus Entrepreneurs) was foreshadowed in a completely different context by the pan-Indian Gadar movement of a century ago, showing a capacity for people of the entire region to unite for a common cause.

Chapter 1

1. "Columbus Had Word for the Natives Here and It's a Nuisance to Visitors from India," *New York Times*, November 17, 1948, 29.
2. Robert Shaffer, "J.J. Singh and the India League of America, 1945-1959: Pressing at the Margins of the Cold War Consensus," *Journal of American Ethnic History* 31 (2012): 68–103.
3. Remarks of Welcome to Prime Minister Nehru of India at the Washington National Airport, http://trumanlibrary.org/publicpapers/viewpapers.php?pid=1245.
4. Hannah Arendt, *The Origins of Totalitarianism* (New York: Houghton Mifflin Harcourt, 1973), 278.
5. John F. Kennedy, *A Nation of Immigrants* (New York: Harper Perennial, 2008), 2.
6. David Scott FitzGerald and David Cook-Martin, *Culling the Masses: The Democratic Origins of Racist Immigration Policy in the Americas* (Cambridge, MA: Harvard University Press, 2014), 5.
7. Richard Alba and Victor Nee, *Remaking the American Mainstream: Assimilation and Contemporary Immigration* (Cambridge, MA: Harvard University Press, 2003), 17. The cycle of each new immigrant group being seen as "alien" by those already settled, and in turn after a few generations viewing the next new immigrant group with similar suspicion, has been a perennial feature of American immigration history.

8. This argument is made forcefully by FitzGerald and Cook-Martin, *Culling the Masses*. It is difficult to judge the relative contribution of the various factors (changing race and labor relations, the demise of eugenic ideology, the cold war, etc.) that led to the social conditions that enabled the change in immigration policy.

9. Earl Robert Schmidt, "American Relations with South Asia, 1900–1940" (unpublished doctoral dissertation, University of Pennsylvania, 1955), 276.

10. India Bicentennial Week, Invitation by the Medical College of Pennsylvania, www.saadigitalarchive.org/sites/all/themes/saada/bookreader.php?title=JnF1b3Q7SG9ub3JpbmcgdGhlIE1lbW9yeSBvZiBBBbmFuZGliYWkgSm9zaGVGVlLCBNLkQuJnF1b3Q7&folder=MjAxNC0wNw==&object=aXRlbS1hMjY2LTE4ODNNoaS1yZWYwMDMt&pages=Ng==#page/1/mode/1up.

11. "Swami Vivekananda: Hindoo Monk of India," www.asia.si.edu/explore/yoga/object.asp?id=V22_vsnc-v2.

12. Vivek Bald, *Bengali Harlem and the Lost Histories of South Asian America* (Cambridge, MA: Harvard University Press, 2013).

13. Gary R. Hess, "The "Hindu" in America: Immigration and Naturalization Policies and India, 1917-1946," *Pacific Historical Review* 38, no. 1 (1969): 59–79.

14. Ibid., 62.

15. Philip Q. Yang, *Asian Immigration to the United States* (Cambridge: Polity Press, 2011), 91.

16. Werter D. Dodd, "The Hindu in the Northwest," *World Today* 13 (1907): 1157–60.

17. Hess, "The "Hindu" in America," 62.

18. Ibid., 62.

19. Dodd, "The Hindu in the Northwest," 1158.

20. Ibid.

21. "Progressive Era to New Era, 1920-1929," www.loc.gov/teachers/classroommaterials/presentationsandactivities/presentations/timeline/progress/immigrnt/.

22. "U.S. Population from 1900," www.demographia.com/db-uspop1900.htm.

23. There is a large literature on this subject. See Manfred Bornewasser, "Social Psychological Reactions to Social Change and Instability: Fear of Status Loss, Social Discrimination and Foreigner Hostility," *Civilisations* 42, no. 2 (1993): 91–103. Also Christopher S. Parker and Matt A. Barreto, *Change They Can't Believe In: The Tea Party and Reactionary Politics in America* (Princeton, NJ: Princeton University Press, 2013).

24. Cheryl Lynee Shanks, *Immigration and the Politics of American Sovereignty, 1890–1990* (Ann Arbor: University of Michigan Press, 2001), 32–34.

25. Yang, *Asian Immigration*, 92.

26. Cong. Record, 63 Cong., 2 sess. (1914), Appendix, 842–45.

27. Committee on Immigration, House of Representatives, "Hindu Immigration," February 13, 1914.

28. Ibid., 51.

29. Ibid., 70.

30. Ibid., 74.

31. Ibid., 76.

32. Ibid., 77. The distinction was clarified later in testimony by another Indian immigrant.

33. "Hindu Invasion Is Headed Off," *Los Angeles Times*, October 3, 1915, 11.

34. *Immigration Act of 1917*, Sec. 3, 64th Congress (1917).

35. Maia Ramnath, *Haj to Utopia: How the Ghadar Movement Charted Global Radicalism and Attempted to Overthrow the British Empire* (Berkeley: University of California Press, 2011).

36. Toward the end of the trial, one of the defendants, Chakravarty, was assassinated by one of the other defendants, further adding to the negative public image of the community. Joan M. Jensen, "The "Hindu Conspiracy": A Reassessment," *Pacific Historical Review* 48, no. 1 (1979): 65–83.

37. Yang, *Asian Immigration*, 54–55.

38. Karen Leonard, *Making Ethnic Choices: California's Punjabi Mexican Americans* (Philadelphia: Temple University Press, 1992), 20.

39. Ibid., 23.

40. *United States v. Bhagat Singh Thind*, 261 U.S. 204 (1923).

41. *Naturalization Act of 1790*, Revised Statutes, Sec. 2169, 1st Congress (1790).
42. *United States v. Bhagat*, 215.
43. Thind finally got (and kept) his citizenship on this third attempt in 1936 in the state of New York.
44. FitzGerald and Cook-Martin, *Culling the Masses*, 89.
45. Susan Koshy, "Category Crisis: South Asian Americans and Questions of Race and Ethnicity," *Diaspora* 7, no. 3 (1998): 285–320; Susan Koshy, "Historicizing Racial Identity and Minority Status for South Asian Americans," www.sscnet.ucla.edu/history/faculty/henryyu/APACHP/teacher/research/koshy.htm.
46. Prior to this, Indian Americans working in and near the national capital had lobbied for, and gained, eligibility to compete for federal contracts as minorities; see chapter 6, this volume, "Rags to Riches."
47. Joan M. Jensen, *Passage from India: Asian Indian Immigrants in North America* (New Haven, CT: Yale University Press, 1988), 261.
48. Ibid., 262.
49. *Married Women's Independent Nationality Act*, 1922. Ch. 411. 42 Stat. 1021, 67th Congress.
50. Jensen, *Passage from India*, 267.
51. "Send Us Your Best and Brightest Students Yearning to Study Here," *San Francisco Examiner*, October 19, 2011, 17.
52. Hess, *The "Hindu" in America*, 68.
53. "Hindus Too Brunette to Vote Here," *The Literary Digest* for March 10, 1923. Source: South Asia Digital Archive.
54. Jensen, *Passage from India*, 265.
55. Leonard, *Making Ethnic Choices*, 53.
56. A well-known case reflected the consequences of such an arrangement falling through. Pakhar Singh had leased his ranch via verbal agreement to two Anglo partners who at the end of the year refused to give him the proceeds of his lettuce crop. Enraged, he murdered the two men and was sentenced to fifteen years in prison, a lesser sentence stemming from the jury's acceptance of the aggravated circumstances leading to the murders. See Jensen, *Passage from India*, 267.
57. Leonard, *Making Ethnic Choices*, 135.
58. Ibid., 158.
59. Ibid., 133.
60. Ibid., 133.
61. Harold S. Jacoby, *History of East Indians in America* (Amritsar: Bhai Chattar Singh Jiwan Singh, 2007), 145–47.
62. Jacoby, *History of East Indians*, 194.
63. Ibid., 180.
64. The Hindu temple opened by the Vedanta Society in 1908 in San Francisco was arguably the first visible religious establishment of the community.
65. Dalip Singh Saund, *Congressman from India* (New York: E.P. Dutton, 1960), 36.
66. Leonard, *Making Ethnic Choices*, 167. As new migrants arrived after 1965, and possibilities for what it meant to be "American" broadened, most of these adaptations of Sikh religious practice were reversed.
67. Leonard, *Making Ethnic Choices*, 168.
68. Ross Bassett, *The Technological Indian* (Cambridge, MA: Harvard University Press, 2016), 129.
69. Siddhartha Mukherjee, *The Emperor of All Maladies: A Biography of Cancer* (New York: Simon and Schuster, 2010), 31.
70. Saund, *Congressman*, 80.
71. Ibid., 112.
72. Jacoby, *History of East Indians*, 180–81.
73. Ibid., 208–209.
74. See Nile Green, *Terrains of Exchange: Religious Economies of Global Islam* (New York: Oxford University Press, 2014), chap. 6.
75. This paragraph and quote draws from, Sidin Vadukut, "My enemy's enemy," *Livemint*, November 22, 2014.

76. Friends of Freedom for India, India Freedom Dinner Address, www.archive.org/details/indiaireland00deva.
77. Daniel Immerwahr, "Caste or Colony? Indianizing Race in the United States," *Modern Intellectual History* 4, no. 2 (2007): 275–301.
78. Ibid., 283.
79. A perceptive analysis of this tension can be found in Aishwary Kumar, *Radical Equality: Ambedkar, Gandhi, and the Risk of Democracy* (Stanford, CA: Stanford University Press, 2015).
80. For an illuminating treatment, see Sudarshan Kapur, *Raising up a Prophet: The African-American Encounter with Gandhi* (Boston: Beacon Press, 1992).
81. Shaffer, "J.J. Singh and the India League of America."
82. Harold A. Gould, *Sikhs, Swamis, Students and Spies: The India Lobby in the United States, 1900-1946* (New Delhi: Sage Publications, 2006), 411–19.
83. Hess, "The "Hindu" in America."
84. Aristide Zolberg, *A Nation by Design: Immigration Policy in the Fashioning of America* (Cambridge, MA: Harvard University Press, 2009), 304–305.
85. Maria P. P. Root, ed., *Racially Mixed People in America* (Newbury Park, CA: Sage Publications, 1992), 67–68.
86. Jacoby, *History of East Indians*, 258.
87. Leonard, *Making Ethnic Choices*, 159–60.
88. Jacoby, *History of East Indians*, 232–33. This story is told in detail in chapter 6, this volume.
89. U.S. Bureau of the Census, www.census.gov/population/www/documentation/twps0029/tab04.html.
90. W. Norman Brown, *The United States and India and Pakistan* (Cambridge, MA: Harvard University Press, 1953), 266.
91. For a detailed analysis of this argument, see chap. 6 in Devesh Kapur, *Diaspora, Development and Democracy: The Domestic Impact of International Migration from India* (Princeton, NJ: Princeton University Press, 2010).

Chapter 2

1. We disagree with the popular "triple package" explanation—based on unobservable psychological characteristics—for immigrant success offered by Chua and Rubenfeld. See Amy Chua and Jed Rubenfeld, *The Triple Package: How Three Unlikely Traits Explain the Rise and Fall of Cultural Groups in America* (New York: Penguin, 2014). Later in this chapter we explain why. Even later, in chapter 3, we show how the heterogeneity of the Indian population in the U.S. belies any claims made on the basis of averages.
2. For a good discussion on the subject, see Vinay Lal, *The Other Indians: A Political and Cultural History of South Asians in America* (Los Angeles: UCLA Asian American Studies Center, 2008). His list includes names that are hangovers from the past (such as "Hindoos") and ones that are advocated by Hindu nationalists (such as "Bharatiya").
3. It is necessary to note that the cutoff year we use to distinguish between the Early Movers and the Families—1979-1980—is imprecise. Later in this chapter we show that this transition was fuzzy (more so than the sharper transition to the IT Generation in 1995) and could have begun as early as 1977.
4. We do not fully understand why Gujaratis were the first to pick up the signal of change in U.S. immigration policy and at the same time were willing to undergo the sacrifices of moving to a country that was still strongly racialized (the civil rights successes were only beginning then, the American South was largely segregated, and the tumult of assassinations and urban riots was palpable everywhere). The facile explanation—that Gujaratis have "always" been emigrants; "look at their success in East Africa"—seems plausible but less than explanatory, especially when one compares the experience in, say, Southeast Asia (where Tamils immigrated in large numbers during British colonialism) or the Middle East (where Malayalis have worked for decades); neither of these regions is known for Gujarati immigration and neither of these language speakers was dominant in immigration streams to the United States.

5. See Sharon M. Lee, "Racial Classifications in the U.S. Census: 1890–1990," *Ethnic and Racial Studies* 16 (1993): 75–94.
6. The U.S. Census is a large and complex data compendium. Appendix 1 contains details on what is in the census, what we have used and why, and the cautions that should be used in interpreting these data.
7. We do not get into the debates over the meanings of different categorical systems here, but use them in a general sociological sense that race refers to "a group that is socially defined but on the basis of physical criteria" just as ethnic groups are also socially defined but on the basis of cultural criteria. Pierre L. Van den Berghe, *Race and Racism* (New York: John Wiley, 1967), 9–10.
8. Lee, "Racial Classifications." On Asian and specifically Indian racial identity in the U.S. Census, also see Susan Koshy, "Category Crisis: South Asian Americans and Questions of Race and Ethnicity," *Diaspora* 7, no. 3 (1998): 285–320; Ronald Takaki, *Strangers from a Different Shore: A History of Asian Americans* (New York: Penguin, 1990), 299–300.
9. Campbell Gibson and Kay Jung, "Historical Census Statistics on Population Totals by Race, 1790 to 1990, and by Hispanic Origin, 1970 to 1990, for Large Cities and Other Urban Places in the United States," February 2005, U.S. Census Bureau Working Paper No. 76, www.census. gov/population/www/documentation/twps0076/twps0076.pdf.
10. We take note of recent scholarship on "ethnic attrition," a phenomenon in which second- and especially third-generation descendants of immigrants tend not to self-identify with their ethnic roots in data-gathering exercises like the Current Population Surveys (CPS) in the United States. As a result, they tend to get undercounted. Duncan and Trejo find that that rate of attrition of second-generation Indians could be as high as 24 percent in the CPS. However, as we show later, the number of adult second-generation Indians in the United States is so small that even a high attrition rate is unlikely to affect the total numbers to any appreciable degree because it is the adults who do the identification in the census; children do not. This may, nonetheless, be an issue to be attentive to in future studies of the community. Brian Duncan and Stephen J. Trejo, "The Complexity of Immigrant Generations: Implications for Assessing the Socioeconomic Integration of Hispanics and Asians," 2016, National Bureau of Economic Research Working Paper 21982, www.nber.org/papers/w21982.
11. The estimate of mixed-race Indians is an illustration of the reasons to be careful about data sources and their meanings. The PUMS 2012 estimate of mixed-race Indians was 250,000, but the ACS 2007–2011 estimate of the same was 58,000. It is very unlikely that in a matter of three years or so the quantity of multiracial Indian Americans could have quintupled. It is more likely that for this very small subpopulation (mixed-race Indian Americans) of a small population (Indian Americans), PUMS 2012 had provided an overestimate while the ACS 2007–2011 had provided an underestimate. Therefore, in light of the growth of the Indian-American population, the top-line numbers in the PUMS 2012—that is, the number of Asian Indians (alone) and the numbers that were India-born and America-born—were more indicative of conditions at the moment of writing than the ACS 2007–2011. But the subpopulation data on diversity of language speakers and national origins were likely to be more robust and reliable in the ACS 2007–2011. Nonetheless, in order to be consistent, we use the PUMS 2012 for all data in figure 2.2.
12. The census attempts to count individuals regardless of the legality of their presence in the country. The Department of Homeland Security estimates the number of undocumented aliens by subtracting the number of individuals for whom they have documentation from the number estimated by the Census Bureau. In the most recent estimate for 2011, there were 240,000 undocumented aliens with Indian citizenship, up from 120,000 estimated in 2000. Michael Hoefer, Nancy Rytina, and Bryan Baker, "Estimates of the Unauthorized Immigrant Population Residing in the United States, Department of Homeland Security, 2012," March 2013, www.dhs.gov/xlibrary/assets/statistics/publications/ois_ill_pe_2011.pdf.
13. The estimates were rather different in PUMS 2012 and ACS 2007–2011. The rankings of countries varied (Pakistan was first in one and third in the other), as did the lists themselves. The basic numbers also varied widely in several cases, Pakistan being the most significant (providing 67,000 of the born-elsewhere in ACS 2007–2011, but less than 49,000 three years

later in PUMS 2012); the data for Fiji were proportionally even more variable—over 12,000 in 2007–2011 but just around 8,000 in 2012.

14. Out of 159,000 Bangladesh-born in the United States, about 73,000 identified with the Bangladeshi "race" at the same time that about 63,000 identified with the Asian Indian "race." Similarly, out of 309,000 Pakistan-born, about 194,000 identified with the Pakistani "race," whereas about 67,000 identified with the Asian Indian "race."

15. There are three reasons for our skepticism. First, this method of using some categories as selectable boxes and others as write-ins was used by the Census for other identities (for American Indians, for instance); we are not aware of such discrepancies in other cases. Second, given the mutually hostile relationship between the states of India and Pakistan, it is hard to imagine that almost one-fourth of Pakistan-born individuals could have inadvertently or lazily chosen an Indian identity in the census. Third, we believe that the racial identity question opens spaces of imagination and desire. For instance, almost 15,000 Pakistan-born, 5 percent of the total in the United States, claimed to be white (not mixed race, but white); only 147 claimed to be Bangladesh-born. This was quite unlikely to be true. There may be some complex identity issues at work here. The difficulties and quandaries faced by South Asian Muslims after 9/11, for instance, could create incentives for non-Indians to identify— sometimes, in some contexts—as Indian. As a Pakistani-Punjabi-Muslim put it: "To simply avoid all these questions [about terrorism and violence in Pakistan], many times I would say I was from India." Hassan Majeed, "A Punjabi in New York: Juggling Multiple Identities," *The Dawn*, January 2015, www.dawn.com/news/1156177/a-punjabi-in-new-york-juggling-multiple-identities. The complexity of self-identification of race/national origin in the United States is highlighted in the emerging phenomenon of "ethnic attrition" discussed above (Duncan and Trejo, "The Complexity of Immigrant Generations").

16. Though the largest number of foreign-born in the United States were Mexico-born—about 11.8 million in PUMS 2012—we did not include this group as a comparator. The size of the undocumented Mexico-born population made it unlikely to be comparable to the India-born.

17. The Philippines and India ranked second and third as sending countries, and each had close to 2 million representatives in the United States in 2010–2012. China was next, and along with it we chose Taiwan, which was not one of the top-sending countries, but as we shall see, was the closest equivalent of India in terms of the material achievements of its population. A couple of interesting points emerged here. It is generally believed that the China-born outnumber all other Asia-born in the United States. This is true, however, only if those born in Taiwan and Hong Kong are added to the China-born. The China- and Taiwan-born are distinct populations in the United States, as distinct as in their home countries, and these distinctions should give pause and cause for reflection to those who propose grand racial theories about "achievement" ethics or psychology. We chose South Korea over Vietnam (though the latter was somewhat larger as a sending country) because, as we shall see later in chapter 5 on entrepreneurship, South Korean immigrants provide interesting comparisons to the India-born. We chose Japan as an example of an old and established successful Asian community.

18. We use family income for comparison because the family is a more organic earning (and spending) unit than an individual or a household (which, in the United States, often includes large numbers of unrelated individuals). It is necessary to note that the India-born had the highest average family income but not the highest average household or average personal income. (This is a point about the significance of families that we expand upon in the following pages.)

19. It is interesting to note the extraordinary degree to which the foreign-born possess advanced degrees in the United States compared to the native-born.

20. The most interesting and unexpected members of this elite club are South Africa and Zambia, the only ones, aside from India, that are not developed nations. We note that our surprise at finding Zambia (and to a lesser extent, South Africa) so high on the list is probably no more than a Zambian (or South African) finding India on top of the list. For these two countries we found a strong racial selection process at work. South Africa's population was 79 percent black and 9 percent white at the time the data were collected. However, these figures were reversed for South Africans in the United States, who were 80 percent white, 14 percent black, and 5 percent Indian. Zambia was 99.5 percent black and 0.5 percent white and Asian; however, one-third of the Zambians in the United States were white or Indian. It appears as if the highest income minorities in these two countries—who occupied economic positions far above

their country averages—were self-selecting and being selected to locate in the United States. As a result, the South Africa- and Zambia-born in the United States were not at all representative of their home countries.

21. Here is a small but representative sample of gender inequality in the HDI. The number following each country was its global rank in gender equality in 2013, 1 being most equal. In East Asia: Singapore–13, Japan–21, S. Korea–27, China–35, Vietnam–48, Thailand–66, the Philippines–77, Indonesia–106. In West and South Asia: Jordan–99, Iran–107, Bangladesh–111, Syria–118, Iraq–120, Pakistan–123, India–132, Saudi Arabia–145, Yemen–148. The data are at http://data.un.org/.

22. "In South Asia and China marriage remains near-universal, with 98% of men and women tying the knot. In contrast, in some Western countries, a quarter of people in their 30s are cohabiting or have never been married, while half of new marriages end in divorce. Marriage continues to be the almost universal setting for child-bearing in Asia: only about 2% of births took place outside wedlock in Japan in 2007. Contrast that with Europe: in Sweden in 2008 55% of births were to unmarried women, while in Iceland the share was 66%." From "Asian Demography: The Flight from Marriage," *The Economist*, August 20, 2011, www.economist. com/node/21526329.

23. Susheela Singh and Renee Samara, "Early Marriage Among Women in Developing Countries," *International Family Planning Perspectives* 22 (1996): 148–57.

24. The recent data on the age of first marriage of females provides abundant evidence. In South Asia: Bangladesh–18.6 years, India–20.2 years, Pakistan–22.7 years; in East Asia: the Philippines–24.4 years, China–24.7 years, S. Korea–28.8 years, Japan–29.7 years. The data are at www.quandl.com/society/age-at-first-marriage-female-by-country. The most reliable data for India comes from the National Family Health Survey, last undertaken in 2005–2006. They report that the median age of first marriage was 17.2 years for women and 23.4 years for men; and though there was little difference between the genders at the level of primary education (ages 6–10), by the age of secondary education (ages 15–17) there was a significant gender gap: 49 percent school attendance for males, 34 percent for females. International Institute for Population Sciences (IIPS) and Macro International, "National Family Health Survey (NFHS-3), 2005–06, India: Key Findings" (2007), http://dhsprogram.com/pubs/pdf/SR128/SR128.pdf; Sonalde Desai, Amaresh Dubey, Brij Lal Joshi, Mitali Sen, Abusaleh Sharif, and Reeve Vanneman, *Human Development in India: Challenges for a Society in Transition* (New Delhi: Oxford University Press, 2010).

25. The term was introduced by Dana Pierce, "The Feminization of Poverty: Women, Work, and Welfare," *Urban and Social Change Review* 11 (1978): 28–36. Also see Sakiko Fukuda-Parr, "What Does Feminization of Poverty Mean? It Isn't Just Lack of Income," *Feminist Economics* 5, no. 2 (1999): 99–103; and Sylvia Chant, "Re-thinking the 'Feminization of Poverty' in Relation to Aggregate Gender Indices," *Journal of Human Development* 7, no. 2 (2006): 201–20. The evidence for this phenomenon has been provided in numerous studies, including Sanjoy Chakravorty, "Urban Inequality Revisited: The Determinants of Income Distribution in U.S. Metropolitan Areas," *Urban Affairs Review* 31 (1996): 759–77; and K. Christopher, P. England, T. M. Smeeding, and K. R. Phillips, "The Gender Gap in Poverty in Modern Nations: Single Motherhood, the Market, and the State," *Sociological Perspectives* 45 (2002): 219–42.

26. Of the 216 U.S. states and countries we had data for, the five lowest rates of female-headed households were in the populations born in Nepal (4.4 percent), Bhutan (5.3 percent), Bangladesh (6.4 percent), Pakistan (6.4 percent), and India (6.6 percent). Again, if we add Sri Lanka to this group (with 13.3 percent female-headed households), we get the definition of South Asia. In the United States as a whole, one-fourth of all households were headed by single women.

27. The number of India-born quadrupled in the 1970s (from around 50,000 to over 200,000). It more than doubled in the 1980s and again in the 1990s. It did not double in the 2000s (it grew by about 60 percent), largely because the base population had grown too large for a doubling to take place every decade.

28. There are other visa categories used by foreign students. A small number of India-born students used J-1 Exchange Visitor visas, and an even smaller number used M-1 Vocational Student visas.

29. Bachelor's and master's degree holders constituted a little over 40 percent each of the total H-1B visa pool; doctoral degree holders made up a little over 10 percent, and the remainder held professional degrees (mainly in medicine).

30. "It is clear that the cap is of limited importance to the actual number of H-1B petitions approved each year: the numbers reported . . . show the approval of 3–4 times as many H-1B visas as stipulated by the cap. This is by legislative intent, as the law exempts all H-1B visas for continuing employment . . . as well as H-1Bs for initial employment, if the petitioner is an institution of higher education (or its affiliated or related nonprofit entities), a nonprofit research organization, or a government research organization." See Jacob Funk Kirkegaard, *The Economic Scope and Future of US-India Labor Migration Issues*, Peterson Institute for International Economics Working Paper Series WP 15-1, 2015. piie.com/publications/wp/wp15-1.pdf.

31. The L-1A visa is for intra-company executives and managers and can be extended by two two-year periods to a total of seven years, while the L-1B visa is for intra-company employees with specialized knowledge and can be extended by only one two-year period to five years.

32. Neil G. Ruiz, "*The Geography of Foreign Students in U.S. Higher Education: Origins and Destinations*," 2014, Global Cities Initiative: A Joint Project of Brookings and JPMorgan Chase, www.brookings.edu/research/interactives/2014/geography-of-foreign-students#/M10420.

33. This category included the following preference ordering: first, the unmarried children of U.S. citizens and their children; second: spouses, children, and unmarried children of resident aliens; third: married children of U.S. citizens and their spouses and children; fourth: siblings of U.S. citizens and their spouses and children.

34. The findings were unambiguous. For the India-born, 70 to 80 percent of the professional services sector was made up of a single subsector—"computer systems design and related services." Before 1995 this sector and subsector were indistinguishable from the other sectors, but from then on it far outstripped the other sectors in bringing the India-born to the United States. So dominant was this subsector that by the end of the data series (in 2011) it was larger than the combination of the four other leading sectors for India-born employment (financial services, medical services, education, and retail). These latter sectors saw some India-born growth from the mid-1980s, especially the financial services sector from the mid-1990s to about 2000, but these growth rates were modest and appeared to have plateaued around 2000. There was some growth in the education sector, but again it was dwarfed by the computer subsector.

35. Dan Breznitz and John Zysman, eds., *Re-Examining the Service Revolution* (New Haven, CT: Yale University Press, 2012), 156–78; Rafiq Dossani and Martin Kenney, "The Next Wave of Globalization: Relocating Service Provision to India," *World Development* 35, no. 5 (2007): 772–91.

36. AnnaLee Saxenian, *The New Argonauts: Regional Advantage in a Global Economy* (Cambridge, MA: Harvard University Press, 2007), 276.

37. Of all U.S. permanent residents in that period, well less than 15 percent used the employment-based track, making it the least significant of the four tracks listed above. During the same post-transition period, well over 45 percent of Indian citizens used this track to permanent residency—that is, at three times the rate of everyone else.

38. 2006 was the only odd year in this stretch. That year saw a one-time spike in the number of asylum-status grants to Indian citizens, about 7,000. We are not sure why this happened. In any case, the numbers and shares for the three other categories were affected.

39. To put these figures in context, note that throughout the entire 1970s about 148,000 Indian citizens, and throughout the entire 1980s about 232,000 Indian citizens, had become U.S. permanent residents. The annual average of total permanent residents from India in 1986–1999 (the pretransition period) was about 27,000, less than the annual average of over 30,000 after the transition in just the employment-based category.

40. It is just as important to note that the paths to permanent residency for Indian citizens were distinctly different from the paths taken by all other foreign citizens. The primary source of the difference came from the use of the employment-based path. This meant that proportionally

far fewer used the immediate-relative path, which was the largest category for U.S. permanent residents as a whole, or the diversity/refugee/asylum seeker path.

41. We compared PUMS data for two years, 2004 and 2012 (the first and last years for which these data were available). Consider, for example, the year 2002: we had estimates of the India-born that arrived in 2002 from PUMS 2004 and again from PUMS 2012. PUMS 2004 had estimated that about 66,000 India-born had entered the United States in 2002 and were still resident in 2004. Later, PUMS 2012 estimated that about 60,000 India-born had entered the United States in 2002 and were still resident in 2012. That is, about 91 percent had stayed on for eight years. These figures were more or less replicated throughout the series. For some years, the 2012 estimate was actually higher than the 2004 estimate (which is mathematically impossible), very likely because of sampling issues. These discrepancies fall well within the range of acceptable standard errors.

42. There may be distinct differences between the language groups in their propensity to sponsor family members for U.S. visas. We do not have the data to make a strong claim, but there is an abundance of anecdotes—so much so that there are well-established stereotypes. Gujaratis, for instance, have the reputation of being the most prolific of family sponsors. There are stories of individuals who have sponsored as many as fifty family and clan members.

43. As we write this, there remain significant differences between India and the United States in the distribution of languages. Punjabi is still close to three and a half times higher and Gujarati over three times higher in the United States than their corresponding shares in India. Three of the four major South Indian languages are also overrepresented: Telugu, Tamil, and Malayalam. These five overrepresented languages together account for less than one-fourth of the Indian population in India but more than half the India-born population in the United States. Inevitably, other languages are underrepresented: Bengali (at less than one-third of its Indian share) and Marathi (at about half of its Indian share) are the most underrepresented of the major languages. Hindi, the most widely spoken language in India and among the India-born, is even after the recent spurt also underrepresented (41 percent in India, but 29 percent in the United States).

44. The act declared that physicians and surgeons were no longer in short supply in the United States and mandated the removal of both groups from the Department of Labor's Schedule A, which meant that foreign medical graduates (FMGs) ceased receiving automatic labor certification. As a result, FMG immigration from India toppled from 2,048 in 1977 to 684 the next year and stayed at that approximate level until 1985. John M. Liu, "The Contours of Asian Professional, Technical and Kindred Work Immigration, 1965-1988," *Sociological Perspectives* 35, no. 4 (1992): 673–704.

45. A few weeks before the first draft of this manuscript was completed, the Census Bureau released the PUMS 2013 data set with some new fields of information that allowed us to calculate the distribution of college degrees by field and country of birth. The following fields had the highest shares of the India-born in the United States: electrical engineering technology—24 percent; computer engineering—19 percent; botany—11 percent; computer science—11 percent; metallurgical engineering—10 percent; electrical engineering—10 percent. Note that these shares of India-born were relative to the entire population in the United States. That is, 24 percent of *all* electrical engineering technology graduates and 19 percent of *all* computer engineering graduates in the United States were born in India.

46. See Lisa W. Foderaro, "More Foreign-Born Scholars Lead U.S. Universities," *New York Times*, March 9, 2011. Our partial list of past and present leaders include: university presidents/chancellors at: Carnegie Mellon, University of Buffalo, University of Massachusetts Amherst, University of Texas at Arlington, Cooper Union, U.C. San Diego, Lawrence Technological University, Manhattanville College, University of Houston; business school deans at: Northwestern University's Kellogg School, Harvard Business School, Cornell University, Johns Hopkins University, University of Southern California, University of Chicago's Booth School, Rutgers-Camden, SUNY Binghamton; engineering School deans at: University of Pennsylvania, U.C. Berkeley, UCLA, Duke University; other deans or provosts at: Graduate School, Princeton University, Harvard College, Oregon State University, U.C. Berkeley-Law, Public Policy at U.C. Riverside.

47. In 1990, about 22 percent of the India-born had bachelor's degrees and 26 percent had advanced degrees. By 2000, these proportions had grown to 29 and 32 percent, respectively. And by 2010, these proportions had grown to 32 and 37 percent, respectively. The figures for 2000 and 2010 were derived from the Census Bureau's site DataFerret. The 1990 figures were calculated from the Census Bureau's report. See "1990 Census of Population: The Foreign-Born Population in the United States," www.census.gov/prod/cen1990/cp3/cp-3-1.pdf.

48. In 2004, IIT-Kharagpur had 3,480 registered alumni in the United States and another 739 alumni spread over 59 countries; IIT-Kanpur had 1,897 alumni in the United States and another 186 alumni spread in other countries; IIT-Madras had about 6,000 alumni in the United States and just 500 alumni in all other countries.

49. A recent analysis at Brown University of the educational background of faculty in the top 50 computer science programs in American universities found that of the 25 leading undergraduate sources, 16 were in the United States, 3 were in China, 1 in Taiwan, and 5 in India. The 5 Indian undergraduate institutions were all IITs. IIT-Madras was 4th, IIT-Kanpur 6th—both were ranked above Stanford, Princeton, Yale, Brown, and Caltech; IIT-Bombay was 12th, IIT-Delhi 17th, and IIT-Kharagpur 21st. The full list is at cs.brown.edu/people/alexpap/faculty_dataset.html.

50. While the migration rate for Indian doctors was about 3 percent of the total pool during the 1980s, it was 56 percent for graduates of the prestigious All India Institute for Medical Sciences between 1956 and 1980, and 49 percent in the 1990s.

51. An important question we do not engage with here in a serious way is why social elites should leave. The historical evidence on international migration from India shows a stark contrast between the late nineteenth and late twentieth centuries. While migrants in the nineteenth century came from poorer socioeconomic groups, from poorer parts of the country, and went to (relatively poor) southern countries, a century later virtually the opposite was true—they came from richer and more educated socioeconomic groups, from wealthier parts of the country and, with the significant exception of the large migration to the Middle East, largely went to industrialized countries. While the opening of the U.S. immigration door was a key "pull" factor, there was perhaps an equally important "push" factor—namely, the transformation of the social basis of political power in India as a result of universal franchise. Over time this resulted in a gradual but perceptible political ascendency of hitherto socially marginalized groups and a markedly diminished political status of the upper castes. That erosion of social and political power very possibly led to a search for greener pastures. More recently, however, as education became more widespread, the social base of Indian immigrants was also changing, albeit gradually. See Devesh Kapur, *Diaspora, Development, and Democracy: The Domestic Impact of International Migration from India* (Princeton, NJ: Princeton University Press, 2010).

52. This investment in higher education came at great cost to primary education for all. This is a large subject that we do not engage with here.

53. William Aspray, Frank Mayadas, and Moshe Y. Vardi, eds., "Globalization and Offshoring of Software: A Report of the ACM Job Migration Task Force," 2006, www.acm.org/globalizationreport/.

54. These data are at https://data.gov.in/dataset-group-name/higher-education-statistics.

55. The top two firms granted H-1B petitions in 2013 were Infosys and Tata Consultancy Services, each with over 6,200 visas. The next two firms (Accenture and Cognizant) were not headquartered in India but did most of their hiring there. They had about 3,500 and 5,500 H-1B visas in 2013. Other Indian firms in the top ten of H-1B recipients were Wipro, HCL Technologies, Mahindra Satyam, and Larsen and Toubro Infotech.

56. Xiang Biao, *Global "Body Shopping": An Indian Labor System in the Indian Information Technology Industry* (Princeton, NJ: Princeton University Press, 2006).

57. There is an extensive literature on educational inequality in India. Despite significant improvements, educational inequality "is not only one of the highest in the world, but has also not declined much in the last three decades," according to M. Niaz Asadullah and Gaston Yalontezky, "Inequality of Educational Opportunity in India: Changes Over Time and Across States," *World Development* 40 (2012): 1151–63. On intergenerational educational mobility, see Mehtabul Azam and Vipul Bhatt, "Like Father, Like Son? Intergenerational

Education Mobility in India," 2012, IZA Discussion Paper No. 6549, Bonn, http://ftp.iza.org/dp6549.pdf.

58. See https://data.gov.in/dataset-group-name/higher-education-statistics.

59. Rakesh Basant, "Bangalore Cluster: Evolution, Growth, and Challenges," 2006, Indian Institute of Management, Ahmedabad Working Paper No. 2005-05-02, www.iimahd.ernet.in/publications/data/2006-05-02rbasant.pdf; G. Balatchandirane, "IT Clusters in India," 2007, Institute of Developing Economies, Chiba Discussion Paper No. 85, www.ide.go.jp/English/Publish/Download/Dp/pdf/085.pdf; Narendar Pani, "Resource Cities Across Phases of Globalization: Evidence from Bangalore," *Habitat International* 33 (2009): 114–19.

60. Radhika Ramaswamy, "Indian IT Pros: Demand vs Supply," *The Times of India*, online edition, April 23, 2011, http://timesofindia.indiatimes.com/tech/jobs/Indian-IT-pros-Demand-vs-supply/articleshow/8048970.cms.

61. Hyderabad alone sent over 26,000 students to the United States in 2008–2012; Chennai and Bangalore sent about 9,000 each. The other Indian cities in the global top-20 of foreign student origins were Mumbai (about 17,000) and Delhi (about 9,000). Krishna and Godavari districts in Andhra Pradesh sent over 2,000 students each, more than the *combined total* that came from the states of Assam, Bihar, Jharkhand, Chhattisgarh, and Odisha. There was evidence that some U.S. college destinations were of questionable provenance (for example, Tri-Valley University in California, which appeared to be nothing more than a visa mill for "students" from Andhra Pradesh), but by and large these students were enrolling in recognized, leading academic institutions. All city-level data are from the Brookings report on foreign students. See Ruiz, *Geography of Foreign Students*. The detailed state-level calculations are our own from the detailed (unpublished) data provided to us by the Ruiz project at Brookings.

62. This is a very unusual distribution, with an absurdly low dependency ratio, most typical of populations of recent migrants.

63. Thomas Friedman's "flat world" thesis—see Thomas Friedman, *The World Is Flat: A Brief History of the Twenty-first Century* (New York: Farrar, Straus and Giroux, 2005)—is popular but not taken particularly seriously by scholars, especially economic geographers, several of whom argue convincingly that the world is more concave/curved and spikier than it has ever been. Philip McCann, "Globalization and Economic Geography: The World is Curved, Not Flat," *Cambridge Journal of Regions, Economy and Society* 1 (2008): 351–70; Richard Florida, "The World Is Spiky," *Atlantic Monthly*, October 2005. A more persuasive approach to a general understanding of the processes at play comes from the literature on global value chains (or GVC). See Gary Gereffi, John Humphrey, and Timothy Sturgeon, "The Governance of Global Value Chains," *Review of International Political Economy* 12 (2005): 78–104. "The rise of the rest" was coined by Fareed Zakaria to summarize the economic growth of the BRICS and other nations in a "post-American" globalized world. Fareed Zakaria, *The Post-American World and the Rise of the Rest* (New York: Penguin, 2009).

64. Chua and Rubenfeld, *The Triple Package*.

65. Kapur, *Diaspora, Development, and Democracy*.

66. One of the reviewers of this manuscript had an intriguing question: did the coincidence of upper-caste status and high education and income among the India-born and their strong adherence to endogamy lead to an inadvertent creation by the U.S. immigration system of a new English-speaking super caste that was both upper caste and wealthy? We were intrigued by the boldness of this suggestion, but were hesitant to go so far as to endorse a "super caste" category. Not only did we not have the data to make such a big claim, but took note of some broadening of the selection base in India that may, over a longer run, create more class heterogeneity. This heterogeneity will almost surely not include India's most marginalized groups—Adivasis, Dalits, and Muslims—in large numbers or anywhere close to their proportions in India, but is likely to reflect the pattern of political representation in the homeland in which the middle castes—similar to but not congruent with Other Backward Classes (OBCs)—are better represented.

67. There is compelling evidence that education significantly affects selectivity into the country of migration (Kapur, *Diaspora, Development, and Democracy*). Generally the highly educated Indians migrate to industrialized countries, while the less educated go to middle-income

labor-intensive economies (such as in the Middle East). The education level of the emigrant is strongly linked to household income, and in turn affects the selection of the country of immigration. The income effect on selection—that immigrants tend to come from higher income groups in their countries of origin—appears to work in a wide range of settings when the United States is the destination. See George J. Borjas, Ilpo Kauppinen, and Panu Poutvaara, "Self-Selection of Emigrants: Theory and Evidence on Stochastic Dominance in Observable and Unobservable Characteristics," CESIFO Working Paper No. 5567, www.econstor.eu/bitstream/10419/123212/1/cesifo_wp5567.pdf. For a recent summary of the associated argument that unrestricted immigration can raise global GDP by "trillions of dollars," see George J. Borjas, "Immigration and Globalization: A Review Essay," *Journal of Economic Literature* 53, no. 4 (2015): 961–74.

Chapter 3

1. Only seven out of the 15,300 settlements with at least 1,000 residents had Indian-American populations larger than 25 percent of the local total. These seven were all small communities (like Iselin, New Jersey, and Loudon Valley, Virginia), each with fewer than 20,000 people overall.

2. The literature on "ethnic clustering" tends to focus on the positive externalities of proximity—that is, the advantages created by living in a group that could not be derived in scattered living arrangements. George J. Borjas, "Ethnicity, Neighborhoods, and Human-Capital Externalities," *American Economic Review* 85, no. 3 (1995): 365–90. Michael Davern, "Social Networks and Economic Sociology: A Proposed Research Agenda for a More Complete Social Science," *American Journal of Economics and Sociology* 56, no. 3 (1997): 287–302.

3. James Kunstler coined the term "geography of nowhere" to describe American suburbs created by the automobile and distinguished by their indistinguishableness. His work fits in a tradition that began perhaps with Jane Jacobs's championing of the industrial city a la Brooklyn as an ideal urban form. Kunstler's lament on the disappearance of urban identity and distinction is balanced by a celebration of the same processes and outcomes by Joel Garreau in his important work on "edge cities." James Howard Kunstler, *The Geography of Nowhere: The Rise and Decline of America's Man-Made Landscape* (New York: Free Press, 1994). Jane Jacobs, *The Death and Life of Great American Cities* (New York: Vintage, 1961). Joel Garreau, *Edge City: Life on the New Frontier* (New York: Anchor Books, 1992).

4. The census geography of the United States follows a size hierarchy going from the largest political unit, the state, to the smallest sampling unit, the census block. There are 51 states and over 11 million census blocks. The data are widely available from the second-largest scale in this hierarchy, the census block group, each of which is composed of around 40 census blocks. A block group generally contains 600 to 800 people, but can have as many as 3,000. Block groups are combined into census tracts. On average, about four block groups make up a census tract, which contains, on average, around 4,000 people.

5. First, as explained in appendix 1, given the small sizes of these spatial units and the much smaller sizes of the Indian-American populations within them, the estimates for the latter tend to be unreliable, with high standard errors. Second, these small spatial units have little organic meaning; they are nameless units that do not convey any sense of place to nonexperts.

6. Minor civil divisions (MCDs) are subdivisions of counties, the primary administrative divisions of a county, typically incorporated as a legal entity, such as a town, township, municipality, borough, precinct, or magisterial district. MCDs have place names and are recognizable entities. Large urban regions are typically made up of several MCDs and other unincorporated places. The Census Bureau uses the term "census county division" (CCD) to cover all these county subdivisions, including MCDs, and we do the same in this chapter.

7. The terminology used by the Census Bureau are metropolitan statistical areas (MSAs), standard metropolitan statistical areas (SMSAs), and combined metropolitan statistical areas (CMSAs). We make no distinction between them and call them "metropolises" or "metropolitan regions."

8. PUMAs are nested within states, and in urban areas, within counties, and are aggregated from census tracts. Each PUMA typically has a population of around 100,000, but there is

significant variation whereby the population can range from 50,000 to 200,000. A densely populated place, such as a large city, is typically broken into several PUMAs, none of which has a place name. In sparsely populated areas, on the other hand, a single PUMA can include several communities, especially CDPs or recognizable places.

9. The data for table 3.1 are all from the Census Bureau's summarized data for the 2005–2009 and 2008–2012 ACS. It was possible to use other, more recent, sources (such as the PUMS data) for the state-level discussions, but those were not substantially different from what is presented here, they had higher standard errors (because they were single-year estimates rather than the five-year estimates presented here), and they were inconsistent with the data at the county and smaller scales.

10. John Iceland, *Where We Live Now: Immigration and Race in the United States* (Berkeley: University of California Press, 2009), 37–38.

11. See, for instance, Maxine L. Margolis, *An Invisible Minority: Brazilians in New York City* (Gainesville: University Press of Florida, 2009).

12. Michigan was the only other state with a comparable decline in significance, very likely as a result of the decline of Detroit, the first city in the modern period that was beginning to revert to agriculture as its economic base. The Indian-American population grew by single digits during this period in Michigan, the only state other than New York in the top twenty in this situation.

13. Of the 3,200-odd counties in the United States, only about 1,800 had any Indian-origin population and 1,660 had any India-born population. Of those 1,660 counties, about 1,000 had less than 100 each. To put this in another way, about half the U.S. counties did not contain a single India-born person; only about one-fifth contained 100 or more India-born persons. Note that since these numbers were drawn from a sample (rather than a census), it is possible that many of these counties may have had a non-zero but very small India-born population.

14. Note that though Queens County had the largest number of Indian-origin people, for the India-born, Queens ranked sixth; Kings County (Brooklyn) did not make the top-25 list of the India-born.

15. This—the proportion of the Indian-origin population that is India-born—provides valuable temporal information; the higher the proportion of India-born in the Indian-origin population, the more recent the migration.

16. The eight types of income are from Subject Definitions, pages 79–83, available at http://www2.census.gov/programs-surveys/acs/tech_docs/subject_definitions/2014_ACSSubjectDefinitions.pdf.

17. We chose family income over household income because, as shown in chapter 2, India-born households differed fundamentally from general American households in that they were strongly centered on family units—in fact, more so than all other sizable immigrant or native-born groups. We argue, therefore, that the appropriate income-earning and expenditure unit for the India-born is the family rather than the household (which, by definition, includes unrelated individuals).

18. The Census Bureau cautions that "care should be exercised in using and interpreting mean income values for small subgroups of the population. Because the mean is influenced strongly by extreme values in the distribution, it is especially susceptible to the effects of sampling variability, misreporting, and processing errors." The approach we took was to give careful attention to the standard error (SE). The smaller the SE, the more reliable the income estimate.

19. It may be possible to make a weak claim that India-born incomes were highest in the Northeast; Maryland, Virginia, Massachusetts, New Jersey, and Connecticut fit this pattern, but New York (which was a special case; more on which soon) and Pennsylvania did not.

20. The India-born family income in Alabama and Mississippi (not shown in figure 3.5 because of the small size of the India-born population) was lower than the average family income of the general populations in Maryland, Virginia, and California. That is, the general populations in the latter states earned more, on average, than the India-born in the former states.

21. This is not unexpected because, as a general rule, when spatial units are aggregated, the dispersion between them decreases. For example, there is greater income inequality between counties in the United States than between states.

22. PUMAs are too large to be called "neighborhoods." They cannot be called "cities" or "places" because these terms have specific meanings (which PUMAs do not match) and are used by the Census Bureau in those specific meanings. "Settlements," we believe, is a reasonable compromise.

23. Recall that on average each PUMA contains about 100,000 residents; for this analysis we considered PUMAs in which the standard error of the India-born family income was less than one-fourth of the income itself. There were 469 such PUMAs in the United States (that is, a little under one-fourth of all PUMAS).

24. See Wilson's classic work on deindustrialization and the consequent concentration of poverty in inner-city America. William Julius Wilson, *The Truly Disadvantaged: The Inner City, the Underclass, and Public Policy* (Chicago: University of Chicago Press, 1987). For recent data and a large compendium of case studies on the location of poverty in urban and rural America, see Alan Berube and Elizabeth Kneebone, *The Enduring Challenge of Concentrated Poverty in America* (Washington, DC: Brookings Institute Press, 2008), www.brookings.edu/research/reports/2008/10/24-concentrated-poverty.

25. For example, from August 2012 to August 2013, the growth in tech job openings in New Jersey led all other states, and was twice the growth rate in New York. Stacy Jones, "Tech Jobs Growing Like Weeds in N.J.," *Star Ledger*, August 13, 2013, www.nj.com/business/index.ssf/2013/08/tech_jobs_growing_like_weeds_i.html. A specific illustration is the relocation of Wall Street's technology infrastructure to New Jersey. See Michael Khouw, "The Real Wall Street Is Actually in Secaucus, New Jersey," *The Street*, July 9, 2015, www.thestreet.com/story/13213317/1/the-real-wall-street-is-actually-in-secaucus-new-jersey.html.

26. The state-level distribution of doctorates in the leading states in PUMS 2013 were California—16,790, New Jersey—9,313, Texas—6,413, New York—5,156, Illinois—5,073, and Massachusetts—4,025.

27. We calculated the share of doctorates in the state-level India-born populations in states that had at least 10,000 India-born using the PUMS 2013 data. The figures were remarkable: Alabama—12.2%, Missouri—10.5%, Oregon—10.3%, Tennessee—9.7%, Maryland—8.8%, Colorado—7.5%.

28. We do not have a ready explanation for this, especially because the India-born were more likely to have degrees in better-paid technical fields than did Americans. One possibility lies in the location of those degrees (India vs. United States) and another in differences in years of U.S. work experience.

29. These communities have, in some ways, a long history, as outlined in chapter 1. Further discussion of the Punjabis of rural California, who are almost all Sikhs, is in chapter 6.

30. Edward L. Glaeser and Joshua D. Gottlieb, "The Economics of Place-Making Policies," *Brookings Papers on Economic Activity*, Spring 2008, 155–239, 162–63.

31. Note that the Census Bureau provides detailed information on "industry," a category that is related to but different from "occupation." "Occupation" refers to the specific work done by a person; hence, it is connected to education. "Industry" refers to the sector of the economy in which a person is employed; hence, a biologist may be employed as faculty at a university (placing her in the "education" category) or as an administrator for the EPA (placing her in the "public administration" category).

32. Pew Research Center, *The Rise of Asian Americans*, 2013, www.pewsocialtrends.org/files/2013/04/Asian-Americans-new-full-report-04-2013.pdf. The Pew report divided the workforce into 15 groups. We aggregated eight of those groups into a meta-group called "low-skilled labor" (which includes low-skill services such as food preparation and physical labor such as construction). The category "sales" was of indeterminate skill. We did not classify it into "low-skilled labor" but retained it as a separate category.

33. The India-born were also overrepresented in the "management," "business and finance," and "healthcare" categories, but not by as much as in the CES category. The India-born were underrepresented in two skilled categories ("education, arts, and media" and "legal, community, and social services").

34. "Managers" included the subcategory "managers of computers and information systems." This was the largest subcategory under "managers" and included about one-fifth of the India-born workers categorized under "managers." It could be argued that these workers, too, belonged in

the "computers" category rather than the "managers" category. That is, in reality, when properly coded, computer-related work employed more than one-fourth of the India-born labor force.

35. The range of personal incomes of the India-born by the leading occupation subcategories (all subcategories with at least 10,000 India-born workers are shown in table 3.4) went from under $19,000 for cashiers to close to $200,000 for physicians and surgeons. Only one occupation—legislators and chief executive officers—came in at around $185,000, close to the earnings of physicians and surgeons. The remaining occupations could be divided into two income ranges: a middle-income range that began with accountants and auditors (earning around $65,000) to financial managers (who earned around $114,000); and a low-income range from cashiers ($19,000) to first-line supervisors of retail sales workers ($45,500). Note the $20,000 gap between the top of the low-income range and the bottom of the middle-income range. The dominant India-born professions in the field of computers all fell in the middle-income range.

36. See World Bank, *World Development Report 2009: Reshaping Economic Geography* (Washington, DC: World Bank, 2009), for a good overview of the subject; and for applications of these ideas to industry in India, see Sanjoy Chakravorty and Somik V. Lall, *Made in India: The Economic Geography and Political Economy of Industrialization* (New Delhi: Oxford University Press, 2007).

37. Note that many of these settlements (PUMAs) with large numbers of India-born workers were adjacent or proximate (see figures 3.2, 3.3, and 3.4)—Silicon Valley (Santa Clara and Alameda Counties) and Middlesex County, New Jersey, are good examples. Hence, the density of India-born workers was, in organic terms, more pronounced than the disaggregated settlement-level data indicate.

38. There is an emerging scholarly literature on taxi drivers in Queens; see Diditi Mitra, *Punjabi Immigrant Mobility in the United States: Adaptation through Race and Class* (London: Palgrave MacMillan, 2012). There is also recognition of the phenomenon in the mainstream middlebrow press; see Amitava Kumar, "The Venerable, Vulnerable Taxi Drivers of New York," *Vanity Fair*, August 26, 2010. The Bollywood movie industry is also interested in Queens, especially its taxi drivers. Big-budget movies like *Kal Ho Na Ho, Aa Ab Laut Chalen, Kabhi Alvida Na Kehna, English Vinglish*, and *Jo Bole So Nihal* were partially or entirely set in that borough. Many of them featured Indian taxi drivers.

39. Hindi is by far the most common language in India, spoken by over 41 percent of the population, but covers too diverse a territory (from Bihar and Jharkhand to Delhi and Rajasthan) for us to find clear and unambiguous patterns among its speakers in the United States. The settlement data show that absence of pattern. In general, we found Hindi speakers to be in the middle of every ranking. Had it been possible to differentiate Hindi speakers from Delhi, for instance, from Hindi speakers from Bihar, it is quite likely that the patterns observed in India (say, on educational attainment or income) would also be observed in the United States.

40. We have not shown the details of the settlement-level geography of languages here. They are available on request.

41. Malayalis followed a settlement pattern distinct from Telugus and Tamils. They were significantly overrepresented in New York and Pennsylvania, at the same time as they were significantly underrepresented in the leadings states of California and New Jersey.

42. Gujaratis appeared to be making new settlement forays into the American South, especially in Georgia and North Carolina. It remains to be seen whether these will become new Gujarati strongholds in the United States.

43. All data in this paragraph are from PUMS 2012.

44. Note that Punjabis and Gujaratis were well represented in the healthcare industry, very likely as a result of the Early Mover advantage created in the 1970s. The healthcare industry had one outlier language group—Malayalis—about one-third of whom were in this single industry. They tended to be less present in the best-paid positions such as physicians and more present in tertiary care, like nursing. Another outlier, noted before, were Bengalis in the education industry. More than one-fifth of all Bengalis worked in education, at twice the rate of any other language group.

45. "Isolation" and "contact" are constructs developed in the segregation literature in sociology to measure the degree to which different groups live in proximity. For a recent analysis of isolation by income and race, see John R. Logan, *Separate and Unequal: The Neighborhood Gap for Blacks, Hispanics and Asians in Metropolitan America*, 2011, www.s4.brown.edu/us2010/Data/Report/report0727.pdf.

46. The argument is that income inequality can be measured at many scales (from the local to the global), but is perceived or understood at the local scale. Punjabi farmers in the Central Valley of California are very likely to be sensitive to who makes how much money in their communities but to be unaware of and indifferent to how much Telugu software developers earn in Silicon Valley. For an elaboration, see Sanjoy Chakravorty, *Fragments of Inequality: Social, Spatial, and Evolutionary Analyses of Income Distribution* (New York: Routledge, 2006).

47. Douglas Massey, "Ethnic Residential Segregation: A Theoretical Synthesis and Empirical Review," *Sociology and Social Research* 69 (1985): 315–50.

48. Robert Park, Ernest W. Burgess, and Roderick D. McKenzie, *The City* (Chicago: University of Chicago Press, 1925).

49. John R. Logan, Richard D. Alba, and Wenquan Zhang, "Immigrant Enclaves and Ethnic Communities in New York and Los Angeles," *American Sociological Review* 67 (2002): 299–322, 299–300.

50. Susan W. Hardwick, "Toward a Suburban Immigrant Nation," in *Twenty-First Century Gateways: Immigrant Incorporation in Suburban America*, ed. A. Singer, S. W. Hardwick, and C. B. Brettell (Washington, DC: Brookings Institute Press, 2008), 31–52.

51. The term "ethnopolis" is used to characterize Chinatowns in different countries by Bernard P. Wong and Tan Chee-Beng, eds., *Chinatowns around the World: Gilded Ghetto, Ethnopolis, and Cultural Diaspora* (Leiden, The Netherlands: BRILL, 2013). Also see Michel S. Laguerre, *The Global Ethnopolis: Chinatown, Japantown, and Manilatown in American Society* (London: Palgrave Macmillan, 2000). Geographer Wei Li conceptualized and has worked extensively on the details of American "ethnoburbs." Wei Li, "Anatomy of a New Ethnic Settlement: The Chinese Ethnoburb in Los Angeles," *Urban Studies* 35, no. 3 (1998): 479–501. Wei Li, *Ethnoburb: The New Ethnic Community in Urban America* (Honolulu: University of Hawai'i Press, 2009).

52. We considered using the term "techno ghetto" in the spirit of the original usage of *ghetto* as a place marked by ethnicity, but not necessarily low income, and the term "gilded ghetto" that has been in use for some years (see John F. Kain and Joseph J. Persky, "Alternatives to the Gilded Ghetto," *National Affairs*, Winter 1969) and is gaining acceptance as a descriptor of the contemporary spatial concentrations of the super-rich. Ian Hay and Samantha Muller, "'That Tiny, Stratospheric Apex That Owns Most of the World'—Exploring Geographies of the Super-Rich," *Geographical Research* 50, no. 1 (2012): 75–88. But we decided not to, primarily because the word *ghetto* has been "ghettoized" through common usage in the United States, so that ethnicity and low income have become inextricably linked to it. Whatever other attributes the Indian suburb in the United States may possess, low income is not one of them.

Chapter 4

1. For an excellent discussion of this issue, see Richard Alba and Victor Nee, *Remaking the American Mainstream: Assimilation and Contemporary Immigration* (Cambridge, MA: Harvard University Press, 2003).

2. Jhumpa Lahiri's *The Namesake* poignantly captures this isolation (the movie by Mira Nair, perhaps even more than the book).

3. Nicola Leske and Dhanya Skariachan, "'Wrong Gender, Color, Country'—India-born Aiyengar, JPMorgan's Rising Star," http://in.reuters.com/article/2014/02/04/jpmorgan-retail-banker-anu-aiyengar-idINDEEA130ET20140204.

4. The colonization of Spanish America resulted in the mixing of natives, Europeans, and Africans. Members of mixed races faced considerable discrimination but could free themselves from multiple burdens through the purchase of a *gracias al sacar*—a royal exemption that provided the privileges of whiteness. See Ann Twinam, *Purchasing Whiteness. Pardos, Mulattos, and the Quest for Social Mobility in the Spanish Indies* (Palo Alto, CA: Stanford University Press, 2010).

5. "Personal Side of Indra Nooyi," *Economic Times*, February 7, 2007, http://articles.economic-times.indiatimes.com/2007-02-07/news/28471801_1_indra-nooyi-nandan-nilekani-personal-side.

6. Correspondent Lesley Stahl on *60 Minutes*, CBS-TV, January 12, 2003, www.csee.wvu.edu/~juggy/60minutes_iit_TRANSCRIPT.htm.

7. Tanya Benedicto Klich, "Top 50 Universities for VC-Backed Entrepreneurs," www.entrepreneur.com/article/236912.

8. Stuart W. Leslie and Robert Kargo, "Exporting MIT: Science, Technology, and Nation-Building in India and Iran," *Osiris* 21, no. 1 (2006): 110–30. See also Ross Bassett, *The Technological Indian* (Cambridge, MA: Harvard University Press, 2016).

9. Indeed, all three authors of this book came to the United States along this route.

10. Romesh Wadhwani, personal communication, October 25, 2014.

11. John M. Liu, "The Contours of Asian Professional, Technical and Kindred Work Immigration, 1965-1988," *Sociological Perspectives* 35, no. 4 (1992): 673–704.

12. Amelie F. Constant, Konstantinos Tatsiramos, and Klaus F. Zimmermann, eds., *Ethnicity and Labor Market Outcomes* (Bingley: Emerald Group, 2009), 91–130.

13. Mary C. Waters and Marisa Gerstein Pineau, eds., *The Integration of Immigrants into American Society* (Washington, DC: National Academies Press, 2016), 4–11.

14. A caveat is in order here since this is based on data on who is allowed to enter the United States rather than who may want to leave. According to USCIS data, while 513 people applied for asylum in 2013, the number jumped to 1,309 in 2014 and to 2,271 in 2015.

15. Catherine Simpson Bueker, "Political Incorporation among Immigrants from Ten Areas of Origin: The Persistence of Source Country Effects," *International Migration Review* 39, no. 1 (2005): 103–40.

16. Alexis de Tocqueville, "On the Use Which Americans Make of Associations in Civil Life," *Democracy in America*, Volume Two (New York: Harper and Row, 1966).

17. S. Karthick Ramakrishnan and Irene Bloemraad, eds., *Civic Hopes and Political Realities: Immigrants, Community Organizations and Political Engagement* (New York: Russell Sage, 2011), 45–194.

18. The story of the India Community Center is described in more detail in chapter 6.

19. NetIP, "Our Mission," http://na.netip.org/aboutus/our-mission.

20. It should be pointed out that the first Indian physicians trained in the United States, Anandibai Gopalrao Joshee and Kadambini Ganguly, were both women who obtained their degrees in 1886.

21. The data in this and the next few paragraphs was obtained by the authors from the American Medical Association.

22. The procedure for getting ECFMG certification is lengthy and difficult. It takes an average of four years for a foreign medical school graduate to complete the process. In 2014, an applicant was required to (a) pass the medical science examinations (US Medical Licensing Examination), which included (i) a medical science test administered electronically at testing centers worldwide; (ii) the Clinical Knowledge (CK) exam, which is administered electronically at testing centers worldwide; and (iii) a Clinical Skills Assessment (CSA), which is an in-person test conducted at one of five clinical skills evaluation centers in the United States; (b) pass the English language proficiency examination; and (c) document the completion of educational requirements. We are grateful to Jack Boulet and the ECFMG for providing the data related to the ECFMG.

23. ECFMG certification is just the beginning of the long path toward practicing medicine in the United States. After receiving certification, IMGs must apply and be accepted into a residency program even if they have already done residency in their own country. If accepted, they must apply for a J-I visa. India has continually provided the largest share of J-1 physician visas. During the 2012–13 academic year, 28.2 percent of J-1 visas for visiting physicians were for Indians. The most popular specialties were internal medicine and pediatrics.

24. Structural changes in the certification process, however, may impact Indian graduates in the future. ECFMG is currently designing an accreditation system through a Directory of Organizations that Recognize and Accredit Medical Schools (DORA). After 2023, it will become a requirement that IMGs have received their degree from an accredited medical school before application.

25. An experience he described in Abraham Verghese, "The Cowpath to America," *New Yorker*, June 23, 1997.
26. Cited in Vibha Bhalla, "'We Wanted To End Disparities at Work': Physician Migration, Racialization, and a Struggle for Equality," *Journal of American Ethnic History* 29, no. 3 (2010): 40–78.
27. John J. Norcini, John R. Boulet, W. Dale Dauphinee, Amy Opalek, Ian D. Krantz, and Suzanne T. Anderson, "Evaluating the Quality of Care Provided by Graduates of International Medical Schools," *Health Affairs* 29, no. 8 (2010): 1461–68.
28. Eui Hang Shin and Chang Kyung-Sup, "Peripherization of Immigrant Professionals: The Case of Korean Physicians in the United States," *International Migration Review* 22, no. 4 (1988): 609–26.
29. N. R. Rao, "A Little More than Kin, and Less than Kind: U.S. Immigration Policy on International Medical Graduates," *Virtual Mentor* 14, no. 4 (2012): 329–37.
30. Brenton D. Peterson, Sonal S. Pandya, and David Leblang, "Doctors with Borders: Occupational Licensing as an Implicit Barrier to High Skill Migration," *Public Choice* 160 (2014): 45–63.
31. Founding President of AAPI cited in Vibha Bhalla, "We Wanted to End Disparities," 40.
32. A founding member of AAPI cited in Vibha Bhalla, "We Wanted to End Disparities," 60.
33. Ibid., 61.
34. Ibid., 63–64.
35. Patricia Cortes and Jessica Pan, "Relative Quality of Foreign Nurses in the United States," Centre for Research and Analysis of Migration (University College) Discussion Paper No. 1231, www.afd.fr/webdav/shared/PORTAILS/RECHERCHE/evenements/Migrations-developpement-2012/nurses_june.pdf.
36. B. DiCicco-Bloom, "The Racial and Gendered Experiences of Immigrant Nurses from Kerala, India," *Journal of Transcultural Nursing* 15, no. 1 (2004): 26–33; Patricia Pittman, Carolina-Nicole Herrera, Franklin A. Shaffer, and Catherine R. Davis, "Perceptions of Employment-Based Discrimination Among Newly Arrived Foreign-Educated Nurses," *American Journal of Nursing* 114, no. 1 (2014): 26–35.
37. It has been assumed that immigrants with limited human capital organize along ethnic lines, often in the process of reactive formation to a hostile context of reception. See Nathan Glazer and Daniel P. Moynihan, *Beyond the Melting Pot: The Negroes, Puerto Ricans, Jews, Italians, and Irish of New York City* (Cambridge, MA: MIT Press, 1963); Alejandro Portes and Ruben G. Rumbaut, *Immigrant America: A Portrait* (Berkeley: University of California Press, 1996).
38. "Prime Minister Narendra Modi at Madison Square Garden in New York City, Live Blog," *Times of India*, September 28, 2014, http://timesofindia.indiatimes.com/Prime-Minister-Narendra-Modi-at-Madison-Square-Garden-in-New-York-City/newsliveblog/43725506.cms.
39. Data from table 2.3 in Janelle Wong, S. Karthick Ramakrishnan, Taeku Lee, and Jane Junn, *Asian American Political Participation: Emerging Constituents and Their Political Identities* (New York: Russell Sage, 2011).
40. Sidney Verba, Kay Lehman Schlozman, Henry Brady, and Norman H. Nie, "Race, Ethnicity and Political Resources—Participation in the United States," *British Journal of Political Science* 23, no. 4 (1993): 453–97; Robert D. Putnam, "Tuning In, Tuning Out: The Strange Disappearance of Social Capital in America," *Political Science and Politics* 28, no. 4 (1995): 664–83.
41. The arguments in this paragraph draw on an insightful Ph.D. dissertation. Shankar K. Prasad, "Red, Brown and Blue: The Political Behavior of Asian Indian Americans" (Ph.D. diss., Brown University, 2006).
42. Jean Bacon, *Life Lines: Community, Family, and Assimiliation Among Asian Indian Immigrants* (New York: Oxford University Press, 1996), 4.
43. Kathleen Bubinas, "Gandhi Marg," 171.
44. Sofya Aptekar, "Organizational Life and Political Incorporation of Two Asian Immigrant Groups: A Case Study," *Ethnic and Racial Studies* 32, no. 9 (2009): 1511–33.
45. Johanna Lessinger, "Class, Race, and Success: Indian-Americans Confront the American Dream," in *Migration, Transnationalization, and Race in a Changing New York*, ed. Héctor R. Cordero-Guzmán, Robert C. Smith, and Ramón Grosfoguel (Philadelphia: Temple University Press, 2001), 167–90.

46. A complete list can be found at http://saalt.org/the-coalition/meet-the-ncso/.

47. Kay Lehman Schlozman, Sidney Verba, and Henry E. Brady, *The Unheavenly Chorus: Unequal Political Voice and the Broken Promise of American Democracy* (Princeton, NJ: Princeton University Press, 2012).

48. Martin Gilens, *Affluence and Influence: Economic Inequality and Political Power in America* (Princeton, NJ: Princeton University Press, 2013).

49. Chatwal was chairman of the Hampshire Hotels & Resorts group. He was caught on tape by a wired informant and pleaded guilty to violating federal election law by using straw donors. See http://news.yahoo.com/obama-s-attorney-general-pick-wants-to-throw-the-book-at-convicted-hillary-clinton-bundler-234614909.html.

50. Karen Leonard, *The South Asian Americans* (Westport, CT: Greenwood Press, 1997), 89.

51. This paragraph is partly based on conversations with Kapil Sharma who was involved in the discussions.

52. Gordon H. Chang, ed., *Asian Americans and Politics: Perspectives, Experiences, Prospects* (Stanford, CA: Stanford University Press, 2001), 258–84.

53. Robert M. Hathaway, "Unfinished Passage: India, Indian Americans, and the U.S. Congress," *Washington Quarterly* 24, no. 2 (2001): 21–34.

54. Ethnic news outlets play a relatively small role in shaping the political views of Indian Americans. In a survey conducted among Asian Americans after the 2012 election, when asked what news sources Indian Americans used to gain information about politics and their community, only 9 percent said ethnic, non-English language outlets, with 25 percent tuning into Indian English-language outlets, and two-thirds saying they used non-ethnic outlets. This rate of information assimilation is much greater than other Asian-American groups; Chinese Americans derived 87 percent of their news from Chinese ethnic news sources, both Chinese and English-language editions.

55. Until 2014, the FBI only tracked hate crimes against the following races and religions: white, black, or African American; American Indian or Alaska Native; Asian; multiple races; native Hawaiian or other Pacific Islander; Jewish; Catholic; Protestant; Islamic (Muslim); other religions; multiple religions; atheism/agnosticism.

56. George Joseph, "Dandekar becomes first Indian American woman lawmaker," November 6, 2002. At http://www.rediff.com/us/2002/nov/06us.htm.

57. Sandip Roy, "South-Asian Americans Discover Political Clout." At: http://www.npr.org/templates/text/s.php?sId=130853516&m=1.

58. Jay Nordlinger, "Pioneers! Rangers! Indians!" *National Review*, December 27, 2004. In reality, a representative survey of the Indian-American community at the time found that 37.3 percent were in favor of affirmative action in India, 22 percent were opposed, 25.6 percent were indifferent to such policies, and another 15.1 percent said, "Don't know." Devesh Kapur, *Diaspora, Democracy and Development* (Princeton, NJ: Princeton University Press, 2010), table 8.15.

59. Ibid. The sample size was 2,132.

60. Karthick Ramakrishnan and Taeku Lee, "Public Opinion of a Growing Electorate: Asian Americans and Pacific Islanders in 2012," www.naasurvey.com/resources/Home/NAAS12-sep25-election.pdf. The sample size was 3,042 Asian Americans, including 386 Indian Americans.

61. "The Asian American Vote: A Report on the Multi-Lingual Exit Poll from the 2012 Presidential Election," Asian American Legal Defense and Education Fund, http://aaldef.org/AALDEF percent202012 percent20Exit percent20Poll percent20Presentation.pdf.

62. Pew, "Rise of Asian Americans," 157.

63. A superlative account of the crisis and the bigotry of Nixon and Kissinger can be found in Gary J. Bass, *The Blood Telegram: Nixon, Kissinger, and a Forgotten Genocide* (New York: Alfred A. Knopf, 2013).

64. A survey by the Pew Center on attitudes among religious groups in the United States toward each other found that while Hindus (along with Buddhists and Mormons) had neutral ratings on average (and atheists and Muslims were perceived more coldly), the coldest thermometer ratings for Hindus came from white evangelical Christians, with only Muslims and atheists faring worse. See www.pewforum.org/2014/07/16/how-americans-feel-about-religious-groups/.

65. Prasad, "Red, Brown and Blue," 199.
66. Francine Blau, Lawrence Kahn, and Kerry Papps, "Gender, Source Country Characteristics, and Labor Market Assimilation among Immigrants," *Review of Economics and Statistics* 93, no. 1 (2011): 43–58. Also see chap. 2 on the gender gap in education in South Asia.
67. Francine Blau, Lawrence Kahn, Albert Liu, and Kerry Papps, "The Transmission of Women's Fertility, Human Capital, and Work Orientation across Immigrant Generations," *Journal of Population Economics* 26, no. 2 (2013): 405–35.
68. Thomas DiPrete and Claudia Buchmann, *The Rise of Women: The Growing Gender Gap in Education and What It Means for American Schools* (New York: Russell Sage Foundation, 2013).
69. See http://www.pewresearch.org/fact-tank/2014/03/06/womens-college-enrollment-gains-leave-men-behind/.
70. U.S. Department of Labor, "The Economic Status of Asian Americans and Pacific Islanders in the Wake of the Great Recession," 2014, www.dol.gov/_sec/media/reports/20140828-AAPI.pdf. Figure 2.9 provides the numbers of H-4 and L-2 visas that have seen a large increase in the past few years.
71. Pallavi Banerjee, "How Dependent Visas Shatter the American Dream," July 2, 2014, www.rediff.com/news/column/column-how-dependent-visa-shatters-the-american-dream/20140702.htm.
72. At the time of this writing, the U.S. government was considering a bill that would change this policy and allow H-4 visa holders to work; however, this would be only after at least six years of living in the country during the first stage of the permanent residency application.
73. While citizenship status is not required to work in the United States, it is a requirement to work in the large government sector. It can be assumed that many noncitizens do not have the legal right to work in the United States, while all naturalized citizens do.
74. Our analysis of the foreign-born and U.S.-born Indians in the United States (based on 2007–2011 ACS five-year pooled sample) shows that the mean age of the former was 39.5 years and the latter was 13.4 years. Indian Americans overall are much younger than other Asian groups and Non-Hispanic whites, given their relatively more recent immigration history to the United States. In the 25+ age group, about 40 percent of foreign-born Indians were between ages 25 and 35, compared to 70 percent of U.S.-born Indian Americans.
75. Douglas Almond and Lena Edlund, "Son-biased Sex Ratios in the 2000 United States Census," *PNAS* 105, no. 15 (2008): 5681–82.
76. Yen Le Espiritu, "Gender and Labor in Asian Immigrant Families," *American Behavioral Scientist* 42, no. 4 (1999): 628–47; Nancy Foner, "Benefits and Burdens: Immigrant Women and Work in New York City," *Gender Issues* 16, no. 4 (1998): 5–24; Shireen Jejeebhoy and Zeba A. Sathar, "Women's Autonomy in India and Pakistan: The Influence of Religion and Region," *Population and Development Review* 27, no. 4 (2001): 687–712.
77. Margaret Abraham, "Domestic Violence and the Indian Diaspora in the United States," *Indian Journal of Gender Studies* 12, nos. 2–3 (2005): 427–51, 434.
78. Prema Kurien, "Gendered Ethnicity Creating a Hindu Indian Identity in the United States," *American Behavioral Scientist* 42, no. 4 (1999): 648–70.
79. There are various ways to define *autonomy*, but here we mean a simple intuitive definition: a sense of control over one's life.
80. Shamita Das Dasgupta, "Gender Roles and Cultural Continuity in the Asian Indian Immigrant Community in the U.S." *Sex Roles* 38, nos. 11–12 (1998): 953–74; Kurien, "Gendered Ethnicity."
81. Abraham, "Domestic Violence," 11.
82. See Banerjee, "Dependent Visas Shatter."
83. Shamita Das Dasgupta, ed., *Body Evidence: Intimate Violence against South Asian Women in America* (New Brunswick, NJ: Rutgers University Press, 2007), 3. The author estimated that there were at least 146 domestic violence fatalities or near fatalities within the Indian-American community between March 1990 and February 2006, based on reports in community newspapers.
84. These include Manavi, Sakhi for South Asian Women, SEWAA (Service and Education for Women Against Abuse), Apna Ghar, Maitri, Raksha and Sneha.

85. Philip Kasinitz, John H. Mollenkopf, Mary C. Waters, and Jennifer Holdaway, *Inheriting the City: The Children of Immigrants Come of Age* (New York: Russell Sage, 2008). The book does not, however, look at children of Indian-American immigrants.

86. Alejandro Portes and Ruben Rumbaut, *Legacies: The Story of the Immigrant Second Generation* (Berkeley: University of California Press, 2001).

87. Alejandro Portes, Patricia Fernández-Kelly, and William Haller, "The Adaptation of the Immigrant Second Generation in America: A Theoretical Overview and Recent Evidence," *Journal of Ethnic and Migration Studies* 35, no. 7 (2009): 1077–104.

88. The 2007–2011 ACS contains information on 77,117 foreign-born Indians and 34,019 U.S.-born, or second-generation, Indians. A subsample of persons over the age of 24 was used for most of the analysis so that the child and school-going population could be excluded. This group is small for the second-generation Indian Americans because of the low median age. There were 66,968 first-generation and 5,639 second-generation Indian Americans in the 2012 ACS subsample above the age of 24, which forms the basis of the analysis in this section. "Second generation" refers to second and all subsequent generations. The population that has been in the United States for longer than two generations is relatively minor.

89. Herbert J. Gans, "Second-generation Decline: Scenarios for the Economic and Ethnic Futures of the Post 1965 American Immigrants," *Ethnic and Racial Studies* 15, no. 2 (1992): 173–92; Alejandro Portes and Min Zhou, "The New Second Generation: Segmented Assimilation and Its Variants," *Annals of the American Academy of Political and Social Science* 530, no. 1 (1992): 74–96.

90. Peggy Levitt and Mary C. Waters, eds., *The Changing Face of Home: The Transnational Lives of the Second Generation* (New York: Russell Sage Foundation, 2002), 16.

91. Margaret Gibson, *Accommodation without Assimilation: Sikh Immigrants in an American High School* (Ithaca, NY: Cornell University Press, 1988).

92. Prema Kurien, "Being Young, Brown, and Hindu. The Identity Struggles of Second-Generation Indian Americans," *Journal of Contemporary Ethnography* 34, no. 4 (2005): 434–69.

93. Prema Kurien, "Gendered Ethnicity Creating a Hindu Indian Identity in the United States," *American Behavioral Scientist* 42, no. 4 (1999): 648–70.

94. The authors are deeply grateful to Jasmeet Ahuja, who interviewed numerous Indian-American military officers (serving and retired) to help us with this discussion. All errors are ours. For a short discussion, also see http://indiaspora.org/blog/a-life-of-service-indian-americans-and-the-u-s-armed-forces/.

95. Dave Philipps, "Sikh Captain Says Keeping Beard and Turban Lets Him Serve U.S. and Faith," *New York Times*, April 1, 2016. The permanent accommodation would only be revoked if the beard and turban affected "unit cohesion and morale, good order and discipline, health and safety."

96. Josh White, "Intolerance Found at Air Force Academy," *Washington Post*, June 23, 2005, www.washingtonpost.com/wp-dyn/content/article/2005/06/22/AR2005062200598.html.

97. Pew, "Rise of Asian Americans," 165.

98. Note that the African Indian group had a small sample size in the ACS. These statistics are based on a sample of 1,832 individuals.

99. Natasha Warikoo, "Gender and Ethnic Identity among Second-Generation Indo-Caribbeans," *Ethnic and Racial Studies* 28, no. 5 (2005): 803–31.

100. Governor Bobby Jindal, Remarks to the Henry Jackson Society, January 19, 2015. At: http://americanxt.org/remarks-to-the-henry-jackson-society-in-london-england/.

101. "Indian Culture Helped Me Win Title, Says Miss America," *The Hindu*, December 28, 2014, www.thehindu.com/news/cities/Vijayawada/indian-culture-helped-me-win-title-says-miss-america/article6731083.ece.

102. Rajiv Shankar, "South Asian Identity in Asian America," in *A Part, Yet Apart: South Asians in Asian America*, ed. Lavinia Shankar and Rajini Srikanth (Philadelphia: Temple University Press.1998), ix; Nazli Kibria, "Not Asian, Black, or White? Reflections on South Asian American Racial Identity," *Amerasia Journal* 22, no. 2 (1996): 77–86.

103. Anne Morning, "The Racial Self-Identification of South Asians in the United States," *Journal of Ethnic and Migration Studies* 27, no. 1 (2001): 61–79.
104. Ariela Schachter, "Finding Common Ground? Indian Immigrants and Asian American Panethnicity," *Social Forces* 92, no. 4 (2014): 1487–512.
105. SAALT, "Under Suspicion, Under Attack: Xenophobic Political Rhetoric and Hate Violence against South Asian, Muslim, Sikh, Hindu, Middle Eastern, and Arab Communities in the United States," 2014, http://saalt.org/wp-content/uploads/2013/06/SAALT_report_full_links1.pdf.
106. Schachter, "Finding Common Ground."
107. Janelle Wong, S. Karthick Ramakrishnan, Taeku Lee, and Jane Junn, *Asian American Political Participation: Emerging Constituents and Their Political Identities* (New York: Russell Sage Foundation, 2011).
108. Caroline Brettell, "Experiencing Everyday Discrimination: A Comparison across Five Immigrant Populations," *Race and Social Problems* 3 (2011): 266–79.
109. The Pew Survey of Asian Americans, 2012, 110.
110. Michael Matza and Joelle Farrell, "Indian Population Booming in Philadelphia Area," *Philly.com*, July 03, 2011, http://articles.philly.com/2011-07-03/news/29733219_1_indian-churches-immigrant-physician-training.
111. Harpalani Vinay, "Desicrit: Theorizing the Racial Ambiguity of South Asian Americans," *NYU Annual Survey of American Law* 69, no. 1 (2013): 77–184.
112. Stephanie M. DiPietro and Robert J. Bursik, Jr., "Studies of the New Immigration. The Dangers of Pan-Ethnic Classifications," *Annals of the American Academy of Political and Social Science* 641, no. 1 (2012): 247–67.
113. Paul Taylor et al., *When Labels Don't Fit: Hispanics and Their Views of Identity* (Washington, DC: Pew Hispanic Center, 2012).
114. *The Rise of Asian Americans* (Washington, DC: Pew Research Center, 2013).
115. Donna R. Gabaccia, "Is Everywhere Nowhere? Nomads, Nations, and the Immigrant Paradigm of United States History," *Journal of American History* 86, no. 3 (1999): 1115–34.
116. Mary Waters, *Ethnic Options: Choosing Identities in America* (Berkeley: University of California Press, 1990).
117. Brian Duncan and Stephen J. Trejo, "The Complexity of Immigrant Generations: Implications for Assessing the Socioeconomic Integration of Hispanics and Asians," 2016, NBER Working Paper 21982. The analysis is based on 2003–2013 CPS data.

Chapter 5

1. Economist Brad DeLong provided a pithy description of what was happening: "Information technology and the Internet amplify brain power in the same way that the technologies of the industrial revolution amplified muscle power," quoted in Frances Cairncross, *The Death of Distance: How the Communications Revolution Is Changing Our Lives* (Cambridge, MA: Harvard Business School Press, 2001), 4–5.
2. See Stuart Anderson, "Immigrants and Billion Dollar Startups," National Foundation for American Policy, Policy Brief, March 2016, http://nfap.com/wp-content/uploads/2016/03/Immigrants-and-Billion-Dollar-Startups.NFAP-Policy-Brief.March-2016.pdf. The role of immigrants in high-growth firms had previously been documented in David Hart, Zoltan Acs, and Spencer Tracy, "High-tech Immigrant Entrepreneurship in the United States," July 2009, Small Business Administration Office of Advocacy Report No. 349, www.sba.gov/sites/default/files/advocacy/rs349tot_0.pdf. See also Stuart Anderson and Michaela Platzer, "American Made: The Impact of Immigrant Entrepreneurs and Professionals on U.S. Competitiveness," 2006, National Venture Capital Association Study, www.contentfirst.com/AmericanMade_study.pdf. As its title implies, the latter study also considers the economic impact of nonentrepreneurs.
3. This quote and subsequent ones for this work are from Alexis de Tocqueville, *Democracy in America and Two Essays on America*, trans. Gerald Bevan (London: Penguin Books, 2003).
4. See Mike Maddock, "Why Americans Make the Best Entrepreneurs . . . For Now," *Forbes*, September 25, 2013, www.forbes.com/sites/mikemaddock/2013/09/25/why-americans-make-the-best-entrepreneurs-for-now/.

5. The overall job-creation impact of small vs. large firms has been the subject of some academic controversy, but see David Neumark, Brandon Wall, and Junfu Zhang, "Do Small Businesses Create More Jobs? New Evidence for the United States from the National Establishment Time Series," *Review of Economics and Statistics* 93, no. 1 (2011): 16–29; the authors carefully examine earlier studies and reach strong conclusions concerning the positive impact of small firms on job creation, both in absolute terms and relative to large firms.

6. As well as the studies cited in n. 2, see Zoltan J. Acs, William Parsons, and Spencer Tracy, "High-Impact Firms: Gazelles Revisited," June 2008, Small Business Administration Office of Advocacy Report No. 328, http://archive.sba.gov/advo/research/rs328tot.pdf.

7. See "The United States of Entrepreneurs: America Still Leads the World," *The Economist*, March 12, 2009, www.economist.com/node/13216037. As brought out in this article, an entrepreneurial culture, such as acceptance of risk-taking and failure, translates into institutions and policies that support entrepreneurship, such as liberal bankruptcy laws, a strong venture capital industry, close industry-university ties, and relatively open immigration policies. Another purely cultural factor that has been adduced is "venturesome consumers." See Amar Bhidé, *The Venturesome Economy: How Innovation Sustains Prosperity in a More Connected World*, (Princeton, NJ: Princeton University Press, 2010). The interplay of cultural factors, on the one hand, and institutions and policies, on the other, is also discussed in Andreas Freytag and Roy Thurik, "Entrepreneurship and its Determinants in a Cross-Country Setting," in *Entrepreneurship and Culture*, special issue of *Journal of Evolutionary Economics* 17, no. 2 (2007): 117–31.

8. It is also true that rates of entrepreneurship have varied over time in the United States, owing to secular forces associated with the rise of large-scale corporations: see Ingrid Verheul, Niels Bosma, Fonnie van der Nol, and Tommy Wong, "Determinants of Entrepreneurship in the United States of America," in *Entrepreneurship: Determinants and Policy in a European-US Comparison*, ed. David Audretsch, Roy Thurik, Ingrid Verheul, and Sander Wennekers (New York: Kluwer Academic Publishers, 2002), chap. 6. Presumably, similar trends were at work in comparator countries, preserving the qualitative ranking of entrepreneurialism across nations.

9. Schumpeter's concepts are introduced in Joseph A. Schumpeter, *Capitalism, Socialism and Democracy* (London: Harper & Brothers, 1942). For a modern formalization of Schumpeter's ideas, see Philippe Aghion and Peter Howitt, "A Model of Growth through Creative Destruction," *Econometrica* 60, no. 2 (1992): 323–51. In that model, growth is driven by innovation within existing firms, but it is easy to think of a modification where new firms replace old ones in the process of new products and services replacing old ones.

10. This quote comes at the end of the abstract of Ian Hathaway and Robert E. Litan, "Declining Business Dynamism in the United States: A Look at States and Metros," May 2014, Economic Studies at Brookings, Brookings Institution, www.brookings.edu/~/media/research/files/papers/2014/05/declining%20business%20dynamism%20litan/declining_business_dynamism_hathaway_litan.pdf. A somewhat more breathless assessment of the current importance of immigrant entrepreneurship to the United States is that of Richard T. Herman and Robert L. Smith, *Immigrant, Inc.: Why Immigrant Entrepreneurs Are Driving the New Economy (and How They Will Save the American Worker)* (Hoboken, NJ: John Wiley & Sons, 2010).

11. See Vivek Wadhwa, AnnaLee Saxenian, and F. Daniel Siciliano, *America's New Immigrant Entrepreneurs: Then and Now* (Kansas City, MO: Ewing Marion Kauffman Foundation, 2012).

12. For example, the study by Wadhwa and his co-authors led to an Internet piece with a catchy title; see Tim DeVaney and Tom Stein, "Why Are Indians So Entrepreneurial in the U.S.?," October 19, 2012, http://readwrite.com/2012/10/19/why-are-indians-so-entrepreneurial-in-the-us. This is one of the questions to be addressed in this chapter and the next, but another question is whether its premise is true. In fact, overall entrepreneurship rates among Indian Americans are not particularly high. Note also that the story of Indian-American entrepreneurship is broader and richer than Silicon Valley, or even high-tech generally. As has been the case for many immigrant groups, Indian Americans have engaged in a range of enterprises, with varying impacts and degrees of success. While the case of high-tech is important, and may be more so as digital technology continues to transform the industrial structure of the United States, one needs a broader understanding of the experience of Indian-American entrepreneurs. Interestingly, despite a decades-old literature on immigrant and ethnic

entrepreneurship in America, Indian Americans were not analyzed systematically as a distinct group until recently. Quantitative studies, in particular, have often been for the much broader category of Asian Americans.

13. The survey's exploration of motivations and success factors is related to the existing theoretical literature on ethnic entrepreneurship. For example, see Roger Waldinger, Howard Aldrich, and Robin Ward, *Ethnic Entrepreneurs: Immigrant Business in Industrial Societies* (Newbury Park, CA: Sage Publications, 1990); the authors frame ethnic entrepreneurship in terms of an interaction of opportunity structures and group strategies. Their analysis also discusses ideas of ethnic clustering and "middleman minorities," the latter referring to ethnic minorities serving niches underserved by mainstream organizations.

14. These included Bhagat Singh Thind, whose citizenship case was mentioned in chapter 1, and as discussed in Philip Deslippe, "Sikh Immigrants and the History of Yoga in the United States," panel presentation on enterprise abroad, Conference on Sikh Studies in the 21st Century, University of California, Santa Barbara, May 2014.

15. See Juan L. Gonzales, Jr., "Asian Indian Immigration Patterns: The Origins of the Sikh Community in California," *International Migration Review* 20 (1986): 40–54.

16. See Pawan Dhingra, *Life Behind the Lobby: Indian-American Motel Owners and the American Dream* (Stanford, CA: Stanford University Press, 2012).

17. For example, see Moses Rischin, *The Promised City: New York's Jews, 1870–1914* (Cambridge, MA: Harvard University Press, 1962).

18. On the other hand, the argument has been made, at least qualitatively, for broad positive impacts of immigration; see Joel Millman, *The Other Americans: How Immigrants Renew Our Country, Our Economy, and Our Values* (New York: Viking Penguin, 1997). The title of that book encapsulates its thesis. Similar themes are in Joel Kotkin, *The Next Hundred Million: America in 2050* (New York: Penguin Press, 2010).

19. For example, Min Zhou remarks as follows, "Indeed, few would regard Computer Associates International (a large public firm specializing in computer technology based in New York) and Watson Pharmaceuticals (a large public firm based in Los Angeles) as ethnic businesses and their founders, Charles B. Wang, an immigrant from China, and Allen Chao, an immigrant from Taiwan, as ethnic entrepreneurs. These immigrant or ethnic group members appear to have successfully shed their ethnic distinctiveness and have incorporated their businesses into the core of the mainstream economy" (1041). See Min Zhou, "Revisiting Ethnic Entrepreneurship: Convergencies, Controversies, and Conceptual Advancements," *International Migration Review* 38 (2004): 1040–74.

20. For discussions of these concepts, and further references, see Howard Aldrich and Roger Waldinger, "Ethnicity and Entrepreneurship," *Annual Review of Sociology* 16 (1990): 111–35; Waldinger, Ward, and Aldrich, *Ethnic Entrepreneurs*, 49–78; Min Zhou, "Revisiting Ethnic Entrepreneurship."

21. This point is made explicitly by Zulema Valdez, "Beyond Ethnic Entrepreneurship: An Embedded Market Approach to Group Affiliation in American Enterprise," *Race, Gender & Class* 15, no. 1/2 (2008): 156–69, with her own framework being derived from K. Polanyi, C. M. Arensberg, and H. W. Pearson, eds., *Trade and Market in the Early Empires* (Glencoe, IL: Free Press, 1957), 243–70.

22. See Aldrich and Waldinger, "Ethnicity and Entrepreneurship."

23. These statistics and those immediately following are originally from various U.S. government sources, including the Census and the Bureau of Labor Statistics, and here are taken from Waldinger, Ward, and Aldrich, *Ethnic Entrepreneurs*, and Ivan Light and Angel A. Sanchez, "Immigrant Entrepreneurs in 272 SMSAs," *Sociological Perspectives* 30, no. 4 (1987): 373–99.

24. The national average business participation rate in 1980 was 48.9, and was 47.1 for Indian Americans. This figure is calculated in a manner that makes it ten times the percentage reported in the previous paragraph.

25. These were Russian, Lebanese, Romanian, and Swiss. Given the year the data pertain to, it is a safe inference that the great majority of those of Russian ancestry were Jewish, but data on religion are not collected, and so this cannot be confirmed. This group was also second in the average income rankings.

26. It was 7.1 percent vs. 9 percent for Korean Americans, 7 percent for Japanese Americans, and 6.6 percent for Chinese Americans. The original source for the data is "The State of Small Business," Bureau of the Census, U.S. Department of Commerce, 1987.

27. This result was derived by Light and Sanchez, "Immigrant Entrepreneurs." They also found no negative effect on the native black population's participation in self-employment. However, with subsequent data, Robert Fairlie and Bruce Meyer, "The Effect of Immigration on Native Self-Employment," *Journal of Labor Economics* 21, no. 3 (2003): 619–50, showed that immigrants did displace nonblack natives in self-employment.

28. See John Sibley Butler and Cedric Herring, "Ethnicity and Entrepreneurship in America: Toward an Explanation of Racial and Ethnic Group Variations in Self-Employment," *Sociological Perspectives* 34, no. 1 (1991): 79–94.

29. See Robert Fairlie and Alicia Robb, *Race and Entrepreneurial Success: Black-, Asian-, and White-Owned Businesses in the United States* (Cambridge, MA: MIT Press, 2008).

30. This number is not directly comparable with those reported earlier in the chapter, which did not separate out Hispanics, who have significantly lower rates of self-employment. The figure for 1986, for Non-Hispanic whites, was 11.2 percent, indicating little change in self-employment rates over the two decades. In 1990, self-employment rates for the foreign-born and native-born were 11.6 percent and 10.5 percent, respectively, while Indian Americans had a rate of 12.3 percent. The three groups with the highest self-employment rates in 1990 were Greeks, Koreans, and Iranians, based on figures compiled by Robert Fairlie: see Robert Kloosterman and Jan Rath, eds., *Immigrant Entrepreneurs: Venturing Abroad in the Age of Globalization* (Oxford: Berg, 2003), 17–38.

31. A study using a different data set (the Panel Study of Entrepreneurial Dynamics, 1988–2000) found that startup capital did not affect the decision to become an entrepreneur, although education and experience did; see Phillip H. Kim, Howard E. Aldrich, and Lisa A. Keister, "Access (Not) Denied: The Impact of Financial, Human, and Cultural Capital on Entrepreneurial Entry in the United States," *Small Business Economics* 27, no. 1 (2006): 5–22.

32. See Zulema Valdez, "The Effect of Social Capital on White, Korean, Mexican and Black Business Owners' Earnings in the U.S.," *Journal of Ethnic and Migration Studies* 34, no. 6 (2008): 955–73.

33. See AnnaLee Saxenian, *Silicon Valley's New Immigrant Entrepreneurs* (San Francisco: Public Policy Institute of California, 1999), 24.

34. Rekhi's story is considered in more depth in the next chapter. The distinction of being the first venture-funded Indian-American entrepreneur seems to belong to Narinder Singh Kapany, whose company was founded in 1960 and went public in 1967. However, this was a relatively isolated example.

35. Rekhi himself has written, "By the late 1970s many [Indian immigrants in Silicon Valley] had reached the top rungs of technical ladders and were beginning to butt against the glass ceilings of American corporations which would not admit them into management ranks. By the early 1980s, a handful of frustrated but talented engineers including myself took matters in their own hands and turned entrepreneurs." See Kanwal Rekhi, "Rise of Indian in Silicon Valley and Rise of India," (undated), www.inventuscap.com/rise-of-indians-in-silicon-valley-rise-of-india-by-kanwal-rekhi/.

36. See Vivek Wadhwa, AnnaLee Saxenian, Ben Rissing, and Gary Gereffi, "America's New Immigrant Entrepreneurs: Part I," January 2007, Duke Science, Technology & Innovation Paper No. 23, http://people.ischool.berkeley.edu/~anno/Papers/Americas_new_ immigrant_entrepreneurs_I.pdf.

37. See Hart, Acs, and Tracy, "High-tech Immigrant Entrepreneurship."

38. See Vivek Wadhwa, AnnaLee Saxenian, and F. Daniel Siciliano, "America's New Immigrant Entrepreneurs: Then and Now," October 2012, www.kauffman.org/~/media/kauffman_ org/research%20reports%20and%20covers/2012/10/then_and_now_americas_new_ immigrant_entrepreneurs.pdf . The numbers reported here are calculated from percentages reported on p. 3 and pp. 26–27.

39. See Robert W. Fairlie, Julie Zissimopoulos, and Harry Krashinsky, "The International Asian Business Success Story? A Comparison of Chinese, Indian and Other Asian Businesses in the

United States, Canada and United Kingdom," in *International Differences in Entrepreneurship*, ed. Josh Lerner and Antoinette Schoar (Chicago: University of Chicago Press, 2010), 179–208; and Robert Fairlie, Harry Krashinsky, Julie Zissimopoulos, and Krishna B. Kumar, "Indian Entrepreneurial Success in the United States, Canada and the United Kingdom," December 2013, CESifo Working Paper No. 4510, www.cesifo-group.de/ifoHome/publications/working-papers/CESifoWP/CESifoWPdetails?wp_id=19100667.

40. A cautionary note is that these comparisons do not control for other variables such as wealth or industry choice.

41. The SBO includes businesses that are classified by the IRS as sole proprietorships, partnerships, 1120 corporations, or employers, and that have sales of $1000 or more.

42. Close to another 800,000 firms were either public and therefore not closely held, or otherwise had ownership that was not identifiable by ethnicity. The latter includes foreign-owned and not-for-profit firms. Ethnic ownership of a firm is determined when 51 percent or more of the business is owned by a member of a racial group. Firms with multiple-ethnicity owners may be counted in multiple categories, but this is a relatively small number.

43. Note that aggregate sales figures can involve double counting, and so are not comparable to national income or output figures.

44. All these percentages and calculations exclude firms that are public or do not have owners with identifiable ethnicity.

45. This occupational clustering is also somewhat distinct from the geographical clustering discussed in chapter 3, although occupations were also considered in that chapter. In the SBO data, the distribution of Indian-American business owners across states was similar to that of the overall Indian-American population, as analyzed in chapter 3. In other words there did not seem to be major geographic differences in propensities for self-employment for Indian Americans.

46. This finding is stronger than the pattern reported in Fairlie, Krashinsky, Zissimopoulos, and Kumar, "Indian Entrepreneurial Success." It is also related to the analysis in Roger Waldinger, ed., *Strangers at the Gates: New Immigrants in Urban America* (Berkeley: University of California Press, 2001), 228–71. They quantify the importance of immigrant occupational niches in major U.S. cities, including Indian Americans in Los Angeles and New York, for 1980 and 1990.

47. Wadhwa, Saxenian, and Siciliano, "America's New Immigrant Entrepreneurs," found that Indians were highly represented in several technology sectors, leading all immigrant groups in biosciences (35 percent of immigrant-founded companies), computers/communications (28 percent), innovation/manufacturing-related services (29 percent), semiconductors (32 percent), software (33 percent), environmental (39 percent), and defense/aerospace (29 percent). Anderson and Platzer, "American Made," had documented the importance of immigrants in key technology and science sectors: immigrant-founded venture-backed public companies were heavily concentrated in science and technology sectors. Of the 144 companies identified by Anderson and Platzer, "American Made," 32 (22 percent) had founders born in India.

48. The other Asian groups also tended to be underrepresented in Construction, and had more concentrated distributions across industries, but nowhere as great as that of Indian Americans. Other notable features of the three Asian-American comparison groups were the heavy concentration of Chinese-American firms in Accommodation and Food Services, and the relatively high proportion of Korean-American-owned businesses in Other Services, which may include businesses such as dry cleaners and beauty salons. Min Zhou uses a combination of Census and survey data to analyze ethnic clustering, occupational niches, and evolution of networks for Chinese Americans. See Min Zhou, *Chinatown: The Socioeconomic Potential of an Urban Enclave* (Philadelphia: Temple University Press, 1992); John Sibley Butler and George Kozmetsky, eds., *Immigrant and Minority Entrepreneurship: The Continuous Rebirth of American Communities* (Westport, CT: Praeger, 2004), 37–60. Similarly, for Korean Americans, see Pyon Gap Min, ed., *Koreans in America: Their Twenty-First Century Experiences* (Lanham, MD: Lexington Books, 2013).

49. Recall that these figures tell us nothing about overall employment in different sectors, only about business owners, so they are consistent with Indian Americans having a relatively strong working presence in the Information sector.

50. For example, in an email interview, Pawan Dhingra responds to a question about the second generation: "Are the children of Gujarati motel owners keen on taking over the family business?"

> Yes and no. Many who grew up in the motel swear they do not want to come back into the business after they go to college (and practically all children of motel owners go to college—a remarkable achievement by the families). They get jobs in the white-collar workplace, such as being engineers or in the sciences. But they encounter a glass ceiling or feel that they could make more money and have more freedom if they owned their own business instead of working for someone else. So they gradually come back to the motel industry. They have the resources of their families and community to draw from to help them succeed. And they will own places that often are a bit higher status than that of their parents, so they feel that they are moving up the ladder and improving upon what their parents have established. Other children know from an early age that they want to stay in the industry. Some may go to hospitality school or business school with the intent of expanding the family operations.

See Amardeep Banerjee, "Room at the Top," *The Times of India: The Crest Edition*, July 14, 2012, www.timescrest.com/world/room-at-the-top-8316.

51. Surprisingly, in the ACS data, Indian-American business owners earn less than the national average in both Wholesale and Retail Trade: this ranking contrasts with the SBO data, and suggests some caution in drawing overly detailed conclusions from the ACS data. It is also true that sales and earnings measure different things.

52. The relationship between wealth and entrepreneurship is not well understood because of obvious problems of identifying the direction of causality. See Robert Fairlie and Harry A. Krashinsky, "Liquidity Constraints, Household Wealth, and Entrepreneurship Revisited," *Review of Income and Wealth* 58, no. 2 (2012): 279–306.

53. The industry in which the earnings took place did matter for the level of earnings, as did location. These results are similar to those of Fairlie and Robb, *Race and Entrepreneurial Success*.

54. Presumably, English fluency increases wage and salary earnings as well. The relative impact, and therefore the impact on choices between employment and entrepreneurship, is unclear. See Robert Fairlie and Chris Woodruff, "Mexican American Entrepreneurship," *The B.E. Journal of Economic Analysis & Policy* 10, no. 1 (2010), ISSN (online) 1935–1682, doi: 10.2202/1935-1682.2479; Fairlie and Woodruff found that greater English fluency was associated with more self-employment, whereas Timothy Bates, *Race, Self-Employment and Upward Mobility: An Illusive American Dream* (Baltimore: Johns Hopkins Press, 1997), among others, found that lack of command of English acted as a barrier to wage and salary employment for Asian immigrants, thereby increasing self-employment.

55. Many of these trends are encapsulated in Richard Florida's idea of a "creative class," although he focuses more on regional clustering and creativity in general, rather than the implications for business enterprise. See Richard Florida, *The Rise of the Creative Class and How It's Transforming Work, Leisure, Community and Everyday Life* (New York: Basic Books, 2002).

56. Most of the responses were obtained through an anonymous online survey and came from a panel of individuals who had indicated a willingness to participate in such surveys. A small number of responses were obtained through telephone interviews from subjects on an alternative list of business owners obtained from a provider of databases for research and marketing.

57. Almost one-fourth of the respondents lived in California and other Pacific Coast states, with another 24 percent in the Northeast, including New England, New York, New Jersey, and Pennsylvania. Illinois, Texas, the Mid-Atlantic states, and Florida were also well represented in the sample. The sample includes both business owners and professionals, but recall that the SBO data did not suggest any major differences in propensities for business ownership across different states.

58. This was highest for current entrepreneurs (29.7 percent), followed by past entrepreneurs (24.3 percent), nonentrepreneurs (23.5 percent), and aspiring entrepreneurs (22 percent). Aspiring entrepreneurs also had the lowest proportion of born-elsewhere respondents (3.3 percent), and therefore the highest proportion born in India (74 percent) compared to 65 percent of current entrepreneurs born in India. A reasonable conjecture is that many of

this group were part of the IT Generation: this is also reflected in a slightly lower average time lived in the United States.

59. This pattern is consistent with much other work on intergenerational influences on entrepreneurship, including Thomas A. Dunn and Douglas J. Holtz-Eakin, "Financial Capital, Human Capital, and the Transition to Self-Employment: Evidence from Intergenerational Links," *Journal of Labor Economics* 18, no. 2 (2000): 282–305; Robert Fairlie, "The Absence of the African-American Owned Business: An Analysis of the Dynamics of Self-Employment," *Journal of Labor Economics* 17, no. 1 (1999): 80–108; Michael Hout and Harvey S. Rosen, "Self-Employment, Family Background, and Race," *Journal of Human Resources* 35, no. 4 (2000): 670–92.

60. As with its language, Kannada (see chapter 2), the state of Karnataka does not fit the southern state pattern, with figures of 4.2 percent of the sample and 5 percent of India's population.

61. Those in the sample who were born in Gujarat were the most likely to be experienced entrepreneurs and to have parents who had been entrepreneurs. They were least likely to work in information technology or professional and technical services, were second least likely (after those born in West Bengal) to have undergraduate degrees in computer science or engineering, worked for the smallest employers on average, and were the second-oldest group by birth states (after those from Kerala). Other patterns associated with birth states in the sample reflected the differences identified in chapter 3: those born in Andhra Pradesh and Tamil Nadu were on average the youngest in the sample, and those from the four southern states were by far the most likely to have undergraduate degrees in engineering or computer science. However, for the case of Punjab, there was less alignment between birth state and language spoken. Furthermore, it is highly unlikely that the survey sample picked up the rural-based or less-educated segment of Punjabi speakers in America.

62. For example, see T. M. Begley and D. P. Boyd, "Psychological Characteristics Associated with Performance in Entrepreneurial Firms and Smaller Businesses," *Journal of Business Venturing* 2 (1987): 79–93.

63. See, for example, R. D. Hisrich, "Entrepreneurship: Past, Present, and Future," *Journal of Small Business Management* 26, no. 4 (1988): 1–4; and "Entrepreneurship/Intrapreneurship," *American Psychologist* 45, no. 2 (1990): 209–22. Other work does suggest considerable heterogeneity among entrepreneurs; see W. B. Gartner, "A Conceptual Framework for Describing the Phenomenon of New Venture Creation," *Academy of Management Review* 10, no. 4 (1985): 696–706.

64. Other studies have found this to be an important motive for entrepreneurship in some circumstances; see Fairlie and Krashinsky, "Liquidity Constraints, Household Wealth, and Entrepreneurship Revisited."

65. As reported in a *Wall Street Journal* article by Deborah Gage, "Of the 6,613 U.S.-based companies initially funded by venture capital between 2006 and 2011, 84% now are closely held and operating independently, 11% were acquired or made initial public offerings of stock and 4% went out of business, according to Dow Jones VentureSource," September 20, 2012, http://wsj.com/articles/SB10000872396390443720204578004980476429190. Other data on failure rates suggest that they are higher than in our sample or the Dow Jones VentureSource data.

66. Sen makes a case that Indian traditions incorporate strong elements of public debate and intellectual pluralism; see Amartya Sen, *The Argumentative Indian* (New York: Farrar, Strauss and Giroux, 2005).

67. A large literature exists on possible psychological differences between entrepreneurs and non-entrepreneurs. Our survey results on attitudes toward thrift are reminiscent of Max Weber, *From Max Weber: Essays in Sociology*, trans. H. H. Gerth and C. Wright Mills (London: Routledge & Kegan Paul, 1948). Cross-country studies indicate that some entrepreneurial traits are not necessarily culture-specific in the Weberian mold; see, for example, Anisya S. Thomas and Stephen L. Mueller, "A Case for Comparative Entrepreneurship: Assessing the Relevance of Culture," *Journal of International Business Studies* 31, no. 2 (2000): 287–301.

68. Respondents were also asked about the value of current strategic relationships, and partners and suppliers in India appeared to be the most valuable. Related questions asked respondents how often they had discussed jobs or business opportunities existing in the United States with

anyone working in India, and also whether opportunities in India had been discussed with anyone working in the United States during the previous 12 months. Over half of the respondents reported multiple such discussions in each direction, with aspiring entrepreneurs being the most active, and nonentrepreneurs the least.

69. Those data are consistent with individual stories such as those of engineering graduates running motels; for example, see Rick Romell, "State's Asian Indians Thrive in Entrepreneurial Society," *Milwaukee Wisconsin Journal Sentinel*, February 7, 2010, www.jsonline.com/business/83779312.html.

70. These results may be compared to those of J. McGrath Cohoon, Vivek Wadhwa, and Lesa Mitchell, "Are Successful Women Entrepreneurs Different from Men?," May 2010, www.kauffman.org/~/media/kauffman_org/research%20reports%20and%20covers/2009/07/successful_women_entrepreneurs_510.pdf. They find many similarities between successful male and female entrepreneurs, with some differences in motivations and sources of funding. Patricia Gene Green and Candida Greer Brush, "The Minority Community as a Natural Incubator," in *Immigrant and Minority Entrepreneurship: The Continuous Rebirth of American Communities*, ed. John Sibley Butler and George Kozmetsky (Westport, CT: Praeger, 2004), 123–48; survey studies of women's entrepreneurship, not restricted to Indian Americans, or even to immigrants.

71. Based on 1992 Census data from the precursor of the SBO, Fairlie and Robb found that female-owned businesses were less successful than male-owned businesses (measured by survival, profits, sales, and employment) because they had less startup capital, less business human capital acquired through prior work experience in a similar business, and less prior work experience in a family business. Key differences from the analysis of Fairlie and Robb are the time of the data, which is more recent for Cohoon et al., "Are Successful Women," and the use of a selected sample, rather than national Census data. See Robert Fairlie and Alicia Robb, "Gender Differences In Business Performance: Evidence From The Characteristics Of Business Owners Survey," *Small Business Economics* 33 (2009): 375–95.

Chapter 6

1. See AnnaLee Saxenian, *Regional Advantage: Culture and Competition in Silicon Valley and Route 128* (Cambridge, MA: Harvard University Press, 1994).

2. See Vivek Wadhwa, AnnaLee Saxenian, and F. Daniel Siciliano, "America's New Immigrant Entrepreneurs: Then and Now," October 2012, www.kauffman.org/~/media/kauffman_org/research%20reports%20and%20covers/2012/10/then_and_now_americas_new_immigrant_entrepreneurs.pdf.

3. Ibid. These numbers can also be compared with those presented in the introduction to chapter 5.

4. As quoted in Melanie Warner, "The Indians of Silicon Valley: The Hidden Geniuses of the Tech Revolution Are Indian Engineers," *Fortune*, May 15, 2000.

5. An important precursor of TiE was the Asian American Manufacturers Association (AAMA), which was a network of Taiwanese and Chinese entrepreneurs and professionals, founded in 1979. In 2002, the "M" was changed to stand for "MultiTechnology." See Rafiq Dossani, "Chinese and Indian Engineers and Their Networks in Silicon Valley," March 2002, report for Asia/Pacific Research Center, Stanford University, for a seminal early comparison of AAMA and TiE.

6. Khosla was one of five Indian-American entrepreneurs in *Forbes* magazine's 2014 list of the 400 richest Americans. See "Five Indian-Americans in Forbes List of America's Richest," *The Times of India*, http://timesofindia.indiatimes.com/nri/us-canada-news/Five-Indian-Americans-in-Forbes-list-of-Americas-richest/articleshow/43876804.cms. This was higher than the previous year. See Deepak Chitnis, "Three Indian-American Entrepreneurs in Richest Americans list," *American Bazaar*, September 17, 2013, www.americanbazaaronline.com/2013/09/17/three-indian-american-entrepreneurs-richest-americans-list/. The others were Bharat Desai, founder of Syntel; Romesh Wadhwani, founder of Aspect Development, Symphony Technology Group, and two previous companies; Silicon Valley angel investor Kavitark Ram Shriram; and John Kapoor, founder of two successful pharmaceutical

companies. Interestingly, Kapoor also owns a small chain of fast-casual Indian restaurants in Arizona and several franchised Japanese restaurants; see www.forbes.com/profile/john-kapoor/.

7. Ajay was also asked about the changing nature of entrepreneurship, and offered some precise observations: "The way I look at the future of entrepreneurship, I feel that because now that we are living in a digital connected world, the need for monolithic organizations is far decreasing. . . . My contention is that if you're living in a perfectly fluid information flow between all of these actors and the interchange of companies, and you can create that kind of an ecosystem, then this is going to be more nimble, more agile, and more innovative to have large networks of independently run companies than to have large monolithic companies, which often times lose innovation under the bureaucracy and the burden of management and people."

8. Another Indian-American Internet pioneer, Sabeer Bhatia, became instantly rich and famous when he and his cofounder sold Hotmail to Microsoft at about the same time. Bhatia went on to try several other startups, but gained the most publicity for his attempt, ultimately unsuccessful, to build a "knowledge city" in northern India; see T. E. Narasimhan, "Life after Hotmail: How Successful Is Sabeer Bhatia?," January 2013, www.rediff.com/business/slide-show/slide-show-1-special-life-after-hotmail-for-sabeer-bhatia/20130121.htm.

9. In the interview, Anil Godhwani described himself as unusual in his family in not wanting to be an engineer. He studied economics, and his first job experience was in sales. He spoke of wanting to use his money to "make the world a better place," and of being continually active in such efforts. He described the supportive web of knowledge and networks of Silicon Valley in making his first venture succeed smoothly and quickly. He mentioned funding and talent as challenges for entrepreneurship, even in the rich environment of the Valley. When asked about changes in entrepreneurship over the years, he described the new environment as more competitive and crowded than before, but did not see differences in the spirit or motivations of entrepreneurs then and now. He judged persistence and desire to be the most essential traits for successful entrepreneurs.

10. Quoted in Richard Springer, "New Indian Community Center Merges with ICSC," *India West*, May 15, 2002, http://news.newamericamedia.org/news/view_article.html?article_id=255. See also Sandip Roy-Chowdhury, "Putting Down Roots," *India Currents*, January 30, 2003, www.indiacurrents.com/articles/2003/01/30/putting-down-roots, for a similar account of the Godhwanis' role in the ICC.

11. Recall that this was the most important motivation for the Indian-American entrepreneurs in the survey described in chapter 5.

12. In previous published interviews, Meera had suggested that she faced much more skepticism, especially as a mother and not just a woman, when seeking funding, than men would have. She had also provided a more general analysis of the challenges faced by women in the work-place, not just as entrepreneurs, and had been categorical in her opinion that the playing field is not level for women, but that it could and ought to be so, especially with the flexibility offered by new technologies. She is well known for mentoring new women entrepreneurs in Silicon Valley. In the interview, she also noted that there were reasons, such as child-bearing decisions, for women perhaps taking longer to become entrepreneurs, something revealed in the survey discussed in chapter 5.

13. Similar observations were made by Ajay, Chetan, and Neena in their interviews. An analysis along these lines is in Ludwig Siegele, "Tech Startups: Special Report," *The Economist*, January 18, 2014, http://media.economist.com/sites/default/files/sponsorships/%5BKY 56b%5DHuawei/180114_SR.pdf.

14. Meera herself has been very active with nonprofit organizations since retiring as an entrepreneur a few years ago.

15. According to Krishnendu Ray, "The Immigrant Restaurateur and the American City: Taste, Toil, and the Politics of Inhabitation," *Social Research: An International Quarterly* 81, no. 2 (2014): 373–96, the first such restaurant was the Ceylon India Inn, opened in 1913. Ray offers a meditation on the role of ethnic food in urban America, but the dimensions of this engagement are even more complex. One of the early Indian restaurants in the Bay Area became a small chain, the basis for a real estate empire, and also associated with illegal immigration and sex trafficking, ultimately collapsing due to these transgressions.

16. This section is based on Mumtaz Alam and Atif Jaleel, "From Azamgarh to America: The Success Saga of Frank Islam," *India Tomorrow*, March 17, 2014, www.indiatomorrow.net/eng/from-azamgarh-to-america-the-success-saga-of-frank-islam, and Frank Islam's personal website, www.frankislam.com.

17. See Madhu Jain, "Living the American Dream," *Washingtonian*, December 1, 2007, www.washingtonian.com/articles/people/living-the-american-dream/: "In 1974, he [Tak] lobbied for Indian-Americans to be considered minorities, enabling them to take advantage of incentives given to minority-owned businesses." As quoted in Jain's article, Islam credits Tak with his start in entrepreneurship: "'Sharad was my boss,' Islam says. 'He inspired my entrepreneurship.'" Tak also happens to be an IIT Bombay graduate, like Rekhi and several other Silicon Valley star entrepreneurs.

18. See Scott Preston, "TiE DC honors Ken Bajaj, Frank Islam and Sharad Tak," *American Bazaar*, December 13, 2014, www.americanbazaaronline.com/2014/12/13/tie-dc-honors-ken-bajaj-frank-islam-sharad-tak/.

19. See Deepti Nair, "From a Farm Labourer to an IT Millionairess: How Jyothi Reddy Beat All Odds to Emerge a Winner," *Your Story*, September 14, 2015, http://her.yourstory.com/jyothi-reddy-0914. Many similar news stories about Reddy are also available.

20. This section draws on Stephanie Carrie, "Valiant Comics: Two Students Did Not Want to See Their Favorite Comic Book Brand Die, So They Bought the Company," *LA Weekly*, September 2014, www.laweekly.com/publicspectacle/2012/05/16/valiant-comics-two-students-did-not-want-to-see-their-favorite-comic-book-brand-die-so-they-bought-the-company; Brooks Barnes, "In the Footsteps of Marvel," *New York Times*, July 8, 2012, www.nytimes.com/2012/07/09/business/media/comics-publisher-valiant-sees-its-future-on-film.html; "Valiant Comics Aim to 'Smash' Marvel and DC," *India West* 37, no. 45 (2012): C8; and "The Story of Two Indian-American Entrepreneurs Who Are Redefining the Global Comics Industry," *Techcircle.in*, October 10, 2012, http://techcircle.vccircle.com/2012/10/10/the-story-of-two-indian-american-entrepreneurs-who-are-redefining-the-global-comics-industry/.

21. In our interviews, other Indian-American entrepreneurs from that generation said that they would never have started a business if they had remained in India—it was just not done since they came from "professional" backgrounds.

22. The interview with Oprah Winfrey can be viewed at www.youtube.com/watch?v=DhOU14E3UOE. The TV program can be found at www.youtube.com/watch?v=zMAKwl1GW-I. The photograph can be found at http://en.wikipedia.org/wiki/Gurbaksh_Chahal.

23. See Gurbaksh Chahal, *The Dream: How I Learned the Risks and Rewards of Entrepreneurship and Made Millions* (New York: Palgrave MacMillan, 2008).

24. See, for example, Nitasha Tiku, "Gurbaksh Chahal Fired for Domestic Violence, Calls Victim a Whore," *Valleywag*, April 27, 2014, http://valleywag.gawker.com/gurbaskh-chahal-fired-for-domestic-violence-calls-vict-1568339976; Maria Bustillos, "Gurbaksh Chahal's Ugly Revenge," *The New Yorker*, May 1, 2014, www.newyorker.com/tech/elements/gurbaksh-chahals-ugly-revenge; and Randi Davenport, "Gurbaksh Chahal Has Lost His Job, His Girlfriend Has Lost More, *Salon.com*, May 6, 2014, www.salon.com/2014/05/06/gurbaksh_chahal_has_lost_his_job_his_girlfriend_has_lost_more/.

25. See, for example, Jack Marshall, "Fired RadiumOne CEO Gurbaksh Chahal Returns with New Ad Tech Venture," *Wall Street Journal*, July 21, 2014, http://blogs.wsj.com/cmo/2014/07/21/fired-radiumone-ceo-gurbaksh-chahal-returns-with-new-ad-tech-venture/. See also Lindsey Bever, "The Rise And Fall Of An Indian-Origin Silicon Valley Mogul," *The Washington Post*, August 12, 2016, https://www.washingtonpost.com/news/morning-mix/wp/2016/08/12/the-rise-and-fall-of-a-silicon-valley-mogul-accused-of-domestic-violence/.

26. The lists include media and sports stars, as well as professionals and business people. See Caroline Howard, "30 Under 30 Who Are Changing The World 2014," *Forbes*, January 20, 2014, www.forbes.com/sites/carolinehoward/2014/01/06/30-under-30-who-are-changing-the-world-2014/; "The 30 Under 30 List," *Forbes*, January 5, 2015, www.forbes.com/sites/forbespr/2015/01/05/forbes-the-30-under-30-list/; and Caroline Howard, "30 Under 30 2016: Today's Brightest Young Stars and the Future Leaders of Everything," *Forbes*, January 4, 2016, www.forbes.com/sites/carolinehoward/2016/01/04/

30-under-30-2016-todays-brightest-young-stars-and-the-future-leaders-of-everything/
#11c0b0ef32f2.

27. See Joanna Sugden, "Meet the People on Forbes' 30 Under 30 List with Indian or South Asian Origins," *Wall Street Journal, India Real Time Blog*, February 16, 2016, http://blogs.wsj.com/indiarealtime/2016/02/16/meet-the-people-on-forbes-30-under-30-list-with-indian-or-south-asian-origins/.

28. The Thiel Fellows program, created by PayPal founder Peter Thiel, pays students to drop out of college and start their own enterprise.

29. Two others of Indian origin in this group are Indo-Canadians.

30. See Shivani Vora, "Indian Additions to NYC's Chocolate Scene," *New York Times blog*, July 4, 2012, http://india.blogs.nytimes.com/2012/07/04/indian-additions-to-nycs-chocolate-scene/?_r=0.

31. See "The Gujarati Way: Going Global: Secrets of the World's Best Businesspeople," *The Economist*, December 19, 2015, www.economist.com/news/christmas-specials/21683983-secrets-worlds-best-businesspeople-going-global.

32. Early accounts of the trajectory of Gujaratis into the U.S. motel and hotel industry include Joel Millman, *The Other Americans: How Immigrants Renew Our Country, Our Economy, and Our Values* (New York: Viking Penguin, 1997); and Tunku Varadarajan, "A Patel Motel Cartel?," *New York Times*, July 4, 1999, www.nytimes.com/1999/07/04/magazine/a-patel-motel-cartel.html. See also "The Gujarati Way."

33. The grandson of one of the early Gujarati motel owners estimated that at this time there were still only about 60 or 70 Indian-American-owned motels in the United States, mostly in California; Varadarajan, "A Patel Motel Cartel?"

34. An early but rare analysis of the role of women in this configuration is Suvarna Thaker, "The Quality of Life of Asian Indian Women in the Motel Industry," *South Asia Bulletin* 2, no. 1 (1982): 68–73. See also Shobha Hiatt, "From Motels to Hotels," *India Currents*, September 1, 2005, www.indiacurrents.com/articles/2005/09/01/from-motels-to-hotels; and Shobha Bondre, *Dhandha: How Gujaratis Do Business* (New Delhi: Random House, 2013), for case studies of motel owners that feature the role of women.

35. Dhingra, quoted in Greg Varner, "How a Staple of Americana Became the Indian-American Dream," *ColorLines*, April 27, 2012, http://colorlines.com/archives/2012/04/how_a_stable_of_americana_became_the_indian_american_dream.html), analyzes this realistically: "But they've been successful because they've learned ways to manage the problems they keep encountering, and the way they manage the problems is not necessarily helping to overcome them." He adds: "You want to avoid any of that and just have as non-foreign a motel as you can. That strategic decision about who they hire helps them in the business. It also reinforces this notion of whiteness as better than brownness. It reinforces the hierarchy. The success is real, but so are the hierarchies they've got to navigate. Both of these narratives work together." Pawan Dhingra, "Hospitable to Others: Indian-American Motel Owners Create Boundaries and Belonging in the Heartland," *Ethnic and Racial Studies* 33, no. 6 (2010): 1088–107, discusses the various facets of adaptation, both work-related and social, by Gujarati motel owners.

36. See, for example, Varadarajan, "A Patel Motel Cartel?"; Hiatt, "From Motels to Hotels"; Rick Romell, "State's Asian Indians Thrive in Entrepreneurial Society," *Milwaukee Wisconsin Journal Sentinel*, February 7, 2010, www.jsonline.com/business/83779312.html; and Pawan Dhingra, *Life Behind the Lobby: Indian-American Motel Owners and the American Dream* (Stanford, CA: Stanford University Press, 2012).

37. See Millman, *The Other Americans*; and Varadarajan, "A Patel Motel Cartel?" A collection of case studies of how Gujaratis do business is Bondre, *Dhandha*.

38. Rigorous quantitative analysis is in Arturs Kalnins and Wilbur Chung, "Social Capital, Geography, and Survival: Gujarati Immigrant Entrepreneurs in the U.S. Lodging Industry," *Management Science* 52, no. 2 (2006): 233–47; and Arturs Kalnins and Wilbur Chung, "Ethnic Business Groups, Chain Affiliation, and Survival of Geographically Dispersed Service Firms," *Proceedings of the Academy of Management*, August 2002, http://proceedings.aom.org/content/2002/1/G1.5.abstract. Pawan Dhingra, "The Possibility of Community: How Indian-American Motel Owners Negotiate Competition and Solidarity," *Journal of Asian American*

Studies 12, no. 3 (2009): 321–46, discusses how motel owners balance cooperation and competition.

39. For example, Stanley Turkel, "From Ragas to Riches Part I: A Wonderful American Immigrant Success Story," *International Society of Hospitality Consultants*, May 1, 2006, http://ishc.com/wp-content/uploads/From-Ragas-To-Riches-Part-I.pdf, quotes from a 1981 article in *Frequent Flyer* magazine. Unsurprisingly, negative stereotypes continue: for example, the blog *patelmonopoly* has posts made in 2010 and 2012, and speaks of the "corrupt Patel crime family."

40. For example, AAHOA created and distributes Spanish-Gujarati phrasebooks for motel owners with an increasingly Latino workforce; "Indian Hotel, Motel Owners Finding Spanish Necessary to Do Business," *Lubbock Avalanche-Journal*, August 6, 2006, http://lubbockonline.com/stories/080606/sta_080606119.shtml.

41. Various pieces of this effort are described in Millman, *The Other Americans*; Varadarajan, "A Patel Motel Cartel?"; Hiatt, "From Motels to Hotels"; Turkel, "From Ragas to Riches Part I"; and Stanley Turkel, "From Ragas to Riches Part II: The Growth of AAHOA Tracks the Ascendancy of Indian-American Hoteliers," International Society of Hospitality Consultants, June 1, 2006, http://ishc.com/wp-content/uploads/FromRagasToRiches-PartII.pdf. A measure of the success of AAHOA is Hasmukh P. Rama's 1999 status as chairman of the American Hotel and Motel Association, which is the organization representing America's entire lodging industry; Varadarajan, "A Patel Motel Cartel?". Interestingly, Rama's original surname was Patel, but was changed by his family.

42. For example, see Meenakshi Verma Ambwani, "Indians Taking over Hotels from Distressed Owners in U.S. at Rock-bottom Prices," *Economic Times*, October 4, 2011, http://articles.economictimes.indiatimes.com/2011-10-04/news/30242710_1_hotel-industry-hotel-assets-indian-investors.

43. See Margaret Gibson, "Punjabi Orchard Farmers: An Immigrant Enclave in Rural California," *International Migration Review* 22, no. 1 (1988): 28–50.

44. For a general introduction to Sikhs and Sikhism, see Gurinder Mann, *Sikhism* (Saddle River, NJ: Pearson, 2004). For an overview of Sikhs in the United States, see Gurinder Mann, Paul Numrich, and Raymond Williams, *Buddhists, Hindus, and Sikhs in America* (New York: Oxford University Press, 2002).

45. See, for example, http://en.wikipedia.org/wiki/Murder_of_Balbir_Singh_Sodhi.

46. Kanwal Rekhi and Narinder Singh Kapany (see note 34 in chapter 5) are both Sikhs: the latter maintains that identity fully, while the former consciously abandoned it to become more "American."

47. See Gurpreet Bal, "Entrepreneurship among Diasporic Communities: A Comparative Examination of Patidars of Gujarat and Jats of Punjab," *Journal of Entrepreneurship* 13 (2006): 161–203, who compares Sikhs (more specifically, Jats) and Gujaratis (Patels and related groups).

48. See Jennifer Parker, "Ethnic Social Structures and Mainstream Capital: The Ethnic Anchoring of 'American' Franchise Growth," *Journal of Asian American Studies* 16, no. 1 (February 2013): 25–56.

49. See Katherine Shilcutt, "Little India," *Houston Press*, May 25, 2011, www.houstonpress.com/2011-05-26/restaurants/little-india/.

50. See Monte Burke, "The Secret to Immigrant Entrepreneurial Success Can Be Found in Edison, NJ," *Forbes*, June 6, 2012, www.forbes.com/forbes/2012/0625/investment-guide-12-india-american-finance-new-jersey-ultimate-neighborhood-bank.html.

51. See Nitya Ramanan, "The Social Entrepreneur," *India West*, June 1, 2005, www.indiacurrents.com/articles/2005/06/01/the-social-entrepreneur.

52. Thomas Lyons, ed., *Social Entrepreneurship: How Businesses Can Transform Society*, vol. 2 (Santa Barbara, CA: ABC-CLIO), 85–125, uses SKS Microfinance to discuss a classification of social entrepreneurship.

53. The problems were not entirely SKS's fault—there were many other microlenders operating simultaneously, and some households were simultaneously borrowing from multiple lenders, making repayment impossible. See Vikas Bajaj, "Amid Scandal, Chairman of Troubled Lender Will Quit," *New York Times*, November 23, 2011, www.nytimes.com/2011/11/24/business/global/vikram-akula-chairman-of-sks-microfinance-to-step-down.html?_r=0, and

http://vikramakula.com/about/. Other dimensions of the SKS story include the involvement of other high-profile Indian Americans such as Vinod Khosla, complicated political
maneuvering in India that spilled over into the microfinance industry, and a bitter divorce and
custody battle between Akula and his ex-wife; Srikanth Srinivas, "Abrupt Fall From Grace,"
Business World, May 20, 2011, www.businessworld.in/news/finance/banking/abrupt-fall-
from-grace/304460/page-1.html; Sandeep Bamzai, "Vikram Akula: The Loan Ranger," *India
Today*, November 15, 2010, http://indiatoday.intoday.in/story/vikram-akula-the-loan-
ranger/1/119094.html).

54. AgSri is a venture focused on innovating, packaging, implementing, and scaling farmer-
friendly and ecologically sustainable agricultural technologies. See E. Kumar Sharma, "What
Is Vikram Akula up to These Days?," *Business Today*, September 9, 2013, http://businessto-
day.intoday.in/story/what-is-sks-microfinance-founder-vikram-akula-up-to-these-days/1/
198465.html.

55. The SKS Trust runs 15 schools in India. See Sharma, "What Is Vikram Akula up to these
days?"

56. See Tamal Bandyopadhyay, "Why Many in SKS Love to Hate Founder Vikram Akula," *Mint*,
December 4, 2013, www.livemint.com/Companies/b4iGFgvmHotiKUaF0wK91L/Why-
many-in-SKS-love-to-hate-founder-Vikram-Akula.html. SKS has started selling other financial products, including insurance and gold.

57. See Aziz Hanifa, "B. P. Agrawal Wins Prestigious MIT award," *Rediff.com*, May 11, 2010, www.
rediff.com/news/report/bhagwati-agarwal-wins-mit-award/20100511.htm; http://si-usa.
org/, http://lemelson.mit.edu/winners/bp-agrawal; and B. P. Agrawal, "Social Enterprises
for Water," Indian Diaspora Initiative, http://diasporaalliance.org/social-enterprises-for-
water-indian-diaspora-initiative/.

58. See Colleen Taylor, "Tech Entrepreneur Priya Haji, Founder and CEO of SaveUp, Has Passed
Away at 44," *TechCrunch CrunchBase*, July 16, 2014, http://techcrunch.com/2014/07/
16/tech-entrepreneur-priya-haji-founder-and-ceo-of-saveup-has-passed-away-at-44/; Sue
Dremann, "Groundbreaking Social Entrepreneur Priya Haji Dies," *Palo Alto Weekly*, July 17,
2014, www.paloaltoonline.com/news/2014/07/17/groundbreaking-social-entrepreneur-
priya-haji-dies; and Chuck Salter, "Remembering Priya Haji: The Best Social Entrepreneur
of Our Generation," *Fast Company Co.Exist*, July 29, 2014, www.fastcoexist.com/3033635/
remembering-priya-haji-the-best-social-entrepreneur-of-our-generation.

59. See Suzanne Hall, "This Bar Saves Lives: A Day with the Founders of This Life-Changing
Snack," *The Chalkboard*, January 10, 2014, http://thechalkboardmag.com/bar-saves-lives-
day-founders-life-changing-snack; J. Jennings Moss, "Whole Foods Deal a Boost to These
Actor-slash-Social Entrepreneurs," *Upstart Business Journal*, September 2, 2014, http://
upstart.bizjournals.com/entrepreneurs/hot-shots/2014/09/02/forget-the-actor-slash-
model-the-new-model-is-the.html?page=all; and Sujeet Rajan, "Indian-American Actor
Ravi Patel's Granola Bars Business Gets a Huge Boost with Endorsement by Whole Foods,"
American Bazaar, September 3, 2014, www.americanbazaaronline.com/2014/09/03/
indian-american-actor-ravi-patels-granola-bars-business-gets-huge-boost-endorsement-
whole-foods/.

60. See Madhulika Khandelwal, *Becoming American, Being Indian: An Immigrant Community in
New York City* (Ithaca, NY: Cornell University Press, 2002), which focuses on New York;
and Vinay Lal, *The Other Indians: Politics and Culture of South Asians in America* (Los
Angeles: UCLA Asian American Studies Center, 2008).

61. These estimates are from Elizabeth Kolsky, "Less Successful Than the Next: South Asian
Taxi Drivers," *WNYC Online*, March 2002, www.modelminority.com/joomla/index.
php?view=article&catid=47%3Asociety&id=328%3Aless-successful-than-the-next-
south-asian-taxi-drivers-&format=pdf&option=com_content&Itemid=56, as well as
Lal, *The Other Indians*; and Amitava Kumar, "The Venerable, Vulnerable Taxi Drivers of
New York," *Vanity Fair*, August 26, 2010, www.vanityfair.com/online/daily/2010/08/
the-venerable-vulnerable-taxi-drivers-of-new-york.

62. Kolsky, "Less Successful Than the Next."

63. See Diditi Mitra, "Social Capital Investment and Immigrant Economic Trajectories: A Case
Study of Punjabi American Taxi Drivers in New York City," *International Migration* 50, no. 4

(2012): 67–84; and Mitra, *Punjabi Immigrant Mobility in the United States: Adaptation through Race and Class* (New York: Palgrave Macmillan, 2012).

64. In 2006, Joe Biden, then a Senate candidate, notoriously remarked that "you cannot go to a 7-Eleven or a Dunkin' Donuts unless you have a slight Indian accent"; Indo-Asian News Service, "Indian-Americans Pay a Price for Running Convenience Stores," *NDTV Diaspora*, www.ndtv. com/article/diaspora/indian-americans-pay-a-price-for-running-convenience-stores-584925).

65. See Roger Waldinger, ed., *Strangers at the Gates: New Immigrants in Urban America* (Berkeley: University of California Press, 2001); Roger Waldinger, *Still the Promised City? New Immigrants and African-Americans in Post-Industrial New York* (Cambridge, MA: Harvard University Press, 1999); Roger Waldinger, *Through the Eye of the Needle: Immigrants and Enterprise in New York's Garment Trades* (New York: New York University Press, 1986); and Roger Waldinger, Howard Aldrich, Robin Ward, et al., *Ethnic Entrepreneurs: Immigrant Business in Industrial Society* (Newbury Park, CA: Sage, 1990). Donatella Lorch, "An Ethnic Road to Riches: The Immigrant Job Specialty," *New York Times*, January 12, 1992, www. nytimes.com/1992/01/12/nyregion/an-ethnic-road-to-riches-the-immigrant-job-specialty. html, references additional studies, especially for Korean ethnic entrepreneurship.

66. Lorch, "An Ethnic Road to Riches."

67. See Brian Berk, "Ethnic Convenience Store Associations Make Their Mark," *Convenience Store News*, November 17, 2011, www.csnews.com/industry-news-and-trends/special-features/ ethnic-convenience-store-associations-make-their-mark; and Indo-Asian News Service, "Indian-Americans Pay a Price for Running Convenience Stores."

68. In addition to the following case, the example of Edison, New Jersey, discussed earlier in the book, is also instructive. Entrepreneurial success did not translate easily into community acceptance, with the community facing hostility from the police and having to struggle for a political presence. See Sofya Aptekar, "Organizational Life and Political Incorporation of Two Asian Immigrant Groups: A Case Study," *Ethnic and Racial Studies* 32, no. 9 (2009): 1511–33.

69. Satish Shah studied chemical engineering at BITS Pilani, and earned an MBA from Roosevelt University in the United States. He remains chairman of the company.

70. See Danny Ecker, "Local Exec Aims to Train Indian Business Leaders through Basketball," *Crain's Chicago Business*, January 20, 2014, www.chicagobusiness.com/article/20140120/ BLOGS04/140129990/local-exec-aims-to-train-indian-business-leaders-through-basketball.

71. Ibid.

72. See http://dreamindiaacademy.com/about/.

73. Vivek Ranadive, a successful Indian-American technology entrepreneur and basketball fan, as well as now an NBA team owner, famously coached his daughter's basketball team to success by reanalyzing how the game is played and instituting changes in the strategy of play; Malcolm Gladwell, "How David Beats Goliath: When Underdogs Break the Rules," *The New Yorker*, May 11, 2009, www.newyorker.com/magazine/2009/05/11/how-david-beats-goliath. Anil Godhwani is a table tennis player and fan, and table tennis has been a huge success as an ICC activity. The game is played individually, but teams compete in tournaments.

74. Another arena in which Indian Americans seem to have done disproportionately well is in becoming deans of business schools and engineering schools, which certainly qualifies as an executive management position, though not in the corporate world.

75. The issue here is whether playing sports together matters more for creating social networks of the "old boy" variety than it does for building individual leadership and teamwork skills, as a determinant of corporate success. Many of the same issues have been faced by women in business. An early study of the complex set of issues involved is Aidan Dunleavy, Andrew Miracle, and Roger Rees, eds., "Studies in the Sociology of Sport," Refereed Proceedings of the 2nd Annual Conference of the North American Society for the Sociology of Sport, Fort Worth, Texas, November 1981 (Fort Worth: Texas Christian University Press, 1982).

76. For example, research shows the continued importance of race, height, gender, and even speech patterns in determining corporate success; Adrian Wooldridge, "The Look of a Leader," *The Economist*, September 27, 2014, 68.

Chapter 7

1. Jennifer Ludden, "1965 Immigration Law Changed Face of America," *NPR*, May 9, 2006, www.npr.org/templates/story/story.php?storyId=5391395.

2. For overviews of the economic and political effects of immigration on sending countries, see Marc Rosenblum and Daniel Tichenor, eds., *Oxford Handbook of the Politics of International Migration* (New York: Oxford University Press, 2012), 131–52; Devesh Kapur, "The Political Impact of International Migration on Sending Countries," *Annual Review of Political Science* 17 (2014): 479–502.

3. Yossi Shain, *Kinship and Diaspora in International Affairs* (Ann Arbor: University of Michigan Press, 2007).

4. Roger Waldinger, "Engaging from Abroad: The Sociology of Emigrant Politics," *Migration Studies* 2, no. 3 (2014): 319–39.

5. R. S. Bourne, "Transnational America," *Atlantic Monthly*, July 1916, 86–97.

6. Nina Glick Schiller, Linda Basch, and Cristina Blanc-Szanton, "Towards a Definition of Transnationalism," *Annals of the New York Academy of Sciences* 645, no. 1 (1992): ix–xiv, ix.

7. Alejandro Portes, Luis E. Guarnizo, and Patricia Landolt, "The Study of Trans-nationalism: Pitfalls and Promise of an Emergent Research Field," *Ethnic and Racial Studies* 22, no. 2 (1999): 217–37.

8. Alejandro Portes, Luis E. Guarnizo, and William J. Haller, "Transnational Entrepreneurs: An Alternative Form of Immigrant Economic Adaptation," *American Sociological Review* 67, no. 2 (2002): 278–98; Luis Eduardo Guarnizo, Alejandro Portes, and William Haller, "Assimilation and Transnationalism: Determinants of Transnational Political Action among Contemporary Migrants," *American Journal of Sociology* 108, no. 6 (2003): 1211–48.

9. Possible exceptions involve the role of Indian-American entrepreneurs in shaping some aspects of economic policy reform. In 1999, India's stock market regulator, the Securities and Exchange Board of India, included Indian-American entrepreneurs Sabeer Bhatia and K. B. Chandrasekhar in a committee to advise on attracting more venture capital to India. In 2000, the recently constituted Ministry of Communications and Information Technology set up a "Select Group with Overseas Indians" to provide it with advice: the group, in addition to Bhatia and Chandrasekhar, included Vinod Khosla, Suhas Patil, and Kanwal Rekhi, all Indian Americans. In both cases, Indian Americans had more than a marginal impact on subsequent reforms in these narrow domains. See Sadanand Dhume, "From Bangalore to Silicon Valley and Back," in *India Briefing: Quickening the Pace of Change*, ed. Alyssa Ayres and Philip Oldenburg (New York: M. E. Sharpe, 2002), 91–120.

10. Rina Agarwala, "Tapping the Indian Diaspora for Indian Development," in *The State and the Grassroots: Immigrant Transnational Organizations in Four Continents*, ed. Alejandro Portes and Patricia Fernandez-Kelly (New York: Berghahn Press, 2015), 84–110.

11. Indiaspora was founded in 2012 by M. R. Rangaswami.

12. Rukmini Banerji, CEO of Pratham, personal communication, April 10, 2016.

13. Agarwala, "Tapping the Indian Diaspora."

14. For a detailed discussion and analysis of the evidence, see Devesh Kapur, *Diaspora, Democracy and Development: The Impact of International Migration from India on India* (Princeton, NJ: Princeton University Press, 2010), chap. 8.

15. Agarwala, "Tapping the Indian Diaspora."

16. A study based on survey data from the Netherlands found that Muslims have relatively high levels of religious philanthropic behavior and relatively low levels of secular philanthropic behavior, whereas Hindus have relatively low levels of religious philanthropic behavior and higher levels of secular philanthropic behavior. One explanation offered by the authors was that the stronger the group orientation in worship rituals, the stronger the relation between religion and philanthropic behavior. Christine L. Carabain and René Bekkers, "Explaining Differences in Philanthropic Behavior Between Christians, Muslims, and Hindus in the Netherlands," *Review of Religious Research* 53 (2012): 419–40.

17. Examples of the latter include the Satish and Yasmin Gupta College of Business at the University of Dallas, the Patel College of Global Sustainability at the University of South Florida (courtesy of Kiran and Pallavi Patel), the Krishna P. Singh Center for Nanotechnology

at the University of Pennsylvania, and the Tandon School of Engineering at New York University (with $100 million from Chandrika and Ranjan Tandon).

18. The three Indian-American entrepreneurs are Manoj Bhargava, Vinod and Neera Khosla, and Romesh and Kathleen Wadhwani.

19. The migration of Sikhs from Punjab did not quite fit this pattern of upper-caste migration, reflecting both the somewhat different nature of the caste composition of Punjab and the longer and more complex history of emigration from that state.

20. Devesh Kapur, *Diaspora, Democracy and Development: The Impact of International Migration from India on India* (Princeton: Princeton University Press, 2010), Chapter 6.

21. Kapur, *Diaspora, Democracy and Development*, chap. 8.

22. Palaniappan Chidambaram, "Commanding Heights: The Battle for the World Economy," *PBS*, 2002, www.pbs.org/wgbh/commandingheights/shared/pdf/int_palaniappanchidambaram.pdf.

23. Min Ye, *Diasporas and Foreign Direct Investment in China and India* (New York: Cambridge University Press, 2014).

24. Saon Ray, Smita Miglani, and Neha Malik, "Impact of American Investment in India," February 2015, ICRIER Working Paper No. 296. Similar linkages were seen in the survey responses of nonentrepreneurs reported in chapter 5, http://icrier.org/pdf/Working_Paper_296.pdf.

25. A more typical action has been the creation of a "team" in India that serves the company headquartered in the U.S, as part of a more general phenomenon of offshoring; see, for example, Rafiq Dossani and Martin Kenney, "The Next Wave of Globalization: Relocating Service Provision to India," *World Development* 35, no. 5 (2007):772–91. This team may include returnees from Silicon Valley. See Sean Randolph, "Silicon Valley Expats Spur Innovation in India," *Yale Global Online*, September 2, 2010, http://yaleglobal.yale.edu/content/silicon-valley-spur-innovation.

26. One can also make the argument that the success of Indian-American technology entrepreneurs paved the way for their compatriots to rise to these major CEO positions through reputational effects.

27. This idea is formalized as the Stolper-Samuelson theorem in trade theory.

28. It is possible to take this argument further and examine the consequences of NRI investments in India's booming land markets, one part of the reason for the boom itself being these NRI investments. See Sanjoy Chakravorty, *The Price of Land: Acquisition, Conflict, Consequence* (New Delhi: Oxford University Press, 2013), for an argument that inequality imposes a tax on India's urban poor by operating through polarized urban land markets.

29. Thomas Faist and Peter Kivisto, "Dual Citizenship" in *Global Perspective: From Unitary To Multiple Citizenship* (Houndmills, UK: Palgrave Macmillan, 2007); Tanja Brøndsted Sejersen, "'I Vow to Thee My Countries' - The Expansion of Dual Citizenship in the 21st Century," *International Migration Review* 42, no. 3 (2008): 723–38.

30. United Nations Department of Economic and Social Affairs (Population Division), *International Migration Policies: Government Views and Priorities*, http://www.un.org/en/development/desa/population/publications/pdf/policy/InternationalMigrationPolicies2013/Report%20PDFs/z_International%20Migration%20Policies%20Full%20Report.pdf#zoom=100.

31. Rogers Smith, *Stories of Peoplehood: The Politics and Morals of Political Membership* (Cambridge: Cambridge University Press, 2003).

32. This complex emotional response that combined resentment and disdain was reflected in popular culture in Hindi films of the period like *Purab aur Paschim* and *Hare Rama, Hare Krishna*. By the late 1990s, Hindi cinema was celebrating the diaspora in popular films like *Dilwale Dulhania Le Jayenge*, *Pardes*, *Kuch Kuch Hota Hai*, and *Kabhi Khushi Kabhie Gham*.

33. Daniel Naujoks, *Migration, Citizenship, and Development: Diasporic Membership Policies and Overseas Indians in the United States* (New Delhi: Oxford University Press, 2013).

34. Daniel Naujoks, *Migration, Citizenship, and Development. Diasporic Membership Policies and Overseas Indians in the United States* (Delhi: Oxford University Press, 2013).

35. There are several well-researched accounts of India–U.S. relations. These include: Kenton Clymer, *Quest for Freedom: The United States and India's Independence* (New York: Columbia

University Press, 1995); H. W. Brands, *The Specter of Neutralism: The United States and the Emergence of the Third World, 1947–1960* (New York: Columbia University Press, 1989); Dennis Merrill, *Bread and the Ballot: The United States and India's Economic Development, 1947-1963* (Chapel Hill: University of North Carolina Press, 1990); Robert McMahon, *The Cold War on the Periphery: The United States, India, and Pakistan* (New York: Columbia University Press, 1994); Andrew Rotter, *Comrades at Odds: The United States and India, 1947-1964* (Ithaca, NY: Cornell University Press, 2000); Jarrod Hayes, *Constructing National Security: U.S. Relations with India and China* (New York: Cambridge University Press, 2013); Dinshaw Mistry, *The U.S.–India Nuclear Agreement: Diplomacy and Domestic Politics* (New Delhi: Cambridge University Press, 2014); Rudra Chaudhuri, *Forged in Crisis: India and the United States Since 1947* (New York: Oxford University Press, 2014).

36. See "The Calcutta Key," Services of Supply Base, Section Two, Information and Education Branch, United States Army Forces in India - Burma, 1945. At: http://www.cbi-theater.com/calcuttakey/calcutta_key.html.

37. Rudra Chaudhuri, *Forged In Crisis. The United States and India since 1947* (New York: Oxford university Press, 2014), 17.

38. In late 2014, Raphael emerged as the subject of an FBI counter-intelligence investigation but was eventually cleared.

38a. Frank Pallone and Bill McCollum served as co-chairs of the Caucus from 1993 to1998, Gary Ackerman and Jim Greenwood from 1999 to 2000, Jim McDermott and Edward Royce between 2001 and 2002, and Joseph Crowley and Joe Wilson from 2003 to 2014. Congressmen Ami Bera (D–California) and George Holding (R–North Carolina) were elected to serve as the new co-chairs of the Congressional Caucus on India and Indian Americans after the 2014 elections.

39. John Lancaster, "Activism Boosts India's Fortunes," *Washington Post*, October 9, 1999, A01.

40. Mike McIntire, "Indian-Americans Test Their Clout on Atom Pact," *New York Times*, June 5, 2006, www.nytimes.com/2006/06/05/washington/05indians.html?pagewanted=all.

41. Cited in Jason Kirk, "Indian-Americans and the U.S.–India Nuclear Agreement: Consolidation of an Ethnic Lobby?," *Foreign Policy Analysis* 4, no. 3 (2008): 275–300.

42. Subsequently on learning of his mistake, the congressman issued a sport-themed apology: "I made a mistake in speaking before being fully briefed, and I apologize … I'm a quick study, but in this case I shot an air ball."

43. Peter Beinart, "Whiteness Is Still a Proxy for Being American," *The Atlantic*, July 27, 2014.

44. The United States is not an exception in this regard. Migration from India and a growing Indian diaspora has led countries like Australia, the United Kingdom, and Portugal to post envoys of Indian origin to New Delhi in recent years; Suhasini Haidar, "'Desi' Diplomats Don't Have it Easy," *The Hindu*, July 29, 2014, www.thehindu.com/news/national/desi-diplomats-dont-have-it-easy/article6258867.ece.

45. William J. Burns, former U.S. Deputy Secretary of State, on *Charlie Rose*, February 26, 2015, http://carnegieendowment.org/2015/02/26/william-j.-burns-on-charlie-rose-pub-59207.

46. Zahir Janmohamed, "U.S. Evangelicals, Indian Expats Teamed Up to Push Through Modi Visa Ban," *New York Times*, December 5, 2013, http://india.blogs.nytimes.com/2013/12/05/u-s-evangelicals-indian-expats-teamed-up-to-push-through-modi-visa-ban/?_r=0.

47. Maldwyn Allen Jones, *American Immigration* (Chicago: University of Chicago Press, 1992).

48. Oscar Handlin, *The Uprooted: The Epic Story of the Great Migrations that Made the American People* (Boston: Little, Brown, 1973), 3.

49. Alejandro Portes and Ruben G. Rumbaut, *Immigrant America: A Portrait* (Berkeley and Los Angeles: University of California Press, 2006).

50. Devesh Kapur and John McHale, *Give Us Your Best and Brightest: The Global Hunt for Talent and Its Impact on the Developing World* (Washington, DC: Center for Global Development and Brookings Institute Press, 2005).

51. Philip Cafaro, *How Many Is Too Many? The Progressive Argument for Reducing Immigration into the United States* (Chicago: University of Chicago Press, 2015).

52. Marie Gottschalk, *Caught: The Prison State and the Lockdown of American Politics* (Princeton, NJ: Princeton University Press, 2014), 206.

53. Philip Kasinitz, John Mollenkopf, Mary C. Waters, and Jennifer Holdaway, *Inheriting the City: The Children of Immigrants Come of Age* (New York: Russell Sage Foundation, 2010), 368.
54. Matthew Frye Jacobson, *Roots Too: White Ethnic Revival in Post-Civil Rights America* (Cambridge, MA: Harvard University Press, 2008).
55. James Hampshire, *The Politics of Immigration: Contradictions of the Liberal State* (Cambridge: Polity Press, 2013), 2.
56. Lant Pritchett, *Let Their People Come* (Washington, DC: Center for Global Development, 2006).
57. See www.igmchicago.org/igm-economic-experts-panel/poll-results?SurveyID=SV_5vuNnqkBeAMAfHv.
58. David Card, "Immigration and Inequality," *American Economic Review: Papers & Proceedings* 99, no. 2 (2009): 1–21, 3.
59. Gaetano Basso and Giovanni Peri, "The Association between Immigration and Labor Market Outcomes in the United States," 2015, IZA Discussion Papers 9436, Institute for the Study of Labor (IZA), http://ftp.iza.org/dp9436.pdf.
60. Jens Hainmueller and Daniel Hopkins, "The Hidden American Immigration Consensus: A Conjoint Analysis of Attitudes toward Immigrants," *American Journal of Political Science* 59, no. 3 (2015): 529–48.
61. Marisa Abrajano and Zoltan L. Hajnal, *White Backlash: Immigration, Race, and American Politics* (Princeton, NJ: Princeton University Press, 2015).
62. Larry M. Bartels, *Unequal Democracy: The Political Economy of the New Gilded Age* (Princeton, NJ: Princeton University Press, 2010); Paul Pierson and Jacob S. Hacker, *Winner-Take-All Politics: How Washington Made the Rich Richer and Turned Its Back on the Middle Class* (New York: Simon & Schuster, 2010).
63. Martin Wolf, "The Economic Losers Are in Revolt against the Elites," *Financial Times*, January 26, 2016, www.ft.com/cms/s/0/135385ca-c399-11e5-808f-8231cd71622e.html.
64. Sandra L. Colby and Jennifer M. Ortman, "Projections of the Size and Composition of the U.S. Population: 2014 to 2060," *Current Population Reports*, P25-1143, U.S. Census Bureau, March 2015, www.census.gov/content/dam/Census/library/publications/2015/demo/p25-1143.pdf
65. Laura B. Shrestha and Elayne J. Heisler, "The Changing Demographic Profile of the United States," *Congressional Research Service*, March 2011, table 2.
66. Colby and Ortman, "Projections of the Size."
67. See Nadwa Mossaad, "U.S. Lawful Permanent Residents: 2014," at: https://www.dhs.gov/sites/default/files/publications/LPR%20Flow%20Report%202014_508.pdf.
68. In 2014, 331,000 out of 1.13 million international students in the United States were from China, an almost fivefold increase since 2000. After India, China has also been an important source of new legal permanent residents admitted through employment-based visa categories, and while the overall numbers are small, Chinese nationals have received more than 80 percent of EB-5 visas for immigrant investors in recent years (a visa that Indians do not have access to). At the other end of the spectrum, China was also the leading country of origin for individuals granted asylum in the United States, accounting for 34 percent in 2013.
69. A striking characteristic of Indian migration to the Organization for Economic Co-operation and Development (OECD) countries is its concentration in English-speaking countries with the United States, United Kingdom, Canada, and Australia having the largest numbers of people born in India. In turn, people born in India ranked 1, 2, 3, and 4 among the foreign-born in the United Kingdom, United States, Canada, and Australia in 2013. Indeed, of the countries where Indians rank among the top ten of the foreign born, only one (Italy) is in continental Europe. See Devesh Kapur, "Europe's India Aversion," *Business Standard*, April 13, 2015, www.business-standard.com/article/opinion/devesh-kapur-europe-s-india-aversion-114041300674_1.html.
70. Jacob Funk Kirkegaard, "The Economic Scope and Future of U.S.–India Labor Migration Issues," Peterson Institute for International Economics Working Paper 15-1, February 2015, Washington, DC, https://piie.com/publications/working-papers/economic-scope-and-future-us-india-labor-migration-issues.
71. F. Qin, "Global Talent, Local Careers: Circular Migration of top Indian Engineers and Professionals," *Research Policy* 44, no. 2 (2015): 405–20.

Appendix

1. In this geographical hierarchy, counties are especially important because they are the primary legal subdivisions within each state. Also, they are small enough to provide some disaggregated information at the sub-state scale. For example, the state of Kentucky is composed of 120 counties. Of these, there are 12 for which single-year estimates are available (that is, these counties belong in a metropolitan statistical area), 43 that have three-year estimates starting in 2008, and 65 that have five-year estimates available starting in 2010.

2. How to interpret these data? The 2012 population estimate for California was 382,852 with a standard error of ±15,788. Hence, the ACS estimated, with 95 percent confidence, that the India-born population of California was between 367,064 and 398,640. The standard error for the three-year estimate was ±7,805, about half of the one-year estimate. This was the more reliable estimate.

3. See https://www.census.gov/geo/reference/puma.html for more detail on PUMA geography. It is useful to note that PUMAs are "made-up" geographies in the sense that they do not correspond to recognizable political units like counties or cities/townships. A large city is made up of several PUMA units, whereas several rural counties often make up a single PUMA unit.

4. Some PUMA data are allocated to smaller geographical units (such as minor civil divisions). In regions that have large numbers of India-born, these estimates are reliable and usable. The detailed maps in chapter 3 show information at the scale of minor civil divisions.

INDEX